Measuring and Managing Information Risk

Measuring and Managing Information Risk
A FAIR Approach

Jack Freund and Jack Jones

ELSEVIER

AMSTERDAM • BOSTON • HEIDELBERG • LONDON
NEW YORK • OXFORD • PARIS • SAN DIEGO
SAN FRANCISCO • SINGAPORE • SYDNEY • TOKYO

Butterworth-Heinemann is an imprint of Elsevier

Acquiring Editor: Brian Romer
Editorial Project Manager: Keira Bunn
Project Manager: Poulouse Joseph
Designer: Matthew Limbert

Butterworth-Heinemann is an imprint of Elsevier
The Boulevard, Langford Lane, Kidlington, Oxford, OX5 1GB, UK
225 Wyman Street, Waltham, MA 02451, USA

Library of Congress Cataloging-in-Publication Data
Application submitted

British Library Cataloguing in Publication Data
A catalogue record for this book is available from the British Library

ISBN: 978-0-12-420231-3

For information on all Butterworth-Heinemann publications
visit our web site at http://store.elsevier.com/

This book has been manufactured using Print on Demand technology. Each copy is produced
to order and is limited to black ink. The online version of this book will show color figures
where appropriate.

Working together
to grow libraries in
developing countries

www.elsevier.com • www.bookaid.org

Contents

Acknowledgments
by Jack Jones

Something like FAIR doesn't come about in a vacuum, and there are a lot of people who deserve my deepest gratitude for the role they played in its development. Sometimes their role was subtle and unintentional; perhaps an offhand comment that spurred deeper thinking or a twist in thinking that unlocked some conceptual obstacle I faced. In other cases the role was explicit and obvious; perhaps as a sounding board, support in the face of skeptics, or mentoring me through political mine fields that litter the information security and risk management landscape. Regardless, the following list (in alphabetical order except for the last two entries) inevitably is incomplete and I beg the forgiveness of anyone who feels I have left them out.

- Dr. Henry Beker—whose deep wisdom and strong support have been so crucial to the ongoing success of FAIR and CXOWARE. It is a true privilege to know someone like Henry, let alone have the opportunity to work with him.
- The team at CXOWARE—how lucky can one person get, to be surrounded by such great energy, intelligence, and skill. These people seem able to work magic, both in building a business and taking my sometimes half-baked ideas and turning them into truly remarkable software.
- Jack Freund—whose mental quickness may be unmatched in my experience. Jack has been a dear friend, great colleague, and outstanding partner in writing this book. In fact, without his gentle persistence this book likely would not exist.
- Mike Keller and Susan Gueli—two amazing people, both of whom I had the privilege of working for during my tenure as CISO at Nationwide. It is entirely accurate to say that without their support my career would have been quite different and far less successful than it has been. I am deeply indebted to both of them.
- Cindi Hart—who was my right hand (and very often my saving grace) in each of my CISO roles. I hold no other professional in higher regard, and her friendship has been a true blessing.
- Kirk Herath—whose support and friendship has been so important over the years. You will not encounter a more courageous professional, or anyone more expert in the field of privacy.
- Jim Hietala and Ian Dobson—whose support for FAIR within the Open Group has been so critical over the years. These gentlemen define the word "class," and it has been a privilege to work with them.
- Douglas Hubbard—perhaps unmatched as a risk guru, Douglas' books and insights continue to stoke my internal flame for trying to get this right.
- My team and colleagues at Huntington Bank—as with Nationwide, there simply are too many amazing people to list. Here again, my success was largely due to them, and I am deeply grateful for their support and hard work.

- Alex Hutton—great friend, tireless sounding board, and truly remarkable risk professional. It was his hard work in the early years that kept FAIR alive long beyond what would have happened if I had been trying to do it alone.
- Ryan Jones—whose exceptional work developing and providing FAIR training was responsible for keeping CXOWARE afloat in the early days. His unique combination of creativity, critical thinking, work ethic and pragmatism make him a privilege to work with.
- Marty Miracle—another great friend, deep thinker, and brilliant risk professional. Few people have provided more honest feedback, and fewer yet can match the quality of Marty's analyses.
- Brooke Paul—great advocate and amazing businessman. Brooke's business advice in the early days, though not always followed by me, was always spot-on.
- My team and colleagues at Nationwide Insurance—any success I realized while at Nationwide was largely a function of the amazing team of professionals around me. There are simply too many to list here, but in my mind and heart they all stand out.
- Eddie Schwartz—easily one of the sharpest minds I have ever encountered. Despite this, he seemed to believe there was something worthwhile in me and mentored me in many ways. I learned an awful lot from Eddie, and am truly grateful for his friendship, guidance, and the opportunities he gave me.
- Steve Tabacek—dear friend and phenomenal business partner. I can't imagine a harder working more ethical person, and FAIR would have certainly died on the vine without his tireless support and exceptional business acumen.
- Chad Weinman—another great friend and outstanding colleague. I've never worked with anyone so completely dedicated to the customer. This combined with Chad's energy and positive attitude continue to be critical to CXOWARE's success.
- I am also deeply indebted to all of the early adopters who found value in FAIR and advocated for it even in the face of criticism. These are the people who had the guts to advocate for something that sometimes ran counter to conventional wisdom. Without their timely support I would have likely given up somewhere along the path.
- Last and most important: my wife Jill, son Ryan, and daughter Kristen. They are my inspiration, my heroes, and my reason for being. Their support has meant everything to me. With them I am truly blessed.

About the Authors

Dr. Jack Freund is an expert in IT risk management specializing in analyzing and communicating complex IT risk scenarios in plain language to business executives. Jack has been conducting quantitative information risk modeling since 2007. He currently leads a team of risk analysts at TIAA-CREF. Jack has over 16 years of experience in IT and technology working and consulting for organizations such as Nationwide Insurance, CVS/Caremark, Lucent Technologies, Sony Ericsson, AEP, Wendy's International, and The State of Ohio.

He holds a BS in CIS, Masters in telecommunication and project management, a PhD in information systems, and the CISSP, CISA, CISM, CRISC, CIPP, and PMP certifications. Jack is a visiting professor at DeVry University and a senior member of the ISSA, IEEE, and ACM. Jack chairs a CRISC subcommittee for ISACA and has participated as a member of the Open Group's risk analyst certification committee. Jack's writings have appeared in the *ISSA Journal, Bell Labs Technical Journal, Columbus CEO* magazine, and he currently writes a risk column for @ISACA. You can follow all Jack's work and writings at riskdr.com.

Jack Jones, CISM, CISA, CRISC, CISSP, has been employed in technology for the past 30 years, and has specialized in information security and risk management for 24 years. During this time, he has worked in the United States military, government intelligence, consulting, as well as the financial and insurance industries. Jack has over 9 years of experience as a CISO with three different companies, with five of those years at a Fortune 100 financial services company. His work there was recognized in 2006 when he received the 2006 ISSA Excellence in the Field of Security Practices award at that year's RSA conference.

In 2007, he was selected as a finalist for the Information Security Executive of the Year, Central United States, and in 2012 he was honored with the CSO Compass award for leadership in risk management. He is also the author and creator of the Factor Analysis of Information Risk (FAIR) framework. Currently, Jack is cofounder and president of CXOWARE, Inc.

Preface
by Jack Jones

Two questions and two lame answers. Those were the catalyst in 2001 for developing FAIR. At the time, I was the newly minted CISO for Nationwide Insurance, and I was presenting my proposed security strategy to senior executives in hopes of getting additional funding. One of the executives listened politely to what I had to say, and asked two "simple" questions:

1. How much risk do we have?
2. How much less risk will we have if we spend the millions of dollars you're asking for?

If he had asked me to talk more about the "vulnerabilities"[1] we had or the threats we faced, I could have talked all day. Unfortunately (or, I guess, fortunately), he didn't. He wanted to understand what he was going to get in return for his money. To his first question, I answered, "Lots." To his second question, "Less." Both of my answers were accompanied by a shrug of my shoulders—tacit admission that I didn't have a leg to stand on (he knew when he asked the questions that I wouldn't have a useful answer). The good news was that I got most of the money I was asking for, apparently out of blind faith. The even better news was that I left the meeting determined to find a defensible answer to those questions.

When I began working on FAIR, I had absolutely no idea that an international standards consortium like The Open Group would adopt it as a standard, that people would be building software to implement it, or that organizations would pay to have their people trained in it. Nor had the idea of a book crossed my mind. It also never crossed my mind that what I was developing could be used to evaluate other forms of risk beyond information security. All I wanted was to never have to shrug my shoulders and mutter lame responses to those questions again. This, I have accomplished.

WHAT THIS BOOK IS NOT, AND WHAT IT IS

If you are looking for a book that spoon-feeds you answers to the daily questions and challenges you encounter as an information security professional, you've come to the wrong place. This book doesn't provide much in the way of checklists. You will likewise be disappointed if you're looking for a book based on deep academic research, complete with references to scores of scholarly resources. There are only a handful of references to other works, very few of which would probably qualify as "scholarly" in nature. If you're looking for highly sophisticated math and formulas that make the average person's eyes roll back in their heads—my apologies again. FAIR simply is not that complicated.

---

[1]You will see later in the book why I put the word "vulnerabilities" in quotes.

First and foremost, this is a book about critical thinking. And if you get nothing else out of it, I hope it helps you to think critically and perhaps differently about risk and risk management. It represents the current state of my exploration into risk and risk management, and how it's being applied today. And as with many explorations, the path has been anything but simple and straight. The experience has been like trying to unravel a tangled ball of twine. You pull on a thread for a while, thinking you are on the right track, only to realize you created a nasty knot that you have to pick apart—and then start over. Some of those knots were due to my own logical failures or limited background. Other times, too many times, the knots existed in large part due to risk-related fallacies I had (and the industry still has) bought into for years. You will find in here that I take square aim at a number of sacred risk management cows, which is certain to have me labeled a heretic by some folks. I'm more than comfortable with that. This book attempts to lay out before you the current state of this twine, which is now much less tangled. There are still strings to pull though, and knots to unravel, and there always will be. Maybe you will take what you read here and do some pulling and unraveling of your own. And if you find and unravel knots that I inadvertently created, so much the better.

A snippet from a T.S. Eliot poem does a great job of capturing my experience with FAIR:

> ... and the end of all our exploring will be to arrive where we started and know the place for the first time.
>
> **T.S. Eliot**

That pretty much nails it. My exploration may not be over but there is no question that I know risk and risk management far better than if I hadn't bothered to explore. I hope you'll feel the same way after you've read this book.

Cheers,
Jack Jones
March 2014

Preface
by Jack Freund

While writing this book, Jack Jones and I had a conversation about some of the difficulties faced by those in this profession, and especially those who are interested in bringing quantitative methods into common practice. During this discussion I did what I always do when I'm full of myself and waxing eloquent: I use Socratic Method to help summarize and build analogies to help illustrate key points. I have one friend who called me "The Great Distiller" (with tongue firmly planted in cheek). Jack liked the point I made, and suggested that I write about it here to help frame the book and the work being done on FAIR. Essentially, the point I made went something like this.

What is one of the first things that a new leader in IT risk and security needs to do? Well, there are a lot of tasks to be sure: building relationships, hiring staff, diagnosing problem areas, and building out new and/or enhanced processes. This list could be written about most leadership jobs in any profession. However one task that will show up on that list is something like "identify risk assessment methodology." How unique that is to our profession! Think about that for a minute: you could have a fully implemented risk function that is rating issues and risk scenarios everyday. Yet, when a new leader joins your organization, they may wipe all of that away because they disagree with the method being used. And this may be for reasons as simple as it's unfamiliar to them, they prefer another method more, or a little from column A and a little from column B.

I was discussing this with someone who runs a chemistry lab. She has a PhD in organic chemistry, runs a peptide laboratory, and who modestly refers to herself simply as "a chemist." I asked her if this is a routine practice in chemistry. "Does one of the early tasks of a new lab manager involve choosing the method of chemical interaction they are going to use? Do they define their own approach and methodology for handling volatile chemicals?" "Certainly not," she replied. Once it is determined the type of chemistry they are going to be doing (organic, inorganic, nuclear, etc.), they will need to supply the lab with the materials necessary to do their job. She said there are five basic chemicals she uses in her peptide lab and once those are selected, it is a matter of outfitting the lab with the correct safety devices and handling precautions (fume hoods, storage containers, etc.). "Do any of these tasks involve explaining to your staff your view on how these chemicals interact? Do you have to have conversations to get their minds right on how to do chemistry?" I asked. She told me this is not the case (although we had a good chuckle over those that still insist on pipetting by mouth). There are well-known principles that govern how these chemicals work and interact. In areas where there is dispute or cutting-edge work, those involved in its practice use the scientific method to gain a better understanding of what "truth" looks like and present their work for peer review.

We may never get to the equivalent of a periodic table of risk, but we need to try. We need to set stakes in the ground on what truth looks like, and begin to use scientific method to engage each other on those areas where we disagree. I genuinely want to get better at the practice of IT risk, and I know that Jack Jones does too. It is for this reason that FAIR has been publicly reviewed and vetted for several years now and why Jack Jones placed the basic FAIR taxonomy discussed in chapter 3 in the hands of a neutral standards body (The Open Group). By all means, let us have an open dialogue about what works and what does not. But let us also use impartial, unbiased evidence to make these decisions.

I wrote this book to accomplish several things. First, it is a great honor to be able to author a book with one's mentor. It is an even bigger honor to help your mentor write a book about their life's work. That really is significant to me, but it is also a weighty responsibility. I learned FAIR from Jack early on in the part of my career where I was beginning to do Governance, Risk, and Compliance (GRC) work in earnest. By that time, I had been studying, training in, and writing about various methods of risk assessment and it was becoming clear to me that what passed for a method was more *process* than *calculation*. Indeed, if you compare most major risk assessment methods, they all bear a striking resemblance: you should consider your assets, threats to them, vulnerabilities, and the strength of the controls. Somehow (although rarely ever explicitly identified), you should relate them to one another. The end result is some risk rankings and there you go. Except that is the problem: no one tells you how to do this exactly, and often times you are encouraged to make up your own solution, as if we all know the right way to go about doing that.

What I learned from Jack was simple and straightforward. The relationship between the variables was well reasoned and well designed. It was easy to understand and explain. It also included some sophisticated math, yet was still easy for me to use (I always scored higher on verbal than math sections on any standardized test). I have often been accused of knowing only a single method for assessing risk (a statement that is wildly inaccurate). I know many *methods* for *assessing* risk, yet only one that seeks to *calculate* and *analyze* risk in a defensible way. Knowing how to do that gives you a sense of composure, and perhaps even some bravado. You do not shy away from difficult or hard problems because you have learned how to model these scenarios even when you do not have the best data available. This can be off-putting to some people. But you will come back to the FAIR taxonomy and calculation method over and over again. It is like learning the quadratic formula after years of solving quadratic equations using factoring. Why go back to something that is harder to do and takes longer to complete? I will tease Jack often by saying that he has "ruined me" for other types of risk analysis methods. He takes my good-natured ribbing well. What I mean is that he has showed me the right way to do it, and it is difficult for me to go back to other approaches since their flaws have been laid bare before me. So to that end, yes I only know one (good) method for practicing risk and I have been thoroughly ruined for all the other (not as good) methods for doing risk assessments. And for that I thank you Jack Jones.

The second major reason I decided to write this book is because I believe we are on the precipice of something really amazing in our profession. IT risk is really starting to become its own distinct function that is slowly separating from Information Security proper while simultaneously becoming more intertwined with it. In my role as an educator, I often have discussions with students who are looking to break into the risk and security profession I often tell them that these jobs are really IT specialties and what they really need is to gain some experience in a reference discipline; they need a strong foundation in networking or application development as an example. Only after a few years of work in these roles will they be able to provide useful security work to a future employer. This used to be the way that people entered the security function. Often it was only after many years of work administering servers or working on network routing tables that you were given the chance to be a security practitioner full time. The industry is changing now, and more and more I find that there are paths into risk and security that do not involve even a moderate level of knowledge of something else first.

This is not necessarily bad, however it has some implications. Since we can no longer depend on someone having a solid skillset to draw upon, they may not know a lot about the environments they are now charged with assessing. Second, if they were trained with specific security knowledge that often means that they missed some of the foundational elements that are a part of a core liberal arts education (critical thinking and scientific method as an example). It is also important to learn how to be more autodidactic (a word I learned while being an autodidact).

This book is written in part to help fill out the knowledge gap that a lot of people have when faced with a job that is primarily risk-based. I often draw a diagram for people, which I think adequately reflects the real nature of the skills necessary for working in this job (Figure P.1):

FIGURE P.1

IT risk job skills.

By and large, most of the job is talking to people. You have to learn how to perform technical interviews of IT people and business process reviews with business people. You have to learn how to talk with the person running backups on mainframes, as well as to be able to present risk information to the board of directors. Do not forget the importance of being able to write: risk communication also includes the ability to write e-mails and reports. Essentially, you have to develop a skillset that includes general soft skills and some specialized techniques. This book will aid with some of this.

Good risk practitioners also have technical knowledge. Most of this is not covered here. Like my (aging) advice to college kids, find some way to gain that knowledge either by education or practice. This is probably the easiest of the three to get better at, given the proliferation of free and near-free training available today.

Lastly are the risk skills necessary for success. Addressing this is a big reason we wrote this book. We will go over the definitions for risk variables, how to apply them, how to gather data, taxonomies, ontologies, range estimation, Monte Carlo method, metrics, and reporting. But do not be thrown off by this: our approach is to focus on applied techniques and methods necessary to do the job of an IT risk practitioner today. This is not a book that is heavy with theoretical and complex notions of risk and mathematics. There are many other great books out there that cover this written by authors far more qualified to discuss the topic than we are. My focus in the practice of risk has been on its practical application. It is an irony not lost on me: the guy with the PhD ends up constantly complaining about being practical to those around him. However beautiful and elegant the theory may be, I personally find practical application to be a much better indicator of reality. That and I like to get my hands dirty. To this end, I have always found motivation in this quote from Albert Einstein:

> Any intelligent fool can make things bigger, more complex, and more violent. It takes a touch of genius—and a lot of courage—to move in the opposite direction.

I do not want risk to be complicated. It should be no more complicated than it needs to be, and I have been on record for a long time that I do not believe the people charged with running the businesses and organizations where you work are incapable of understanding IT risk (when properly explained). It is easy to make it complicated; it takes dedicated practice to make it easy.

That brings me to the third and final reason that I wanted to write this book. In my family, it is generally understood that I do "something with computers." And although I imagine many in the various and sundry nooks and crannies of the practice of Information Technology have similar experiences, I have always wanted to be able to find a better (simpler) way to describe the work that I and we as a profession do everyday to the layperson. This explanation I have sought alongside the rapidly changing profession that we labor in daily. As I have outlined above, it is changed enough that it is no longer sufficient to simply say Information Security is our job. The well informed will find it obtuse (what kind of InfoSec do you do?) and the IT civilian still will not know what you are talking about really. Over the years, I have practiced with certain words and phrases to help make it clearer; I tend to use some tactile examples such as how I protect people's bank and retirement accounts from hackers (but even that really is not precisely true). However, given the proliferation of these kinds of attacks and their growing impact, there is usually something in my descriptions that is sufficient to satisfy the cursory inquiry of most. However, I have found that some of those closest to me are routinely curious enough such that they deserve a more complete and full answer as to what exactly I do at work everyday (and most evenings); Mom, this is for you.

Jack Freund, PhD
March 2014

Introduction

How much risk do we have?
How much risk is associated with…?
How much less (or more) risk will we have if…?
Which of our risk management options are likely to be most cost-effective?
What benefit are we getting for our current risk management expenditures?

These are the core questions that FAIR (Factor Analysis of Information Risk) is intended to help us answer. But how is FAIR any different than what the profession has been doing for years? That's what this chapter is about—describing the reasons why "being FAIR" about risk is different and, in many ways, better.

HOW MUCH RISK?

Pick a risk issue. Doesn't matter what the issue is. It could be an information security issue like "cloud computing," a business issue like entering a new market, or a personal issue like buying a used car. Now, if someone asked you how much loss exposure (risk) is associated with that issue, can you answer him or her? Let us rephrase that. Can you answer them and stand behind your answer? With a straight face? If you are using FAIR effectively, you can.

The reason you can rationally answer questions like these using FAIR is because it provides a well-reasoned and logical evaluation framework made up of the following elements:

- An ontology of the factors that make up risk and their relationships to one another. This ontology provides a foundational understanding of risk, without which we could not reasonably do the rest. It also provides a set of standard definitions for our terms.
- Methods for measuring the factors that drive risk
- A computational engine that derives risk by mathematically simulating the relationships between the measured factors
- A scenario modeling construct that allows us to apply the ontology, measurements, and computational engine to build and analyze risk scenarios of virtually any size or complexity

TALKING ABOUT RISK

How complicated is FAIR? Not very. The concepts and ontology are quite straightforward, and measuring the variables can often be downright simple. Unfortunately, the world in which we have to apply FAIR (or any other analysis framework) is often very complex, and that is where we face the learning curve in analyzing risk. What FAIR does is simplify the problem by providing a relatively noncomplex lens through which to view and evaluate the complex risk landscape.

THE BALD TIRE

Those of you who have had some exposure to FAIR in the past might expect this section to be "old news." Well, yes and no. Although you may already know how it turns out, some of the discussion and terms have evolved. As a result, it is probably worth your time to read it. If you have never of heard of FAIR or the Bald Tire, then know that this is a thought experiment to help us uncover some of the challenges with the current state of risk analysis.

The bullets below describe a risk scenario in four simple stages. As you proceed through each of the stages, ask yourself how much risk is associated with what's being described:

1. Picture in your mind a bald car tire. Imagine that it is so bald you can hardly tell that it ever had tread. How much risk is there?
2. Next, imagine that the bald tire is tied to a rope hanging from a tree branch. Now how much risk is there?
3. Next, imagine that the rope is frayed about halfway through, just below where it's tied to the tree branch. How much risk is there?
4. Finally, imagine that the tire swing is suspended over an 80-foot cliff—with sharp rocks below. How much risk is there?

Now, identify the following components within the scenario. What was the:

- Threat,
- Vulnerability, and
- Risk?

Most people believe the risk is "high" at the last stage of the scenario. The answer, however, is that there is very little risk given the scenario exactly as described. Who cares if an empty, old bald tire falls to the rocks below? But, but…what about the person using the tire swing?! Ah, what person? We never mentioned any person.

ASSUMPTIONS

Was our question about the amount of risk unfair? Perhaps, and we've heard the protests before…"But what if someone climbs on the swing?" and, "The tire's purpose is to be swung on, so of course we assumed that somebody would eventually climb on it!"

Both are reasonable arguments. Our point is that it is easy to make assumptions in risk analysis. In fact, assumptions are unavoidable because the world is infinitely complex.

That is our first point—assumptions are unavoidable. Assumptions are also the most likely source of problems within most analyses because, too often, people do not examine their assumptions or even recognize when they are making them. They just shoot from the hip. "That scenario is high risk!" they'll say. Unfortunately, the person next to them may be making a different set of assumptions and react with, "Are you nuts? Clearly that scenario is low risk!" Most of the time, the disagreement is based on different assumptions.

One of the significant advantages to using FAIR is that its ontology and analysis process help you to identify and clarify your assumptions. That way, when someone questions your results, you are in a position to explain the assumptions underlying the analysis.

TERMINOLOGY

Our second point is that from any group going through the Bald Tire scenario, we will typically get several different descriptions of what constitutes the threat, vulnerability, and risk within the scenario. We've heard the frayed rope described as threat, vulnerability, and risk. We have also heard the cliff and rocks described as threat and risk.

The simple fact is that much of the risk profession (including the operational risk discipline) has not adopted standard definitions for these terms. Compare this to other professions. Physicists do not confuse terms like mass, weight, and velocity, and financial professionals do not confuse debit and credit—even in informal discussions—because to do so significantly increases the opportunity for confusion and misunderstanding. It also makes it tough to normalize data. This is important to keep in mind when we're trying to communicate to those outside our profession—particularly to executives who are very familiar with the fundamental concepts of risk—where the misuse of terms and concepts can damage our credibility as professionals and reduce the effectiveness of our message. After all, our goal is not to create a secret risk language that only we can talk about—effectively isolating ourselves from other risk professionals.

TALKING ABOUT RISK

Go to your local bookstore or library and pick up two different books on risk by two different authors. There is a very good chance that you will find that they have used foundational terminology differently from one another. For that matter, there's a decent chance that each author uses fundamental risk terminology inconsistently within his or her own book.

So, what are the threat, vulnerability, and risk components within the Bald Tire scenario? The definitions themselves are described in Chapter 3, but within this scenario:

- The threat is the earth and the force of gravity that it applies to the tire and rope.
- The frayed rope introduces some amount of vulnerability, but is NOT a vulnerability itself. Huh? Vulnerability (in FAIR) is a probability statement. In other words,

it is the probability that a threat event (e.g., the force of gravity on the tire and rope) will become a loss event (e.g., the rope breaks). In FAIR, we use the term vulnerability in a way that answers the question, "How vulnerable are we?" In answer to that question, a FAIR practitioner may answer something like, "between 30 and 45%." Simply stated, the rope represents a control, and its frayed condition simply increases the probability of a loss event. If this still doesn't entirely make sense to you, it will later as we get into the framework in more detail.

- What about risk? Which part of the scenario represents risk? Well, the fact is, there isn't a single component within the scenario that we can point to and say, "Here is the risk." Risk is not a thing. We can't see it, touch it, or measure it directly. Similar to speed, which is derived from distance divided by time, risk is a derived value that represents loss exposure. It's derived from the combination of factors described in FAIR's ontology.

Having made an issue of terminology, the following paragraphs introduce and briefly discuss some basic definitions.

THREAT

A reasonable definition for threat is anything (e.g., object, substance, human, etc.) that is capable of acting in a manner that can result in harm. A tornado is a threat, as is someone driving a car, as is a hacker. The key consideration is that threats are the actors (a.k.a., "agents") that can cause a loss event to occur. This is in contrast to some common usage, where conditions may be referred to as threats. For example, someone might refer to a puddle of water on the floor as a "threat," when in fact it is not. It is passive, inanimate, and not an actor in any meaningful way. A person stepping on it is the threat actor. The water simply increases the probability that the threat action (stepping on the wet floor) results in a loss event (a slip and fall accident).

VULNERABILITY

Although the word "vulnerability" is commonly referred to as a "weakness that may be exploited by a threat," that isn't how we view things in FAIR. Similar to the term risk, vulnerability is considered a value rather than a thing. As a result, you can't point to something and say, "Here is a vulnerability!" What you can do is point to a control (like a frayed rope) and declare, "Here is a condition that increases our vulnerability." It may feel like a fine point, but trust us, it is a critical distinction. The relevance of this distinction will become clearer as you progress through this book.

RISK

The following definition applies regardless of whether you are talking about investment risk, market risk, credit risk, information risk, or any of the other common risk domains:

Risk—*The probable frequency and probable magnitude of future loss.*

In other words—how often losses are likely to happen, and how much loss is likely to result. Rest assured, we'll get into much more detail on this in Chapter 3.

THE BALD TIRE METAPHOR

In large part, risk management today (particularly operational risk management) is practiced as an art rather than a science. What is the difference? Science begins by analyzing the nature of the subject—forming a definition and determining the scope of the problem. Once this is accomplished, you can begin to form and then substantiate (or not) theories and hypotheses. The resulting deeper understanding provides the means to explain and more effectively manage the subject.

Art, on the other hand, does not operate within a clearly defined framework or definition. Consequently, it isn't possible to consistently explain or calculate based upon an artistic approach. In fact, it doesn't even seek to explain. It just "is." A useful example is shamanism. The shaman rolls his bones or "confers with his gods." He then prescribes a remedy based upon what his ancestors have passed down to him (analogous to "best practices"). Now, some shamans may be extremely intuitive and sensitive to the conditions within a scenario and may be able to select a reasonable solution on most occasions. Nevertheless, the shaman can't rationally explain his analysis, nor can he credibly explain why the cure works (or sometimes doesn't work). In addition, while we would like to believe that best practices are generally effective (as we strive to reuse what we think has been successful in the past), this can be a dangerous assumption. Best practices are often based on long-held shamanistic solutions, tend to be one-size-fits-all, may evolve more slowly than the conditions in which they are used, and can too often be used as a crutch— e.g., "I can't explain why, so I'll just point to the fact that everyone else is doing it this way."

There is, however, no question that intuition and experience are essential components of how we do our jobs. The same is true for any profession. Yet these alone do not provide much traction in the face of critical examination, and are not strong formulas for consistency.

In order for the risk management profession to evolve, we have to begin to approach our problem space more rigorously and scientifically (note that we did not say "purely scientifically"). This means we have to seek to understand why and how, we have to measure in a meaningful way, and we have to be able to explain things consistently and rationally.

RISK ANALYSIS VS RISK ASSESSMENT

Many people don't differentiate "assessment" from "analysis," but there is an important difference. From a FAIR perspective, risk analysis is often a subcomponent of the larger risk assessment process.

The broader risk assessment process typically includes:

- Identification of the issues that contribute to risk,
- Analyzing their significance (this is one place where FAIR fits in),
- Identifying options for dealing with the risk issue,
- Determining which option is likely to be the best fit (another opportunity to apply FAIR), and
- Communicating results and recommendations to decision-makers.

As you can see, "analysis" is about evaluating significance and/or enabling the comparison of options. Unfortunately, much of what you see today in risk management is assessment without meaningful (or accurate) analysis. The result is poorly informed prioritization and cost-ineffective decisions.

Bottom line—The purpose of any risk analysis is to provide a decision-maker with the best possible information about loss exposure and their options for dealing with it.

EVALUATING RISK ANALYSIS METHODS

FAIR is just one approach to risk analysis. There are many people working to develop other methods with the same goals in mind. This is terrific news to those of us who are trying to be as effective as possible in managing risk. However, regardless of the methods you consider using, we encourage you to evaluate any risk analysis method on at least three points:

1. Is it useful?
2. Is it practical?
3. Are the results defensible?

A methodology is useful when the results are accurate and meaningful to decision-makers. If an analysis method provides results that are expressed in qualitative or ordinal scales, then meaningfulness must be questioned. Why? Well, what does a risk score of 3.5 mean? We suppose it's better than a risk score of 4.1 (assuming one is good and five is bad), but ultimately, how do you compare that kind of value statement, or something like "medium," against the other more quantitative considerations (like revenue projections or expenses) that inevitably play a role in decisions? As for accuracy, a precise ordinal rating like 3.5 or 4.1 is just begging to be picked apart because it implies a level of precision that is unrealistic in risk analysis. Why 3.5 and not 3.6 or 3.7? Or, if the risk rating is qualitative (e.g., "medium"), then accuracy is often a matter of what assumptions were being made and how rigorous the thinking was that underlies the analysis (typically not very rigorous).

Now, some decision-makers find qualitative or ordinal results acceptable. That's fine. Fine, that is, until you have to defend those risk statements when you are asking for significant funding or telling them that their pet project can't proceed because it has "high risk." (Good luck, by the way, defending 3.5 or "high" to a strong critical thinker.) In our experience, the underpinnings of those kinds of risk values are arrived at through very little rigor, through questionable methods, or both. The executives might not push back, but don't count on it.

Practicality is a crucial matter. It does little good to apply rocket science when all you really need to do is cross the street. Don't get us wrong, though. You can go deep into the weeds with FAIR if you want or need to. However, you don't have to. The same should be true for any practical risk analysis approach—i.e., you should be able to apply it quick-and-dirty if need be, or go deep.

There are "risk analysis" methods in use today whose logic falls apart under close examination. Often, these methods call themselves risk analysis when what they are really analyzing is a subcomponent of risk (e.g., control conditions). Keep in mind, however, that these methods may be excellent at what they actually do, so don't disregard their value. It's simply a matter of recognizing what they do and do not provide. A simple way of identifying a bona fide risk analysis method is to determine whether it includes an analysis of threat frequency, vulnerability, and loss magnitude, and whether it treats the problem probabilistically. If one or more of these components is missing, or if the problem is not treated from a probabilistic perspective, then it likely can't be defended as a true risk analysis method.

Let's look at an example risk "analysis" against this three-point litmus test:

Risk issue: Absence of segregation of duties for system administrators.
Asset at risk: Corporate financial data that supports financial reporting (a SOX concern for publicly traded companies in the United States)
Risk rating: High risk. The assessing individual felt that it was possible for system administrators to manipulate data feeding the financial reporting process, which would require restatement of finances. This could result in significant penalties and reputational damage.

My, that does sound scary.

In this case, executives are presented with a situation they may only superficially understand (i.e., they may understand the concept of segregation of duties, but they couldn't explain it in this technology context). They *do* know that they do not want to be in violation of SOX rules, so the "high risk" rating makes them very nervous. The options they're presented with though, expensive monitoring technologies and/ or an increase in system administrator staff levels so that duties can be segregated, are unattractive because they are trying to reduce budget rather than increase it. So the question is, is this "analysis" useful, practical, and logical?

Is it useful? Well, it is darned difficult to compare "high" against the increased budget implications. As a result, the executives have to mentally compare the two considerations (requiring many unexamined assumptions). In cases like this, it usually boils down to how risk averse the executive is and how much credibility they place in the person doing the risk rating.

Is it practical? Sure…we guess…at least if all you are concerned with is simplicity. We mean, how hard is it to wave a wet finger in the air and declare something to be high risk, medium risk, or whatever. In fact, it's not unusual in cases where a regulation or other scary element is involved, for people to skip the wet finger in the air. They just hear the terms SOX and noncompliant, and go straight to "high" in their risk rating.

Is it defensible? Well, now it gets interesting. So let's poke this analysis with a stick and see if it squeals. With risk being the probable frequency and probable magnitude of future loss, let's first examine the likelihood aspect. How likely is it that a system administrator, by virtue of their having unsegregated access to this data, would act in a manner that creates inaccurate financial reporting?

Certainly, it *could* happen, but this is not a question of possibility, it's a question of probability (more on this later). Examining the available data and considering that we are talking about a population of five system administrators (in this organization) who have all undergone background checks and have impeccable work records, you would be hard-pressed to say that this is anything but very unlikely to occur.

Even if they did attempt to manipulate the data, there are four points of validation farther along in the financial report generation process that would almost certainly catch the discrepancy. This means that the threat event (manipulation of data) is very unlikely to result in a loss event (inaccurate financial reporting). In FAIR-speak, this means that loss event frequency is low. Quantitatively, the estimates might come to somewhere between once every 50 years to once every 20 years (we will cover how we get to numbers like these later in the book). Regarding loss magnitude, after speaking with subject matter experts both inside and outside the company, the losses were estimated to be between $100,000 at the low end, to $10 million at the high end.

Plugging these values into a Monte Carlo tool, the annualized exposure is somewhere between $60,000 and $330,000. However, because the company has predefined risk thresholds stating that high risk is anything greater than $1 million, it seems the initial "high risk" rating does not stand up, and is in fact misrepresenting the level of risk to the organization. We could swear we hear the sound of squealing.

Clearly, this was a quick and dirty (but real) example, but you get the point. The off-the-cuff analysis was not accurate. In addition, when pressed, the person who did the initial analysis argued that it did not matter how likely it was. It *could* happen and if it did, it would be painful. That's true, but it reflects possibility rather than probability, which means it is not a risk analysis. By that person's line of thinking, we should worry equally about our sun turning into a white dwarf.

In presenting the quantitative analysis of this scenario to management, you would include a description of the worst-case outcome, but you would also present the annualized view and rationale. This allows the decision-makers to operate from a clearer and richer understanding of what they are up against, which is the whole purpose of analyzing anything.

RISK ANALYSIS LIMITATIONS

Risk analysis is never perfect. The fact is, all risk analysis models are approximations of reality because reality is far too complex to ever model exactly. Furthermore, the future is uncertain. Making matters even more interesting is that fact that all data are imperfect. Nonetheless, by decomposing a complex subject into clearer, more readily analyzed components, we can understand and make reasoned judgments about the subject. Additionally, we can optimize the use of imperfect data by using methods like Monte Carlo, which is inherently designed to deal with the uncertainty in data.

Of course, the question sometimes comes up, "Well, if models are imperfect and data are imperfect, is quantitative risk analysis even legitimate?" Let us put it to you this way:

- You are always using some kind of risk analysis (whether quantitative or qualitative, formal or informal) to inform decisions.
- Decisions are going to be made, regardless of what method you used to inform those decisions.
- Even qualitative scoring is using a model—often, this is your mental model of how you think the risk world works, and that model may or may not be complete or biased, but it is unlikely to have been examined and vetted. Consequently, the odds are lower (perhaps much lower) that your mental model is as good as a well-vetted formal model.
- Even qualitative scoring uses data. By this we mean, how else do you justify a medium rating versus a high rating? Also, those data are certainly no better than what would be applied to a quantitative method, and stand a good chance of being less complete because they are typically developed with much less rigor.

Given the above, there is virtually no way a qualitative result is more accurate or reliable than a well-developed quantitative result.

WARNING—LEARNING HOW TO THINK ABOUT RISK JUST MAY CHANGE YOUR PROFESSIONAL LIFE

Risk management is about setting priorities. Every day, we make decisions about what to spend our money on, where to go, and what to do. In every one of those decisions, we make a trade-off between perceived benefits and costs associated with pursuing one end or another. In all that we do, the truth is that we will never have enough time, money, or resources to accomplish all that we desire. In many ways, it's a uniquely human condition to be able to analyze our choices and options for spending our limited resources to achieve our goals as best we can. This is a book about learning how to think about risk as much as it is a book for calculating and implementing risk management programs in your organization.

Using FAIR to manage risk in your organization is an effective way to bridge the largest gap you may experience in your work: communicating effectively with stakeholders. Because as you will discover, not everyone will have the same keen sense of the technological issues you wish to raise to senior management. As a result, there are bound to be vocabulary issues among the various groups with which you wish to speak. Utilizing the FAIR risk ontology can help even the uninitiated grasp the concepts necessary to communicate effectively with the various parties interested in the outcome of a risk scenario.

However, you should be warned that within the pages of this book are concepts and ideas that may change your professional life. We often warn people before taking FAIR training classes that learning FAIR can be a real "red-pill blue-pill moment" in reference to the movie "The Matrix," when the protagonist takes a pill and his whole world changes when he is awoken from an involuntary sedentary state. FAIR tends to challenge the established way of doing things in information security. Once you learn the highly productive, practical, and defensible way to analyze risk using FAIR, it will be very difficult to ever go back to what you learned previously. No longer will you be able to stare at risk labels like "High", "Medium", and "Low" and not wonder what assumptions were made, or what ranges they map back to. No longer will you be content with multiplying two ordinal numbers together to come up with a risk score that no one really understands. And you will never be able to look at ordinal scales again without feeling concern regarding their imprecision (look out annual review time).

USING THIS BOOK

This book provides a thorough review of what FAIR is and how it works. As such, it can be used to evaluate whether FAIR will fit your organization's risk analysis needs, and where it fits among the many other risk-related frameworks and methods that are out there. It can also be used to help you prepare for The Open Group Level-1 FAIR Analyst certification exam. Beyond that, we would like to think that it can also enrich your understanding of risk and risk management, and help you to be better calibrated when you are faced with making decisions that entail risk (as all decisions do).

It is best read from beginning to end, but if you are already familiar with the concepts, feel free to jump around to areas where you need help. We've tried to include many "Talking About Risk" boxes through the text to share our experiences and help give you ammunition to address concerns regarding quantitative methods generally, and aspects of FAIR particularly. Furthermore, these boxes can give you valuable insights into practitioner-level techniques for how best to model, frame, and discuss risk and risk management using FAIR.

The book will next dive into some basic risk concepts where we'll give you the 10-cent version of some really complex philosophical foundations on risk. This is a practitioner's guide, not a dissertation on risk, so we really only want to focus on the most topical aspects of risk to get you going. This also tends to be where some classically trained information security professionals have some critical misconceptions about risk, which can limit their ability to be productive in dealing with the topic. From there, we'll delve into describing the FAIR framework's particular ontology and terminology. Additionally, an entire section on measuring risk components is offered to help you come up with quantitative numbers for your analysis. This is a challenging, yet critical area, so it's important to have the tools in your box to be able to handle this soundly. After that is a detailed section on the process of conducting an analysis. There will also be a *lot* of examples to help guide you down the right path when faced with some complicated scenarios. How to communicate the results of an analysis is another section that is given prominent treatment here. Never underestimate just how important it is that you be able to speak about your work to upper management. The last several chapters focus on leveraging FAIR we will address how to position in the context of an overall risk decision-making and a risk management program. Most of this has never before been published, and we think you will find it especially interesting and helpful.

Basic Risk Concepts

The winning general is the one who can best act on imperfect information and half formed theories
Napoleon Bonaparte

Any discussion of risk can easily become mired in mathematics and complex theories. These debates can be important and useful for the advancement of the profession. However, as a risk practitioner, you will rarely find yourself in these deep academic debates over the nature of risk. Instead, you'll find that when discussing risk "in the trenches," you need to arm yourself with a number of basic concepts. This isn't just for your own understanding, but also because you will likely find yourself defending your risk analysis work on occasion, and it's always good to stay light on your feet! Anyone who has spent time preparing and presenting risk analyses knows that it is part of the job to be able to defend your work, sometimes against logical fallacies. We will provide you with some pointers to keep you out of the line of fire and redirect the discussion back to the risk decision-making business at hand.

Very often, the points we will discuss in this chapter—predictions, probability, subjectivity, precision and accuracy—are raised as criticisms of quantitative analysis. Some of the commonly raised concerns are valid, and we will talk about those. We'll also talk about where there are weaknesses in those arguments.

POSSIBILITY VERSUS PROBABILITY

It's a very common practice for risk analysts to consider all the bad things that could happen when conducting their assessments. Some organizations even consider it a high water mark of the maturity of a risk program if they're able to point to a long list of risk scenarios that represents everything everyone on the team could think of that might go wrong. Although it's often useful to think about all the possibilities that exist, decisions generally are better served by focusing on probabilities…or at the very least probabilities have to be part of the deliberation. The problem is, not everyone clearly understands the difference between possibility and probability.

There is a metaphor we like to use that's helpful in thinking about the difference between possibility versus probability. Let's say that you had the "opportunity" to play Russian roulette (we are glass-half-full kinda guys). If you are unfamiliar with the term, this is a gruesome game where one or more people use a gun with at least one empty chamber. The player will take the weapon, point it at his or her head (or in some variations someone else's head), and pull the trigger. If you're in luck, you hear a click; otherwise… But there is a twist in our version of the game! You get to pick which weapon you would use: a six shot revolver or a semi-automatic pistol, both loaded with a single bullet. Which would you choose?

Well, if you approach risk analysis as purely a possibility issue, then you would consider either gun an equivalent choice. Yup, either gun will, ahem, "do the job." That's all you need to know, right? Heck, if we were in a snarky mood we might even call both options "high risk," but we both know there is a real distinction between the two. Let's put on our risk analysis hats and dig into this scenario (see Figure 2.1).

We could choose the six-shot revolver. That will give us about an 83% chance of walking away from this with only significant emotional scars and a promissory note for decades of therapy. However, say you choose the semi-automatic pistol. Your odds of having a big therapy bill plummet to near zero (eh, maybe it jams, or the bullet is a dud or something).

This is a horribly grisly example of the difference between possibility and probability. The point here is that the possibility perspective gives you absolutely no help in making a good decision because you aren't well informed. It's 100% possible with either weapon that you will have a bad day. It's really only when we start talking about probabilities that we have useful information. Suddenly, we go from having to worry about everything (Squalls! Stalactites! Sinkholes! Oh my!) to having a more manageable list of concerns. The same thing is true in information security or any risk discipline. It is useful to think of what events are possible, but only as a means of surfacing events on which to analyze probability. Decisions should be informed by probabilities.

Now, we aren't naive, there are often some low probability risk scenarios that need to be accounted for. As an example, most organizations have established

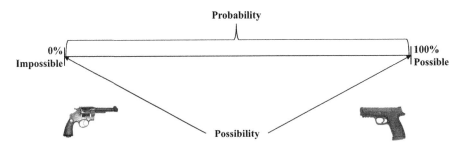

FIGURE 2.1

A deadly game of possible versus probable.

measures for dealing with the loss of their data center in a horrible natural disaster. However, if you are tracking meteors, then perhaps you aren't managing risk at the right level.

An argument we've heard raised about quantitative analysis, especially if there isn't much empirical data available to inform an estimate, is that because we don't know the probability of an event exactly, we have to treat it as a possibility—i.e., not distinguish it from a likelihood perspective. In fact, in one case, an individual insisted that because he didn't have hard data, he would be just as likely to bet that the network administrators in his organization were compromising sensitive information on the network a million times per year, as he would be to bet on one such compromise per year. Not a million compromised records per year—a million distinct attacks— by perhaps a couple of dozen network administrators. We kid you not. Apparently, those network administrators have a lot of spare time on their hands. Clearly, not being able to make that kind of distinction means prioritization goes right out the window.

One other thing that comes up a lot when working in risk is the difference between probability, likelihood, and frequency. Consider a look at a typical 5-day forecast. What if, instead of knowing which day it's most likely to rain, you only knew that there was a 63% chance it would rain sometime during the upcoming week. Without a more specific time-frame reference, we can't make good decisions. Yet, even this scenario is more helpful than many risk analyses that don't provide a time-frame reference: in that case, you wouldn't know if the 63% applied to Wednesday, the whole week, month, year, or eternity.

Yes, some assessment methods simply apply a probability rating to a risk scenario. No mention of time frame is ever made, and it often feels like you're supposed to consider the event on an infinite timeline (as in, the probability that this will ever happen, also known as a possibility). This isn't very helpful in understanding risk because, without a timeline, it can be argued that all things are highly likely to occur. One helpful illustration of this is the line from the movie Fight Club, in which the narrator says that "on a long enough timeline the survival rate for everyone drops to zero." Likewise, for any risk scenario, on a long enough timeline, the chance of it happening, whatever "it" is, approaches 100%.

Certainly for events that are expected to occur more than once a year, the logical thing to do is express them in terms of frequency—e.g., three times per year. This is, in fact, an example of a limitation associated with "probability" and "likelihood." Neither of them easily allows you to account for events that are expected to occur more than once in a year (or whatever time-frame is being used). For example, within an annual time-frame, the "likelihood" of a computer virus infection occurring within an organization may be the same as, for example, a facility power outage. They may both be "highly likely." One is almost certain to be more frequent than the other though, and thus frequency is the more useful term. This is one of the reasons why you will hear us use frequency in our analyses more often than probability or likelihood. On the other hand, frequency has a limitation as well. You can't use it for events that can only happen once.

For example, you wouldn't use frequency when you're talking about the risk associated with our sun turning into a white dwarf. That event only happens once.

The good news is that you can easily convert a probability estimate into frequency in almost all cases. Simply annualize it. For example, let us say there is a 5% probability of an externally facing system being hacked this year. This 5% probability is equivalent to a frequency of once in 20 years.

PREDICTION

Here we'll discuss the sometimes subtle but important difference between forecasts and predictions, helping you to have a realistic understanding of the nature of risk analysis, and giving you some talking points if someone wants to argue about whether your analysis is a prediction.

Obviously, if anyone were truly able to predict the future, they would be ridiculously wealthy by now. They would not be writing books about risk (as an example…but we aren't bitter). Risk analysis is inherently about looking at the future and decision makers want to know what will or could happen, and what they should do about it. It's for this reason that some people may pose questions like these:

"Are you telling me that we will get hacked in the next year?"

or

"Are you sure that a patient will file a lawsuit against us in the next 6 months?"

Sometimes questions like these are intended to undermine the results you've presented. People can be skeptical of quantified risk results, and this is one of the ways they may attempt to poke holes in your work.

Fundamentally, risk analyses conducted with FAIR provide a measure of *temporally-bound probability*. Put more plainly, this means you are offering a measure of the probability of occurrence in some given time period (typically annually). Note that probability is not the same thing as certitude. Therefore, you would be able to say, for example, that a risk scenario is likely to occur sometime between once in a decade and once a year. Think about it this way—you are making forward-looking statements based on a series of assumptions, models, and data about things over which you may have no direct control. Clearly, you aren't predicting anything.

So if we aren't predicting, then how is a risk analysis even helpful? Well, first know that regardless of whether an analysis is performed, someone is going to make a decision to fix (or not fix) whatever the issues are. Your goal in risk analysis should always be to make sure that whatever the decision is, you have done your best to keep the decision maker well-informed about the probabilities of different outcomes. Therefore, with that goal in mind, there are some useful techniques to answer questions about the nature of "prediction" in risk analysis.

The first is the language you use to discuss the analysis. Never call your analysis a prediction. Just don't use the word; purge it from your vocabulary. A more useful alternative is "forecast." Forecast is useful because people inherently understand the uncertain nature of, for example, weather forecasting (even though meteorologists do a significant amount of quantitative analysis). People just know that when it says 50% chance of rain on Thursday that it may or may not rain (but they might still bring an umbrella). Not to be disparaging of the many fine meteorologists out there, but their work is certainly not prediction in a mystical, "I know your destiny" kind of way. (Note that forecast differs from prediction in connotation only. We offer this approach here as a means to help the layperson come to terms with quantitative risk analysis.)

The other thing to keep in mind is the idea of an event being probable within a period of time. Because that's what a risk analysis is—a representation of the reality that you think exists today. It may change tomorrow. The risk landscape changes all the time—tomorrow there could be a brand new wave of computer hacks or the introduction of a new patient's rights bill that could allow for more frequent patient lawsuits. But if you have collected the data properly, and followed the other guidelines in this book about how to perform the analysis and present it, then you should be confident that your results, while not a prediction, accurately represent what you believe the probabilities are for your organization. Be forthright about how you came up with the numbers (you should have done your legwork here). Indicate the subject matter experts from your organization or elsewhere that were sources, the reports you referenced on the topic (there are a lot of information security resources available that can assist you in coming up with these values), and that through this information gathering, you feel confident that this range represents reality. Be clear that you don't know when an attack would occur, but that you have quantified your uncertainty around how often you think it will happen.

An analogy we find useful for getting the point across involves a pair of six-sided dice. Examining the dice and considering the factors as we know them (the number of sides, the symmetry of the dice, etc.), we can confidently state there is a 1/36 chance of them coming up snake eyes with any roll. That is a probability statement. We would be fools, however, to believe we could predict on which roll this would happen. It might happen on the first roll or the fortieth. In either instance, the probability estimate was not wrong. Nonetheless, even though we can't predict exactly when snake eyes will occur, someone faced with betting on the dice would benefit from knowing the probabilities of the different outcomes.

SUBJECTIVITY VERSUS OBJECTIVITY

The question of subjectivity comes up in virtually every conversation with skeptics of quantitative risk analysis. The argument usually is that in order for an analysis to be valid, it has to be objective. The problem is that very few people seem to take the time to understand the nature of subjectivity and objectivity. Furthermore, whether an analysis or data set are more objective or subjective in nature is far less important than whether they are useful.

TWO ENDS OF A CONTINUUM

From a practical perspective, subjectivity and objectivity are not binary in nature; they are two ends of a continuum. There is no bright yellow line that you cross in your analysis whereby it's all of a sudden objectively objective. This is because any time a human being is involved in a process (which is all the time if you think about it), some amount of subjectivity will creep in. Even in "hard" sciences like physics, human judgment (and thus subjectivity) play a role. Humans formulate the theories under analysis, devise and perform the experiments to prove or disprove the theories, decide which data are relevant and which are noise, and interpret the results. At each stage, some amount of subjectivity in the form of personal bias or opinion inevitably creeps into the process, which ultimately means it isn't a question of whether subjectivity exists in an analysis; it's a matter of how much.

One of the goals in any analysis should be to drive as much objectivity as possible into the process and data, while recognizing that there is no such thing as a purely objective analysis. Achieving this increased objectivity can come from things like controlled experimentation and empirical data. It can also come from a clearly defined model, unambiguous terminology, the rigor that comes from having to document rationale for the estimates used in an analysis, peer reviews, as well as the dialogue and critical thinking that should be a natural part of the analysis process.

TALKING RISK

Many times, people who express concerns regarding subjectivity in quantitative risk analysis seem to forget that qualitative estimates of risk are inherently as subjective, and often times more subjective, than quantitative estimates. This greater subjectivity stems from the lack of rigor that usually occurs when making qualitative estimates. Reminding them of this can be an effective way of focusing the conversation on more relevant concerns.

HOW OBJECTIVITY AND SUBJECTIVITY REALLY WORK

Imagine that you are driving to work and you approach a traffic light just as it starts to turn yellow. Do you stop or speed up? It depends, right? It depends on how fast you're driving, how close you are to the intersection, road conditions, other traffic, whether you are late for work, whether law enforcement is in the vicinity, etc. In the instant you see the light turn yellow you take in these objective, but imprecise, pieces of information. In that same instant you apply your mental models regarding how all of these elements work together and generate informal probabilities of various positive and negative events—and then you make a decision. A very personal, subjective decision based on how you *feel* about the results of your analysis within the context of everything else on your plate and how you are wired as a risk taker.

This is no different, really, than our circumstances in risk analysis. We pull together data of varying quality (more on this shortly), apply models to interpret what the data mean, and then someone (an executive, perhaps) makes a personal decision in the context of their own interpretation of the analysis, given how they are wired emotionally and the broader set of considerations they have to deal with (e.g., profitability, other forms of risk, etc.).

This combination of data and personal interpretation guarantees that some amount of subjectivity is inherent in every decision, regardless of the level of objectivity that went into an analysis.

MEASUREMENT QUALITY

Ultimately, though, the question is not (or should not be) about whether data are more "subjective" or "objective" in nature; the focus should be on measurement quality. So what are the characteristics of a quality measurement? For the purposes of this discussion, there are two: repeatability and validity. Repeatable measures are those that will be consistent when performed by different means and perhaps by different analysts. A "valid" measurement is one that measures what it is intended to measure. For example, attempting to measure distance by using a volume metric like bushels wouldn't qualify as valid.

Repeatability

Whenever we teach classes on FAIR, we ask someone in the class to estimate our heights. Invariably, the person says something like, "6 feet tall" or "5 feet, 10 inches". The next question for the class is whether that estimate was subjective or objective. Almost without exception, the answer has been that it was "subjective." The class believes the estimate was subjective because it wasn't arrived at using a tape measure or some other measurement tool. We point out to them, though, the first thing that happens when we ask someone to estimate our heights is their eyes look us up and down, and often side-to-side. In other words, they compare us (measure us) against objective (but imprecise) references in the room, like the whiteboard, podium, etc. But are these legitimate measurement references, and what makes a reference "legitimate" for measurement purposes?

Repeatability is often a function of who is doing the measurement, the environment, as well as the quality of measurement tools and processes. If you have skilled personnel, a controlled environment, and good measurement tools, it becomes much more likely that you will get repeatable results. Unfortunately, risk scenarios rarely exist in controlled environments. Furthermore, sources of data may be few and not always reliable. Although this makes repeatability more challenging, it doesn't make it impossible. Furthermore—and this is critical—the question of repeatability is inextricably tied to the notion of precision.

Let's assume for a minute that you aren't buying the idea that the whiteboard we're standing next to is a legitimate measurement reference. You may grudgingly accept that it is generally objective in nature, but seriously, a measurement tool? Okay, suppose instead that we handed someone in class a tape measure and asked them to measure our height. They would probably ask us to stand next to the wall, where they would lay something flat (like a book) on top of our heads and use that to mark a point on the wall. They would then use the tape to measure from the floor to that point and arrive at a height somewhere around 5 feet, 10 inches. If you asked 100 people to repeat this measurement process, you would probably get measurements ranging from roughly 5 feet, 9 inches, to 5 feet, 11 inches, depending on the time of day (we get shorter as the day wears on) and how careful they are in the measurement process. Clearly, the results are repeatable within a certain range of precision.

What is interesting is that after asking the question regarding our height within dozens of risk analysis classes, the answers we get have ranged from 5 feet, 8 inches, to 6 feet, 1 inch. In other words, this measurement has been repeatable within a range of roughly 4% (plus or minus). The point we're trying to make here is that both measurement methods were repeatable, just to different degrees of precision. This notion of a useful degree of precision is key because we are making a measurement in order to facilitate a decision. Perhaps it is something simple like, "Can Jack fit through this door?" or maybe something morbid like, "Is this pine box big enough to fit Jack?" When dealing with risk, particularly information security related risk, high degrees of precision are a pipe dream in the vast majority of analyses. The aim of analyses should be to be better informed in our decision making through better models, assumptions that are more clearly understood, and better use of whatever data we have. This does not require high degrees of precision.

TALKING RISK

Claims are often made that qualitative measurements are more consistent than quantitative ones. The only reason this would be true is that qualitative measurements are, by design, very imprecise. The range of actual values that might be contained within something labeled "medium risk" are generally undefined and large, which inherently increases the odds of getting consistency from analyst to analyst. After all, how much less precise can you get than when you carve the entire continuum of possible outcomes into three parts—high, medium, and low? Of course, if we define the width of quantitative ranges widely enough, we could certainly guarantee an equal degree of repeatability. This lack of precision, whether qualitative or quantitative, comes at a price, though, in terms of usefulness. As with most things in life, the key is to strike the right balance between precision and utility.

Measurement validity

What reaction do you believe someone would receive if they gave a presentation to their CEO that exclaimed, "Next quarter our profit will reach an all-time high of five!" Unless "five" was already understood to translate to something meaningful, we're guessing that this would be the last presentation this hapless soul would give to that CEO. What does "five" mean in the context of profit? Who knows? It doesn't intuitively translate as a measurement of profit and so its validity is (or should be) suspect. Perhaps if profit was a "four" last year we can at least feel good that it is improving, but it still lacks important informational value. We can think of this apparent disconnect between a measurement and its relevance as an abstraction problem—i.e., the true value is abstracted, and thus must be translated, from its given value. This doesn't necessarily mean that the measurement isn't valid; it just forces us to work harder to understand what it really means. That said, because we don't always go to the trouble to do that translation, we are more susceptible to making decisions based on abstracted measurements that are not valid or are misunderstood.

Another common validity problem occurs when a measurement is purported to be risk-relevant, but it isn't relevant at all or it has some relevance but is applied to a "broken" risk model that misapplied the measurement. Both of these circumstances occur when the person performing the measurement (or the one who developed the model) doesn't understand how risk works. For example, let's say that we are measuring the efficacy of an authentication control (such as a password), which can be a legitimate factor in some risk scenarios. Unfortunately, let's also say that the model we're using to derive risk applies that efficacy value in the loss magnitude component of the equation rather than loss event frequency. In that instance, the measurement isn't valid given how it's being used, and the resulting risk values will be wrong. You might scoff at this example, but we've seen these sorts of errors repeatedly in the risk measurement world.

Making up numbers

Unfortunately, some of the risk scenarios we have to analyze don't even appear to have the equivalent of us standing next to a whiteboard for reference. For example, we might be asked to analyze the loss exposure associated with some event that has not happened yet (a nuclear strike on New York City, for example). In some of these scenarios, we might not have a way of even knowing with certainty when an event takes place (someone cheating on a test, for example). When faced with this situation, an argument is often presented that the analyst is forced to "just make up numbers." In these circumstances, skeptics sneer at the notion of subject matter expert estimates as nothing more than one person's "opinion." The implication is that these estimates are inherently flawed. In some cases, these concerns are valid. Studies have shown that human beings are notoriously bad at estimating. In the Measurement chapter, we will spend some time discussing this further, and we will also discuss methods for significantly improving the quality of estimates.

TALKING RISK

It's interesting that skeptics who offer their derogatory views of subject matter expert opinions have overlooked the fact that they are subject matter experts offering their opinions on the matter. Seems a little hypocritical to us, but then, that is just our opinion... By the way, how many expert opinions does it require before something is perceived to be a fact? We guess it depends on which expert you ask...

Let's say we're doing an analysis regarding the amount of risk an organization has from a database administrator "going rogue" and stealing sensitive customer data. Most organizations haven't had this happen (that they know of), so trying to estimate the frequency of such an event is challenging. Does this mean they:

1. get to ignore the possibility of it occurring and not make decisions regarding controls that might be useful to manage it, or
2. assume it happens continuously and do everything humanly possible to prevent it?

Probably neither. Probably they need to evaluate it as best they can so that they can prioritize this concern appropriately against all the other scenarios they have to worry about. An evaluation also puts them in a better position to choose which remediation option is likely to be most cost-effective.

So how do we put numbers around something so nebulous? We examine the various known factors (recognizing there will always be some amount of unknowns) and make reasoned estimates based on those factors. Invariably, this approach is less precise than if we had good data, but as long as we apply decent critical thinking skills and are calibrated in our estimates (calibration is covered in a later chapter), we improve the odds that our numbers will be accurate.

Questions we might ask to help us estimate the frequency of malicious acts by rogue DBAs will include things like:

- How many database administrators are there? (With a larger population, you increase the odds of a bad apple.)
- How good is the HR employment screening process?
- How long have they been with the company? (Long tenure suggests, but does not guarantee, a greater personal investment in organizational welfare and a feeling of "stewardship" over its assets.)
- Have there been any instances of impropriety by any of them that might be a precursor to a more significant event? (Small misbehaviors can snowball.)
- How tightly knit are they as a team? (Teams that are tightly knit are more likely to recognize aberrant behavior.)
- How good is employee morale in general, and in this team in particular?
- What kinds of controls exist that might increase the odds of an act like this being prevented or detected (e.g., encryption, logging, joint responsibilities, etc.), and how immune are those controls to tampering or circumvention?

Clearly, these factors do not answer the question for us, but they inform our estimates and can help us defend those estimates. Nonetheless, in circumstances like this, our estimates will almost always consist of wide ranges. If we're using distributions (as we do in FAIR), they will invariably be much less peaked. In these hard-to-estimate situations, wide, flat distributions faithfully reflect the low quality of our data and our higher level of uncertainty. This, too, is informative for decision-makers, as they may choose to provide additional resources that might help us improve our data. Or, depending on the scenario, they may simply take a conservative approach and apply risk mitigation resources to the scenario even if the estimated frequency is low. In either case, at least they have a better sense for what is not known.

TALKING RISK

One of the funniest arguments we get into is when a skeptic of quantitative risk makes the claim that, when faced with no data, you are left with no choice but to use a qualitative measure. "Okay," we'll say. "What likelihood—qualitatively—would you assign to the probability of this event?" Let's say they answer, "Low." When we ask them what they mean by "Low," the conversation almost always ends up with them saying something like, "Not very often, maybe once or twice every few years." Sometimes they realize as soon as they say this that they have just quantified their estimate. Other times, we have to point it out to them. Either way, the point is that many qualitative estimates seem to be based on subconscious quantitative values.

PRECISION VERSUS ACCURACY

In earlier sections of this chapter, we mentioned the notion of "a useful degree of precision." We also said that precision and repeatability are inherently linked. But where does accuracy fit into the picture?

Very often, people don't differentiate between precision and accuracy, yet understanding the difference is critical in risk analysis. For example, you can have high degrees of precision and yet not be accurate. Likewise, you can have accuracy and a very low level of precision. For example, if we estimated that the loss exposure associated with a scenario was $501,277.15, that is a precise number. It is right down to the penny. If, however, the actual loss exposure was $200,000, then our estimate was inaccurate—i.e., it was not representative of the truth. If, instead, we'd estimated the loss exposure to be between $1 and $1,000,000,000, then our estimate was accurate, but the level of precision left something to be desired. For that scenario, an estimate of between $100,000 and $500,000 might represent an appropriate balance between accuracy and precision.

The bottom line is that risk measurements will always be a trade-off between accuracy and precision. That said, of the two, accuracy is king. In the Measurement chapter, we will show you how to balance the two, but we always place a higher priority on accuracy than on precision. Always. The trick is arriving at a useful degree of precision. There's more to come on that.

TALKING ABOUT RISK

Another commonly heard, and often valid, concern about quantitative analysis regards "false precision." The basis for this concern is that numbers with high degrees of precision (e.g., loss exposure values of $501,277.15 or risk ratings of 3.1) may be believed to be more credible than they deserve. We've also heard this called the "monkey with a spreadsheet" problem—i.e., if it's in a spreadsheet then it must be good. Whether a number is "good" or not has much more to do with how it was arrived at than how it's expressed. That said, although the tools we use may provide precise values for points along the distribution (e.g., the minimum, maximum, average, etc.) based on the underlying data and mathematical functions, when presenting the results to decision-makers, we are careful to round the numbers to help reinforce the imprecise nature of such analyses. Of course, the fact that our outputs are represented as distributions also drives home this point.

The FAIR Risk Ontology

Those of you who have some previous exposure to Factor Analysis of Information Risk (FAIR) may be familiar with its "taxonomy." However, the FAIR framework is more accurately described as an ontology (in the technical versus metaphysical sense) (see Figure 3.1). The difference is that taxonomies are used to classify things (e.g., mammals versus amphibians versus reptiles), whereas ontologies describe relationships between elements (e.g., the molecular and biological processes surrounding genes). The term "taxonomy" was inaccurately applied early in FAIR's existence and gained common use and recognition. Live and learn.

Regardless of what you call it, FAIR's ontology is the secret sauce that is largely responsible for its effective and pragmatic nature. Simply stated, the ontology represents a model of how risk works by describing the factors that make up risk and their relationships to one another. These relationships can then be described mathematically, which allows us to calculate risk from measurements and estimates of those risk factors.

As mentioned earlier, inconsistent and poorly defined terminology is one of the most significant challenges the information security and operational risk profession faces. As a result, the consistent and logical terms and definitions that make up FAIR's ontology can significantly improve the quality of risk-related communication within an organization and between organizations.

TALKING ABOUT RISK

How much credibility would the physics profession have if practitioners could not agree on foundational terms like mass, weight, and velocity? As silly as that may seem, the risk profession struggles with foundational terminology on this profound a scale. As long as this is true, the profession will struggle to mature.

Unfortunately, some people's answer to the problem is to simply take a subset of existing terms and definitions, and declare that those should be the "official" nomenclature. What we have not seen happen in those instances, though, is any real critical examination of whether those terms and definitions make sense. In other cases, you have standards bodies that seem to want to avoid any (useful) controversy and declare that all definitions are okay with them. Their glossary of terms can be remarkably unhelpful.

You will probably find much of FAIR's terminology to be intuitive and familiar. On the other hand, some of the terms may have either profoundly or subtly

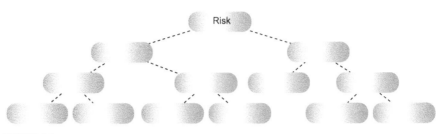

FIGURE 3.1

Factor analysis of information risk (FAIR) ontology.

different meanings than you are used to. This isn't arbitrary. Unfortunately, some of the nomenclature that's been in common use in the risk profession are…let's be generous and say imprecise. This imprecision leads to inconsistent and sometimes confusing usage (e.g., terms like "risk" being used to mean different things even in a single sentence: *The risk of that risk occurring is high risk*). Since FAIR diverged from "conventional wisdom" in other ways, we figured we might as well take this opportunity to refine terms and definitions rather than limp along with terminology that was an obstacle to our profession's maturity. Of course, there are detractors out there who claim that these refinements just further muddy the water. This is unfortunately true to some degree until the profession gets its terminology act together.

Keeping in mind that no models are perfect, FAIR's ontology has evolved over the years to reflect growth in our understanding of risk, risk analysis and, in some cases, analyst behaviors. It's reasonable to expect the ontology to continue to evolve as more organizations apply FAIR and we learn from its use. In this chapter, we'll also include some discussion about where different types of controls may be applied within the model. This is critical to understand in order to evaluate control effectiveness in the scenarios we analyze.

Please note: This chapter is intended to introduce the terms and concepts that make up the ontology. The Analysis chapter book will cover in depth how to use the ontology when evaluating risk.

TALKING ABOUT RISK

We often get questions about how a legitimate model for information security risk could be developed when so little data are available. These questions stem from the fact that the risk models people are most familiar with (e.g., insurance) are derived using an inductive approach.

In an inductive approach to modeling, you take data (usually lots and lots of data) and infer from the data how the world appears to work. That's great when you have a lot of good data, but that was not an option when FAIR was first being developed.

The other approach to model development is deductive in nature (à la Sherlock Holmes). In other words, we infer model elements and their relationships based on our experience, logic, and critical thinking. This was the approach used to develop the FAIR ontology, which to-date is holding up very nicely to scrutiny.

Neither approach is necessarily better than the other, as both can work marvelously or fail miserably. Inductive modeling is sensitive to data quality. Deductive modeling is sensitive to the experience and quality of thinking that goes into it. In either case, users of any model should continuously evaluate whether there are opportunities to improve the model or even replace it entirely with something better. Dogma regarding models can be a very dangerous thing.

DECOMPOSING RISK

The FAIR ontology begins with the concept that risk equates to "Loss Exposure." With this as a starting point, the following definition for risk is derived:

The probable frequency and probable magnitude of future loss

The wording of this definition is important for a few reasons:

- Any analysis of risk must include both the frequency and magnitude components in order to be meaningful. It does little good to know the magnitude of some potential event if we don't also understand its frequency. Likewise, knowing the frequency of an event is relatively meaningless without understanding its magnitude.
- Because risk analysis is based on imperfect data and models, any statement of frequency or magnitude should be considered probability based (i.e., uncertain).
- From a practical perspective, we perform risk analysis in order to inform decision makers of the future potential for loss.

With this as a starting point, the first two factors become obvious: Loss event frequency (LEF) and Loss Magnitude (LM) (see Figure 3.2). The next sections will decompose these two sides of the risk equation, beginning with LEF.

FIGURE 3.2

FAIR top-level ontology.

TALKING ABOUT RISK

As is true for many words in the English language, there are multiple definitions for risk. Rather than engage in a religious debate about which is the right definition, we want to make it clear that FAIR is strict in its use of the word risk. If you feel strongly that "risk" means something other than exposure to loss, then feel free to mentally substitute the term "loss exposure" any time you see the word "risk" in this book. Loss Exposure appears to generate less controversy, which can help refocus dialogue away from open-ended and passionate debates.

LOSS EVENT FREQUENCY

The probable frequency, within a given time-frame, that loss will materialize from a threat agent's action

The definition for LEF is fairly straightforward but could be thought of even more simply as a measure of how often loss is likely to happen. The only aspect of the LEF definition that may deserve specific mention is the statement, *within a given time-frame*. This is important because, as was mentioned earlier in the book, in order for frequency, likelihood, or probability to be meaningful there must be a time-frame reference. Within FAIR, the most commonly used time-frame reference is annual. Experience suggests that consistently using this annualized time-frame reference (versus monthly, weekly, etc.) is important to avoid confusion in interpreting analysis results.

TALKING ABOUT RISK

An argument has been made that the term Frequency implies a time-frame reference and therefore "time-frame" is redundant in the definition. True enough. Regardless, we have retained it in the definition to emphasize its importance and minimize the probability of being overlooked, particularly by people who are newer to risk analysis.

Examples of loss events would include:

- A data center outage due to extreme weather
- A corrupted database
- An employee injuring themselves on a wet floor
- A hacker stealing sensitive customer information

It's extremely important that this notion of a "loss event" be firmly cemented in your mind because it is a cornerstone to performing analyses. There is *no way* you are going to be able to come up with defensible frequency or magnitude values if the event you are evaluating isn't clearly defined. We'll discuss this further in the Analysis section, but consider this fair warning (pun intended) of how important this is.

LEF can either be estimated directly, or derived from Threat Event Frequency (TEF) and Vulnerability (Vuln). In either case, it is generally expressed as a distribution using annualized values, for example: Between 5 and 25 times per year, with the most likely frequency of 10 times per year.

There are some scenarios where LEF is more appropriately expressed as a probability than as a frequency. For example, we wouldn't talk about the frequency of our sun becoming a white dwarf star because that is something that can only happen once. In those kinds of scenarios, we'd express LEF as a probability within a given time-frame (e.g., the probability of our sun becoming a white dwarf this week is, well, we don't know what it is but it's a really small number—we hope). The two factors that drive LEF are TEF and Vuln (see Figure 3.3).

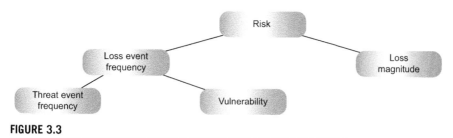

FIGURE 3.3

FAIR loss event frequency ontology.

THREAT EVENT FREQUENCY

The probable frequency, within a given time-frame, that threat agents will act in a manner that may result in loss

Those who are just learning FAIR occasionally confuse TEF with LEF, and this is in fact one of the most commonly missed questions on the certification exam. We suppose the fact that the definitions and acronyms are almost identical doesn't help. That said, once you gain even a little experience using FAIR, this will become second nature to you.

The operative phrase in the TEF definition that distinguishes it from LEF is "may result in loss." In other words, the key difference between LEF and TEF is that loss may or may not result from Threat Events. For example:

- Rolling a pair of dice while gambling is a threat event. Having the dice come up "snake eyes" is a loss event.
- A hacker attacking a website is a threat event. If they manage to damage the site or steal information, that would be a loss event.
- Pushing a new software release into production is a threat event. Having a problem with the release that results in downtime, data integrity problems, etc., would be a loss event.
- Having someone thrust a knife at you would be a threat event. Being cut by the knife would be the loss event.

Note that in the first sentence of each bullet above, loss is not guaranteed; it isn't until the second sentence that loss is clear. The probability of loss occurring in each threat event is a function of Vulnerability, which we will discuss in detail a little later.

TEF can either be estimated directly or derived from estimates of Contact Frequency (CF) and Probability of Action (PoA). Similar to LEF, TEF is almost always expressed as a distribution using annualized values, for example: Between 0.1 and 0.5 times per year, with a most likely frequency of 0.3 times per year. This example demonstrates that annualized frequencies can be less than one (i.e., the frequency is expected to be less than once per year). The example above could thus be restated: Between once every 10 years and once every other year, but most likely once every 3 years. Similarly, TEF can also be expressed as a probability rather than as a frequency in scenarios where the threat event could occur only once in the time-frame of interest. The factors that drive TEF are CF and PoA (see Figure 3.4).

FIGURE 3.4

FAIR threat event frequency ontology.

CONTACT FREQUENCY

The probable frequency, within a given time-frame, that threat agents will come into contact with assets

The contact referred to here can be physical or logical (e.g., over the network). Regardless of contact mode, three types of contact can take place:

- Random—the threat agent randomly encounters the asset (e.g., a tornado strike)
- Regular—contact occurs due to regular threat agent activity. For example, the cleaning crew regularly comes by the office (and its contents) at 5:15 PM each workday.
- Intentional—the threat agent seeks out the asset (e.g., a burglar who targets a particular house thought to contain valuables of interest)

Examples of contact events would include:

- A burglar cruising through your neighborhood
- A scan of your website
- A bear smelling or seeing your campsite
- A database administrator seeing sensitive information while troubleshooting the database

CF would seem to be a relatively straightforward concept, and most of the time it is. That said, there are times when people confuse it with TEF. For example, some people are mistakenly inclined to call it a threat event when a network engineer encounters sensitive data while troubleshooting the network. Why isn't this a threat event? Because although there is an opportunity to act maliciously, the act isn't guaranteed. The PoA (discussed in the next section) determines whether a contact event becomes a threat event. Just as described for LEF and TEF, CF can be expressed as a probability in some scenarios where contact could occur only once in the time-frame of interest.

TALKING ABOUT RISK

Some people will argue that, for example, a network engineer encountering sensitive patient information on the network during troubleshooting actually represents a loss event because "a loss of privacy has occurred." However, unless the organization is required to notify regulators and/or the patient whose information was exposed, and thus incur the costs associated with investigation, notification, etc., it would be inaccurate to consider this a loss event. In order to keep analysis pragmatic, we have to stay focused on events where tangible loss to the organization is reasonably likely. The key to making this distinction is to ask yourself whether the organization is going to incur loss or liability from the event.

THINKING ABOUT CONTROLS

When we want to reduce risk by reducing CF, we look for ways to reduce the probability/frequency of a threat agent coming into contact with the asset(s). Examples include:

- Moving a facility away from an earthquake zone
- Implementing a firewall that blocks network access to a server or application
- Killing the spiders in the basement by using poison

PROBABILITY OF ACTION

The probability that a threat agent will act upon an asset once contact has occurred

It's important to recognize that PoA only applies to threat agents that can think, reason, or otherwise make a decision like humans and some other animals. As far as we know, tornados and other acts of nature don't exercise conscious choice and decide whether to act on or against an asset or not.

The choice of whether to act is driven by three factors:

- The perceived value of the act from the threat agent's perspective
- The perceived level of effort and/or cost from the threat agent's perspective
- The perceived level of risk to the threat agent (e.g., the probability of getting caught and suffering unacceptable consequences)

Note that it's uncommon to perform an analysis where you have to derive TEF from estimates of CF and PoA. That said, it's often very helpful to examine your assumptions at the CF and PoA level of abstraction, particularly when there are disagreements between analysts.

THINKING ABOUT CONTROLS

Understanding the factors that drive PoA is also useful when considering control opportunities. If we can implement measures that affect the apparent value of the asset (e.g., camouflage), increase the apparent level of effort required by the threat agent (e.g., enhance the hardened appearance of the target), or increase the perceived level of risk to the threat agent (e.g., large dogs, cameras, etc.), then we can drive down the PoA, which reduces TEF.

VULNERABILITY

The probability that a threat agent's actions will result in loss

The FAIR definition for Vuln (shorthand for Vulnerability) is probably the single greatest point of variance from common usage out of all of the FAIR terms. In common usage, things like a weak password or an unlocked window would be called vulnerabilities. The notion being that these conditions represent weaknesses that can be exploited. This perspective though, can be misleading. Too often, people infer that a locked window or a strong password are not vulnerable, which is clearly not the case. The truth is, the only difference between the locked window and the unlocked window is the level of effort required by the threat agent. It's a matter of degree rather than a difference of whether a loss event can happen or not.

From a FAIR perspective, Vuln is a percentage representing the probability that a threat agent's actions will result in loss. For example,

- That house is 100% vulnerable to damage from a Tornado (duh)
- That lock is 10% vulnerable to compromise through lock-picking
- That password is 1% vulnerable to brute force attempts

As we discuss elsewhere in this book, most of the time we represent Vuln as a distribution. For example: that lock is between 5 and 20% vulnerable to lock-picking, with a most likely value of 10%. In other words, between 5% and 20% of the lock-picking attempts, (most likely 10%) will be successful given what we know about the threat community under analysis and the characteristics of the lock.

The reason we express Vuln in this way is that there are almost always aspects of the problem that introduce uncertainty. Of course, when we're talking about something like a tornado or other circumstance where some amount of loss is assured, we can feel pretty confident in saying we are 100% vulnerable (i.e., 100% of the time there will be some amount of loss from the threat event).

Vulnerability can be estimated directly, or it can be derived from Threat Capability (TCap) and Difficulty (Diff) (see Figure 3.5). In later chapters of the book, we will talk at length about when to estimate Vuln directly versus when to derive it from TCap and Diff.

FIGURE 3.5

FAIR vulnerability taxonomy.

THREAT CAPABILITY

The capability of a threat agent

The definition for TCap (FAIR shorthand for Threat Capability) is a little sparse for a reason. In earlier versions of FAIR, it was defined as the level of force a threat agent could apply. Well, this is fine if the only scenarios you're ever going to evaluate are malicious or natural (e.g., earthquakes), but the fact is you will also very likely evaluate scenarios that involve human error. In those scenarios, it usually isn't a matter of force, but rather skills, resources, or both (which is ultimately true for malicious actors as well). So in order to remain agnostic regarding the type of scenario under analysis, the definition has been generalized.

Estimating TCap can be one of the toughest elements in an analysis. This is because most of the time you aren't analyzing something as straightforward as wind speed or pounds per square inch. Most of the time, you're dealing with much more ambiguous factors like human knowledge and experience. In order to deal with that, we had to introduce the notion of a relative scale referred to as the TCap Continuum.

The TCap Continuum is simply a percentile scale from 1 to 100, which represents the comprehensive range of capabilities for a population of threat agents. The least capable threat agent in the population is considered to represent the first percentile, while the most capable threat agent in the population is considered to represent the 100th percentile. Everyone else falls somewhere in between. An example will help.

If we're evaluating a malicious scenario where the threat community of interest is cyber criminals, we can estimate the TCap for Cyber Criminals given where we believe they stand relative to the broader population of threat actors. We might say that the least capable cyber criminal is at the 60th percentile on the continuum, the most capable is at the 100th percentile, and that most cyber-criminals are at approximately the 90th percentile. Our rationale for this estimate might be a belief that cyber criminals are more skilled and have better resources than the average cyber-focused threat agent. We can also use the concept of TCap if we're evaluating a human error scenario where the threat community is programmers who might inadvertently introduce software flaws into an application. Programmers who are at the higher end of the TCap continuum have greater skills and resources with which to make and introduce these flaws.

As some of you have no doubt figured out, higher TCap is bad in malicious scenarios, and good in human error scenarios. We'll spend more time on the relationship between TCap, Diff, and Vuln in later chapters so that you can feel confident in how the concepts work and how to apply them. If TCap estimation seems squishy, you're right. Nonetheless, it can be an effective approach to evaluating some very challenging scenarios, particularly if you are able to leverage solid threat intelligence from experts in the field.

THINKING ABOUT CONTROLS

Given that TCap (in scenarios where humans are the threat agents) boils down to skills and resources, let's examine a couple of examples of how we might be able to reduce our risk by affecting TCap.

- In a human error scenario, we could improve TCap (and thus reduce Vuln) by providing additional training, improved tools, or more time
- In a malicious scenario, we could reduce TCap (and thus reduce Vuln) by reducing the amount of time the threat agent has to complete their attempts to breach resistive controls. For example, we might deploy cameras and a rapid response force that can detect and intervene before a breach is completed

DIFFICULTY

The level of difficulty that a threat agent must overcome

Those readers who are familiar with older versions of FAIR may be scratching their heads and wondering what happened to resistance strength (or control strength if they learned FAIR a very long time ago). Resistance strength replaced control strength some years ago because we found that people would include controls of *all* kinds when estimating control strength, even things like backup tapes. This was a problem because not all controls play a role in minimizing Vuln, and thus accounting for nonresistive controls within this branch of the ontology resulted in inaccurate results. Later, we realized that resistance strength was not an ideal term either because it didn't fit human error or other scenarios where it wasn't about resistance to force. To-date, the term Difficulty appears to be the best fit for all of the scenarios we have encountered.

Similar to TCap, Difficulty can be a very tough concept for some folks to wrap their heads around. Like TCap, we usually can't measure Difficulty in tensile strength, compression strength, or any of the other physical measures we normally might think of. Fortunately, the TCap Continuum discussed earlier gives us an option. We can use the TCap Continuum as a measurement scale for evaluating the effectiveness of controls that affect Difficulty. For example, if we need to estimate the effectiveness of a particular authentication control, we might estimate that it is expected to stop anyone below the 70th percentile along the TCap Continuum. We might also estimate that anyone above the 90th percentile is certain to succeed. This would give us the two ends of our distribution. The most likely value (mode; the peak of our distribution) might be estimated to be the 85th percentile, meaning that is what we believe the control's effectiveness is most likely to be.

The thing to keep in mind (and where many people make mistakes in their analyses) is that Difficulty is *always* measured against the TCap Continuum (our measurement scale) and *never* against the specific threat community you are analyzing against in your scenario. Let's use a simple example from the physical world. Let's say we're analyzing the probability that a rope will be able to hold a steel bar. The rope has, through its design and construction, a certain ability to withstand longitudinal stress. Let us also say we measured or estimated the rope strength to be 500 pounds (i.e., the rope should be able to hold 500 pounds before it breaks, give or take a few pounds). We didn't have to know what this specific steel bar (the threat agent in this scenario) weighs in order to measure the strength of the rope because the rope's strength is independent of the steel bar.

We'll cover this more thoroughly later so that you can become more comfortable thinking in these terms. Something we should point out though, is that you don't have to estimate TCap and Difficulty in most analyses. In fact, you may only need to work at this level of abstraction in the model rarely.

THINKING ABOUT CONTROLS

In order for a control to be relevant to Difficulty it must make the threat agent's job more difficult (in a malicious or act-of-nature scenario) or easier (in a human error scenario). If a control decreases the probability of contact (avoidance controls), deters the threat agent from acting (deterrence controls; which affect TEF), or limits the magnitude of loss that occurs (containment or minimization controls; in the yet-to-be-discussed Loss Magnitude section), then it should be accounted for in those parts of the analysis but not in Difficulty. Examples of controls that commonly are relevant to Difficulty in malicious scenarios include:

- Authentication
- Access privileges
- Patching and configuration
- Encryption

Examples of controls that may be relevant to Difficulty in human error scenarios include:

- Training
- Documentation
- Process simplification

Examples of controls that may be relevant to Difficulty in acts of nature scenarios include:

- Reinforced construction materials and designs

TALKING ABOUT RISK

We have to use the TCap Continuum if we are going to estimate Diff. The reason is because Vuln is determined by comparing whether TCap is greater than Diff. The only way you can do that is if both TCap and Diff are measured using the same scale. Think of it this way: you couldn't effectively evaluate whether a rope was likely to break if you measured the longitudinal force being applied in pounds, and the rope's strength in some other scale, like bushels.

LOSS MAGNITUDE

The probable magnitude of primary and secondary loss resulting from an event

On the surface, LM is conceptually very simple—it's about how much tangible loss is expected to materialize from an event. That's the good news. The reality, however, is that there can be some important subtleties that distinguish where and how we account for different types of loss. These subtleties will become clear very quickly after you have begun performing FAIR analyses.

Here again, people who are familiar with older versions of FAIR (particularly from the 2005 white paper) will find significant differences in the LM side of the ontology. The newer version of the ontology is a much more effective model when evaluating how losses actually materialize.

STAKEHOLDERS AND PERSPECTIVE

One of the most important considerations when evaluating LM is determining whether losses fall into what are referred to as primary or secondary loss. In order to understand these two dimensions of loss, it's critical to understand the concept of stakeholders and analysis perspective.

Primary stakeholders are those individuals or organizations whose perspective is the focus of the risk analysis. For example, if we're doing an analysis to understand the loss exposure an organization has from not complying with environmental policies, then it is that organization that is the primary stakeholder. It's that company's loss exposure that we're trying to ascertain.

Secondary stakeholders are defined as anyone who is not a primary stakeholder that may be affected by the loss event being analyzed, and then may react in a manner that further harms the primary stakeholder. For example, let's say that Company XYZ has an event occur that damages public health or diminishes surrounding homeowner property valuations. Odds are, the company will incur direct losses as a result of this event (e.g., cleanup, etc.). These direct losses are referred to as primary loss, which we'll discuss in more detail shortly. In this scenario, the public (a secondary stakeholder), has also been adversely affected and may, depending on circumstances, react negatively toward the company through legal actions, protests, taking their business elsewhere, etc. The costs and losses incurred by the company in dealing with secondary stakeholder reactions would constitute the secondary losses in the analysis. Something else to keep in mind is that you can have more than one relevant secondary stakeholder in an analysis. In our example above, environmental regulatory agencies may also react negatively and drive additional secondary losses for Company XYZ.

The question sometimes comes up asking where in the risk formula we put the losses incurred by secondary stakeholders? Simply stated: we don't. Not directly, anyway. Remember, this analysis is from the company's perspective, and therefore the company's losses are the only losses we plug into the formula. As a result, the only time we account for the losses incurred by secondary stakeholders is when and if those losses are going to flow through to the primary stakeholder. For example, Company XYZ might have to compensate the affected members of the community for their damaged property or injuries, which would be included in the secondary

FIGURE 3.6

FAIR loss magnitude ontology.

loss component of the analysis. Note that we can always do a separate risk analysis from the public's perspective if that were useful to us.

LOSS FACTORS VERSUS LOSS FORMS

The LM factors shown in the ontology in Figure 3.6 (primary loss magnitude (PLM), secondary risk (SR), secondary loss-event frequency, and secondary loss magnitude (SLM)) represent a logical breakdown of how loss works computationally. This is different from something we'll cover later referred to as FAIR's six forms of loss, which are simply categories that have been defined to help analysts think through and account for the different ways in which loss materializes. The diagram illustrates the relationship between these elements of the model. If this still feels unclear, rest assured that the fog will lift when we cover forms of loss later in the book.

PRIMARY LOSS MAGNITUDE

Primary stakeholder loss that materializes directly as a result of the event

The key terms in this definition are "primary stakeholder" and "directly," which are what differentiates primary loss from secondary loss. Consequently, in order for a loss to be considered primary, it has to be unrelated to secondary stakeholder reactions.

Common examples of primary loss include:

- Lost revenue from operational outages
- Wages paid to workers when no work is being performed due to an outage
- Replacement of the organization's tangible assets (including cash)
- Person-hours spent restoring functionality to assets or operations following an event

You may be asking how lost revenue isn't related to secondary stakeholder reactions. After all, revenue invariably comes from customers or business partners, both of whom are secondary stakeholders. If this question came to mind, give yourself a gold star for critical thinking. This is, in fact, an example of one of those subtleties mentioned earlier. The bottom line is that an operational outage prohibits business transactions from occurring, versus a decision by the customers, etc., to no longer do business with the company. In many cases, business transactions are automated and no decision is actually made by a secondary stakeholder to terminate the relationship. The question of lost market share—i.e., customers going elsewhere—is accounted for in secondary loss. Sure, it's a fine point; however, it is a very useful distinction when performing analyses.

THINKING ABOUT CONTROLS

Some examples of controls that can help minimize or contain PLM include:

- Disaster recovery and business continuity processes and technologies
- Efficient incident response processes
- Process or technology redundancy

SECONDARY RISK

Primary stakeholder loss-exposure that exists due to the potential for secondary stakeholder reactions to the primary event

This is the longest and most complicated of our factor definitions. Boiled down, though, you can think of this as fallout from the primary event. In many scenarios, the potential LM from things like reputation damage, fines and judgments, and other forms of fallout can be much different and often times greater than primary losses from an event. However, as we'll see, it's also true that in many scenarios the frequency of these secondary effects occurring can be quite small. Consequently, the fact that a risk scenario can have a substantially different frequency and magnitude for secondary effects makes it imperative that we treat secondary effects as a separate but related risk scenario. The factors that drive SR are secondary loss-event frequency and SLM (see Figure 3.7).

FIGURE 3.7

FAIR secondary risk taxonomy.

TALKING ABOUT RISK

The name of this factor is yet another change from earlier versions of the ontology. Previously, this was referred to as secondary loss, but that term created confusion with the SLM factor we'll cover shortly. Besides the confusion these terms introduced, there was another reason for the change—from a model perspective, the secondary risk branch is almost identical to the overall risk ontology, having frequency and magnitude sub-branches. Consequently, using the term risk in the name of this factor seemed to make more sense.

SECONDARY LOSS EVENT FREQUENCY

The percentage of primary events that have secondary effects

The bottom line is, not all events have secondary effects. Furthermore, of those scenarios that do have the potential for secondary loss, in many cases only a relatively small percentage of the events would experience secondary loss. The secondary loss event frequency (SLEF) factor allows us to represent this characteristic of loss as a percentage of primary LEF. For example, using the Company XYZ scenario mentioned earlier, if the environmental loss event being analyzed has a frequency (LEF) of 10 times per year but is of a nature where secondary losses would only materialize 20% of the time (SLEF), the derived frequency of secondary losses would be two times per year.

THINKING ABOUT CONTROLS

Any measures we can take to minimize the frequency of costs or losses associated with secondary stakeholders will be accounted for here. For example, encrypting laptops can be a great way of minimizing SLEF, because if the customers' personal information is encrypted, you typically don't have to incur the cost of notification, etc.

TALKING ABOUT RISK

The name of this factor is confusing to some people when they are first learning FAIR. The term frequency in the name implies the data type would be a real number (e.g., 1, 57, 0.33, etc.), but the definition refers to it as a percentage (e.g., 50%). Why then don't we just call it secondary loss event probability? Actually, it was pretty much a coin toss when naming this factor, but since the formula uses this value in combination with LEF to derive the frequency of secondary effects, frequency seemed to be the more appropriate term.

SECONDARY LOSS MAGNITUDE

Loss associated with secondary stakeholder reactions

The definition kind of says it all. The costs and losses associated with secondary stakeholders comprise SLM. Examples of secondary loss include but are not limited to:

- Civil, criminal, or contractual fines and judgments
- Notification costs
- Credit monitoring
- Covering secondary stakeholder monetary loss
- Public relations costs
- Legal defense costs
- The effects of regulatory sanctions
- Lost market share
- Diminished stock price
- Increased cost of capital

Note that later in the book, we'll describe the six categories of loss these examples will fall into.

THINKING ABOUT CONTROLS

Examples of controls that may affect SLM include:

- Timely notification of secondary stakeholders
- Offering credit monitoring (at least in the United States)
- Strong public relations efforts

Although each of these incurs a cost that would be accounted for as part of the secondary losses, they each also help to minimize the severity of secondary stakeholder reactions that likely would drive even greater losses.

TALKING ABOUT RISK

When first publishing the *Introduction to FAIR* white paper in 2005, LM was one of the toughest nuts to crack in an analysis. We aren't sure that is as true anymore. We've learned and experienced a lot since then. Besides improved sources of hard data from actual incidents, one of the most important things we've learned is the importance of talking to the right subject matter experts when estimating loss. In the vast majority of instances, the information security professional is *not* the right subject matter expert to give you loss estimates. They simply do not have the background, information, or frankly, investment in the outcome, to get it right.

ONTOLOGICAL FLEXIBILITY

FAIR's ontology can be viewed as flexible in terms of which layer of the model that you make your measurements and estimates. It can even be viewed as flexible in that you can substitute names (but not meaning) for the different factors if you have some reason to. What you *can not* do, though, at least without being extremely careful and prepared to defend your decision, is add to or subtract from the model, or change the relationships. We have seen examples where people took the FAIR ontology and added a branch, deleted a branch, changed the relationships between branches, or even added weighted values. In every instance we've encountered, these changes broke the model, i.e. the results no longer made sense. This is like deciding to say, "speed equals distance divided by time plus bananas." It just doesn't work that way. This isn't to say that FAIR can't be improved upon. We are pretty sure it can and will be over time. However, if there is an idea about how to improve upon it, we suggest that it be tested and evaluated in an open forum to ensure that the change helps the model better represent reality.

TALKING ABOUT RISK

For those with a statistics and/or scientific background, the FAIR ontology may resemble a Bayes-ian Network. In fact, Bayesian network concepts did contribute significantly to FAIR's early devel-opment in two important ways. First was the adoption of a Bayesian-like approach to decomposing the risk factors and their relationships into the ontology. Second, was the acceptance of the Bayesian concept that you can begin performing statistical analysis by leveraging subject matter expert esti-mates ("priors" in Bayesian terminology) and then refine your probabilities as more and better data become available. The very earliest versions of FAIR even used Bayesian formulas to derive results, but we found that using Monte Carlo worked just as well and was *much* easier.

FAIR Terminology

RISK TERMINOLOGY

How likely would you be to climb into a spaceship if you knew that the scientists who designed the technology and planned the voyage could not agree on foundational terms? You know, things like mass, weight, and velocity. How likely would you be to put your money in financial institutions if you knew that the professionals within that industry were inconsistent in their understanding and use of foundational terms like debit and credit? Not very likely in either case, we're guessing. Yet that is exactly the state of information security (and in many respects the broader risk management profession). This is, in our opinion, one of the biggest challenges facing the profession today. You don't believe us? Just ask any group of information security professionals to name the biggest risk facing organizations today. You would likely get a wide variety of answers ranging from advanced persistent threats (APTs), to "the cloud," to mobile technology, to insiders. Or give them a list of risk landscape elements like the one below and ask them to label each one as either a threat, vulnerability, or risk:

- Disgruntled insider
- Unencrypted backup tape
- Policy violation
- Unpatched Internet-facing server
- Database full of sensitive customer information

We do this regularly and get a remarkable amount of variance in the answers. This is a pretty strong indicator that our profession is still in its infancy. All the fancy tools and professional certifications don't make up for the fact that we haven't made our way out of the crib yet. You'd think that standards documents would be helpful in clarifying these terms, but not so much. There is little consistency from glossary to glossary. In some glossaries, multiple definitions for terms are provided, perhaps in an effort to avoid offending some group or because the glossary creators couldn't decide.

One of the objectives of, and value propositions for, FAIR is a relatively precise set of definitions for foundational terms. In some cases, you'll find that our definitions more or less align with what you're used to. In other cases, you'll find that our definitions are quite different. This chapter intends to shed some light on foundational risk terms as they are used in FAIR in order to better clarify what we mean when we use them, how we need to apply them for the purpose of risk analysis, and how to communicate them to nonrisk professionals using natural language.

ASSET

Assets are things that we value. It is amazing how often when doing a risk analysis we fail to explicitly name the thing that we value in the analysis. If it's true that we can't have risk without loss, then we need something with value (or consequences) that can be lost, stolen, or affected in some negative way. So let's start with that. Assets are usually something that have intrinsic value, are fungible in some way, or create potential liability. If you work in financial services, the cash in customer accounts is an asset you should care about. Health care? Yes, human lives have that intrinsic value that we care about. Fungible assets get a little trickier. Things like account numbers, social security numbers or other government issued health services or tax identification numbers, as well as the magic mix of data types that trigger breach notifications—things like name and address. What's useful to remember is that these data assets have value in that they enable business functions, and, at the same time, they create potential liability if they become corrupted or inappropriately disclosed.

Decomposition of the scenario is usually pretty helpful in getting to the real asset in an analysis. Countless times we've sat and listened to someone describe a risk scenario that ends with a server of some kind being compromised. "Because, you know, once I own the server I can do anything," is often the summary of their analysis. It seems very conclusive to the person speaking but often leaves the rest of the room (especially if there are representatives from the business) thinking "So what?" What's often left unstated is the asset at risk. After the server is hacked into by some nefarious attacker, they will take the customer records off that server and monetize them somehow. Or maybe the attacker will lay in wait on that server until some important bit of data comes across the wire upon which they can act.

Many newbie risk analysts will list the server as the asset, which it is. Very often though, it isn't the primary asset of interest in an analysis. It may be the point of attack through which an attacker gains access to the data, but unless the existence of the server or its operational integrity is the focus of an analysis, it is really just a container of data that, hopefully, provides a means of applying controls to protect the data. In a confidentiality-focused analysis, the negative press, lost clients, legal action by the State Attorney General, and other losses associated with the data may dwarf the actual cost of the server's hardware and software. Of course, that isn't what is meant when people say the server is the asset. They implicitly recognize data as the asset of interest and are simply conflating all the things that could happen if that server were compromised. It's just easier to refer to the server as the asset. This is one of those examples of why being a good risk professional is at least half communication. Learning when to leave terms and examples high level, and when to delve deeper to get to the root of the matter (decomposition) is really as much art as science. Take it from a couple of guys who have been at this art and science thing for a while: the business cares about the asset. The real asset. Make sure you take the time to really unearth the asset and how it is affected by, or affects, business practices, processes, sales cycles, etc. This will gain you credibility in the eyes of the business and leads to better risk analyses.

Thus, understanding the business gives us a much better sense of the assets that we care about for a particular scenario; for example, not all customer records are the same from a value or liability perspective. It also gives us some credibility with the business if we present our risk analysis findings and can talk intelligently about how their business works. Finally, yet importantly, it also sets us up much better to effectively estimate values for the loss forms, which we'll discuss in more detail later in this chapter.

THREAT

Several years ago, one of us sat through a presentation by a very successful and highly intelligent security architecture executive. He was trying to outline what he felt were emerging threats that needed to be prepared for. There was a slide deck in a very high-end teleconference room where the results of his analysis were presented, and it was clear that this slide deck had been meticulously crafted and reviewed. The list of threats he presented included the following:

1. APT
2. Hacktivist
3. Cloud
4. Voice over IP (VoIP)
5. Social engineering
6. Organized crime
7. State sponsored attacks
8. Social networking
9. Mobile devices and applications
10. Distributed denial of service

So what's the problem with this list? We'll give you a hint—it isn't logically consistent. Before we kibitz about this list, let's spend some time thinking about threats.

In order for loss to materialize, an action has to occur that may result loss. In FAIR, we refer to these actions as "threat events." Every action has to have an actor to carry it out. We refer to these generally as threat agents or threat communities (TComs) for groups of threat agents with similar characteristics. Sometimes when speaking generally about them, we will refer to them as threats.

A way to think about threats is that they need to represent an ability to actively harm the organization, person, or for whoever you're performing this risk analysis. One technique that we sometimes use during training to clarify the term is to actually threaten somebody. We'll point to somebody in the room and say something like "If you don't shut your face we'll beat it in." By the way, it's actually quite hard to threaten somebody without cursing. We watched one YouTube.com video clip of 100 of the greatest movie threat scenes of all time and easily 85–95% had some curse words in it. However, we refuse to work blue so we'll stick with a clean example, namely, the following line from Kevin Costner's 1991 movie *Robin Hood: Prince of Thieves*:

> *Sheriff of Nottingham: Locksley! I'll cut your heart out with a spoon!*

This is a great line for a number of reasons. First, it sets up a running gag about spoons and second offers a very disturbing image when Guy of Gisborne asks why a spoon and not a knife, to which the Sheriff replies "Because it's dull, you twit. It'll hurt more." It also offers us insight into the Sheriff as a person (they call this character development). What you need to keep in mind about threats is that they must have the potential to inflict loss.

Not uncommonly, we'll hear someone refer to an employee who chooses a weak password or misconfigures a server as a threat. On the surface, this makes sense. They are clearly an actor and they are acting in an unacceptable manner. Technically, however, within the context of a risk analysis they don't qualify as a threat because there is no resulting loss. To be sure, this kind of event affects the level of vulnerability the organization has, which typically increases risk, but it does not result in direct loss in the vast majority of cases. Usually, we refer to these types of events as "vulnerability events," which we'll cover later in the chapter.

TALKING ABOUT RISK

When we offer our empty threat to someone in training, it is interesting to watch their face and hear their reaction. They know we're faking it but they still react emotionally. They can't help the rush of adrenaline that shoots through them as they search for some words to let us know that they get the point (and were not really feeling threatened anyway). It's hard not to respond to a threat in some physiological way. So too should you imagine your organization being threatened when enumerating threats.

So let's apply these concepts to the list we presented at the beginning of this chapter. First, here is the original list:

1. APT
2. Hacktivist
3. Cloud
4. VoIP
5. Social engineering
6. Organized crime
7. State sponsored attacks
8. Social networking
9. Mobile devices and applications
10. Distributed denial of service

Now let's arrange them in Table 4.1 and we want you to try classifying which of these elements are legitimate threats. Go on, take a couple minutes to go through these.

Table 4.1 Threat Identification Exercise

Item	Threat—Yes or No
Advanced persistent threat (APT)	
Hacktivist	
Cloud	
Voice over IP (VoIP)	
Social engineering	
Organized crime	
State sponsored attacks	
Social networking	
Mobile devices and applications	
Distributed denial of service	

Done? All right, let's review the results. First, APT, despite its name, is not a threat. It certainly has a threat component, but it isn't a threat as defined here. For those that don't know or recall, APT is a loosely defined scenario involving an ongoing attack by a highly skilled attacker (perhaps a nation state threat community). Many definitions include the notion that the attackers take advantage of some deficiency in the computer systems that is heretofore unknown. Typically, APT represents a class of threat events.

Next up is Hacktivist. Yes, they are threats. The term typically defines a person or persons who attack a computer network and systems in order to advance a personal or group agenda without necessarily being driven by criminal motivations.

Cloud is not a threat. It's a computing infrastructure, platform, service, or some combination thereof that exists in a large data center and not in your company's four walls. Many information technology (IT) strategists actually think of this as a potential source of competitive advantage. Regardless, it's just technology; an inanimate thing. It is not threatening anybody. The same thing applies to VoIP. It's just a way to send voice-based phone calls over general purpose or specialized computing equipment.

Social engineering is not a threat. It's just a technique that attackers use to gain the trust of someone in order to perpetrate some sort of attack.

Organized crime is a threat (a TCom to be exact). Again, they represent a person or persons that can bring to bear some form of attack against your computing systems.

State sponsored attacks are not a threat. Similar to APT it represents a class of threat events.

Social networking isn't a threat. Again, it's just a potential method or avenue of attack. People use social media to stay connected to each other and many companies use it to market and sell their products so it can be a revenue stream. Sure, bad things may come through this channel, but the potential for misuse does not make something a threat.

Mobile devices and applications are all the rage these days. So, as a result, it's a threat, right? Once again, it's just a thing and not a threat. Applications can do all sorts of good and bad stuff. Mobile devices and computing are changing the face of our lives every day, some for good and some for not quite so good. Again, just because it has the potential to be misused doesn't make it a threat.

Last, denial of service (distributed or otherwise) is also not a threat. It's just a form of attack. It is the form by which some threat agent may attempt to take your computing systems offline. If you noticed, as we boiled down each item in the list, we uncovered many assumptions. We used terms that encompassed lots of risk elements (like APT) and others that were very clearly defined (organized crime).

So, anyway, here is how Table 4.1 looks now as Table 4.2:

Table 4.2 Threat Identification Results

Item	Threat—Yes or No	Why?
APT	No	Form of attack
Hacktivist	Yes	Person(s)
Cloud	No	Thing
VoIP	No	Thing
Social engineering	No	Form of attack
Organized crime	Yes	Person(s)
State sponsored attacks	No	Threat event
Social networking	No	Thing
Mobile devices and applications	No	Thing
Distributed denial of service	No	Form of attack

Basically, don't confuse things and attacks with actors. That's a good rule of thumb, but, like all rules, there are exceptions. Sometimes technology or processes in and of themselves can exhibit emergent properties or behave in ways that aren't intended and can result in harm. It may be a system with a power supply that dies, a business process that results in unintended harmful outcomes, or software that has a malicious component to it. We have to keep in mind these sorts of emergent behaviors when we think about and model threats.

THREAT COMMUNITY

When using FAIR to model threats, it is usually far more effective to treat them as groups rather than as individuals. For instance, it's usually more accurate to model the characteristics of a group of system administrators versus Bob, the system administrator, who has been with the company for 20 years. Remember, we aren't in the business of prediction, so, intuitively, doing the analysis on Bob will come very close to an attempt at prediction of whether or not Bob goes rogue.

It is highly unlikely we will ever be able to predict Bob's actions. He may go rogue or not, but if we modeled the entire group we will get closer to a more characteristic rate of malicious insider activity for this group, which also applies to Bob. It applies in many scenarios, for example, no matter how many different people in your company take laptops to China, the rate of them being lost is probably more uniform and easier to estimate effectively than the odds on whether or not George loses his. Furthermore, we typically don't need to model an individual's behavior to offer decision-makers the information they need to make a well informed choice in the matter. A simple risk profile for offshore travel with laptops that is characteristic of the entire population is probably helpful enough.

You can use any group to build your own TComs. It could be various groups in your office—marketing, accounting, IT programmers, executives, etc. Attackers can be modeled the same way also—the Mafia, Russian mob, Ukrainian cyber criminals, New Jersey ATM skimmers, etc. However, before you go hog wild building out details on dozens of TComs, think about the sort of decision-making you want these distinctions to drive. We've seen people get highly granular with how they carve up the threat landscape, and we always want to know how useful this is to the decision-makers. For instance, if your organization will end up treating risk scenarios involving the Sicilian Mafia (the Cosa Nostra) the same as the Russian Mafia, then don't bother splitting them out. Just lump these two groups, along with the Yakuza, together into a big bucket called "organized crime" and call it a day. If, however, you find that one group has a significantly higher rate of attack or skillset (effectively making them outside the norm), then go ahead and split them out. Fundamentally, this is about finding and placing attackers into useful buckets to aid in the decision-making process.

Common TComs used in FAIR include the following:

- Nation states—State sponsored professional groups that are engaged in espionage and either clandestine or overt action.
- Cyber criminals—A generic term for any group of criminal enterprises or loosely organized criminals. They are reasonably well-funded but not as well as a nation state.
- Insiders—People inside your organization, typically divided into two subgroups.
  - Privileged insiders—Those with specific access levels, knowledge, or otherwise some other privilege which enables them to overcome any controls and cause harm. In other words, we have invested organizational trust in these people such that if they wanted to do some harm, they could. We may catch them later, but there is effectively nothing to stop them. People in this group might be information security people (oh no!—who is watching the watchers!?!), executives, database administrators, those involved in mergers and acquisitions; you get the drift.
  - Non-privileged insiders—Everyone else. These are the people who have to overcome some form of resistive control in order to affect harm.

Each of these TComs is defined in a way that differentiates them in some fashion from the rest of the threat landscape. Either they bring to bear something unique in terms of their attack methods, capabilities, or intent, or they have levels of access that are distinct from other members of the threat landscape. Defining TComs also allows us to be more effective in estimating how often these groups attack us. Again, this may be a function of their intent, capability, size, or access. For instance, no organization with which we have worked knowingly hires criminals, at least not intentionally, and at least not often. In fact, standard hiring and personnel management practices are intended to reduce the probability of malicious acts by insiders. Thus, the internal rate of seriously malicious activity for most organizations tends to be extremely low when compared to how often external attacks occur. At the end of the day, it's about drawing lines and differentiations within a threat landscape that is otherwise fairly nebulous. We can also draw some inferences from this division about what our control opportunities could be for each TCom. What we have begun to do by making these delineations in our threat landscape is something called "threat profiling." Let's learn more about this now.

THREAT PROFILING

Quick! Tell us what label you would apply to the threat profile below (Table 4.3).

Table 4.3 Threat Profile

Factor	Value
Motive	Ideology
Primary intent	Damage/destroy
Sponsorship	Unknown/unofficial/unrecognized
Preferred general target characteristics	Entities or people who clearly represent conflicting ideology
Preferred targets	Human, critical infrastructure (water, communications, power, etc.), high profile buildings
Capability	Varies by attack vector, yet technological skills vary from virtual luddite to highly advanced engineering
Personal risk tolerance	Very high; up to and including death
Concern for collateral damage	Low

If you said "terrorists," congratulations! We use profiles to help describe who or what a TCom is based upon demographic data, intentions, and preferred modes of attack. As in this case, an observer will usually be able to name the TCom based on the information in the profile. The form and content of a threat profile can be anything you find useful in fleshing out the characteristics of a TCom. Think of it as a way of documenting the assumptions underlying a TCom definition so that answering questions regarding this aspect of an analysis doesn't require dredging from memory.

That said there are a few specific FAIR factors that usually are included when creating a threat profile:

- Threat capability (TCap)—What is the relative skillset that this group can bring to bear against my organization? We'll cover the process of estimating threat capabilities in detail a little bit further on.

- Threat Event Frequency (TEF)—In general, often do they attack us? For this one, it's important to be able to draw a distinction from other TComs in terms of attack frequency. For instance, unless you work in the government, have some special intellectual property (IP), or work in a critical infrastructure industry, Nation State TComs probably are not targeting you very often.
- Asset—Are they interested in the asset under review in this scenario? Do you even have what they're interested in? This is an interesting aspect to keep in mind when forming TCom profiles. For instance, perhaps you work for a company that invests in other companies (a holding company). One day you wake up and the chief executive officer announces they're buying a company engaged in harvesting timber. Now you may be in the crosshairs of environmental terrorists. Better make a profile for them too.
- Harm—What do they intend to do? The information security CIA triad (Confidentiality, Integrity, Availability) works well here—are they looking to affect the availability of a critical system? Or perhaps they just want to steal data from you (confidentiality). Or maybe they are so evil they want to mix up the patient medication records on a critical medication application (integrity). Kinetic types of events work here too—maybe they want to blow up your building (availability). Last, good old-fashioned greed is always in vogue—consider whether they want to steal money from you (another availability scenario—availability of money). Another consideration that cannot be overlooked: your insider TComs will have different TEFs if you consider whether they want to knock systems offline (perhaps rare) versus if they want to exfiltrate data (not as rare).

One way to start building these threat profiles is to put together a Threat Agent Library (TAL) to store this information and to make it accessible to others.

THREAT AGENT LIBRARY

A TAL is a collection of information about TComs that was first described by Matthew Rosenquist at Intel in his whitepaper called "Prioritizing Information Security Risks with Threat Agent Risk Assessment."[1] In that document, the author describes the construction of a table that he calls the Threat Agent Library. It's really little more than a table for various attributes associated with the lists of threat agents. It is a great technique for articulating the differences between threats. In FAIR, we advocate the creation of standard templates for threat identification and, further, the creation of standard ranges for two of the FAIR threat factors (TEF and threat capability).

There are two factors to consider when building out a TAL. First, there is the need to create a common list of relevant TComs for the organization and default values for their variables. This provides a common base from which all analysts can begin their analysis. We say begin, because the second factor to consider is that the default values will very often need to be adjusted based on the scenario under analysis. We offer a caution here. We have seen some analysts rely completely on the default

[1] Rosenquist, M. (2010). *Prioritizing Information Security Risks with Threat Agent Risk Assessment.* Retrieved from http://communities.intel.com/docs/DOC-4693.

values and not make the scenario-based adjustments. This isn't a good idea. In fact, it is the opposite of a good idea. The default values and the rationale behind them are a starting point to help analysts break any analytical inertia they might struggle with when starting an analysis. They also act as a landmark so that any extreme variation in estimates is easier to recognize and validate. An organization that has fully deployed and integrated FAIR risk assessment into its environment may be conducting dozens of analyses a month. The level of quality amongst these will naturally vary (as all work products do). Building these values in a TAL or other threat profile will improve efficiency and consistency from analyst to analyst. As we cautioned though, a careful eye has to be kept out for analysts being "overly efficient." Some TAL examples will be helpful.

EXAMPLES OF A STANDARD SET OF THREAT PROFILES

The following table represents an example of the threats an organization might use to populate a TAL (Table 4.4).

Table 4.4 Internal and External Attackers for Cyber Security Concerns

Internal	External
• Employees • Contractors • Vendors • Business partners	• Cyber criminals (professional hackers) • Organized crime • Spies • Nonprofessional hackers • Activists/hacktivist • Nation state intelligence services • Malware/malicious code authors • Thieves

This is a big list, and if you're just starting out, it might be too much for you to deal with, so we recommend the following five high-level TComs as a basic set for most organizations concerned with information security or cyber security:

- Nation states
- Cyber criminals
- Privileged insiders
- Non-privileged insiders
- Malware

As always, you need to choose groups that are useful and meaningful to your organization—don't build a big list just for the sake of being complete; that does little to engender management support for your effort. If they don't care that much about the difference between cyber criminals and organized crime, then don't bother with differentiating them. If, however, you want to draw a distinction between the

Table 4.5 Nation State Threat Profile

Factor	Value
Motive	Nationalism
Primary intent	Data gathering or disruption of critical infrastructure in furtherance of military, economic, or political goals.
Sponsorship	State sponsored, yet often clandestine.
Preferred general target characteristics	Organizations/individuals that represent assets/targets by the state sponsor.
Preferred targets	Entities with significant financial, commercial, intellectual property, and/or critical infrastructure assets.
Capability	Highly funded, trained, and skilled. Can bring a nearly unlimited arsenal of resources to bear in pursuit of their goals.
Personal risk tolerance	Very high; up to and including death.
Concern for collateral damage	Some, if it interferes with the clandestine nature of the attack.

two because your company is a bank with many ATMs that are in the crosshairs of organized crime, yet they are not targeting your web presence, then perhaps that will be worthwhile. Your mileage will vary. So let's build some standard risk profiles for each of these five groups, along with some TEF and TCap ranges (Table 4.5).

Table 4.5 shows us the profile card for a nation state attacker. It's meant to give the reader an impression of the kind of attacker that we're looking at—and what some of our assumptions are. Now let's quantify characteristics of the TCom (Table 4.6) using two FAIR factors—TEF and TCap:

Table 4.6 Nation State FAIR Risk Factors

TCom	TEF Min	TEF ML	TEF Max	TCap Min	TCap ML	TCap Max
Nation states	0.20 (once in 20 years)	0.06 (once in 15 years)	0.10 (once in 10 years)	95	98	99

TCap, threat capability; TCom, threat community; TEF, threat event frequency; Max, maximum; Min, minimum; ML, most likely.

Table 4.6 shows us a few aspects of the nation state attackers that are important for our analyses. The first is how often they're expected to attack your organization. Keep in mind, however, that when performing an analysis you estimate how often the attack happens in reference to the asset under consideration. The values in a TAL threat profile are simply generalizations - reference points to aid analysts.

These are also not a measure of how often the nation state actors are attacking all American companies (as an example). However, because we are applying this as a base value for analyses at our firm, we have to include all attacks against all assets in these frequency estimates. So using our estimation skills (more on this later), we determine that our firm is subject to attacks from this group sometime between once in 20 and 10 years. We also think the most likely attack frequency will be about once in 15 years. Clearly, these estimates reflect an assumption that your organization is not a prime target for this TCom, in which case we might wonder whether a nation state TCom is relevant enough to be included in your TAL, at least starting out. However, at the same time, there are an increasing number of reports indicating that the frequency of attacks from this TCom is increasing. The point is that whatever your estimates are today, it is important to revisit them periodically to update them based on whatever new information might be available.

TCap is the measure of the attacker's capability so from this table it's clear that these threat agents are well-funded, trained, and outfitted. It's hard to think of a group of attackers that are better than they are. This assumption drives the most likely and maximum numbers. However, not every nation state can afford the best (there are a lot of tin-pot dictators out there), so that drives our 95% rating. Again, this will depend on your organization and assumptions about the nature of the work your firm does. (*Note*: Do not sweat how these numbers are arrived at just yet. We'll get into the details on TCap further on.)

Okay, with that done, let's take a look at another threat profile (Table 4.7), that of the cyber criminals:

Table 4.7 Cyber Criminal Threat Profile

Factor	Value
Motive	Financial
Primary intent	Engage in activities legal or illegal to maximize their profit.
Sponsorship	Non-state sponsored or recognized organizations (illegal organizations or gangs). The organization, however, does sponsor the illicit activities.
Preferred general target characteristics	Easy financial gains via remote means; prefer electronic cash transmission over physical crimes involving cards. Needs money mules or other intermediary to shield them from reversed transactions.
Preferred targets	Financial services and retail organizations.
Capability	Professional hackers. Well-funded, trained, and skilled. May employ relatively desperate actors with or without native skillsets.
Personal risk tolerance	Relatively high (criminal activities); however, willing to abandon efforts that might expose them.
Concern for collateral damage	Not interested in activities that expose themselves or others from their organization. Prefer to keep their identities hidden.

Table 4.8 Cyber Criminal FAIR Risk Factors

TCom	TEF Min	TEF ML	TEF Max	TCap Min	TCap ML	TCap Max
Cyber criminals	0.5 (once in 2 years)	2 (twice a year)	12 (once a month)	60	85	98

Cyber criminals are our professional hacker category (Table 4.8). They may work alone, but often are involved in some sort of community or organization of dubious sponsorship. Many hackers are involved in this activity through organized crime as well.

The frequency of these attacks is really going to depend on the types of business in which you participate and the assets your organization has. If your organization is in their target demographic, such as financial services, banking, retail, ecommerce, or restaurants, then you may experience attacks more often than expressed here. These values (somewhere between once every 2 years to every month) may be too high for a nonprofit organization focused on a generic cause unless they raise funds over the web and run their own ecommerce site. However, if you are Amazon.com, then this estimate is way too low. In other words, your mileage will vary.

Okay, so we have a couple of profiles defined for external threats. Now let's turn and examine your internal people, but first, some level setting. Do we think we experience more attacks from internal or external sources? This is a question that our industry is faced with on a regular basis. The answer is, it depends. It depends on what you consider to be an attack. Insiders frequently do things they aren't supposed to do or intend to do. They take sensitive information home to work on during off-hours. In the course of troubleshooting, system and network administrators encounter sensitive information they don't normally have access to. Personnel regularly lose assets or mistakenly send sensitive information to unintended recipients. Or at least these things occur regularly in the places we've worked. If you consider these events "attacks," then that's going to be an entirely different TEF number than if you narrow the definition to malicious acts intended to harm the organization and/or illegally benefit the perpetrator. Likewise, our estimate for external threat agents also has to be based on a clear understanding of what constitutes an attack. If you include those network scans that occur all the time against Internet-facing systems, you are going to have a very different number than if you narrow your definition to events that will directly result in a breach if your defenses fail (which is the preferred method in FAIR). Once again, our point is that clarity is king. If you don't have clarity on what you're talking about and estimating, the numbers will not make sense.

So, back to our question about which has a higher TEF, insiders or outsiders? Assuming your definition for insider attacks is focused more narrowly on truly malicious events, then, unless your organization has truly awful hiring and personnel management practices, your answer should be external. The misconception that exists in the security industry about this question is largely one of terminology. It's often said by various sources in the security press that insiders are our greatest risk. First, if this is true, then, as we said above, there is a serious problem with hiring and you need to improve human resources, not information security. However, if we tweaked this statement a little and asked whether internal or external attackers had the greatest potential to cause loss, well then maybe the statement is more accurate. The good news is they typically don't cause serious loss. As often as we have built these kinds of tables for companies across various industries and sectors, universally, people choose much lower ranges for insiders causing attacks (maliciously) than they do for external attackers. Remember that risk is comprised of two things—how often bad things are likely to happen and how bad they are likely to be. Most people who say insiders are the biggest risk are generally thinking about what could happen given their unconstrained access without considering the likelihood of that worst-case event. To be sure, insiders misbehave in many ways, and not infrequently. However, there is a distinct difference between the high frequency, low impact behaviors versus the lower frequency, high impact actions. Particularly so when it comes to malicious acts. With this in mind, let's take a look at our first insider group, privileged insiders (Table 4.9).

Table 4.9 Privileged Insider Threat Profile

Factor	Value
Motive	Vindictive or personal gain. These tend to be loyal, trusted employees who go bad in extreme conditions.
Primary intent	Gain retribution for perceived wrongs or to acquire money for alleviating a personal stressor.
Sponsorship	None. In rare cases, there is collusion between various bad actors, however, most are lone wolves.
Preferred general target characteristics	Easy yet hidden financial gains or high profile targets that offer vindication for the attacker.
Preferred targets	Prefer to attack targets to which the attacker already has access.
Capability	Skillset varies. Tends to be very well versed in the systems to which they have access. Could have very high general computer science skills, yet may not be well-skilled in hacking.
Personal risk tolerance	Very low. Attacker typically pressured into scenario that compels them to act (backed into a corner). This could be work related pressure such as a layoff, demotion, or a personal pressure, such as an illness in the family or personal financial stress.
Concern for collateral damage	In highly cohesive groups, there is very little tolerance for collateral damage, except in cases where the attacker feels wronged by the group.

Privileged insiders are the people who run your business. To borrow from a medieval metaphor, somebody has to be trusted to dress and feed the king, which necessarily gives him or her privileged access. Are they high-risk people? Hopefully not! You shouldn't put high-risk people in charge of the servers, applications, and systems that run your organization. By high-risk we mean they're highly likely to act in ways that create significant loss. Nevertheless, their actions should be under constant review. Regardless, the actions or mis-actions of these people should (if possible) be monitored both as a deterrent and to provide the means for timely response. With that behind us, let's take a look at the FAIR factors for our trusted insiders (Table 4.10):

Table 4.10 Privileged Insider FAIR Risk Factors

TCom	TEF Min	TEF ML	TEF Max	TCap Min	TCap ML	TCap Max
Privileged insider	0.04 (once in 25 years)	0.06 (once in 15 years)	0.10 (once a decade)	98	99	99

Once again, your mileage may vary on these estimates. We hope that your frequency numbers aren't much worse than this—an insider attack of any severity sometime between once a decade and four times a century may not be too bad. However, always look for data to lead you in this. If there are instances of this kind of behavior (or near instances), then it is important to consider that and whether it should affect just the minimum, maximum, or the most likely value. The other key piece of information to keep in mind about privileged insiders is that the TCap estimates reflect the fact that they don't have to overcome any preventative security controls (e.g., authentication and access privileges) in order to cause harm to your organization, and they are in privileged positions because of their skills. Think about it—they already have access to the things they're likely to affect and they are familiar with the technologies and processes in place. Keep in mind, too, that these estimates reflect serious malicious acts versus minor acts, which may be much more frequent. Also, these estimates reflect intentional acts versus unintentional error, which privileged insiders also inflict on their organizations.

With our trusted employees out of the way, let's move on to the rest. For this next group, we're going to lump in everyone else. Non-Privileged insiders are basically anyone who is not, well, privileged. Depending on your needs, you might include temporary workers (contractors) in this TCom. Some organizations don't include them and instead define a separate TCom for these actors. Factors that might help you decide whether to treat them separately include the number of contractors and whether the frequency of severity of their actions would be any different. Again, think about this with the end in mind—is there a significant difference in the frequency in which they misbehave, their skillset (the FAIR risk factors), or the controls you would use to manage the exposure they represent? If yes, then break them out. In addition, if your temporary workers are engaged in a lot of criminal activity, then we'd suggest you take a look at those hiring practices again. Table 4.11 is a profile card:

Table 4.11 Non-Privileged Insider Threat Profile

Factor	Value
Motive	Spite or personal gain. These could be largely unengaged personnel with little allegiance to the organization.
Primary intent	Gain retribution for perceived wrongs or to acquire money for alleviating a personal stressor.
Sponsorship	None. In rare cases, there is collusion between various bad actors, yet this is rare—most are lone wolves.
Preferred general target characteristics	Easy yet hidden financial gains or high profile targets that offer vindication for the attacker.
Preferred targets	Prefer to attack targets to which the attacker already has access, or to which they have the skills necessary to attack (in which case they'd be considered privileged insiders).
Capability	Skillset varies widely. Likely to have limited access to systems. Most are likely to have limited skills required for pulling off a hacking attack, yet some may be studying and practicing on their own as a hobby or in pursuit of career progression.
Personal risk tolerance	Varies with personal circumstances.
Concern for collateral damage	Varies with personal circumstances.

So, there you have it—the profile for the general populace of your company (Table 4.12).

Table 4.12 Non-Privileged Insider FAIR Risk Factors

TCom	TEF Min	TEF ML	TEF Max	TCap Min	TCap ML	TCap Max
Non-privileged insiders	0.06 (once in 15 years)	0.10 (once in 10 years)	1 (once a year)	40	50	95

The TEF estimates reflect an assumption that these people are less trustworthy than the privileged insiders yet not as criminal as the external threat agents. In part, this is a result of this TCom typically being larger than the privileged community (e.g., you have a lot more general personnel than you do database administrators), and simple statistics would suggest that, everything else being equal, a larger population will have more bad actors than a smaller one. Honestly, once a year may be too often, but our range here pulls toward the low end. Perhaps if you have some near misses with temporary workers then the once a year maximum (or even more) might be a solid estimate for you. As we indicated in the profile card, we see their skills could be below average (40%) yet some may have some very solid skills (95%). The most likely value reflects an assumption that the average non-privileged insider is no better or worse than the average member of the broader community. One assumption of note here is that if the skillsets were much higher, then we would be more likely to see these actors in privileged roles. For your organization, this may be a poor assumption. Take stock of the environment while building these.

We have a solid start on a profile deck for some basic TComs. The last one that is important to build out is one for malicious code (malware) however, we aren't going to spell out the profile here as its nature and purpose varies widely. For instance, you can use malware to exact revenge on being demoted or an external attacker could use it to try to steal money from you (in which case its more of a method of attack by those TComs than one of its own). So why does it get its own category? Again, we look at this with the end in mind. Malware will behave with various levels of capability and frequency in your orientation. It also may have certain properties of emergent behavior. Take a look at Table 4.13:

Table 4.13 Malware FAIR Risk Factors

TCom	TEF Min	TEF ML	TEF Max	TCap Min	TCap ML	TCap Max
Malware	0.5 (once every 2 years)	2 (twice a year)	6 (once every 2 months)	40	60	95

One key determination to make about malware is whether this frequency is per infection or per outbreak (note that the same question applies to phishing as well, where we can call it a campaign instead of an outbreak). You may get 100 infected computers all gummed up with the same piece of malware. Is that 100 attacks? Well, for most analyses, this isn't the case. What you need to do is build a model that reflects the reality you are experiencing. For our purposes here, let's model this as a single event; an outbreak. In our TEF estimate, we are saying that we may experience a malware outbreak in our organization between once every 2 years and once every 2 months. For this, you will often have good information to pull from—your virus scanning software will tell you how often this occurs. Look for the bigger patterns though. You're looking for the currents here, not the individual swim lanes. How good is this malware? Again, these wide ranges (40–95%) reflect the reality that some malware is virtually impotent, most is not much to write home about, and is caught by your antimalware measures, but some is just downright wicked.

So there you have it—the foundation for a threat profile library and some templates to feed our risk analyses. The importance of building these cannot be understated. It can be a critical component in ensuring consistent results regardless of the risk analyst. As we mentioned though, there is the tendency for some analysts to rely too heavily on the templates. Ensuring quality in analyses is a topic that will be discussed later, but the key here is to impart to the risk analysts that these tables are to be used as a starting point; the rough material from which you can get your head wrapped around the factors associated with an analysis. In keeping with the malware example, the values may say that TCap is between 40% and 95%, however, if the particular risk scenario you are modeling involves a piece of password stealing code on the newest tablets, then it may make sense to narrow that range; pull up the low end to 80% and extend the high end to 98%. Another assumption may be that it is harder to get new malware on recently released hardware/software platforms so it takes a higher skillset. Either way, the template we build in the profile helps jump start the analysis and get us better results faster. As the use of FAIR broadens, there will be more research and data available to improve these estimates. In fact, as this book is being written, we are working with a couple of threat intelligence vendors on formalizing threat capability data sources.

One other element that is important to consider is that when you lump together TComs you need to manage the ranges differently. For instance, assume we combined internal employees and temporary employee TEF estimates. The temporary workers may be more likely to behave poorly so that drives our high number (every other month), but the remainder of the internal employees drives the low number (every other year). In this case, the maximum estimate within our analysis would reflect the temporary employee maximum and the minimum estimate within our analysis would reflect the internal employee minimum. The most likely value would come from whichever TCom had the higher most likely estimate. This is a tactic that we will use a lot in FAIR when building ranges, but it's especially important to keep it in mind when we are building broadly applicable templates like these.

THREAT EVENT

A threat event occurs when a threat actor acts in a manner that has the potential to cause harm. These actions can be intentional and malicious, intentional and non-malicious, and unintentional and nonmalicious. Most untrained, uncalibrated risk analysts tend to overestimate the number of threat events to which their organization is exposed. This is one of the common areas where unmitigated bias enters into an analysis. When that happens, it's important to remember the definition of what a threat event really represents.

In FAIR, risk analyses are always specific to the scenario under examination. For example, if you're examining the risk associated with an ecommerce portal, then all the estimated factors need to be specific to that scenario, including how often the portal is attacked. A threat event, in this case, might be how often the TCom under consideration (call it cyber criminals) attacks that portal. It isn't how often they attack websites in general, other bank's websites, etc. It is your estimate of how often this specific ecommerce portal is likely to be attacked during the timeframe under consideration (usually annually). Thinking about the factors this way helps you to keep the values realistic and relevant to the analysis at hand.

Intent also matters when modeling a scenario. In a malicious scenario, the threat actor has to intend to cause the harm. For example, in a physical security scenario—the risk associated with piggybacking through a corporation's main employee entrance. A threat event in this example isn't when an employee comes through the door, and it's not when an employee piggybacks with another employee in order to bypass an authentication mechanism. There is no intended harm. They were already authorized to get in and they just choose a method that isn't compliant with policy. One of us has a friend who did something that illustrates this well. It was morning and this person was late for a meeting. They got to the main employee entrance, which, at the time, were those automated see-through acrylic batwing styled turnstiles. It was at this point he realized that his access badge was not working. So he jumped the turnstiles and made his meeting (the turnstiles were just waist high). Was this a threat event? No. First, he was still employed and had legitimate access to the facility. His badge access was simply turned off by accident. Second, his intent was to attend a meeting; put another way, he intended to do his job. One might even argue that he saved the company money by not missing the meeting! If his access had been turned off on purpose because he had been terminated or because he no longer required access to the facility, and he jumped the turnstile with the intent to inflict harm, it would be a threat event, at least within the context of a malicious threat event.

Going back to our original task, we have to estimate how often people who tailgate intend to cause some harm, which constitutes our TEF for that scenario. Given what we discussed above, we would not count every tailgating incident as a threat event. Instead, we might get estimates on the frequency of tailgating and estimate the percentage of those where the intent is malicious. This may be a very low percentage in many companies. Or we can take the known number of malicious events that occurred by non-privileged insiders within the facility and estimate the percentage of those where entry was gained by tailgating. Regardless, there are a number of ways to approach the estimate but you have to be very clear on what constitutes the threat event itself in order to have any hope of getting the estimate right. A lack of this sort of clarity is a major factor in poorly done analyses.

LOSS EVENT

A loss event is a threat event where loss materializes and/or where liability increases. Recall that a threat event is an event where loss *could* occur. When an event results in loss, then it is called a loss event. We'll talk about the loss categories below, but assume that there is impact to the business processes, internal investigations, lost clients, fines, etc. Some organizations make a distinction between internal dollars and external dollars—sometimes they give them colors (a green dollar is money out the door and blue/red/yellow dollars are internal costs, very often materializing as person-hours spent dealing with an event). For our purposes, a loss is a loss, the color of the money doesn't matter.

What turns a threat event into a loss event? Well, you have to be susceptible to the attack, errors, or extreme weather. Another word for that is vulnerable. This is where vulnerability will make its mark on your risk assessment. The state of being vulnerable is a spectrum and subject to many factors. With that in mind, let us talk about what may be a new term for you; vulnerability event.

VULNERABILITY EVENT

There is no such thing as zero vulnerability. Everything is vulnerable to some degree, even when controls are in place and performing as intended. That being the case, a vulnerability event occurs when there is an increase in vulnerability, either because a control condition changes or threat capability changes. This term allows us to differentiate events that are very often not well differentiated. For example, in many organizations we've worked with, there is no clear differentiation between security-related events where a threat agent acted in a manner that qualifies as a threat event (e.g., attacked your Website) versus someone who bypassed change control and installed a server insecurely. Many times these will both be called a security incident, yet they are very different things. One was a threat event—an attempt to cause harm in this case, while the other created additional vulnerability for the organization—a vulnerability event. Another example is leaving the door open in the back of the building. This is a vulnerability event. It doesn't mean loss has happened, or even that a threat agent is trying to break in. It means that if a threat event were to occur, the organization is more likely to suffer.

We will cover metrics in a separate chapter but this is an example of where better definition enables more accurate and more meaningful metrics.

PRIMARY AND SECONDARY STAKEHOLDERS

Understanding the notion of stakeholders is critical in order to do analysis well. Broadly speaking, primary stakeholders are those who are directly impacted by primary loss. We'll cover primary loss further in the chapter that follows, but think about the things that happen immediately as a result of an event—response functions kick into play, investigation begins, business productivity may fall because of an operational outage, etc. These "primary" losses are experienced by the organization directly as a result of the event. Within an analysis, primary stakeholders are typically considered the executive team, which is often generalized as the organization itself.

However, something interesting happens after these primary losses occur—other stakeholders take notice or are affected. It depends on your organization and industry, but government regulators may make it their business to understand the loss. They may audit your organization, publicly shame it, and levy fines against it. Likewise, customers and business partners might change their relationship with the organization or file their own legal grievances. The media might join the fray and issue scathing reports about the organization. These are examples of secondary stakeholders and their reactions—they have an interest in your organization from a value or liability perspective and they have the ability to inflict harm, sometimes significant harm.

LOSS FLOW

FAIR is, above all else, a model of reality (inasmuch as you can ever model reality), and when modeling reality, the real world is never wrong. It is fruitless to attempt to shoehorn the real world into a model that doesn't fit. In the very early days of FAIR, it became evident that using a single series of losses was not going to represent reality very well for a number of reasons. This was standard fare for the security profession at the time: a simple equation that asks that you fill in a number for "impact." Well, how does one come up with this number? A common approach was to survey the landscape for examples of others that have experienced a security breach. For better or for worse, there hasn't been an overabundance of public data for this kind of thing. Companies are breached every day, but most don't disclose the details, nor do they speak extensively about the money it cost them. Even in the more high profile cases, these loss numbers tend to be kept close to the vest. So, if you do find a number anywhere, it tends to be a big, obscene number from a company that may not be anything like yours.

One of our favorite examples was the time we saw an analysis where the impact number the analyst used was based on Google's 2012 settlement with the Federal Trade Commission (FTC) over tracking Safari users using cookies[2]. For the record, that was $22.5 million—and we do mean "record" as this was a record-breaking fine for the FTC at that time. Now, what are the odds this scenario applies in any way to your firm or the scenario you're analyzing? Are you the largest search engine on the planet? We're hard pressed to expect that this number applies to very many risk analyses today–there are just too many unique factors involved. Yet, there it was staring at us and being rationalized by the presenter as a big number that was used because it was easier than calculating all the other impact costs. In their minds, the fact that it clearly would exceed any fine in their scenario made it a safe and easy number to use. Thus, they concluded, it was a reasonable number.

TALKING ABOUT RISK

A sidebar here is in order. Having frequently had to defend loss amounts in risk analyses to executives, we find this argument untenable at best. The goal is to provide relevant numbers that provide an accurate and defensible result. Properly applied, FAIR will give you the tools to come up with these values. If you are going to bat with the Google numbers (or another similar high dollar fine), then it's going to be a hard sell unless it is directly applicable. You must use numbers that are relevant to your organization and the scenario under analysis.

One of the big revelations in the early development of FAIR was that losses typically follow a two-phase approach. Let's delve deeper into this to understand why this is and how it's useful in your risk analyses.

To illustrate loss flow (see Figure 4.1) let's examine an example risk scenario— a burglar trying to steal a rare artifact from a museum. In this scenario, the burglar

---

[2] http://www.ftc.gov/opa/2012/08/google.shtm.

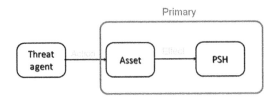

FIGURE 4.1

Loss flow—primary.

is (obviously) the threat agent. They initiate some action against an asset (in this case, the artifact). let's assume they succeed (their TCap exceeds the difficulty or resistance strength of the museum's controls, thus turning the threat event into a loss event). This has an effect on the PSH or primary stakeholder (i.e., the odds are pretty good that executive leadership of the museum is going to be upset). They'll be upset because the museum will have to investigate the incident and bear the costs associated with that. They will also have to close that exhibit as there is nothing to, well, exhibit. Tourists that would have come specifically to see that exhibit probably won't come. If museum security was contracted out, the museum may also have to (or want to) replace the contracted security company that fell down on the job. These are primary losses, but the fun doesn't stop there.

Perhaps most critically, the museum will have to deal with compensating the owner of the artifact (if it is borrowed or on tour) and probably file some insurance claims (the artifact owner and insurance company are examples of secondary stakeholders or SSH). How likely would you be to exhibit your priceless artifact at this museum after you heard of this attack? As the insurer, how would you rate the insurance premiums for this museum going forward? What would you write about this museum in the press if you were a reporter? How likely would you be to advocate for future funding if you were the mayor of the local government where this museum resided? Imagine being the person in charge of fund raising efforts for this museum in the days following the heist. The answer to these questions will vary wildly from scenario to scenario. However, each of these questions hints at one or another form of secondary loss that may materialize (see Figure 4.2). These secondary losses occur as a result of the primary loss event, and stem from secondary stakeholder reactions to the primary event.

EXAMPLES OF SECONDARY STAKEHOLDERS

- Customers
- Competitors
- Community
- Government
- Media
- Business partners

Secondary stakeholders (SSH) will make use of the tools at their disposal to recoup their losses or express their moral outrage. They may file class action lawsuits,

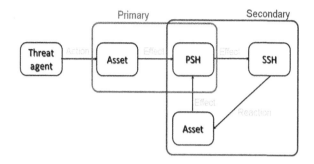

FIGURE 4.2

Loss flow—secondary.

open regulatory investigations that ultimately end in fines, or simply choose to take their business elsewhere. These actions, collectively, are referred to as secondary loss events, and they have an impact on the primary stakeholder that can be measured monetarily.

Cascading losses happen when the results of secondary stakeholder reactions further impact the primary stakeholder such that the same or new secondary stakeholders take additional actions, creating additional losses. Picture the Enron and Arthur Andersen fiascos. There is a snowball effect in play here whereby, for example, a reduction in patronage after an event leaves the museum unable to fund future expansions, which means fewer new exhibits, which means even fewer new customers, ad nauseum.

FORMS OF LOSS

Before we begin a discussion of the kinds of things you should consider when assessing losses, we'll review the approach used in FAIR for tallying up losses. First, it's important to know that FAIR does not solely use asset value to compute impact as do some risk methods that consider risk a percentage of asset value. Instead, it's more similar to what the ISO/IEC 27,005:2008 standard calls "consequences." The metaphor that we think best illustrates the approach is the accounting costing method known as activity-based costing (ABC).

ABC has the user identify the activities used to build a product or deliver a service and then allocates them in a rational way to those work streams to find a way to come up with a cost the firm can use to understand better their profit and loss for a particular offering. There are many ways to accomplish this same task besides ABC, but those distinctions are not critical to our application of this in FAIR. Put simply, when a security breach happens in an organization (for example) there are "activities" that are performed in response (the previous section on Loss Flows gives some examples of this). The FAIR loss forms provide a structured framework to account for, estimate, and capture these costs and allocate them to risk scenarios.

One very important word of caution about using these loss forms: the risk analyst should not typically come up with the values by themselves. It is very important that when assessing business impact, investigation costs, or any other losses, that some-one from those impacted business functions assist in estimating those values. Your role as the risk analyst is to guide the appropriate subject matter experts through the estimating process and to help keep their minds from wandering to include irrelevant factors—focus on the guidance in this chapter and use it to gather good data on the form of loss being considered. The benefits here are twofold: (1) you get much higher quality estimates for losses, and (2) the results have improved credibility with the business. When your analysis is being reviewed by the organization and they question where you got the loss numbers, the best possible answer is "With input from your subject matter experts."

FORMS OF LOSS

There are six FAIR loss forms that can occur in both the primary and secondary loss flows: productivity, response, replacement, competitive advantage, fines and judgments, and reputation. Productivity and replacement costs occur mostly as primary loss, and the latter three materialize primarily as secondary loss. Response losses commonly occur as both primary and secondary loss. There are some exceptions, but this is a good rule of thumb. Let's look at each form of loss in turn and explore how they apply to risk scenarios, as well as where they fit within primary and secondary loss.

Productivity

There are two categories of productivity loss that we commonly use—(1) losses that result from a reduction in an organization's ability to execute on its primary value proposition (the primary value proposition is the reason that the organization exists, usually as a result of the products and services that it offers the marketplace), and (2) losses that result from personnel being paid but unable to perform their duties. An example of the first category of productivity loss would be lost revenue when a retail Website goes down. An example of the second category would be when call center communications fail. In this case, you have a bunch of people collecting a paycheck yet being unable to provide value to the organization.

There are some subtle but important considerations for each of these categories of productivity loss. Very often the effect on revenue from an operational outage is delayed rather than lost, at least in part. If customers are loyal to your organization or you don't sell goods and services that are easy to acquire elsewhere, they will eventually make their purchases. However, if customers can buy what you're offering from a number of different sources, then losses are less likely to simply be delayed. Consider how much business you will lose both permanently and temporarily. For example, we know an online gaming company that was doing a FAIR analysis related to outages on their primary revenue generating game. They at first came to the table with an estimate based on the duration of a potential outage times the average hourly revenue from the game. This was a *big* number. We questioned though whether the revenue was lost or simply delayed.

Would their customer base simply wait for the game to come back online and make up, at least in part, the normal revenue stream? We dug into their data and found that yes, most of the revenue was recovered by a surge in game usage following outages. The resulting productivity loss estimate was much smaller than the original estimate. The point is, it's important to understand the nature of the event, the affected business processes, and your market in order to understand the real effect on revenue.

For personnel productivity, a similar consideration exists. Even though normal activities may be hampered, it is uncommon for employees to be 100% unproductive during most events. As a result, in order to arrive at an accurate estimate, it's often important to estimate the degree of degradation on personnel productivity that an outage would impose (which may be nominal in many cases). Also, keep in mind that very often employees are expected to simply "suck it up" and work as late as needed to make up for downtime during normal work hours.

We encounter a fair number of companies who just don't bother with the personnel productivity aspect of loss. In many cases, this makes perfect sense because the numbers simply aren't large enough to matter relative to some of the other forms of loss. In other cases, organizations just want to focus on hard dollar losses and consider soft costs to be sunk costs.

Response

Response costs are those associated with managing the loss event. Very often these are intuitive to tally, but it's important to understand which response costs belong as primary loss and which should be considered secondary loss.

When tallying primary response costs, many firms have an incident response team, computer security incident response team, or something similar. The costs associated with scrambling these teams to manage an incident are included in this category. How do we calculate their cost? There's a straightforward approach to this. Most companies have something called a "loaded cost" hourly rate for their employees. In some cases, organizations have varied rates based on the type of employee. For instance, the loaded cost number for higher skilled people may be something like $110 an hour. For lower-tiered skillsets, the number may be $85. In assessing what you think the response costs would be, consider how many people would be involved and how much time would be spent on the incident. Consider things like initial kickoff and status reporting via conference calls, meetings in real life, travel (if necessary), and investigation time for various technical specialties. It's often helpful to build this data into a table that allows you to break down time and costs into various subtypes depending on your needs. Also, note that this does not have to be limited to just internal people—if your firm will hire outside organizations to assist in the investigation and response (e.g., forensics), then add those up here as well.

Secondary response costs are focused on those activities and expenses incurred while dealing with secondary stakeholders. This can include a lot of different things, depending on the nature of the incident. For example, if the event involves a confidentiality breach of sensitive customer information, the number of exposed records will strongly affect response costs like notification and credit monitoring expenses. For our response cost estimates, figure on there being notification costs for each record. The requirements will vary from jurisdiction to jurisdiction, but may include things like a notification on a public Website, emails, and a letter in the mail. These things have their costs so it's important that we account for them. Some firms choose to outsource this, which can make it easier to assess the costs (you can get the data from quotes, etc.). Check with the privacy department in your firm to see if they already have a contract, statement of work, or other prearranged firm they would utilize. This will have the benefit of assisting not just with notification but also with credit monitoring cost estimates (a lot of outsourced providers combine the two). Thus, we can also tally how much it will cost to provide credit monitoring for impacted people as well. One key point to remember here, far fewer than 100% of notified people will take you up on your free credit monitoring option. It seems insane, we know, but this number will vary significantly from firm to firm and may be as low as 5% or as high as 70%. The number of compromised records also can significantly affect the probability of fines or judgments by regulators, as they are more likely to get nasty when the number of records is large. Fundamentally, customers and regulators treat a ten record breach much differently than a one million record breach.

Remember our discussion of loss flows? One key thing to recall is that in secondary loss scenarios, the "threat agent" could be customers choosing to participate in a class action lawsuit. This means that your firm will need to staff attorneys in order to address and fend off this new "attack." In that case guess what you're doing? Responding. But the same process applies—figure out a per-hour cost of attorneys (probably higher than for your in-house people) and how many hours of work they will be doing. There's likely to be a lot of variability in this answer, but getting some ranges together should be pretty straightforward. You can use a table to reflect the values you have accumulated from this analysis like the one in Figure 4.3. In this type of scenario, be sure to recognize these legal defense costs as secondary response losses as they are incurred as a result of secondary stakeholder reactions.

Replacement

Replacement costs in many of the scenarios we analyze are considered primary losses. If you've spent time calculating risk by figuring asset value, then this will feel very familiar to you, even though its use here is more robust. For this, consider the intrinsic value of an asset; the book value if you will. This means that if the risk scenario you're modeling involves the loss of physical things (think theft, breakage, violent weather, physical violence, looting, etc.) then this is usually the category where these losses go. This one is straightforward—what will it cost to replace the physical asset under question? This is how many insurance policies are structured— they're interested in how much it would cost to replace your house, not necessarily what the house is worth right now (however, these replacement costs usually have built-in inflation values as well).

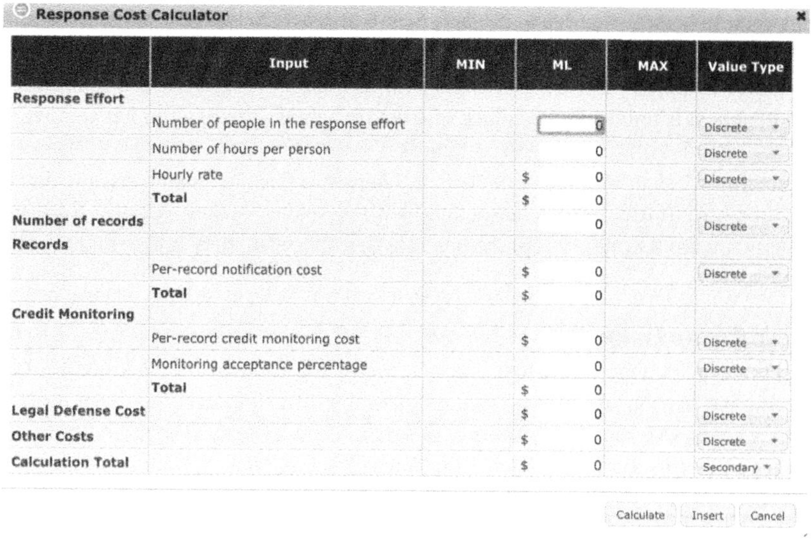

	Input	MIN	ML	MAX	Value Type
Response Cost Calculator					
Response Effort					
	Number of people in the response effort		0		Discrete
	Number of hours per person		0		Discrete
	Hourly rate	$	0		Discrete
	Total	$	0		
Number of records			0		Discrete
Records					
	Per-record notification cost	$	0		Discrete
	Total	$	0		
Credit Monitoring					
	Per-record credit monitoring cost	$	0		Discrete
	Monitoring acceptance percentage		0		Discrete
	Total	$	0		
Legal Defense Cost		$	0		Discrete
Other Costs		$	0		Discrete
Calculation Total		$	0		Secondary

Calculate   Insert   Cancel

FIGURE 4.3

Assessing response cost.

For example, if you're modeling a business continuity scenario and the result is that a hurricane, tornado, or other destructive weather pattern blows through and levels your facility, then there are a lot of costs associated with rebuilding, reacquiring new leased space, replacement furniture, fixtures, computing equipment, and on and on. All of this goes into this category.

But replacement costs can occur as secondary loss too. For example, making customers of financial service firms whole after a theft of funds. Most firms' standing policy is that if an online account is hacked, then they will make the customer whole (replace the stolen funds in their account to bring them back to where they were). Modeling this involves estimating how much money you think will be stolen out of the account multiplied by the number of affected accounts, prior to the firm catching on and shutting it down. This is going to involve spending some time with the fraud and loss prevention people in your organization, and especially with the lines of business to understand the various business processes, paper or online forms, and the reporting, checkpoints, and approvals that are required in order to get money out of an account. In our experience, there tends to be some threshold upon which the business will say "We'd definitely notice transfers of this amount in short order." This may be something like $100,000, $1,000,000, or more.

Also important to note is that for certain types of retirement accounts, there is a limit to the amount of money the customers are allowed to withdraw from the account (some Internal Revenue Service rules limit account withdrawals prior to retirement at 50% or $50,000, whichever is less. Check with the business/legal/compliance groups in your firm for specifics and how this applies to you.). This will limit the amount of money that the attacker can take at one time, assuming the business rules are codified in the application somewhere.

Another example of where secondary replacement costs occur is when a breach of credit card information takes place and the breached organization has to cover the costs associated with replacing credit cards.

Knowing whether replacement costs fall in primary or secondary loss is relatively straightforward. If the costs are associated with secondary stakeholders in some manner, then they are secondary replacement costs. Otherwise, they are primary replacement costs.

Competitive advantage

Competitive advantage (CA) losses are some of the more difficult kinds to assess properly. The first hurdle to overcome is that most firms believe they have more CA than they really do. Largely speaking, these kinds of losses are specifically focused on some asset (physical or logical) that provides your firm an advantage over the competition. This is also something that another firm cannot acquire or develop (legally) on their own. Typical examples here include things like intellectual property (IP), secret business plans (mergers and acquisitions), or market information. If your firm has a patent or copyright on something that no other firm has, then it may have a competitive advantage over them (assuming the patent or copyright is something useful—there are a lot of questionable patents out there). Trade secrets are similar, but a little trickier. Remember that trade secrets are like a patent or copyright, but a firm does not wish to disclose them to the public using one of those legally recognized methods, so they keep them secret and protect them with contracts instead. This is typically what's being done when you sign a non-disclosure agreement—somebody is trying to protect their trade secrets. The classic example is the formula for Coca Cola. They decided it was better protected as a trade secret than to publicly disclose it via a patent and only get 20 years of protection before everyone could make Coca Cola penalty free (patents expire after a period of time).

When considering IP for competitive advantage, you also have to assess how likely the competition will be to take illegally acquired information and act upon it. Essentially, you have to think about how likely your competitors will be to illicitly use your IP and harm you in the process. Keep in mind that illicit use of IP carries some pretty stiff penalties—both legal and reputational—and that (at least in many countries) organizations are very cautious about crossing that line. It happens, but perhaps not as often as the movies and television will have us believe. Factor that into your analysis as well. In fact, ask yourself how likely it would be for your company to use illicitly gained IP and then consider whether your competition is any different in that regard. With regard to patents, keep in mind that the patent details on new product are only really secret up until the patent filing, after which they are publicly searchable. So, if the scenario involves existing patents, those are already public. This may or may not affect your analysis, so pay attention to that as well.

Information about mergers and acquisitions is typically highly regulated and there are specific consequences for disclosing information about it before the appropriate time. However, it's important to include losses associated with a merger partner backing out (and the difference between that deal and the next) as well as what that might do to your competitors. There may be some moves they can make that will block you from making any deal at all, effectively devaluing your company. There can be high levels of uncertainty associated with these deals, so can be important to consider that when building your estimates; You may need to make them much wider ranges to reflect your firm's uncertainty.

One last area to consider is information about the market to which your competition may not have access. We tend to draw a distinction between information held before and after the market closes. After closure, everybody knows about it anyway and has made their trades based upon it. However, sometimes traders legally come across a bit of information for which quick action can benefit the firm. Thus, risk scenarios involving access to trader's personal workstations and workspaces tends to get some CA numbers tallied to account for these losses.

Fines and judgments

Sometimes, as a result of a loss event, a firm will get fined by a regulatory body, incur a judgment from a civil case, or pay a fee based on contractual stipulations. These losses fall into the fines and judgments (F&Js) loss category. Those really big numbers from Google that we mentioned earlier would be included here (if warranted, of course). As with any risk analysis, loss values must be relevant to the scenario under evaluation and F&J numbers are no different. You have to believe that for the scenario you are modeling (say, a hack of your Website) that the FTC, Securities and Exchange Commission, Food and Drug Administration, or any other alphabet soup government agency, will levy fines or impose sanctions. For instance, we might estimate that in failing to uphold the level of security outlined in our privacy policy, the FTC would fine us somewhere between $0 and $10 million. Why such a wide range? Recall our comment earlier that the number of compromised records can have a profound effect on regulatory furor. If the breach is limited in size, F&Js can easily be $0. In fact, there are many scenarios in which both the minimum and most likely values are $0 but the maximum is in the millions of dollars. We may also be worried about customer reaction, so a class action attorney may bring together a few hundred of your affected customers and win a big judgment against your firm. The estimate of that loss will be included here as well. Remember that these numbers are likely to have a high level of uncertainty associated with them. That's okay—the idea is to use numbers that accurately reflect the reality of the scenario, which includes the level of uncertainty in the estimates.

One last thing to consider: bail. Sometimes we have executives that, through their own willful violation of ethics and good judgment, will perform some act that results in them going to jail. Sometimes laws, like the Sarbanes-Oxley Act of 2002, include the potential for prosecution of executives as well. If the firm would bail these executives out of custody, then those costs go here. Bail bond companies usually take a fee (such as 10% of the face value of the bail) for providing the full amount to the court. They usually require some sort of collateral as well (car, house, etc.).

The only time in our experience where F&Js can be counted as primary loss is if the scenario is based on a threat agent (perhaps a competitor) filing legal action for something like a patent violation. In this case, the primary event is this legal action so any resulting F&Js would be considered primary.

Reputation

Discussions regarding reputation damage can be particularly interesting, especially when someone comes to the table claiming that reputation damage can't be measured. We enjoy these debates because, at the end of the day, their argument is inevitably badly flawed. First of all, the only reason anyone cares about reputation damage is because of its effects. That being the case, the next logical question is what these effects look like. For commercial enterprises, it usually boils down to market share, cost of capital, stock price if it is publicly traded, and, in some cases, increased costs associated with hiring or retaining employees following an event. It also can materialize as an increase in insurance premiums because, after all, the premiums are based on the reputation of the organization from a liability perspective. For government organizations, reputation damage is trickier. In some cases, we've seen reputation damage evaluated as the increased costs associated with political leaders being reelected to office. In another instance, it reflected expectations regarding reduced departmental funding. What it boils down to though is that reputation losses occur because of secondary stakeholder perception that an organization's value (or its leadership's competency) has decreased or liability has increased in a way that affects the stakeholder.

Everyone is sure that a hack of their firm will result in serious impacts to their reputation. It may, but consider once again our lesson about primary value propositions—we have to believe that the risk scenario under evaluation will result in damage to our firm's reputation such that secondary stakeholder opinion will materially change. But how could we possibly measure this?

As it turns out, these are relatively straightforward things to measure. In the context of your risk scenario, just consider how many current customers you would lose and what that would mean to your organization in terms of profit. Likewise for new customers. If you believe that a data breach would result in you losing as many as 10 customers and the lifetime value of their business is $10,000 each, then your maximum loss value for this loss form value is $100,000. Now, we can get very advanced with our analyses and consider whether that customer will leave forever or if they will only leave for a short period. Check with the marketing or sales department—they often have concepts like the "lifetime value of a customer" that can help you in making your estimates.

Stock price is similarly estimated, yet different enough from market share that we include it separately. Estimating stock price impact involves some very high levels of uncertainty, yet there is some guidance we once heard from a client that is helpful here. When building FAIR loss tables to aid in an analysis, we gathered people high in the organization and worked through reputational losses. Chief among them was the comptroller. This was for a firm that was in the Fortune 500 and had a very large footprint of stores across the United States. In discussing stock price, this person indicated that there were many things that influenced their stock price, much of which he dismissed as being irrational or the part of greater market trends. As a result, this person doubted whether a specific breach, if it did affect stock price, would have any noticeable impact at all. However, this person did say that assuming they could isolate that as the cause, they still would not consider it a loss unless the price remained depressed for at least 12 months as a direct result of that security breach.

Your mileage may vary, but the lesson here should be very clear—if you want to model stock price losses for an organization, you need to include the right person to aid in doing so. Get some face time with those that manage this on a day-to-day basis and get them to assist you in coming up with ranges that make sense to them.

The last type of reputational loss that we need to review here is cost of capital. Why is this important? Because it's a quantifiable measure of the market's trust in the leadership of the firm. Think of it like this—if Moody's (the credit rating agency) felt that your firm was run by graduates of a clown college, had no background in leading companies, and didn't know anything about the products or services you offered, how do you think they would rate your firm? Alternatively, if leadership graduated from top schools, had a background running similar companies, and a record of accomplishment, they would look favorably upon the firm. The bottom line is that in order for the cost of capital to be materially affected, the nature of an event would have to reflect on the organization's ability to repay loans. For most organization, and most scenarios, this is extremely unlikely. Nonetheless, it's another example of estimates that have to come from the right people in the organization.

When it comes to reputation damage, a key factor is how the firm deals with the incident. If those responsible for public relations and communication perform well, then the reputation damage is far more likely to be muted. Measures of performance here includes being perceived as being honest, forthcoming, sincere about caring for the stakeholder's concerns, and committed to making things right. If, however, they bungle the response, it could easily result in more lost customers and more significant damage to stock price and the cost of capital. There are a number of examples out there where an incident occurred that by all rights should have crushed the company, but the company's response was so deft that they actually improved their market share. On the other hand, there are also examples of incidents that should not have been a big deal but the organizations mishandled them so badly they went out of business. The moral to this story is that the public relations component of event preparation is critical.

Measurement

> *There is literally nothing we will likely ever need to measure where our only bounds are negative infinity to positive infinity.*
> **Douglas Hubbard, *How To Measure Anything***

In this chapter, we confront head-on the single biggest objection to quantitative risk management. Namely, that it can't be done because measuring these things is too hard, impossible, or just plain unknowable. Fortunately for you, all of those objections are inaccurate. You absolutely can measure risk quantitatively and we'll show you how. Throughout this section, it's important to keep in mind that our goal is to reduce management's uncertainty about risk. Also, something else to keep in mind: risk is always a forward-looking statement about what may or may not come to pass in the future. Because we aren't trying to predict the future, you shouldn't expect precision (for more on these themes, see the chapter on Basic Risk Concepts). Before we begin, we should say that we owe a great deal of our understanding and practice of measurement concepts to Douglas Hubbard and his groundbreaking book *How to Measure Anything*.

MEASUREMENT AS REDUCTION IN UNCERTAINTY

We asked this question earlier, and it's a good place to start this chapter:

> *Pick a risk issue. It doesn't matter what the issue is. It could be an information security issue like "cloud computing," a business issue like entering a new market, or a personal issue like buying a used car. Now, if someone asked you how much loss exposure (risk) is associated with that issue, can you answer them? Let me rephrase that. Can you answer them and stand behind your answer? With a straight face? If you're using FAIR effectively, you can.*

Part of the reason we can make these claims is that we have gained a solid understanding of measurement science. By using the approaches we've learned, we can positively assert that our measurements are not just accurate, but that we are 90% confident in their accuracy. Many people, when asked what it means to take a measurement, conclude that it has something to do with quantifying and giving exact answers to questions. But how true is this really?

Let's take a look at this measurement issue from another direction. Assume you have a hole in the drywall of your home that you need to fix. For some reason, this is a situation that I (Jack Freund) have had to deal with on a number of occasions. Typically when this happens, you need to buy some supplies, including a sort of screen, netting, or tape to cover the hole and slather the drywall compound over. But how much screen to buy? Well, let's pull out our trusty tape measure. We'll measure width and height, as the screening is sold in rectangular pieces. Using the tape measure, you measure about 11¾ inches across and 7½ inches down. But wait! How do you know that the tape measure accurately represents 1 inch, or even that each of the tick marks for inch are equidistant from one another? Another problem we have (when we think too deeply about it) is where does the inch actually end—is it the near side of the tick mark or the far side? Or perhaps it's right in the middle? At times like this, we're often reminded of the old measurement gag: How long is the shoreline of the United States? Answer: it's infinite. How can this be you ask? Well, infinite extends not just to the left of the decimal point, but also to the right. If you were to measure all the nooks and crannies, not just of bays and coves, but of rocks, pebbles, and even grains of sand … and this shoreline actually moves, sometimes slowly and sometimes quickly over time, so even after you have started, it is already changed. It would take several lifetimes to get it right and would undoubtedly require technologically advanced measurement and monitoring devices. As clever as this question is, who really cares about that level of precision? Not many people that's for sure. Most are satisfied with the stock answer of 12,283 miles…but that's the general measure, not the tidal shoreline, but who cares? We can work with about 12,000 miles and that is really the point now, isn't it? That number is useful for your general understanding and, more importantly, has gone a great way toward reducing your uncertainty about the measurement. That brings us to our working definition of what a measurement means:

A measurement is a reduction in uncertainty.

Think about this for a second—prior to reading this passage, most of you probably had no idea about how long the coastline was. Now that we know it's about 12,000 miles, you have a good working knowledge of the problem. There is an enormous difference between "I do not know" and "about 12,000." That's the goal of measuring for risk purposes—reducing uncertainty to a useful level of precision. It's what you do with your tape measure—we assume the units are accurate (good enough), take some rough measures, and then head over to the hardware store to buy a 12×8 inch sheet of screening. Nothing is free, either in terms of money or time, so it doesn't work well to focus on the minutiae of measurement when you could save time and get along with the other errands you have to get done.

So what does drywall hole repair and the US shoreline have in common? When we analyze the underlying measurement activities in each, the result is the same—we tend to be very comfortable with some uncertainty in our measurement. This extends to business as well. For example, a common activity in business is forecasting how much money they think the organization will spend next quarter. These expense forecasts happen all the time and they are usually a round number. These values are typically enough for people to get by with in their day-to-day jobs and lives. These rough numbers work well because what we need is a single data point to lift us out of ignorance. There is a vast difference between knowing nothing about something, and knowing a single data point.

Risk works the same way—knowing nothing about the amount of risk associated with a new product launch or a new security attack is a very different thing than having even a single data point. This is how FAIR helps add clarity to ambiguous risk situations—by giving you the tools to add data points to a situation that is purported to be "unknowable." However, there are additional benefits in looking at measurements from the perspective of reducing uncertainty: it also allows you to quantify how uncertain you are about your measurements, which is what we cover next.

MEASUREMENT AS EXPRESSIONS OF UNCERTAINTY

Like most people, when one of us heads out for the evening without our spouse, they often want to know when we will return. Unfortunately, every single time we give an answer we're wrong. Oh we don't mean to be, it's just that this measurement of our view into the future is inherently flawed. It's flawed because we often choose an estimate that doesn't express our uncertainty: "I dunno," we'll say, "I plan on being done at 9:30." See what we did wrong there? No? Let's look at another example. Assume you run a department where you work and you're asked how much travel expenses your people will incur in the coming 90 days: "should be $5000," you say.

In each example, we gave the wrong answer. Why? We provide a single point estimate of what we thought the time and amount was, respectively. Single point estimates are almost always wrong, at least for any complex question. Think about what it would take for you to mosey over the threshold of your door at precisely 9:30. You would have to factor in the travel to your meeting location, activities, games, conversations, dinner, drinks, storytelling…probably more drinks and storytelling, and then a drive home (observing all applicable drunk driving laws of course). Even if you tried your hardest, you would probably still miss it by a minute or two in either direction. To be fair, your spouse is not likely to expect you to come home precisely at the bottom of the 9 o'clock hour (your estimate is a reduction in uncertainty, after all), but still, an expectation has been set and when 9:50 rolls around, they could be worried.

However, an alternative approach to each of these solutions is to offer your measurement as a range. If you told your spouse that you would be home between 9:00 and 10:30 the odds are much better that the right answer is between that range. Further, giving your superiors a cost estimate of between $4000 and $12,000 also better ensures that the right answer is contained therein. This establishes a couple of important elements to the measurement process. The first is bounds—you are indicating that the least amount of money to be spent is $4000, no less. Likewise, the maximum amount of money will not be more than $12,000. The second factor is the spread. Our upper bound is three times as much as the lower. Let's assume that each trip the team takes costs about $2000. That would mean that we are so unsure about our travel plans that we're estimating between two and six trip in the next 90 days. This spread illustrates the other power of ranges—it allows us to quantify and accurately communicate our uncertainty about our measurement. What if our upper bound was not $12,000 but $25,000 instead—a total of about 12.5 trips? Think about the message this would send to management about what you were dealing with in your department? Yes, ranges give us guiderails for making decisions, but can also tell a story about what's happening.

If you have ever been a part of a project at work where the project manager asks you how long it will take to accomplish your part of the job, how do you answer? This is a regular occurrence for many professions. Software developers tend to have to make estimates about how long it will take to do something that hasn't been done before (although things similar to it may have been done—which aides us in our estimating). What so often happens is that we pad our estimates. We say that a job we are pretty sure will take three days of coding should run us about a week. Why? Well, people respond very interestingly to single point estimates—they assume the estimates are right. Just like our spouse expecting us in the driveway at 9:30, and our boss getting upset when we submit that last receipt that takes us over $5,000, we get comfortable with expectations that have been set and things that exceed them upset us. However, using a range gives the software developer the means to express how much he knows about this task—he can tell us that complex things may take as little as 2 days, as many as 5 days, but will most likely take 3 days. With that additional element of most likely, we now have three data points, which incidentally is miles away from "I have no idea," which is so often people's first response to inquiries like this. More to the point, it is exactly what's needed to build a distribution—for example, a bell curve. This is a critical part of how we apply some additional elements of FAIR, discussed later in this chapter.

Project managers have had a tool in their belt to capture estimates this way for some time—it's called the program evaluation and review technique (PERT). PERT was developed in 1950s by the US Navy in an effort to control project cost and schedule overruns. It is an estimating technique that effectively builds a bell curve or normal distribution for a range of answers. It has a prescribed method of implementation that looks like this:

$$\text{Expected Value} = \left(\frac{\text{Min} + (4 \times \text{Most Likely}) + \text{Max}}{6} \right)$$

Expected value is the value you would use as your estimate. Multiplying most likely by four bumps up the middle of the curve so it looks like the line in Figure 5.1:

FIGURE 5.1

A normal curve.

However, you can modify the equation by moving the multiplier to some of the other factors like minimum and maximum to make curves that look like these (see equation and Figure 5.2):

$$\text{Expected Value} = \left(\frac{(4 \times \text{Min}) + \text{Most Likely} + \text{Max}}{6} \right)$$

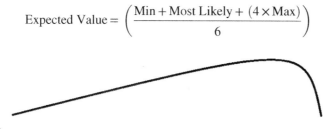

FIGURE 5.2

A left learning curve.

In this case, the distribution indicates that we are more confident in the minimum value than the others; or this distribution (see equation and Figure 5.3), where we feel more confident in the maximum value:

$$\text{Expected Value} = \left(\frac{\text{Min} + \text{Most Likely} + (4 \times \text{Max})}{6} \right)$$

FIGURE 5.3

A right learning curve.

Each of these equations is valuable in communicating a story to the decision-makers about what we believe about our estimates. What we're doing can be called quantifying uncertainty. You are expressing numerically how much you do or do not know about a particular estimate. It's a measurement of not only what you do know, but also what you do not know about a particular value. For instance, if the software developer were asked to estimate how long it would take to rewrite every Java application in their organization (to remediate issues with earlier Java versions); there is likely to be a lot of uncertainty around that estimate. She may say that it will take between 12 months and 48 months. There's a lot of variance between 1 and 4 years her boss may say. However, this gives her the ability to express that there is a lot she doesn't yet know about the applications themselves and, as a result, there are many unknowns in achieving this business goal. Note that we're already past the "I have no idea" stage of this estimate and now are talking about how much. This alone would be a substantial improvement over most conversations we have in information security. However, we can get even better with a little additional effort. Let's take this hypothetical conversation and explore the specific areas where there is uncertainty.

Perhaps the biggest cause for concern is that there isn't any clear count of the number of Java applications, which is a lynchpin in this estimate. One quick measurement task could be to get a better count of how many applications in the organization are built in Java. The next issue in this discussion could be how much effort it would take for each application (assuming our estimate is based on the number of hours multiplied by the number of applications). Perhaps we could break this problem down further by subdividing all the Java applications into subtypes representing relative complexity. Those with fewer than 5000 lines of code might take 2 weeks to review, while those with more than 5000, but less than 20,000 might take a month to look over. Last, those with more than 20,000 lines of code could take as much as 2 months to review. We could make our mini-model here even more complex by estimating costs by labor types (developer, senior developer, outsourced developer) and setting some standard rates (some companies call these loaded cost rates) for each type. This is a real basic example of a measurement technique called decomposition, which means that to measure a big thing we need to break it down into its constituent components and measure those things. Very simple models in Excel can be developed to accomplish this that should take no more than a few hours of work. When compared to the investment at stake, this small amount of time and effort is very well worth the cost. Incidentally, the solution described here was a real-world scenario in which one of us was involved.

BUT WE DON'T HAVE ENOUGH DATA...AND NEITHER DOES ANYONE ELSE

You have seen in these few examples that not only can quantitative measurements be accomplished, but that they can be done with relatively little effort. One quote from Douglas Hubbard that rings true here is that the models being built are never anywhere as complex as the thing being modeled. This is an important point to remember when responding to the primary objection against quantitative measurements—that there isn't enough data.

When reviewing this topic in FAIR training classes, the discussion usually turns toward insurance at some point. As in, "Security isn't insurance; we don't have tons of data." This is true, but it just so happens that both authors have worked in the insurance and financial services industry for some time and have some insight into that. For common types of insurance (auto, home, and life), this assumption is correct—there are a lot of data available from which to make good underwriting decisions. However, there are a lot of insurance types for which history is not available.

One type of specialized insurance is called event cancellation insurance. For example, one of the requirements of the Olympic Games is that the host city carry insurance coverage in the unlikely event that the games are canceled. It has been a while since this has happened, but it isn't without precedent—as of this writing, the games have been canceled five times, each having something to do with the first and second World Wars:

1. 1916 Summer Olympics—to be held in Berlin, Germany. Canceled due to the outbreak of World War I.

2. 1940 Summer Olympics—to be held in Tokyo, Japan. Canceled due to the outbreak of World War II.
3. 1940 Winter Olympics—to be held in Sapporo, Japan. Canceled due to the outbreak of World War II.
4. 1944 Summer Olympics—to be held in London, United Kingdom. Canceled due to the outbreak of World War II.
5. 1944 Winter Olympics—to be held in Cortina d'Ampezzo, Italy. Canceled due to...you guessed it: World War II.

So here it is in 2014—70 years since the last cancellation event. Cell phones weren't invented and certainly not the Internet. Air travel was far less common than it is today. In short, how much about these very distant events could help us make an intelligent choice about insuring an event in South America—like the 2016 Summer games in Rio de Janeiro?

A phrase used by Douglas Hubbard and shared by the authors is that you need less data than you think, and you have more than you think.[1] Even a single data point takes us miles away from "I have no idea." In our Olympic example, there is a very obvious thread that runs through them—war. As we learned in the terminology chapter, decomposition is a valuable tool in breaking down complex problems into measurable units. Because risk is comprised of two primary factors—frequency and magnitude, we can begin by building a frequency table of all instances of war: conventional, unconventional, and civil. Then we can look at the upcoming locations of Olympic events—assuming that past events have some relevance to future outbreaks—and determine how often we think war would occur. To be sure, there are plenty of other potential causes for canceled games—we'd just have to account for those as well. Things like stability of currency, political turmoil (precursors to civil war), and natural disasters to name a few. Many other factors, such as facilities, lodging, and transportation, are also factors that the International Olympic Committee takes into consideration when evaluating cities to host the games. Next, we have to consider the costs associated with canceling the games—lost revenue, sponsorships, etc. Many insurance policies have a "named value" approach where you identify how much money you want them to insure. It doesn't have to be associated with a fixed asset.

What this boils down to from an information security perspective is that we can decompose relevant loss scenarios in a similar manner to help us clarify the ways in which loss can materialize. Following that, we can use what are referred to as calibrated estimates to effectively leverage whatever data do exist to make good estimates. Using those estimates within a FAIR analysis is then very straightforward. It is really no more difficult than that. This process enables us to significantly reduce uncertainty regarding the decisions we face and gives us a foundation to apply even better data as it becomes available. Let's look at an example.

Let's assume we are considering a policy for cyber insurance. Perhaps you were recently involved in a bidding process and the terms and conditions for insurance coverage included the need for a cyber insurance policy. How much should you buy? Well, the obvious question you need to answer is how much money could you end

---

[1] Hubbard, D. (2010). *How to Measure Anything*. John Wiley and Sons, Inc. Hoboken, NJ.

up losing through cyber events? This sounds like loss magnitude, which is something FAIR is designed to handle. To be specific, we would need to determine the single loss event (SLE) losses versus the annualized loss event (ALE) losses. This is because the policy will be written to cover the losses you would experience on a per-event basis; whereas the ALE numbers will spread per-event losses across a number of years (we are assuming you are not experiencing large losses from cyber incidents every year or more). Using FAIR, we know that we will need to identify the assets at risk—perhaps sensitive data, money in accounts, or business process availability. Once this has been done, we need to list out the systems on which these data reside as well as the business processes supported by those systems (if the organization has a business impact assessment this can be a helpful aid in this process). Next, identify the potential attackers/perpetrators that can act against these various systems and processes. Perhaps it's the threat communities we identified earlier: cyber criminals and privileged insiders might be a good starting point here. List the intent of these groups and break them down further if need be. For instance, the cyber criminals would be malicious, as could our privileged insiders; yet privileged insiders could also just make costly mistakes, so list error scenarios for them as well. Last, indicate the effect of their success—confidentiality, integrity, or availability. What we are effectively doing is building permutations of attacker/perpetrator combinations that could apply to this question of insurance (Table 5.1).

Tables like this can be used to articulate the most relevant scenarios that apply to a situation. A relatively thorough risk scenario identification process like this helps to

Table 5.1 Sample risk scenarios for a cyber insurance policy

Target	Threat Community	Threat Type	Effect
Customer portal	Cyber criminals	Malicious	Confidentiality
Customer portal	Privileged insiders	Malicious	Confidentiality
Customer portal	Privileged insiders	Error	Confidentiality
Customer portal	Privileged insiders	Malicious	Availability
Customer portal	Privileged insiders	Error	Availability
Databases	Cyber criminals	Malicious	Confidentiality
Databases	Privileged insiders	Malicious	Confidentiality
Databases	Privileged insiders	Error	Confidentiality
Databases	Privileged insiders	Malicious	Availability
Databases	Privileged insiders	Error	Availability
Bank reconciliation process	Privileged insiders	Malicious	Possession of $
Bank reconciliation process	Privileged insiders	Error	Possession of $
Bank reconciliation process	Customers	Fraud	Possession of $

articulate some of the nuances between attacks—a malicious insider attack is rarer than insiders making mistakes (we hope). It also helps us better identify loss when we get to that part of the FAIR assessment—building out losses for theft of money means we need to account for replacement costs, whereas data theft looks very different. These tables are a valuable starting point for evaluating cyber security needs. After compiling a list like this, the next step is to begin estimating the FAIR values for each scenario—threat capabilities (TCap), difficulty/control strength, etc. It may seem like a daunting task, but many of the values can be reused as the analysis continues. After some computation in FAIR, you can compare these values in the original Table 5.1 like this in Table 5.2:

Table 5.2 Example frequency and magnitude of losses for a cyber insurance policy

Target	Threat Community	Threat Type	Effect	Max LEF	Max LM-SLE
Customer portal	Cyber criminals	Malicious	Confidentiality	0.01	14,329
Customer portal	Privileged insiders	Malicious	Confidentiality	0.06	100,833
Customer portal	Privileged insiders	Error	Confidentiality	0.03	70,809
Customer portal	Privileged insiders	Malicious	Availability	0.17	148,613
Customer portal	Privileged insiders	Error	Availability	0.03	84,581
Databases	Cyber criminals	Malicious	Confidentiality	0.10	214,240
Databases	Privileged insiders	Malicious	Confidentiality	0.04	474,722
Databases	Privileged insiders	Error	Confidentiality	0.04	199,197
Databases	Privileged insiders	Malicious	Availability	0.18	33,986
Databases	Privileged insiders	Error	Availability	0.13	26,356
Bank reconciliation process	Privileged insiders	Malicious	Possession of $	4.05	2257
Bank reconciliation process	Privileged insiders	Error	Possession of $	0.22	1650
Bank reconciliation process	Customers	Fraud	Possession of $	0.22	935

LEF, loss event frequency; LM, loss magnitude; Max, maximum; SLE, single loss event.

Table 5.1 now has two additional columns in Table 5.2—loss event frequency (LEF) and loss magnitude-SLE (LM-SLE). Note that for easy comparison, the values in the LM-SLE column have been converted to SLE values—we will discuss this more later. Our values represent the maximum output from the Monte Carlo simulators. This is because we are interested in insuring against worst-case losses (a usual thing that insurance is for). With a table like this in hand, calculating how much insurance is necessary becomes much easier. Consider that each row could result in an insurance claim of some varying amount. A quick scan shows that your most catastrophic scenario involves your privileged employees misusing their access to steal customer data. Your worst-case losses here look like almost a half million dollars about once in 25 years ($474,722 and 0.04, respectively). Now your company may say that they are willing to self-insure the first $100,000 of that amount (this is called your deductible). A policy that insures up to $1 million dollars after a $100,000 deductible would more than cover your worst-case scenario, while providing some buffer for losses that exceed your estimates. It also has the added benefit of capping your losses at $100,000 for most scenarios—which is in line with your management's risk tolerance.

When dealing with objections to quantitative measurement, it's often important to remember that, regardless of how decision-makers are informed on an issue, a decision is being made. Whether we decide to spend the time measuring and managing risk using quantitative methods or if we accept the limitations associated with qualitative methods, someone is going to be making a decision. If you work in a job that is purported to offer executives decision-making assistance via risk analysis, you had better think long and hard about which approach you want to take.

CALIBRATION

In this section we'll introduce you to an estimation method called calibration that Douglas Hubbard[1] writes about in his books. Calibration is simply a method for gauging and improving a person's ability to estimate effectively. This is a big deal because FAIR and other methods for analyzing risk are often highly dependent upon expert estimates. Unfortunately, most people tend to not be very good at estimating. In fact, when we provide calibration training, the average level of accuracy by people taking the class is about 20% at the beginning of class. In other words, their estimates are right only about 20% of the time. Good news however—studies have shown that people can be taught to be better at it. Much better at it, in fact. In his book, Hubbard outlines an approach that helps you avoid inherent biases in your estimating and enables you to make estimates that are 90% accurate. By the end of our training class, averages have climbed into the 80–90% range. This transformation occurs within the span of a couple of hours, which seems like a pretty good investment in time. Like anything else, the more you practice making estimates the better you get at it. We find ourselves using it several times a day for everything from estimating how long it will take us to complete some task, to how

FIGURE 5.4

FAIR analysis steps.

far it is to the next ridge on our hike. After a while it becomes very unusual for our estimates to be inaccurate even when we're operating from weak data.

The central tenets of measurements in FAIR are based on the notion of estimating using PERT-styled distributions. It is very important however, that the individuals who make those estimates should be the most qualified person available on the subject being estimated. Furthermore, giving those estimates, they should either be trained in, or guided by people who are trained in the estimation techniques outlined below. These estimates are expressed as PERT distributions, which become the input to a Monte Carlo function, perhaps in Excel or a commercial analytic tool. The relationship between these elements is outlined in Figure 5.4.

Look around the room for another person. Anyone will do. How tall are they? Size them up. How tall do you think they are? If you gave a single point answer ("about 5'10," you may have said), then go back and read the section on estimating using ranges. From here on out, always answer questions like this using ranges. Practice all the time: the cost of your grocery store cart as you are waiting to check out, the time you tell your spouse you will be back from that client dinner tonight, when your flight will arrive, how much the monthly rent is on that strip mall business, etc. Once you learn this estimating method, it's hard to give it up—it's just so effective at measuring how much you do or don't know about something. Further, it goes to demonstrate that the whole world is full of natural variability–recognition of which will help you to become more comfortable with uncertainty in general.

If you made your estimate using ranges, you get a gold star! But how did you come up with those ranges? Remember that old adage in computer science—garbage in garbage out? We have to make sure that the values we use for estimation are solid and as accurate as possible.

In the next section we'll describe a technique that helps you to be calibrated in your answers. In addition, it turns out there are a couple of common mistakes people make when coming up with ranges that can make them less likely to be accurate. We'll explore this too and learn how to avoid making these mistakes.

EQUIVALENT BET TEST

The equivalent bet test was popularized by Douglas Hubbard as a technique to improve our range estimations by having us lay wagers on our answers. This works in part because we all tend to estimate better when money is on the line. However, in one of those little human quirks, studies have shown that no real money is required for the process to have its desired effect on improving estimates. The other intended purpose of the bet is to have you mentally weigh the difference between your confidence in your range with that of a known level of confidence.

The "test" works like this. You have the chance to win $1000 in one of two ways: you can bet on whether your range contains the correct answer for a question, or you can spin this board-game styled wheel (see Figure 5.5) where you win nine out of 10 times (if the pointer lands in the larger white area, which covers 90% of the wheel's surface, you win). In this process one of three things happen:

1. The estimator will bet on their range. This means they are more than 90% confident in their range (or else they would pick the wheel). This being the case, they can and perhaps should narrow their ranges until their confidence is lowered. Why reduce their range when they are more than 90% confident in their range? It's because otherwise it is too easy to use ranges that, while accurate, lack a useful degree of precision. There is always a trade-off between accuracy and precision and this is one way to help find that balance.
2. The estimator will pick the wheel. This means that they are less than 90% confident in their range. They should expand their ranges to increase their confidence in the range.
3. They can't decide which option gives them the best odds. It is at this point that they have 90% confidence in their estimate. Effectively, you have weighed a known 90% probability against your estimate and found them to be equivalent. When making estimates, you typically want to seek this point of indecision so that you will know your ranges truly reflect your 90% confidence interval.

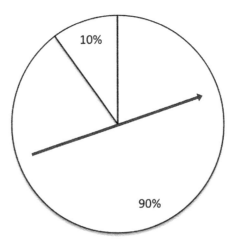

FIGURE 5.5

An equivalent bet test wheel.

ANCHORING

Many people when asked to come up with a range will try to come up with what they believe the "right" answer is. Then they figure they'll just build out from that on either side to offer some buffer in case they were over or under a little bit. This is called anchoring and it leads to ranges that are far more narrow than they need be. It is also a leading cause for inaccurate estimates. For example, say you were estimating the time it would take to mow your lawn. Having done it before, you have some data to pull from, so you think the right answer is 40 min. Well, just to be sure, you add and subtract 10 min to either side of that and the range is somewhere between 30 and 50 min. For simple things that don't matter that much, this is fine. It's not a good idea though when making estimates on more complex or difficult values, and when there is a lot riding on accuracy. Too often, when we give ourselves this starting point, we aren't giving sufficient consideration to variables that might affect the outcome. There is a much more effective way to start developing an estimate, which we will cover next.

I HAVE NO IDEA

It's rare, but occasionally when facilitating estimates, you will find someone who claims they have absolutely no idea how much something could be. Usually, they are just refusing to provide inputs out of some misguided, yet principled objection that some things are just immeasurable. However, for those who need a little push to get going, start with the absurd. Pick minimum and maximum values so extreme that the person making the estimate will have no choice but to agree that the range must include the right value. For instance, if you asked someone to estimate how many cups of coffee your team had to drink that morning they might claim to have no idea and, thus, no measure would be possible. You could counter with "Could it be 100?" Perhaps they stand their ground, so go even higher—"Could it be 1000?" Eventually you will reach a breaking point—"Okay Jack, you got me. No way it's a 1000." This is referred to as "starting with the absurd" and it is an incredibly valuable tool for a couple of reasons. First, it helps break the ice. It gives people a starting point that they have complete confidence in. Second, it helps to overcome some cognitive biases, particularly anchoring. Keep in mind that once you know what something is not (e.g., not greater than 1000 cups of coffee), you have a starting point for what it could be (even one data point helps). Then, incrementally add (to a minimum estimate) or subtract (from a maximum estimate) until you or the estimator reaches that point of indecision between their estimates and spinning the wheel.

The genius of the absurdity test is that it allows the estimator to provide a data point by reversing the question being answered while still providing a positive response. In other words, you don't have to reverse your thinking in order to answer the question, yet you are providing information about what it can't be—no way it is over 1000. Because when you think you have no idea what something is, even a single data point can help to exclude many possible values and move you closer to what the probable answer really is.

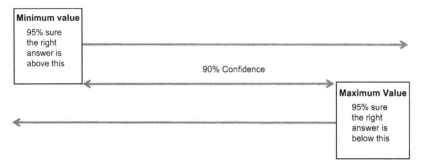

FIGURE 5.6

90% and 95% confidence.

Another approach is to focus on one end of the range at a time. Ask "What is the least it could be?" or alternatively you could ask "Could it be lower than this?" A critical check is to see whether you believe you are 95% confident that the right value is above this minimum value. Once we've checked the minimum value, we can evaluate the maximum value with the same questions: "What is the most that it could be?" "Could it ever be more than this?" "Am I 95% sure that the right answer is less than this?" It's important to keep in mind that each time you consider adjusting the minimum or maximum value of your range, so consider the data or rationale that change is based on. This is so that if someone challenges your estimate you're in a position to defend it well.

This approach will help you make sure that you are 90% confident in your estimate (see Figure 5.6).

ESTIMATING GROUPS OF THINGS

When sizing up your risk scenarios, you may have to group things that are similar, yet dissimilar enough to cause you concern when estimating. This tends to happen a lot in information technology scenarios where there are things like servers involved. Say that we need to estimate a range regarding the percentage of servers that are up-to-date on their patches. Also, assume that we have both Windows and Linux servers. In this scenario, the trouble arises from the different nature of patches when it comes to Windows versus Linux—Microsoft has made it relatively straightforward to patch nowadays, and for some companies it is the Linux servers that struggle with patching (it could be the other way at your firm; this is just an example). So we need to come up with a minimum and maximum percentage of servers that are up-to-date on patches. When you're considering the lower bound number, base that estimate off what you know about the Linux servers and their poor patching, but base the high numbers off the Windows servers. There are, however, a couple of disadvantages to this approach. The first is that if the datasets are too dissimilar your range can become unacceptably wide. The second is that the Most Likely value (the peak of the distribution) might be difficult to decide on. Very often it's easier and even faster to do two separate analyses on distinct sets of objects rather than a single conflated analysis. You also tend to get better precision and more actionable results.

CONFIDENCE DOES NOT EQUAL ACCURACY

There is one very important point we need to make before we end this chapter. Going through a calibrated process to arrive at 90% confidence in your estimate does *not* guarantee that your estimate is accurate. The calibration training, practice, and process simply improve the odds considerably that your estimates will be accurate. Remember that this is about reducing uncertainty. For more information on calibration we strongly encourage you to read Douglas Hubbard's book "How to Measure Anything".

Analysis Process

So far, this book has had to present a somewhat theoretical or abstract approach on risk analysis concepts and measurement. Unfortunately, for the current practitioners of risk analysis (outside of certain professions like actuarial sciences), there hasn't been an abundance of risk courses that train people to think about risk systematically, or even that deeply. We don't intend for this book to replace a full education on statistical methods and probability theory; there are plenty of resources out there that address that better than we can. Instead, we intend for this book to describe a pragmatic sweet spot somewhere between the highly sophisticated end of the analytic continuum and the quick and dirty end, where most of what takes place resides. This chapter takes the next step in describing what we believe is that sweet spot, and begins to more clearly answer the question, "How do I put this into action today so I can help my organization tomorrow?" As a result of this direction, in the upcoming sections, you will learn the step-by-step process for conducting a Factor Analysis of Information Risk (FAIR) risk analysis and see it in action with a couple of examples.

THE TOOLS NECESSARY TO APPLY THE FAIR RISK MODEL

Before we go any further, we need to point out that even though FAIR provides a great framework for doing quantitative risk analysis, we use FAIR every day in nonquantitative ways. In fact, probably more than 95% of our use of FAIR doesn't involve Program Evaluation and Review Technique (PERT) distributions, Monte Carlo functions, graphs, charts, or tables. FAIR is nomenclature, it is a set of models and a framework for thinking through complex scenarios clearly and confidently, and it is a way to explain how you came to your conclusions. None of that requires numbers or tools, but when you want or need to use numbers, it does that too.

Putting FAIR into action quantitatively requires some tools. There are a couple of ways you can come by these tools. The easiest way is to purchase them through a vendor, such as CXOWARE, which makes the official version of the FAIR software. That said, CXOWARE isn't the only company to offer FAIR-based software; more companies have begun to sell licensed products and services. However, the basic FAIR ontology that was covered in Chapter 3 is a series of open source

Measuring and Managing Information Risk.

standards published by the Open Group[1] that can be used to develop your own solution for personal or internal corporate use:

- C081—Risk Taxonomy
- G081—Requirements for Risk Assessment Methods
- C103—FAIR–ISO/IEC 27,005 Cookbook

If you're going to develop your own tool, it's important to ensure that you use a statistical package that can perform Monte Carlo analysis. As an example, for those using Microsoft Excel, it will be necessary to use an add-in that provides this functionality. One nice option is a free Excel add-in called OpenPERT, which was created by two of the sharpest risk professionals we know: Chris Hayes and Jay Jacobs.

However, for the remainder of this chapter, the figures, images, and illustrations will be taken from commercially available FAIR software. A matrix-based approach is described in a later chapter as well as in the Open Group standard if you'd like to use a more qualitative approach to FAIR.

HOW TO APPLY THE FAIR RISK MODEL

One of the biggest differences between FAIR and other risk analysis methods is that in FAIR, you will sometimes assess the same scenario multiple times. It's a bit like a Rubik's Cube—one "thing" but with multiple views, and each turn reveals additional insight into the nature of the truth. What this means in practice is that in FAIR, we consider a more comprehensive scope of risk factors and their permutations to bring the most relevant scenarios to the surface. Don't worry, however; it's not as painful as it sounds (at least not once you've done a few analyses). Like any method or process though, there is a learning curve in FAIR. It's not so much about the FAIR concepts or terminology themselves but rather the application of those to perform analyses. We like to say that risk itself is simple; it's the complex world that makes risk analysis so challenging. That's what we hope this and the next couple of chapters can help you better understand.

To get started, you need a problem to solve—a risk scenario to analyze. There is certainly no shortage from which to choose. Many times, it's related to a control failure or gap of some kind that was identified in an audit. Perhaps it's someone asking for a policy exception or proposing that the organization implement a new technology. Other times, it is simply someone wondering if there is a way to decrease the burden of security on the organization. For example, one question might be, "How risky is it if we don't have a screen saver password?" These are starting points, but you need additional information before you can answer the questions.

Have you ever been caught in a meeting, hallway, restroom(!), instant message chat, or e-mail with somebody asking you if it's okay to send data via e-mail

---

[1] http://www.opengroup.org/subjectareas/security/risk

and you felt that tickle in your brain that made you think this was a trap? That's your subconscious telling you a couple of things: (1) that context matters and you need more information before you answer the question, and (2) you may not be the appropriate person to answer the question. You might be able to answer a different question, "How much risk is associated with sending data via e-mail?" or "Is it against policy to send these data via e-mail?" but blessing someone's request to send data via e-mail may not fall within your scope of authority. This question of authority is dealt with in a later chapter, so for now, let us focus on the first part.

PROCESS FLOW

The overall analysis process is illustrated in Figure 6.1. For several reasons we'll explore later, the actual scenario that has come to your attention is often not framed appropriately to be properly risk assessed. This being the case, the first step is to frame the question appropriately.

FIGURE 6.1

Fair analysis process flow.

SCENARIO BUILDING

We have to begin with scoping the scenarios because that is foundational in structuring our thoughts for proper analysis. Of all the things that you care about for the scenario under consideration, take the time to pull them apart and compartmentalize them using the following factors:

- Asset at risk
- Threat community
- Threat type
- Effect

We will discuss each of these in order, but it is important to recognize right now that the more clarity you have regarding the scope of your scenario, the easier the analysis is going to be. In carpentry, you hear the phrase, "Measure twice, cut once," with the idea being that if you spend the time being careful about what you are about to do, you greatly reduce the odds of screwing things up and wasting material and time. The same principle is true here. Spend the time to get clarity about the scenario up front. If you don't, the analysis is likely to be much more difficult and take longer, and nobody wants that.

ASSET

In many scenarios, more than one asset is involved. Worried about lost or stolen laptops? Is it the laptop you are primarily concerned about or the information on it? Both are assets and both are stolen, but one is the primary focus (usually the information). Passwords written on sticky notes? Yes, passwords can be considered an asset, but are you concerned about the passwords themselves, the applications they provide access to, or the information the applications provide access to? For many scenarios, the focus is on the information, but perhaps the password provides access to a manufacturing application that, if taken down, disables an entire factory production line. A couple of useful terms we sometimes use to help differentiate asset relevance and role in an analysis are "point of attack" and "container." The laptop is a point of attack (i.e., it is the first point of contact and action on the part of a threat agent). Likewise, the password on a sticky note is a point of attack. In that scenario, if it's the information we're worried about, then the application the password provides access to would be the next point of attack in the path. The term "point of attack" is obviously geared toward malicious scenarios. For nonmalicious examples or if you just don't like that term, the word "container" works just as well. An example of a container would be a safe containing cash. The asset of interest is the cash. The safe, although also an asset, is the container in any scenario where the cash is the analytic focus. The bottom line here is asset clarity. You can't even begin an analysis unless you are crystal clear on the asset(s) at risk. Think back to the earlier question, "How risky is it if we don't have a screen saver password?" Given what we just discussed, what would you need to understand before you can even begin to answer the question?

THREAT COMMUNITIES

Who or what is the threat? Is it human, animal, Mother Nature, or mechanical? You wouldn't think this would be too hard to figure out, but there can be more to it than you think. Revisiting our previous screensaver question, who or what might be the threat? The truth is it could be several threat communities: non-privileged employees (i.e., colleagues who don't legitimately have access to the same stuff as the person with an unlocked), visitors and other nonemployees with physical access to the system, or even privileged insiders (i.e., colleagues who do have access to the same stuff but who might prefer to do dastardly things from someone else's account). Why would we need to break the threat landscape into all those different subcommunities? Maybe you don't need to, but if you don't at least consider the potential need to differentiate you run a much greater chance of getting part way through your analysis only to discover you should have differentiated. Think about it, though: would threat event frequency be the same across these different threat communities, and if not, why not? For example, are visitors few and far between or always escorted? Would we expect privileged colleagues to be highly likely to abuse unlocked keyboards for malicious purposes? Similar treatment is due the question of threat capability: is that variable likely to be the same or close enough to the same across these threat communities such that it wouldn't drive a need to differentiate between them?

We also have to consider which threats have a reasonable expectation of reaching the target. For instance, if we are looking to model an application that is used exclusively by internal employees, then it makes sense to use internal Threat Communities (TComs) as the primary attackers. We may include external groups like cyber criminals if we are able to draw a line from them to the target, perhaps through some other point of attack. The fact that those external groups have to make it through additional points of attack means that we almost certainly have to analyze them as a separate scenario.

Although each TCom will increase the number of risk analyses you have to perform, the marginal cost in terms of time to run each scenario is actually pretty small. Much of the data, particularly loss data, are reusable from TCom to TCom. The other good news is that the more analyses you do, the more it becomes second nature to evaluate and scope the threat landscape. We should add that, even though we're stressing the importance of having scenario clarity up front, there is absolutely nothing wrong with getting part way through an analysis only to discover a need to refine the scope and make adjustments. It even happens to us. The less you have to do that, though, the smoother the process. Smoothness is good.

THREAT TYPE

We also have to be clear on the nature of the threat action. Is it malicious, human error, mechanical, process failure, or natural (e.g., weather, geological activity, or animal behavior)? There can often be a significant difference in the frequency of these types of events. Human error, for example, tends to be a much more common cause of loss than malicious acts in many organizations. Furthermore, the impact resulting from one type of event can be much different from another type, and the control options available to you might be different as well. Ultimately, it's the question of whether substantial differences exist in variables, such as frequency, capability, impact, and controls, that drive the importance of knowing whether you are faced with one analysis, or more than one analysis.

Given this consideration, what type or types of threat events might be most relevant to our unlocked screensaver scenario? Which brings up an important point we need to make about relevancy. We have encountered folks who aren't comfortable with an analysis unless every possible thing they can think of is included. For example, we have seen an analysis that included the Israeli Mossad as a TCom against a US financial institution, with the threat event description being attempted financial fraud via mobile banking. Although we won't deny this as a possibility, you have to draw a line somewhere in terms of relevancy. Take care of the obvious stuff first. If, after you have analyzed the more relevant scenarios, you have the time and want to measure the risk associated with a polar bear attack on the streets of Cincinnati, OH, in the summertime, go for it.

EFFECT

Last, we need to identify the nature of the loss event (i.e., its effect on the asset). For information security scenarios, the confidentiality, integrity, and availability (CIA) triad is a useful framework for this.

Sometimes, the classification gets a bit tricky: which category would apply to stolen funds, for instance? At first glance, people often cite confidentiality, but the money is unavailable for use; thus, availability is a better fit. Many scenarios involve more than one effect, such as the stolen laptop. You have an availability effect because the laptop and perhaps some of its contents are no longer available to you, but the overriding concern might be confidentiality. Likewise, loss of customer information confidentiality can ultimately result in the unavailability of funds. However, remember to focus on the most relevant effect (i.e., the one that is likely to trigger the most significant losses for the organization). If the threat agent's intent is to steal data, then confidentiality works well. If they want to steal money, go for availability. Last, if they want to cause harm by modifying data or systems, then integrity is the way to go. If you find that you need more granularity in effects, then you can consider Donn Parker's Parkerian Hexad, which expands on the CIA Triad to include three additional categories: possession or control, authenticity, and utility.

For nonsecurity scenarios, the CIA categories have still proved to be a good starting point. For example, we've used availability as the category for wrongful death lawsuits against a hospital. Integrity can be used for personal injuries or damages to a structure. Confidentiality can be applied outside of security scenarios but is still related to protecting information from unintended disclosure. The point is simply that you need to understand the effect—whatever it is—because that will affect your estimates.

THE ANALYSIS SCOPE

Sometimes, the scope of an analysis is simple and straightforward. For example, you might be faced with a question like, "How much risk is associated with a particular vulnerability (e.g., XSS) in a particular customer-facing web application?" In that case, it might be as simple as naming the asset as customer data, the threat as cyber criminals, the threat type as malicious, and the event type as confidentiality. Simple is good when you can get it. At that point, you can pretty much carry on with data gathering and analysis.

Other times, life isn't so kind and questions aren't so narrowly focused. Take, for example, a situation where the business is proposing to reduce authentication strength for an external website X. The challenge in these cases is to gain an understanding of the various loss scenarios where authentication strength for that website is relevant. It might be one or it might be a dozen. When it is more than a handful, you might find it helpful to document the possible scenarios in a Table 6.1 like the one below.

Table 6.1 Risk Scenarios Associated with Reducing Authentication Strength for External Website X

Asset	Threat Community	Threat Type	Effect
Customer information	Cyber criminals	Malicious	Confidentiality
Customer information	Privileged insiders	Error	Confidentiality
Customer information	Privileged insiders	Malicious	Confidentiality
Customer information	Privileged insiders	Error	Availability
Customer information	Privileged insiders	Malicious	Availability
Customer funds	Privileged insiders	Error	Possession of $
Customer funds	Privileged insiders	Malicious	Possession of $
Customer funds	Customers	Malicious	Possession of $

Each of the rows in Table 6.1 represents a distinct scenario to be analyzed, but don't be concerned by the size of the table. As we previously mentioned and as you will see, much of the data are reusable from analysis to analysis, and the incremental increase in work is not nearly as bad as it seems. You might also be able to reduce the number of analyses by combining scenarios or eliminating scenarios. The analysis scope table, especially early in the analysis process, is simply a way to document potential scenarios to include in the analysis.

The other thing to keep in mind is that clearly scoping an analysis is often the hardest part of the process. If you scope an analysis well, the process of data gathering, estimating, and running the numbers is usually pretty straightforward.

Before we move on, we want to provide another example scoping table. This time, we'll go back to the question mentioned earlier about the possibility of not requiring personnel to use locking screensavers. For that question, we might end up with a scope that looks like the one below Table 6.2.

As you can see, some questions can involve a lot of analyses (particularly questions with broad implications like, "Can we disable screensaver passwords?"). Given the nature of the question and its broad ramifications, the table could perhaps include even more scenarios. For example, in Table 6.2, we didn't differentiate between non-privileged insiders of various types (employees versus contractors versus visitors). If we thought there were relevant differences in frequency, capability, intent, or controls between those subcommunities, we might have carved them out as additional analyses.

We also often have an opportunity to reduce scope by modifying the question just a bit. For example, if the screensaver password question was focused on a particular subset of the user population rather than the entire organization (e.g., screensavers

Table 6.2 Risk Scenarios Associated with Unsecured Desktop and Laptop Screensavers in the Workplace

Asset	Threat Community	Threat Type	Effect
Sensitive customer information	Non-privileged insiders	Malicious	Confidentiality
Sensitive corporate information	Non-privileged insiders	Malicious	Confidentiality
Sensitive customer information	Privileged insiders	Malicious	Confidentiality
Sensitive corporate information	Privileged insiders	Malicious	Confidentiality
Customer information	Non-privileged insiders	Malicious	Integrity
Corporate information	Non-privileged insiders	Malicious	Integrity
Customer information	Privileged insiders	Malicious	Integrity
Corporate information	Privileged insiders	Malicious	Integrity
Customer information	Non-privileged insiders	Malicious	Availability
Corporate information	Non-privileged insiders	Malicious	Availability
Customer information	Privileged insiders	Malicious	Availability
Corporate information	Privileged insiders	Malicious	Availability

for just human resources personnel), we could narrow the scope considerably. In addition, if you look at the purpose statement in the table, you will see that it specifies "the workplace." This reduces the number of analyses by clarifying that the scope doesn't include systems used outside of the controlled workplace. Without that clarification up front, it's likely a question would come up at some point in the analysis regarding whether screensavers would have to be secured outside the workplace. If that had happened, you would need to refine your scope statement and then evaluate whether that refinement would affect any of the estimates (e.g., threat event frequency) you had already made in your analysis. This is a good example of why scope clarity is important.

A last point to make before we move on is that sometimes when you are presented with a question, the simple act of scoping provides sufficient understanding of the problem that it isn't necessary to complete the analysis. We might be able to present the scoping table above to whoever asked the question about screensavers and have that person realize that the risk associated with the question is almost certainly not going to be acceptable. As much as we enjoy doing risk analysis, we do not enjoy doing it when it isn't necessary.

FAIR FACTORS

After having established the scope of an analysis, the next step is to begin gathering data and making estimates for each scenario. Before charging off after data, it is helpful to recognize how the different elements in the scope definition can affect the values you'll be looking for. This can both help you understand where to get the values and how to litmus test the data you get. For example:

- The particular asset under analysis, and where it resides in the landscape, will often help us understand the controls that will likely be part of the analysis, from either a risk mitigation perspective or a data resource perspective. Customer information on a website might suggest that a web application firewall (if deployed) might be an important part of understanding the application's vulnerability. It might also be a great source of threat event frequency data for our analysis. The asset will also dictate from whom the privileged insider threat community is comprised. For example, if the asset is customer funds being processed by the Automated Clearing House (ACH) system, your privileged insiders are that group of people who have legitimate access to the ACH system and the funds it processes.
- The Threat Community in scope for an analysis will naturally dictate threat event frequency and threat capability values. It will also often guide us in understanding which controls are more or less relevant. For example, privileged insiders intentionally have access to the asset under analysis. Therefore, authentication and access privilege controls are irrelevant. Controls that are more relevant could include logging and monitoring. These controls also might be a source of data that can better inform the analysis.
- Threat Type helps us understand threat event frequency and loss magnitude. For example, malicious events tend to be less frequent for insiders than error events. In some cases, they also can result in larger losses because of the intent.
- Especially when combined with the asset at risk (e.g., sensitive customer information combined with a confidentiality effect), the effect can strongly indicate both frequency and magnitude. For example, we would generally expect a higher frequency of malicious confidentiality events against sensitive information than we would availability events. Similarly, loss magnitude can be profoundly affected. By using our example again, the losses generated from a sensitive customer information availability event would be different from a confidentiality event against that same information.

EXPERT ESTIMATION AND PERT

At this point, we can begin to acquire and provide estimates. Of course, we will use the techniques we discussed in the Measurement chapter (namely, the use of calibrated PERT values for each of the factors). Tables 6.3 and 6.4 (based on our earlier table) can aid in a larger-scale analysis containing numerous scenarios. Smaller analyses involving just a couple of scenarios might not benefit from tables like these and can be plugged right into your analysis application.

You may have noticed that we did not include Difficulty as a column in Table 6.1. That's because its value does not change from scenario to scenario and, thus, does

Table 6.3 Quantified Threat Factors for the Risk Associated with the Reduction in Authentication Strength for External Website X

Asset	Threat Community	Threat Type	Effect	Threat Event Frequency	Threat Capability
Customer information	Cyber criminals	Malicious	Confidentiality	0.5–2	0.75–0.95
Customer information	Privileged insiders	Error	Confidentiality	2–6	0.98–0.99
Customer information	Privileged insiders	Malicious	Confidentiality	0.02–0.05	0.98–0.99
Customer information	Privileged insiders	Error	Availability	2–6	0.98–0.99
Customer information	Privileged insiders	Malicious	Availability	0.02–0.05	0.98–0.99
Customer funds	Privileged insiders	Error	$	0.5–2	0.98–0.99
Customer funds	Privileged insiders	Malicious	$	0.1–0.3	0.98–0.99
Customer funds	Customers	Malicious	$	6–12	0.75–0.95

Table 6.4 Quantified Loss Factors for Risk Associated with the Reduction in Authentication Strength for External Website X

Loss Forms	Confidentiality	Availability	Possession of $
Productivity	$5000–$75,000	$5000–$50,000	$15,000–$150,000
Response	$50,000–$250,000	$50,000–$100,000	$50,000–$500,000
Replacement	$0	$0	$50,000–$1.5 million
Fine and judgments	$500,000–$2 million	$50,000–$150,000	$1–$5 million
Secondary response	$100,000–$500,000	$50,000–$100,000	$1–$5 million
Competitive Advantage	$0	$0	$0
Reputation	$500,000–$1 million	$100,000–$1 million	$250,000–$2 million

not benefit from a table. In other words, if it had been included as a column in the table, you would have seen that column with the same RS values for every row/ scenario.

Once we have the values estimated for our analysis, we're almost ready to plug the values into the FAIR risk software, run the analysis, and capture the results. There is just one more step, though, that is absolutely crucial—documenting rationale. You should never complete a FAIR analysis without documenting the scope of the analysis, as well as the reasoning and basis for each value used in the analysis. From our perspective, this is nonoptional, at least if you plan to actually use the results. Please trust us on this. If you do an analysis without documenting the rationale, you are setting yourself up for a fall when, six months later, someone wants to review the analysis and questions where the numbers came from. You won't remember. At least if you're like us you won't, and that is a bad situation.

MONTE CARLO ENGINE

At this point, it's time to use some software product like CXOWARE's RiskCalibrator product, or a homegrown version of your own that uses a Monte Carlo function. The use of a stochastic modeling tool like Monte Carlo can bring additional legitimacy to the analysis and allows you to better defend your results. Assuming this part is complete and the results have been generated, you can then compare them in the software tool, or use something like Excel to review the results. Here is an example of a table of such results (Table 6.5). Using an index number that refers to the scenarios can be helpful for large tables.

Table 6.5 Monte Carlo Analysis Results

Scenario No.	Mode: LEF	Mode: ALE	Max: LEF	Max: ALE
1	0.03	$95,004	0.20	$190,741
2	0.05	$378,132	0.10	$1,228,254
3	2.51	$650	5.00	$1377
4	0.36	$4050	1.11	$102,468
5	0.54	$25,521	1.01	$155,520
6	0.15	$48,243	0.43	$120,956
7	0.60	$28,728	0.80	$2,203,339
8	0.48	$34,444	1.07	$88,005
9	1.72	$2701	3.51	$10,402
10	0.14	$1994	0.21	$6385
11	0.11	$848	1.47	$2230
12	1.22	$1362	2.76	$139,165
13	0.07	$90,874	0.09	$8,035,326

With these results compared in a table like this, it becomes easier to identify the scenario with the highest maximum annualized loss (13) and the loss scenario that you will experience the most (3). You can also use heat maps, like the one shown in Figure 6.2. We'll discuss their use in more detail in the next chapter.

If you're using a FAIR software application, there are more sophisticated representations like the one shown in Figure 6.3, which shows an example of how analysis results can be compared side-by-side. In this example, the loss exposure distribution

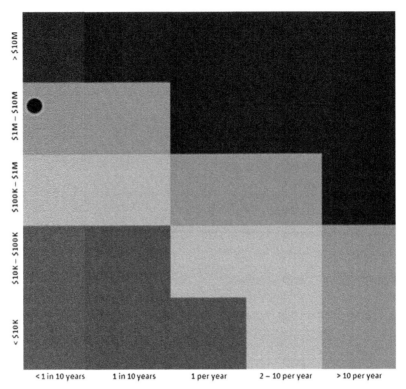

FIGURE 6.2

Example heat map.

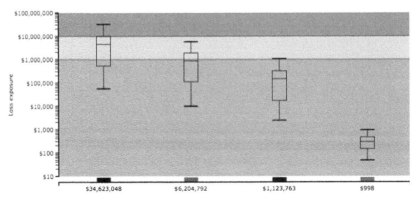

FIGURE 6.3

Analysis results compared side-by-side.

for each scenario is shown as a box-and-whisker plot. The top and bottom "whiskers" show the maximum and minimum loss exposure outcomes, respectively, from the Monte Carlo simulations, whereas the top and bottom of each box represent the 90th and 10th percentiles, respectively. The line in the midst of the box is the average. The colored bands represent thresholds defined by the organization for what it considers high, medium, and low risk.

That's it. That is the process for performing a FAIR analysis. We hope that it seems relatively straightforward even if it is clear that the scoping part of the process can be challenging. But that's the nature of the beast. With that in mind, imagine the unexamined assumptions that invariably occur when someone tries to answer questions like "Can we…" and "Should we…" and "How much risk will we have…" if they haven't gone through an exercise like this. With all of those unexamined assumptions, how likely is it that their wet finger in the air estimate will stand up under critical examination? As we said earlier, among other things, FAIR is a framework for understanding complex conditions. Even without making the quantitative estimates we used in our examples, we would still be in a far better position to understand the "riskiness" of these scenarios having been through this exercise.

LEVELS OF ABSTRACTION

Before we end this chapter, we need to drive home a point that we have only just brushed over so far, on the LEF side of the ontology of FAIR you have the option of choosing the level of abstraction at which you want to make your estimates. For example, you can estimate LEF directly rather than derive it from Threat Event Frequency (TEF), Threat Capability (TCap), and Difficulty. Likewise, you can estimate vulnerability directly rather than derive it from TCap and Difficulty. What we teach people today in our FAIR classes is when beginning an analysis always start at the top of the ontology and ask yourself whether you can make an estimate at LEF directly rather than farther down in the ontology. If not, go down to the next level and ask yourself the same thing about vulnerability. And likewise on down the tree. The point is, do not default to making your estimates at the lowest level of abstraction in the ontology. The lower levels are incredibly useful, but why spend the time down there if you don't need to. Most of the time, we find ourselves estimating TEF and vulnerability in the scenarios we perform. We usually only derive vulnerability by estimating TCap and Difficulty when we need to for some reason. The following guidance should help you recognize when you can or should estimate at higher versus lower levels of abstraction.

LEF LEVEL

If your organization has a reasonable amount of data from past loss events, then you should typically make your LEF estimates directly. Examples include malware infections, weather-related events, and hardware failures. For weather-related events especially, we have found it to be a waste of time to try to draw the line regarding what represents a threat event. Odds are good that if your organization has been in business for any length of time, it will have weather damage experience to draw from, and if it doesn't, other businesses in the neighborhood will. There is no shortage of these data.

VULNERABILITY LEVEL

Vulnerability is by far the most difficult variable to derive well from its factors. Estimating TCap and Difficulty effectively can be challenging in some scenarios, and the shape of these variables (how flat or peaked they are) can have a significant effect on the derived level of vulnerability. For this reason, we generally prefer to estimate vulnerability directly. That said, if you are doing an analysis where the efficacy of a resistive control is being evaluated, then operating at that lower level can be especially useful.

There is one clear rule of thumb regarding the use of TCap and Difficulty, and that is when you are dealing with a privileged insider. By their roles and responsibilities, these people intentionally have unfettered access to the assets that are the focus of the analysis. As a result, except in very rare circumstances don't even bother to estimate TCap and Difficulty in scenarios where they are the threat community because the only answer is that you are 100% vulnerable to them.

TEF LEVEL

We almost never derive TEF from Contact Frequency and Probability of Action. In fact, in all the years we have been doing FAIR analyses, we can probably count on two hands the number of times we've found it useful to go that deep. There are a couple of reasons for this: (1) we rarely have any difficulty making an estimate directly at the TEF level, so why go any deeper, and (2) estimating probability of action effectively can be pretty tough. That said, there have been a couple of times when being able to operate at this deeper level has been tremendously helpful, so leverage it when you need to, but don't count on needing it often.

DEEPER LEVELS

As you know, the ontology goes to even deeper levels. In all our years of doing FAIR analysis, though, we have never had to make estimates at any level deeper than Contact Frequency, Probability of Action, TCap, and Difficulty. Not once. Those deeper levels really just exist to help us flesh out the assumptions that affect our estimates at higher levels, and troubleshoot analyses, particularly when analysts disagree on values at the higher levels of abstraction.

Interpreting Results

"On a long enough timeline, the survival rate for everyone drops to zero."
Narrator, *Fight Club*

This quote illustrates the importance of probability in risk analyses. However, it's also a favorite because it very succinctly communicates a risk truism that can only come from good interpretation. This is one of the goals of a risk analysis; to understand the results so well they can be effectively and succinctly communicated to the risk decision makers. In this section, we will discuss how to interpret results from a FAIR risk analysis. This is an important topic especially for those that have come from a qualitative world and are not well versed in what to do with the numbers that come out of an analysis.

Because most of us haven't done quantitative risk analysis before, a common reaction from first-time FAIR users when they see the numeric output is confusion. It doesn't take long however, before the results become second nature. The output is well structured and presented in various forms in order to fit various reporting needs. Whether you prefer tables, graphs or even qualitative ratings, it's all there.

FAIR helps you analyze risk in a way that can integrate well with the rest of the organization. In order to make this easy though, it often requires some artifacts to aid in interpreting the results. We've talked about some of these generally so far –heatmaps, risk registers, and/or an issue tracking system. However often you need more than that; you need organizational context. We're going to be talking about how context plays into the FAIR results and how you can set up your organization to more easily use FAIR. So with that as backdrop, let's get started!

WHAT DO THESE NUMBERS MEAN? (HOW TO INTERPRET FAIR RESULTS)

We read a lot of security and risk standards. It comes with the territory. If you've done the same, you doubtless have read one of those well-intentioned write-ups about the difference between qualitative and quantitative risk analyses. When you get to the end of those write-ups, they usually have some discussion of the pros and cons of each approach. One of our favorite statements is offered by the NIST 800-30 standard *Guide for Conducting Risk Assessments* (both the older version and the newer one have similar issues). They say this about *qualitative* analysis: *"This*

type of analysis supports communicating risk results to decision makers." This statement implies that there are two types of risk analysis methods: qualitative for those
that want to communicate with executives, and quantitative for those who want to
play math games in their basement (we are being facetious of course). Clearly this
creates a bit of a bias because in case you didn't know, all risk professionals want
to communicate with executives. Our experience has been that although qualitative
scales can be very useful and are often what the executives are used to seeing, quantitative results tend to be far more informative. That said, it is true that executives
are busy people who often need or want to operate off at-a-glance indicators of their
world. That way, things that are amiss jump off the page at them, allowing deeper
investigation and perhaps corrective actions. Qualitative values – the reds, yellows,
and greens of the world – are great at providing that view. Consequently, your risk
reports may need to provide that qualitative perspective. Here's the catch though.
*Providing a qualitative interpretation of an analysis is not the same thing as doing
a qualitative analysis.* We can very effectively represent the results of a quantitative
analysis in qualitative terms. The reverse isn't true.

Let's assume that you want your work to be taken seriously by executives so
you follow the sage advice from 800-30 and do a qualitative analysis. You present
the results (High, Medium, or Low) to the executives and one of two things happen.
Either they ask how you came up with the ratings or they simply accept the information at face value. If there's not a lot at stake (or if your credibility is already in the
toilet) it's very likely they won't dig into how the analysis results were arrived at.
If, however, you're asking for a lot money to remediate an issue, or if what's being
proposed is likely to impact business significantly in some manner then it's much
more likely they'll want an explanation. So if they ask how you came up with the ratings for your analysis, what would your answer be? How much rigor went into your
analysis? If it's like most qualitative analyses you're left with talking at a high level
about some of your reasoning, your experience and training, perhaps what you used
to do at another company, or what best practice is. What they hear is that they need
to trust you and they need to do what the other companies are doing. If they're the
trusting sort, that may be the end of the conversation. If not, it can be an uncomfortable conversation.

Okay, so now let's try it another way: with a quantitative analysis. You do your
analysis and then present just the numbers. What's their reaction? Well, first of all
you are far more likely to get questions about how you came up with the results,
especially the first time or two you put numbers in front of them. This should be
viewed as a good thing. It generates dialog and provides the opportunity to convey
far more information about the scenario. It also provides an opportunity to demonstrate the rigor underlying your approach, which should increase the credibility of
the results. You explain that the estimates were based on this or that data and these
assumptions. You can also describe the level of confidence (or lack thereof) in your
inputs and why, and answer questions related to the number of Monte Carlo simulations that were performed. All this is great but there can be a downside, depending on
the circumstance and the individual inclinations of the executives.

Some executives love numbers and some just want it easy. They have a million things on their plate and they don't always want to gain a deeper understanding of this scenario at this moment. Sometimes all they want to know is whether this is a situation they need to do something about or worry about. Presumably, you wouldn't be bringing this analysis before them if the results weren't important, but setting that aside for the moment, it is important to present analysis results in a form that meets the needs of the decision makers. This introduces a third option – presenting both qualitative and quantitative results. We'll talk about ways in which to do this shortly. The advantage is that executives can have a simple visual cue regarding how much to care about an issue, and you have the numbers and underlying rigor to explain the analysis if they want an explanation. Everybody wins.

Our experience has been that executives ultimately want to feel they can trust the analysis results. That trust can come from their innate faith in you, the rigor that went into an analysis, or both. We've found the combination of the two to be a much stronger formula for trust than just having faith in the person sitting across from them. In fact, very often we appear to gain credibility through the rigor in our analyses. We have yet to encounter an executive who hasn't appreciated our ability to explain our results, be they presented numerically, in colors, or both. Unfortunately, NIST 800-30 and similar references don't appear to recognize the distinction between how results are presented versus how they're arrived at, therefore the people who read those references are misinformed.

UNDERSTANDING THE RESULTS TABLE

Regardless of whether we intend to present results as numbers or colors, we have to start by understanding the numbers. Once again, we will be using the results table from the online FAIR application as our example for this section. Figure 7.1 shows the output from one of our earlier examples.

	Minimum	Average	Most likely @	Maximum
Primary				
Loss events / year	0.02	0.03	0.02	0.03
Loss magnitude	$203,823	$667,221	$496,693	$1,399,591
Secondary				
Loss events / year	0	0.01	0.01	0.01
Loss magnitude	$2,966,595	$5,398,031	$4,535,356	$8,746,812
Total loss exposure	$26,785	$50,125	$46,540	$83,047

Percentiles	10 %	$40,156.81	90 %	$60,507.57	Vulnerability	50%

FIGURE 7.1

FAIR risk analysis results.

The first thing you may notice is that the analysis doesn't generate a single discrete value like "3.75" as a risk score. This is because the inputs to a FAIR analysis are distributions and the Monte Carlo functions that perform the underlying calculations generate distributions as output. Using distributions as inputs and outputs are critical components of any credible risk analysis because they more faithfully represent the uncertainty that's inherent in any analysis. What this table represents is a distribution of results given the inputs you provided. There is a minimum value, which is the lowest value generated by the Monte Carlo function, a maximum value, which is the largest generated value, as well as an average and a most likely value.

TALKING ABOUT RISK

A commonly stated concern is the precise nature of the values in the table (e.g. $203,823), the implication being that stakeholders might misinterpret this to mean the analysis itself has a high degree of precision. There are two things to keep in mind on this score – 1) the output is a *distribution*, which by its very nature isn't highly precise output regardless of how the values at different points in the distribution are displayed, and 2) it can't be helped that the minimum and maximum values from a Monte Carlo function, or the mode (Most Likely) value of a distribution are precise – that's just how math and statistics work. Nonetheless, when presenting results to management we nearly always round the numbers to avoid any misunderstanding.

Next, you will see that the table rows are split vertically between the primary and secondary losses. They are then subdivided between frequency and magnitude. Lastly, there are percentile and vulnerability numbers at the bottom that give us an additional lens into this analysis.

Working down from the top of the table we see primary loss event frequency – i.e. how often loss is expected to occur. Under this are the primary loss magnitude values. It's important to recognize that these loss magnitude values are per-event. In other words, when a loss event occurs this is the distribution of how much loss would be realized. These frequency and magnitude rows are then repeated for secondary losses. Lastly, at the bottom we see the total *annualized* loss exposure, which combines the primary and secondary results.

Multiplying the loss magnitude values by the event frequency annualizes the results (as long as the frequencies are based on an annual timeframe). In other words, an event that occurs once every ten years with a loss magnitude of $10,000 has an annualized value of $1,000. There's good news and bad news regarding annualized values. The good news is that it can be a very helpful perspective for making comparisons – e.g. a scenario with an annualized loss exposure of $100,000 is probably more important to deal with than a scenario having $1,000 of annualized exposure, and putting controls in place that drive $100,000 of annualized exposure down to $20,000 is very important to recognize. It is only one perspective though. Another important perspective focuses on the single event loss magnitude, which ignores frequency altogether. The single event loss perspective helps us understand how bad the events are likely to be when they occur. In order to understand the single event loss from the table above you simply add the primary loss magnitude values to the secondary loss magnitude values - e.g. roughly $500,000 of primary loss plus $4,500,000 of secondary loss (from the most likely column) suggests a most likely single event loss of approximately $5,000,000. This is a much bigger number than the annualized view and adds significantly to our understanding of the scenario and what decision makers might do to deal with it. Based on this information they might choose to simply insure against the event or take measures to reduce loss magnitude from this kind of event rather than try to further reduce an already low frequency. The point is, in order to make well-informed decisions on risk scenarios you can't boil it down to a single number, or even necessarily a single distribution.

When communicating results however, it often makes sense to begin by focusing on the total annualized loss exposure line, and specifically the most likely value. It's easy to talk about the results by starting off with, "the most likely results of the analysis indicate that..." In this case, the most likely total loss exposure, annualized, is roughly $46,000. The dialog can expand from there as appropriate.

VULNERABILITY

Another important result from an analysis is the vulnerability percentage. Recall from previous chapters that vulnerability is designed to answer the question, "How likely is it that a threat event will become a loss event?" Well, here is where you get the answer to that question. In our above example, we are 50% vulnerable. What this means is that roughly half of the threat events are expected to result in loss. If this value said 100% it would mean that every threat event would become a loss event. Likewise, vulnerability of 0% means threat events should almost never result in loss. How does 0% translate to almost never? Read on.

Do *not* interpret 0% vulnerability to mean there is absolutely no chance of a threat event becoming a loss event. Realistically, 0% vulnerability should be interpreted as one of two things – 1) the probability is low enough that the application rounded it to 0%, or 2) none of the Monte Carlo simulations (usually thousands of them) encountered an instance where threat capability exceeded difficulty. Perhaps if there had been just one more Monte Carlo simulation, or a million more, it would have encountered a vulnerable condition. The point is, there are inevitable limitations with any stochastic function, and this is an example. That said, when analysis results show vulnerability at 0% at least it suggests that resistive controls are highly effective.

PERCENTILES

The percentiles are another way to get a sense for how the distribution is shaped. The 10% value means that 10% of the Monte Carlo outcomes fell below this value (in this case $40,156.81). At the other end of the spectrum, it shows that 90% of the results were below $60,507.57, or put another way, only 10% exceeded this value. So think about these as the main body of the distributions absent the tail values. A full 80% of all the results fall between these two values. For some kinds of risk analyses, we specifically target the tails in order to do some stress testing ("what if" testing such as if all events occurred today in their worst-case form).

Earlier we suggested that it often works well to start a conversation about the results by focusing on the Most Likely values. You should be aware that this could vary depending on the risk culture of your organization. We have worked in organizations where decision makers wanted to focus on the 80th percentile instead. What this means in practical terms is that these folks take a more conservative view of risk and want to base their decisions on a more dire representation of loss exposure. There's absolutely nothing wrong with this. You just need to be aware of it as a possibility.

UNDERSTANDING THE HISTOGRAM

The histogram is another common output from the FAIR application. It shows the cumulative annualized loss exposure (ALE) in bins. In Figure 7.2, we can see that about 1,600 of the Monte Carlo simulations resulted in ALE of about $600,000. This is just another way to look at the results of the simulations, spread amongst the various bins to show the most prominent results. This can be a very effective visual for comparing two or more scenarios at a glance.

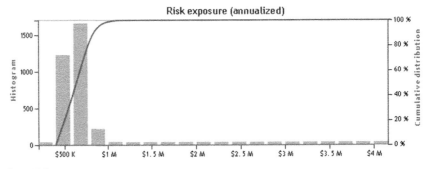

FIGURE 7.2

FAIR histogram.

UNDERSTANDING THE SCATTER PLOT

The scatter plot is another way to visualize results from an analysis. In Figure 7.3, the red and blue blobs are made up of thousands of individual dots, with each dot representing the result from one of the Monte Carlo simulations. The blue dots represent primary loss and red dots represent secondary loss.

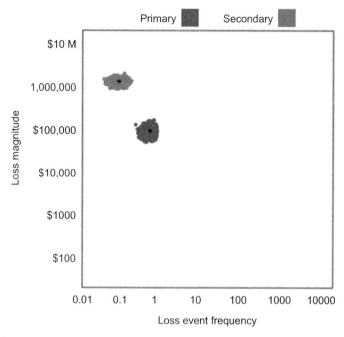

FIGURE 7.3

Scatterplot.

When these blobs are highly concentrated and don't extend very far vertically or horizontally it suggests that the output distributions are relatively narrow, which usually happens when your input distributions are narrow – perhaps because you had good data for this analysis. More widely dispersed dots doesn't necessarily mean your data was sketchy though. You might have a lot of excellent data that simply has a wider range of values.

Very often you will see the red dots higher along the vertical scale than the blue dots, and always to the left of the blue dots. This vertical difference is because secondary loss tends to be higher in magnitude than primary loss. The red dots will always be to the left or vertically in line with the blue dots because secondary loss event frequency is predicated on primary loss events – i.e. only a percentage of primary loss events have secondary effects.

QUALITATIVE SCALES

The first few times you present quantitative results it can feel like your job isn't done. Why? You haven't told the executives how important the results indicate the issue to be (High, Medium, or Low). This is a bit misguided though because information security isn't in (or shouldn't be in) the business of interpreting the relevance of analysis results. We almost never have sufficient visibility into the broader context that determines the business relevance of our results. We might have an opinion on the matter and we might even be relatively well informed and correct in our interpretation. Other times the results are so large or small that their relevance is obvious. The point is, our analyses generate numbers and the significance of those numbers in the business context is for the executives to decide. That said, if we want to provide a meaningful qualitative representation of the results (the importance of which we discussed earlier) then the qualitative scale being used has to be relevant. Ideally, a preexisting severity scale and/or a risk appetite definition exists in the organization. Sometimes the operational risk or business continuity group has already developed a scale similar to the one below:

- Critical: Losses over $25,000,000
- High: Losses between $5,000,000 and $25,000,000
- Moderate: Losses between $500,000 and $5,000,000
- Low: Losses between $50,000 and $500,000
- Very low: Losses less than $50,000

If your organization has a scale like this, count yourself lucky because most organizations we run into either don't have a defined scale or their scale describes each qualitative level using purely qualitative terms – e.g. "High : Large financial losses and/or significant reputation damage." If your organization doesn't have a quantitative scale then you'll be a bit hamstrung in terms of translating quantitative values into qualitative values until one exists.

TALKING ABOUT RISK

In some organizations it can be challenging to get the right stakeholders involved in creating a loss severity scale. They either don't want to think about it that hard or they don't want to feel "pinned down" by a document that could be interpreted to mean that they're okay with, for example, a $1,000,000 loss (falling within the Moderate range in our scale above). If you can't get the right stakeholders involved the next best approach is to take a shot at defining the scale yourself. We know, that runs counter to almost everything we preach about information security practitioners leaving relevance in the hands of the stakeholders. Once you've defined the scale though, begin using it openly. What you'll likely find is that if your scale is too far off the mark stakeholders will provide feedback that allows you to calibrate it. For example, if your scale defined critical risk as anything over $1,000,000 in annualized loss but stakeholders are reacting to loss exposure of that size as a rounding error, then your scale is probably not well aligned.

A useful rule of thumb to keep in mind regarding severity scales is that each level of the scale should drive a different behavior. For example, if something is truly critical in the eyes of business leadership then their reaction should be to call all hands on deck to resolve the issue, and the cost of remediation should be a nonfactor. If something is high risk in their eyes, then they should be willing to adjust current plans and resource allocations to deal with it. Likewise on down the scale. Besides being helpful in creating and calibrating a severity scale, this rule of thumb can shed significant light on some of the qualitative ratings you might encounter. If something is labeled High Risk but nobody seems to care, it likely means the stakeholders see the rating as not credible.

Ultimately, what these scales represent is the organization's tolerance for risk. We'll cover risk appetite and tolerance in detail later so don't sweat it for now.

HEATMAPS

As we've mentioned already, heatmaps can be used effectively as the translation engine between the quantitative results and qualitative ratings. To accomplish this though, you need to develop a heatmap that aligns with the organization's severity scale (mentioned above). In some larger firms you may have to develop several different heatmaps – an overall heatmap for the enterprise based on its scale and heatmaps for different parts of the organization based on their loss scales.

In Figure 7.4 we have our heatmap from previous chapters. In this example, there are four color bands that designate the "levels" of risk as defined by the underlying numbers. Believe it or not, the names of these levels can be contentious in some organizations, or worse; various parts of the organization could use different names for each color band. We prefer the typical Low, Medium, High, and Severe, but it could be Minimum, Moderate, High and Critical or any other combination. Regardless, as we mentioned earlier, it is important to have solid definitions for these labels to help ensure clear communication.

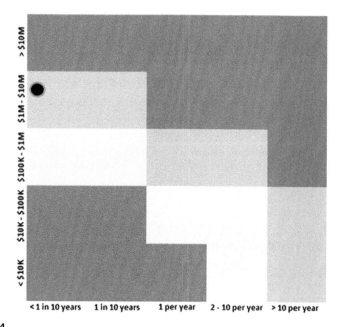

FIGURE 7.4

A heatmap.

The next observation we'll make is that the scales in this example are logarithmic, covering all values from less than once in ten years to greater than ten times per year with just five boxes. This has advantages and disadvantages – a main disadvantage being that people sometimes have to reminded that the scale isn't linear. Nonetheless, we've found it to be an effective way to cover a very broad continuum of values.

Another consideration is that the size of the plotted dot can be large or small, conveying the disbursement of outcomes, or it can represent a specific value within the distribution (e.g., the most likely or 80th percentile). With this in mind comes the inevitable question of how to describe a dot that spans two (or more) bands in the heatmap (e.g. something that sits in both the Moderate and High bands). Here again, how you treat this will vary in part based on the risk culture of your organization. Some organizations will opt to default to the more severe label (rounding up as it were) and simply show the dot there, while others will split the difference, calling the level of risk "Moderate-to-High" and letting the dot span the two bands. Most places we've encountered round up. That's okay, our goal here is to facilitate decision making, and the visual representation of the risk is an aide to the decision makers so they can understand how you have rated risk and where it falls in relation to other risk issues (if you plot more than one on the same map).

These heatmaps can work very well on slide presentations to decision makers. We include the graph and some text describing key points regarding the scenario, along with the specific numbers. For instance, if you are showing a heatmap above, somewhere in the narrative be sure to explicitly call out the frequency and impact you are talking about. Figure 7.5 is an example of what those slides can look like:

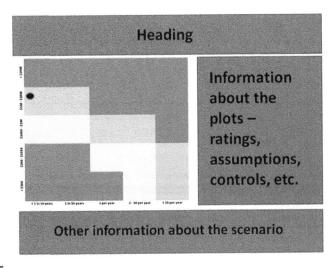

FIGURE 7.5

Example presentation slide.

In addition, as we mentioned above, you will probably want to include both the ALE and SLE values. Leaving this out of the slide could negatively impact the decision maker's ability to make a good decision. For example, they may be comparing the perceived gains from implementing some cool new project against investing in mitigation measures for your risk scenario. If all you present is the scenario's ALE value of $10,000 but leave out the fact that it has a SLE of $100,000 then that may materially change their decision. To help ensure clear communication, we recommend two things – 1) use a consistent scale for the loss magnitude (do not switch the scales from ALE to SLE in different presentations; this will only confuse people), and 2) make sure that the acronyms are spelled out, perhaps with a short definition as well. Something like this would be helpful:

ALE – The Annualized Loss Expectancy is the amount of risk being held on a yearly basis (the total loss is spread over the years before it is expected to happen)
SLE – The single loss expectancy is the total amount of loss that will be experienced in a single loss event.

We have also used terms like "peanut-buttered" to describe the process by which we spread single event losses over the years in the event horizon. You might find this helpful as well. Eventually though you will come to a steady state where your decision makers are used to seeing these slides and will not need hand holding before making their decisions.

SPLITTING HEATMAPS

One interesting aspect of risk decision-making is that questions about, "How much risk are you willing to accept?" will always be influenced by human bias and, frankly, irrationality. It can't be helped. We might argue that $10 million of risk should be treated the same regardless of the nature of the loss however that tends to not be the case. We have seen companies fully comfortable with losing $10 million in investments, yet not willing to accept a single dollar in reputation exposure. Some companies are not comfortable spending that same $10 million in cash outlays but would certainly be willing to risk it in market investments. That companies and executives behave this way should be none too surprising. After all, the Nobel committee gave its top economics prize to Daniel Kahneman, who studied why people didn't make rational economic choices. We are barely able to treat our personal cash flows rationally with regards to risk; it's not reasonable to expect companies and executives to behave much differently.

This being the case a good approach to solving this problem is to take a risk scenario and decompose it in ways that management may find useful in helping them make decisions. This is where multiple heatmaps can be helpful. There are a couple of different ways you can approach this depending on the problem you're faced with. The first approach helps when considering the relative differences in severity levels for different parts of the organization. The second approach can be helpful when you're faced with significant differences in how executives view different forms of loss (e.g. reputation versus productivity) even when the amounts of exposure are the same. It is worth noting that these heatmaps should be created in collaboration with the other risk-related stakeholders in your business, operational risk, etc. One sure-fire way to upset your peers and take political heat is to create a table that purports to represent all the things they need to care about, when it actually does nothing of the sort. Get stakeholder buy-in before you do any of these.

SPLITTING BY ORGANIZATION

For each part of the organization, there can be a different heatmap that represents relevant severity levels (see Figure 7.6). For example, a large line of business may have the capacity to absorb much higher losses than a small affiliate. As a result, each should have a different set of scales for their heatmaps. Likewise, the enterprise (the mother ship) will probably have an entirely different set of scales. With these different scales you can better communicate risk relevance to different audiences in terms that align with their worldview. And by the way, this is often a very humbling experience to those in support functions like IT when they see how what they work on with such fervor every day is reflected in the overall organization's priorities.

Nevertheless, that is how risk works – it isn't what's important to you as the analyst, it's the priorities of the company as a whole that matter. We once saw a company take the quantitatively assessed IT risk for an entire company and display it on a stacked bar chart next to the cumulative operational risk of its primary line of business. Let's just say that the entirety of InfoSec risk was a rounding error in that

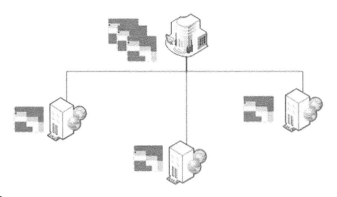

FIGURE 7.6

Organizational heatmaps.

chart. Very humbling and yet freeing as it allows a risk group to focus on those things that are truly important to the company.

SPLITTING BY LOSS TYPE

There may be times when we need to break a scenario down and map it to the FAIR loss categories (see Figure 7.7). For instance, if management is strongly focused on hard dollar financial loss you can map some FAIR categories such as replacement costs to these categories, which would allow your analysis to be compared to other hard dollar risk issues throughout the organization. You can also map other risk categories like reputation without much translation. Remember that the scales just need to be consistent. For instance, frequency and probability are mostly interchangeable as long as the time scale is the same (typically one year), and the losses are equivalent to impact or magnitude. Remember to pay attention to whether the losses are expressed as per event, or annualized (SLE versus ALE).

One inherent challenge with qualitative labeling and heatmaps is that they invite questions about how many lows make a medium and how many of those make a

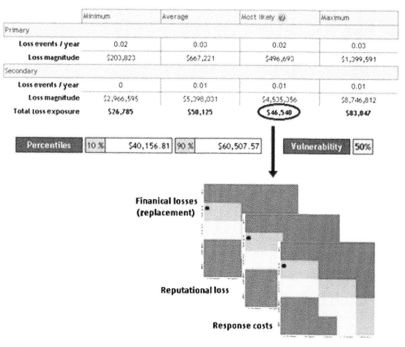

FIGURE 7.7

Multiple impact heatmaps.

high, and so on. In the Metrics chapter we introduce an alternative that works well. However, if you do find yourself in a scenario where you need to present a risk issue in this form, we recommend that you don't hide the dollar amounts associated with the loss forms. At the very least, it will give the decision makers a clear picture of how much risk is being discussed. Lastly, remember that your risk analysis does not set the priority for the organization; it should be reflective of it. Thus, whatever label you use for these multi-tiered analyses should be indicative of what the firm thinks about losses of this type, as best as you possibly can.

SPECIAL RISK CONDITIONS

There are two types of scenarios in risk analysis that warrant special mention; unstable conditions and fragile conditions. To understand why these are important, take a look at the scatter plot in Figure 7.8:

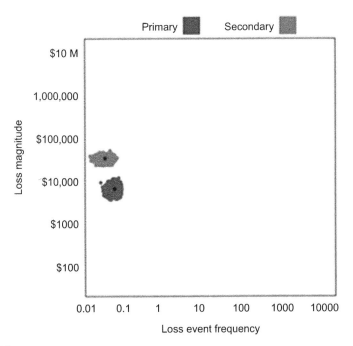

FIGURE 7.8

Another scatterplot.

In this example, we can see both our primary and secondary losses occur in that middle left side of the box. It shows us that there is a moderate loss magnitude (at least as defined on this scale) associated with this scenario but that there's apparently no need to fear because the frequency of these losses are low; in this case somewhere between once every 10 and 100 years. So we're good to go, right? Not necessarily. Sometimes numbers alone aren't enough in order to understand a risk scenario.

UNSTABLE CONDITIONS

The chart above might result from a scenario where resistive controls are nonexistent but the threat event frequency is inherently low – i.e. there just isn't much threat activity. This is referred to as an Unstable Risk Condition. It's unstable because the organization can't or hasn't chosen to put preventative controls in place to manage loss event frequency. As a result, if the frequency changes the losses can mount fast. Another way to describe this is to say that the level of risk is highly sensitive to threat event frequency. Examples might include certain weather or geological events. The condition also commonly exists with privileged internal threat communities (e.g. executive administrative assistants, database administrators, etc.). Since most companies model scenarios related to privileged insiders as a relatively infrequent occurrence with high impact, these risk scenarios will often be unstable.

Perhaps given all of the other risk conditions the organization is wrestling with this just hasn't been a high enough priority. Or perhaps the condition hadn't been analyzed and recognized before. Regardless, it boils down to the organization rolling the dice every day and hoping they don't come up snake-eyes. If you presented the analysis results above without noting that it is unstable management might decide there's no need to introduce additional controls or buy insurance because the odds of it happening are so low. They would be making a poorly informed decision. Designating something as an unstable risk condition is really just a way of providing a more robust view of the situation so decision makers can make better-informed decisions.

FRAGILE CONDITIONS

The other scenario worth calling out to management is something called a Fragile Risk Condition. On a heatmap it can look exactly like an unstable condition – low loss event frequency and moderate or higher loss magnitude. Here again though, these numbers don't tell the whole story.

You may recall that there are a number of things that are required prior to the analysis being calculated. One of these things is an analysis of controls that affect loss event frequency. If you look at the controls that are in place and come up with just a single preventative control, the odds are pretty good that you are knocking on the door of a Fragile Risk Condition.

By calling it out decision makers have the opportunity to institute additional preventative controls or controls that reduce the likelihood of the single control failing.

Or both. In any event, this again is just another opportunity to improve a decision maker's understanding of what they're faced with.

TROUBLESHOOTING RESULTS

The very first thing you should do after running an analysis is gut-check the results. Do they make sense? Would you feel comfortable presenting and defending them to someone whose opinion matters? If you've been diligent while performing the analysis your answer will typically be "yes." If the answer to either of these is no, then it's time to examine the results and see if you can find some clues as to what might be wrong. Note that we have an entire chapter on common problems we see in analyses, so we won't go into too much detail here. Nonetheless, this is a good time for us to share a few things to keep an eye out for in analysis results that might indicate trouble. Many times a screwy analysis will be obvious. Other times, a problem can be tougher to recognize. With that said:

- If the annualized loss exposure in your results is greater than the net worth of the organization, you might have a problem. Very often, this occurs when threat event frequency, vulnerability, or secondary loss event frequency values aren't realistic.
- If the threat community is privileged insiders and you're not 100% vulnerable, you might have a problem. We strongly suggest that for scenarios involving privileged insiders you estimate vulnerability directly (not bothering with deriving it from TCap and Difficulty). It's simpler and faster.
- If loss event frequency is coming out high even though nobody can remember the last time the event happened (if it ever happened), you might have a problem. Your assumptions regarding what constitutes a threat event might need revisiting, or perhaps you need to rethink TCap and Difficulty.
- If secondary loss is huge for events you experience regularly (e.g. virus infections) yet your organization is still in business, you might have a problem. Think hard about either how often you actually experience secondary effects (secondary loss event frequency) or your secondary loss magnitude values.

We tried to think of a tactful way to write this in a manner like Jeff Foxworthy's "You might be a redneck, if..." gag, but worried about people taking it wrong. We could have done a FAIR analysis on this concern but decided instead to simply avoid the exposure.

One of the challenges in troubleshooting your own analyses is that you often "get what you asked for." In other words, the results reflect the inputs you used and your underlying assumptions, even when they're wrong. This is one of the reasons we strongly suggest that you always have at least one other person review your work.

TALKING ABOUT RISK

If you're asking yourself the question, "Are we supposed to run an analysis and if we don't like the answer just continue to change the inputs until we get an answer we like?" the answer is yes. Absolutely. But only if your purpose is to generate the best, most defensible results possible. If you're doing it to drive an agenda or make a point then you're what we call "a monkey with a hammer." The simple fact is that FAIR is no different than any other analytic tool or function; it can be abused and misused. The good news is that one of the advantages to quantitative methods (at least as we apply them) is that the numbers have to be supported by rationale. Absent rationale, we don't place any credibility in a FAIR analysis. If your numbers are designed to drive an agenda then there's a very good chance your rationale will reflect it. What a marvelous way to look stupid and deceitful.

Risk Analysis Examples

OVERVIEW

We could have written an entire book containing nothing but example analyses. Instead, we have tried to provide some examples that will reinforce the concepts and methods we've introduced thus far in the book. If we haven't included an example that is similar to a scenario you are wrestling with, feel free to drop us a note through LinkedIn. We may have one on file that we can share or we might be able to provide an idea that will be helpful. You are not alone.

Please note that you don't have to read all of these example analyses before moving on and reading the rest of the book. These are here as a guide and reference that you will hopefully find valuable as you begin to use FAIR.

INAPPROPRIATE ACCESS PRIVILEGES
PURPOSE

Determine the level of risk associated with inappropriate access privileges in a customer service application.

BACKGROUND

During a recent audit, it was discovered there were active accounts in a customer service application with inappropriate access privileges. These accounts were for employees who still worked in the organization, but whose job responsibilities no longer required access to this information. Internal audit labeled this a high risk finding.

ASSET(S) AT RISK

The account privileges in question permit access to the entire customer database, comprised of roughly 500,000 people. This information includes customer name, address, date of birth, and social security number. No banking, credit, or other financial information exists in these records.

TCOM(S)

The primary threat community (TCom) is made up of employees whose accounts have inappropriate privileges in the account. Given that this group of people has access and experience with the application, they are considered privileged insiders for the purpose of this analysis. You will sometimes get an argument that they aren't supposed to have access, so they shouldn't be labeled privileged insiders. Keep in mind that the label "privileged insider" is not about whether their privileges are approved or not, it's about the fact that they have logical or physical proximity to the assets in question, and they don't have to overcome resistive controls in order to do whatever you are concerned about them doing.

Another potential TCom to consider in this analysis would be nonprivileged insiders who gain illicit access to one of these accounts and leverage the inappropriate access in a malicious act. For example, John, who sits across from Debbie, might not have access to this application, but he knows that Debbie does. He knows this because she mentioned the other day how odd it was that her account could still get into the application 3 months after changing roles. He wants to gain access to the application, so he shoulder surfs Debbie's password the day before she's supposed to go on vacation. The next day, he logs into her account and looks up personal information on a handful of people. He sells this information to someone he met in a bar. This scenario is certainly a possibility and can be scoped into the analysis as well.

Another potential TCom is cyber criminals. The thinking here is that one of these accounts could be compromised via malware that gives remote access to a cyber criminal. The cyber criminal leverages the inappropriate access to steal customer data. We'll discuss some considerations regarding each of these TComs in the Analysis section below.

THREAT TYPE(S)

The primary type of threat event here is clearly malicious. It is difficult to realistically imagine that someone with inappropriate access to an application they're no longer supposed to have access to would accidentally log into that application, and do something that would inappropriately disclose customer information. However, there is a twist here.

What about the possibility of an employee with inappropriate access logging into the application and just rummaging around looking up customer information out of boredom or curiosity but not with an intent to harm—snooping, as it were? That is absolutely a realistic scenario, and it's something that the organization is not okay with, so the question boils down to whether we scope that separately from the truly malicious event.

Deciding whether to combine or separate scenarios like this typically boils down to whether there is likely to be a significant difference in the:

- Frequency of one scenario over the other
- Capability between the threat agents in one scenario versus the another
- Losses that would occur, or
- The controls that would apply

In this analysis, the capability of the threat agents is the same, so that wouldn't be a good differentiating factor. Likewise, the applicable controls should be the same. The losses that would occur might be different, as a malicious actor might on average take more information, and there's a much greater chance for customers to actually experience loss, which would increase secondary losses. There is also likely to be a higher frequency of the events involving nonmalicious actors, because truly malicious acts tend to be less frequent than acts of misbehavior (there are more jaywalkers in the world than there are serial killers). For these reasons, it makes sense to have two distinct threat types for this analysis. We'll label them "malicious" and "snooping."

THREAT EFFECT(S)

The relevant threat effects in this scenario will depend on the type of privileges an account has. If an account has inappropriate read-only privilege, then the only threat effect in play is confidentiality. If an account has change or delete privileges, then integrity and availability come into play. As a result, unless you already know that inappropriate privileges are limited to read-access, you'll need to include all three threat effect types.

SCOPE

Based on the considerations above, our scope table at this point looks like this (Table 8.1):

Table 8.1 The Scope Table for Level of Risks Associated with Inappropriate Access Privileges

Asset at Risk	Threat Community	Threat Type	Effect
Customer PII	Privileged insiders	Malicious	Confidentiality
Customer PII	Privileged insiders	Snooping	Confidentiality
Customer PII	Privileged insiders	Malicious	Availability
Customer PII	Privileged insiders	Malicious	Integrity
Customer PII	Nonpriv insiders	Malicious	Confidentiality
Customer PII	Nonpriv insiders	Malicious	Availability
Customer PII	Nonpriv insiders	Malicious	Integrity
Customer PII	Cyber criminals	Malicious	Confidentiality
Customer PII	Cyber criminals	Malicious	Availability
Customer PII	Cyber criminals	Malicious	Integrity

You'll notice that snooping is limited to confidentiality events. This is because we assume that as soon as someone illicitly changes or deletes a record, they've crossed the line into malicious intent.

At this point, the scoping table consists of 10 scenarios. It would be nice if we could slim this down a bit by eliminating a few of these. The first and most obvious way to accomplish this is to find out whether the inappropriate privileges are limited to read-only, or whether they have change and delete privileges as well. Let's say for the purposes of this example that none of these accounts have delete privileges. This being the case, our scope table now looks like this (Table 8.2):

Table 8.2 The Slimmed Scope Table

Asset at Risk	Threat Community	Threat Type	Effect
Customer PII	Privileged insiders	Malicious	Confidentiality
Customer PII	Privileged insiders	Snooping	Confidentiality
Customer PII	Privileged insiders	Malicious	Integrity
Customer PII	Nonpriv insiders	Malicious	Confidentiality
Customer PII	Nonpriv insiders	Malicious	Integrity
Customer PII	Cyber criminals	Malicious	Confidentiality
Customer PII	Cyber criminals	Malicious	Integrity

There's another very important consideration, though, that can help you skinny-down the number of scenarios you need to analyze in a situation like this. Ask yourself what question these analyses are trying to answer. We know that inappropriate access privileges aren't a good thing, so that's not in question. In this case, what we are trying to understand is the level of risk associated with these inappropriate privileges so that we can accurately report it to management and appropriately prioritize it among all of the other risk issues the organization is faced with.

Our next step, then, is to look at the scenarios in our scope table and try to identify one or more scenarios that are likely to be much more (or less) frequent and/or much more (or less) impactful than the others. This is where your critical thinking muscles can get some serious exercise.

The first scenario that catches our eye in this regard is the one about cyber criminals/integrity. In our minds, there's very little likelihood that a cyber criminal is going to benefit from damaging the integrity of customer records. It's possible that their purpose is not financial gain, but rather to simply harm the company or individuals, but it seems a very remote probability that an actor with sufficient skills to gain this kind of access is going to have that focus. Furthermore, damaging or deleting records is much more likely to be recognized and reacted to than simply stealing data, and it seems especially unlikely that a cyber criminal would sacrifice their hard-won access in this manner. If the scenario were different, however, and instead of customer PII, the information at stake was something a cyber criminal or other threat community would gain significantly from by damaging or deleting, then this scenario might make perfect sense. We are going to delete it from our scope, though.

As we look at our scenarios, it also seems to us that the frequency of nonprivileged insiders hijacking an account that has inappropriate privileges is likely to be much smaller than the malicious or abusive acts of privileged insiders. It also occurs to us that illicit actions by nonprivileged actors would take place against accounts with appropriate access privileges roughly 85% of the time, because there would be little reason for them to single out and attack an account that had inappropriate privileges. For these reasons, we suspect the frequency of privileged insider actions to be much higher than the frequency of nonprivileged insiders, so we'll remove the nonprivileged insider scenarios from scope, too. Now our table looks like this (Table 8.3):

Table 8.3 The Scope Table with Further Omissions

Asset at Risk	Threat Community	Threat Type	Effect
Customer PII	Privileged insiders	Malicious	Confidentiality
Customer PII	Privileged insiders	Snooping	Confidentiality
Customer PII	Privileged insiders	Malicious	Integrity
Customer PII	Cyber criminals	Malicious	Confidentiality

It's looking better all the time. At this point, we aren't sure we're comfortable removing any more scenarios from our scope. That doesn't mean, however, that we have to analyze all four of these. Our approach now is to choose one that we believe will represent the most risk and analyze it. The results of that analysis may tell us everything we need to know to answer the question of how high this audit finding should stand in our list of priorities. The odds are decent that we will need to analyze more than one scenario, but the odds are at least as good that we won't have to analyze all four. This is not about being 100% comprehensive in our measurement of risk. This is about pragmatically reducing uncertainty and having enough information to effectively prioritize this issue against other things on the organization's to-do list.

ANALYSIS

Now that scoping is done, we need to start performing our analyses. The most frequent scenario is almost certainly going to be snooping, but the most impactful is likely to be the cyber criminals because they are certain to try to run off with as much information as possible, which means more compromised records (insiders might do that too, but they are more likely to take fewer records). A cyber criminal compromise is also likely to have a greater impact because they are far more likely to leverage the customer information in a way that will harm customers, and because their compromise included two control failures—failure of controls at the compromised workstation and in account privileges. Regulators and lawyers love a twofer.

At this point, we are pretty sure we'll analyze both of these scenarios because they are so different from each other and because they both seem to have the potential for significant outcomes. We won't know for sure until we have made our estimates and run the numbers, but that's what our gut is telling us at this point.

TALKING ABOUT RISK

This is a good time to point out (if you had not noticed) that the analyst's intuition and experience—those more subjective but vital elements of us as humans—still play a critical role in risk analysis. It will never be a purely objective practice. What you'll find, though, is that the more you do these kinds of analyses, the more finely tuned your critical thinking and analytical instincts will become. You'll be able to glance at a scenario and have a pretty decent notion of how much risk it represents. You'll find that after you've completed the analysis, your initial gut feeling was in the right ballpark. However, there's a warning attached to this. You have to be careful not to let that gut impression you had up-front bias your analysis. It can happen. We think we know something and then we look for things that validate or confirm that initial starting point. We don't do this consciously; it's one of those cognitive biases we humans are subject to.

This is another reason why it is so important to document the rationale behind your estimates. The process of documenting your rationale very often brings to the surface weaknesses in your thinking. It also provides an opportunity for others to examine your line of thinking and poke holes in it. For example, after reading this example analysis, some of you might decide you would approach it differently than we have, perhaps making different assumptions. That's fine. There is no perfect analysis and we all bring our own strengths (and weaknesses) to the process. However, consider the following: without an analytical model like FAIR and the rigor this process introduces, how likely is it that someone sticking a wet finger in the air is going to rate risk accurately? Yes, some people just have a gift for shooting from the hip with their analyses, but in our experience this is not the usual case, which is why we find so many holes in so many of the risk ratings we review.

PRIVILEGED INSIDER/SNOOPING/CONFIDENTIALITY
LOSS EVENT FREQUENCY

Note that we tend to work the loss event frequency (LEF) side of the equation first. That is not a requirement. We know people who prefer to start with loss magnitude, which they feel works better for them. You'll undoubtedly figure out your own approach.

The next decision we need to make is what level of abstraction we want to operate at on the LEF side of the ontology. Do we have sufficient historical loss data specific to this scenario that we can estimate LEF directly? Probably not in this scenario. We may have some data, though. A couple of employees were terminated in the past several years for misuse of privileges, which can be useful information, but it is not enough by itself for us decide to make our estimates at the LEF level. That being the case, let's look at the next lower level in the ontology—threat event frequency (TEF) and vulnerability.

The first thing that should jump to mind is that we already know how vulnerable we are—100%. These are privileged insiders, after all. It's great when one of the values is that easy to figure out. One of the things that being 100% vulnerable tells you is that every threat event is a loss event, which means that estimating TEF is the same thing as estimating LEF. That being the case, we are just going to estimate LEF directly for this scenario. Before we go on, we should point out that in scenarios like this you might find value in making your estimates all the way down at the Contact

Frequency and Probability of action level in the ontology. We very rarely do that, but it is an option when you need it.

As for data to help us with our estimates, we probably don't have confessions of the guilty to guide us, and we doubt that if we sent out a survey asking people who had inappropriate access whether they'd ever snooped around we'd get very useful results. We do have some data that can help us though, as you'll see.

As you'll recall from the chapter on measurement, you always start with the absurd when making a calibrated estimate. For LEF, we could use the following as our starting point:

- Minimum: once every 1000 years
- Maximum: a million times a year

In other words, we are saying that the population of privileged insiders with *inappropriate access privileges in this application* abuse that access by snooping at least once every 1000 years, but no more than a million times a year. (It is critical to keep in mind that our TEF estimate is constrained to this population of privileged users with inappropriate access, rather than all privileged users on that application. This is a very common mistake that we see people make.) Now we have to decide whether we are at least 90% confident in that estimate by asking whether we'd rather bet on that range or spin the wheel in the hopes of winning the hypothetical $1000. We're probably going to bet on our range, but before we make that decision, there's something we've forgotten. Wouldn't it be a good idea to know the size of this user population? How many people does 15% of accounts represent? Let's say that in this organization, 15% represents 30 users. In other words, 30 accounts out of a total population of 200 accounts have inappropriate access privileges in the application. This data point doesn't guide us directly to our estimate, but it's helpful nonetheless.

With the population of potentially abusive insiders defined, we can do some work on the maximum end of our estimated range. If, for example, we reduced our maximum value from 1,000,000 to 1000, would we still prefer to bet on our range or the wheel? A maximum estimate of 1000 abuses for a population of 30 employees seems high, but it raises a question. What constitutes an event? If an employee illicitly peeks at one customer record each day over the span of a week, is that one event with five compromised records, or five events with one compromised record each? The truth is, it usually doesn't matter which approach you choose, you just need to pick an approach and specify it as part of your rationale. You also need to remember the approach you have chosen because it will affect your loss magnitude estimates.

For this example, we are going to consider each instance of snooping to be an event, regardless of how many records were affected—e.g., when a privileged insider illicitly views records on five separate days, it represents five distinct loss events. With this approach in mind, how do we feel about our maximum estimate of 1000 versus spinning the wheel? Think about the 30 people involved. What are the odds that one or more of them do this and, if they do, how often would it be? Also think about the information at which they would be sneaking a peak. It's name, address, social security number, and date of birth. It occurs to us (now) that absent malicious intent, what's the value in looking at this information? It isn't financial or medical information, which is more likely to stimulate voyeuristic viewing. With this question in mind, we reach out to HR again about the two people who were terminated. As it turns out, they were selling the information rather than just snooping in it, which belongs in the malicious scenario and not this one. This means the organization has no history of privileged insiders abusing their access to snoop around in this data. Of course, this isn't saying it hasn't happened. Nonetheless, when we think about the relatively small population of users and the low value proposition for voyeurism, we reconsider whether the likelihood of simple snooping is high enough to warrant spending more time on this scenario. We decide it's not, document this in our analysis rationale, and move on. Here's our scenario table now (Table 8.4):

Table 8.4 The Scope Table with the Most Important Scenarios

Asset at Risk	Threat Community	Threat Type	Effect
Customer PII	Privileged insiders	Malicious	Confidentiality
Customer PII	Privileged insiders	Malicious	Integrity
Customer PII	Cyber criminals	Malicious	Confidentiality

Note that we are not saying privileged insider/snooping does not or could not take place; we're simply prioritizing the time we spend doing analyses.

PRIVILEGED INSIDER/MALICIOUS/CONFIDENTIALITY
LOSS EVENT FREQUENCY

Based on the new information from HR, we have decided to analyze the Privileged Insider/Malicious scenario next. This should go a bit faster because a little bit of the groundwork is already laid. We know that we are 100% vulnerable to this threat community, that we are going to operate at the LEF level of the ontology, that the size of the user population is 30 people, and we have defined what an event looks like. We'll also start with the same absurd estimate for LEF:

- Minimum: once every 1000 years
- Maximum: a million times a year

Now let's see if we can leverage that HR information to help us with our frequency estimate. There were two of these people in the past 3 years, so maybe we can use that to help us nail down an estimated minimum frequency—i.e., two events every 3 years, or said another way, a frequency of 0.67. There's a problem with using that value as our minimum, though. Those two employees didn't have inappropriate access. Their access levels were exactly what they were supposed to be. As a result, they were members of the 170 people with legitimate access and not members of the user population we're focused on. We could, however, assume that the users with inappropriate access privileges have roughly the same rate of abuse as that broader population. Based on that assumption, we figure out that 15%[1] of 0.67 comes to roughly 0.1 or once every 10 years. So how does that affect our estimates? Well, it's just one data point, so it could always be an outlier. Furthermore, these events could happen without ever going detected. Still, never let a good piece of data go to waste. Let's adjust our range to look like the following:

- Minimum: once every 20 years (0.05)
- Maximum: 100 times per year

You'll note that the minimum is actually lower than the 0.1 we came up with in the previous paragraph. We did this primarily because we don't like to narrow our ranges too fast. It's too easy to get aggressive with range narrowing and end up losing accuracy, especially with limited data. Remember we need accuracy with a useful degree of precision. Accuracy rules. We can always narrow the range further if additional considerations or data suggest it's appropriate to do so. With the minimum where it's at, we'd still bet on that end of our range rather than the wheel.

Given our definition of an event, we're also at least 95% confident in our maximum value (recall that we use 95% when we're evaluating our confidence in just one of the range values). We find it very difficult to believe that out of a population of 30 people with no criminal records (per HR hiring policy and background checks), there would be one or more people performing more than 100 malicious acts per year. The folks in HR agreed when we ran our thoughts past them. In fact, they suggested that the number was still too high, so we dropped it to 50. So now our range looks like this:

- Minimum: once every 20 years (0.05)
- Maximum: 50 times per year

We left that as our final range because we could not come up with rationale that allowed us to feel comfortable narrowing it further. It was an equivalent bet between the wheel and our range. It is a fairly wide range, but the simple fact is that we did not have enough data to narrow it further. This is common with privileged insider acts where so little history exists.

For our most likely estimate, we decided to simply go with what our single data point told us, 0.1. We couldn't think of any logical rationale to move up or down from that number. We'll choose a moderate confidence setting to reflect our single data point, as well as the other considerations and assumptions in play, in a combination of less than perfect confidence (Table 8.5).

Table 8.5 LEF Calculations for the Event of Cyber Criminal Analysis

LEF Minimum	LEF Most Likely	LEF Maximum	Confidence
0.05	0.1	50	Moderate

---

[1] A more accurate approach would be to use 17%, because 30 people are 17% of 170 people. This would be a slightly more accurate approach to use when assuming both groups have a similar rate of abuse. The difference in this case is nominal, so we opted to keep it simple in the example above.

Now that the frequency side of the equation is taken care of, it's time to think about loss magnitude—i.e., when/if this happens, how badly is it going to hurt?

LOSS MAGNITUDE

The first thing we have to do is determine which of the six loss forms are likely to materialize as *primary* loss from this type of event.

Productivity loss

We are quite certain that there would be no operational disruption in revenue generation, nor would there be any reason for personnel to sit idle. As a result, productivity loss is not a factor in this event.

Response costs

There would certainly be time spent investigating and dealing with the event, so response costs are a factor.

Replacement costs

Likewise, we would clearly terminate a perpetrator so there would be replacement costs associated with hiring a replacement (unless the organization decided to not backfill the position).

As with most scenarios, competitive advantage, fines and judgments, and reputation loss aren't relevant as forms of primary loss.

Primary response costs for an incident like this tends to fall into three categories: (1) person-hours spent in meetings regarding the incident, (2) investigation into what transpired, and (3) dealing with law enforcement. The magnitude of these costs will depend to some degree on how much information we have about the event and how easy it is to get the information. If the perpetrator confesses and it's easy to know the extent of the compromise, the amount of effort spent in investigation will be smaller. It also helps if we have application logs that narrow down the number of records that were accessed, which can be cross-referenced against legitimate work the employee was doing to determine which customers were compromised. Law enforcement might also have information for us. If we have to bring in external forensic expertise to determine what went on, the dollars start stacking up fast.

Breaking this down, then, we're going to make the following absurd starting estimate for person-hours:

- Minimum: 1 hour
- Maximum: one million hours

The "good news" here is that this type of incident has happened before so we can draw from those experiences. After talking with people who were involved in those earlier incidents, we learned that person-hours involved in response for each incident were somewhere between 100 and 200. Nobody was tracking the number of people involved or the level of effort, so this boiled down to a best guess. Based on this information, we adjusted our estimate to the following:

- Minimum: 50 hours
- Maximum: 400 hours

The minimum value represents a case where there are almost no complicating factors. The perpetrator confesses and very little investigation is required. The maximum represents a worst case where the event is more complicated and it is not even clear who the perpetrator was. When considering best case and worst-case conditions in this type of incident, these estimates are where we landed with an equivalent bet against the wheel. It's broader than the ranges experience in the two previous incidents because neither of those reflected what we considered to be best or worst-case conditions.

For most likely values, we split the difference from the previous events (150 hours), which we thought was a reasonable representation of what to expect. We did not choose high confidence for the most likely value, though, because there are too many uncertainties regarding complexity from one incident to another.

We then multiplied these values times the organization's average loaded employee hourly rate of $55 to come up with the following primary response cost estimates (Table 8.6):

Table 8.6 Primary LEF Response Estimates

Loss Type	Minimum	Most Likely	Maximum	Confidence
Primary response	$2750	$8250	$22,000	Moderate

Replacement costs for a terminated employee are very easy to come by because, unfortunately, there's so much data. Our HR colleagues suggested the following values for replacement costs in our analysis (Table 8.7):

Table 8.7 Primary LEF Response and Replacement Estimates

Loss Type	Minimum	Most Likely	Maximum	Confidence
Primary response	$2750	$8250	$22,000	Moderate
Primary replacement	$20,000	$30,000	$50,000	High

That's it for primary loss, which just leaves secondary loss.

SECONDARY LOSS

The first thing you need to do when thinking about secondary loss is identify the relevant secondary stakeholders. When dealing with customer information, two jump immediately to mind: the customers themselves, and regulators. Once you have the secondary stakeholders identified, you need to identify which forms of secondary loss you would expect to materialize. With that in mind:

Response
In an incident involving sensitive customer information, your response costs almost always include:

- The cost of notifying customers, and perhaps regulators
- The cost associated with increased volumes of customer support calls
- The cost of credit monitoring
- The cost of having people in meetings to strategize how to handle customers and regulators
- If the number of records is large enough, you are also likely to have legal and PR costs

NOTE: Every time you have secondary loss of any form, you have response costs of some sort. Every time. If one person picks up a phone to answer a customer's call regarding the event, that cost is considered secondary response. If one meeting is held to strategize on how to notify or deal with the secondary stakeholders those person-hours represent a secondary response cost.

Fines & Judgments
There is always the potential for fines, judgments, or sanctions of some sort when dealing with sensitive customer information compromises.

Reputation
Reputation damage is also a potential outcome from any breach of sensitive customer information.

Productivity and competitive advantage losses do not typically result from these types of incidents. In fact, productivity loss rarely materializes as secondary loss. If you're surprised about competitive advantage being excluded, you might want to refer to the chapter on Common Problems. In that chapter, we explain why competitive advantage is so commonly misused. Secondary replacement costs usually only apply when the organization has to compensate for a secondary stakeholder's losses (e.g., replacing stolen funds from a bank account).

Having established the relevant secondary loss forms, we can start estimating secondary loss event frequency (SLEF). Because SLEF is a percentage (i.e., the percentage of primary events that have secondary effects) your absurd starting points are always 0% and 100%. However, the good news (analytically) when dealing with sensitive customer information scenarios is that you almost always have to engage the customer if their private information has been breached (at least in the United States). This makes SLEF nearly 100%. We say nearly because there can be situations where notification is not required. Consequently, we used a minimum of 95% and a maximum of 100% for the ends of our distribution, and 98% for the most likely value. When a range is this narrow, we don't worry much about our choice of confidence level, and just leave it at moderate (Table 8.8).

Table 8.8 Secondary LEF Calculations

SLEF Minimum	LEF Most Likely	LEF Maximum	Confidence
95%	98%	100%	Moderate

As we noted above, secondary response costs take various forms, each of which need to be evaluated separately.

In a customer information compromise analysis, you want to answer the question of the number of compromised records. Based on the way the application in this scenario functions, if you have access to one customer, you have access to them all. Consequently, the best-case breach involves just one customer and the worst-case involves all 500,000. We can use those numbers as the minimum and maximum values. The most likely value was estimated to be toward the low end of the range for a couple of reasons. Both of the previous incidents involved relatively low numbers of affected customers (6 and 32), and the expectation is that most insiders are intent on minimizing their chances of being detected and don't want to try to fence half a million records. They're also more likely to be trying to satisfy a relatively marginal financial need. As a result, the most likely value was set at 20 records. The confidence level was set to moderate because of the inherent uncertainty regarding how many records a perpetrator might compromise.

- Compromised records minimum: 1
- Compromised records most likely: 20
- Compromised records maximum: 500,000
- Confidence level: Moderate

Customer notification costs are pretty easy to pin down, particularly if an organization has had to do it before, which most have (at least any that have been around a while and have a large number of customers). You'll want to get these numbers from your privacy office (if your organization has one) or whoever is responsible for notification. In this organization, notification costs were pretty well established for customers at $3 each. The organization has a boilerplate notification document already created, so there's very little effort required in customizing it. Note that this is the cost per notified customer and thus has to be multiplied by the number of affected customers.

- Customer notification cost minimum: $3 \times 1 = \$3$
- Customer notification cost most likely: $3 \times 20 = \$60$
- Customer notification cost maximum: $3 \times 500,000 = \$1.5M$
- Confidence level: Moderate

Customer support calls resulting from an incident are also sometimes included as a response cost. That said, some organizations choose to consider those a sunk cost in all but a worst-case scenario. After speaking with customer support management, we decided to include this cost in the analysis and use estimates they provided regarding the percentage of affected customers who would call and the average cost of each of those calls. Their numbers were 10% of the customers at $10 per call. Note that they opted to not provide a range, but instead gave us discrete values. We can work with that.

- Customer support costs minimum: $0
- Customer support costs most likely: $10\% \times \$10 \times 20 = \$20$
- Customer support costs maximum: $10\% \times \$10 \times 500,000 = \$500,000$
- Confidence level: Moderate

Credit monitoring costs are also well established in many organizations. For this organization, the privacy group provided two values for us to work with—the percentage of customers who would use the offer of credit monitoring, and the cost each of those would represent. Those numbers were 10% and $25, respectively.

- Credit monitoring costs minimum: $0
- Credit monitoring costs most likely: $10\% \times \$25 \times 20 = \$50$
- Credit monitoring costs maximum: $10\% \times \$25 \times 500,000 = \$1,250,000$
- Confidence level: Moderate

The person-hours involved in meetings also can be pretty sensitive to the number of compromised records. Based on the previous events as well as other related events the organization has had that involved customer information disclosures, the estimate ranges were establish as a minimum of 20 hours, maximum of 400 hours, and a most likely of 50 hours. Note that we followed the calibration process for getting these estimates from management. The hourly rate for these meetings was estimated to be higher than what was estimated for primary response losses because there would be more executive involvement. As a result, it was set at $125 per hour.

- Person-hours minimum: $20 \times \$125 = \$2500$
- Person-hours most likely: $50 \times \$125 = \$6250$
- Person-hours maximum: $400 \times \$125 = \$50,000$
- Confidence level: Moderate

The legal cost estimates our legal department provided varied widely based on the number of compromised records. The best-case minimum of course is $0. The maximum, assuming all 500,000 records were compromised, was estimated to be $500,000. The most likely value of $5000 was aligned with the estimated most likely number of compromised records cited earlier (20 records).

- Legal costs minimum: $0
- Legal costs most likely: $5000
- Legal costs maximum: $500,000
- Confidence level: Moderate

By the way, it can sometimes be like pulling teeth to get estimates from our legal brethren because the costs can vary so widely. Eventually they warm up to the idea though.

Public relations (PR) costs are also highly sensitive to the number of affected customers. The best case is always $0. The worst-case, when all customers are affected, can be quite large. The number provided by business management and marketing for a worst-case event of this sort was $3,000,000. The most likely value was $0, based on an expectation that a compromise of 20 records would not result in any PR costs.

- PR costs minimum: $0
- PR costs most likely: $0
- PR costs maximum: $3,000,000
- Confidence level: Moderate

If you haven't noticed, determining secondary response costs can be a lot of work. The good news is that the information is highly reusable from analysis to analysis, so it gets much easier quickly. With the work we've done above, the response costs come together as shown below (Table 8.9):

Table 8.9 Loss Estimates due to a Customer Information Compromise Analysis

	Minimum	Most Likely	Maximum	Confidence
Notification	$3	$60	$1,500,000	Moderate
Customer support	$0	$20	$500,000	Moderate
Credit monitoring	$0	$50	$1,250,000	Moderate
Meetings	$2500	$6250	$50,000	Moderate
Legal	$0	$5000	$500,000	Moderate
PR	$0	$0	$3,000,000	Moderate

These secondary response costs are totaled (and rounded) in the table below (Table 8.10).

Table 8.10 Secondary Response Costs

Loss Type	Minimum	Most Likely	Maximum	Confidence
Sec response	$2500	$11,500	$7,000,000	Moderate

Note that the confidence level in these estimates tracks with the confidence level set for the number of compromised records.

Believe it or not, things get quite a bit simpler for the remaining two forms of secondary loss—fines and judgments, and reputational damage.

Fines and judgment loss estimates come straight from the organization's legal department, and are actually relatively straightforward, or at least the minimum and most likely values are. The minimum value is $0, reflecting an expectation that in a best-case scenario where one record is compromised, there's a very real possibility there would be no fines or judgments. In fact, even with 20 affected customers (the most likely number of compromised records), the legal folks expected no fines or judgments. There could be some, of course, but they didn't anticipate any, so this value is $0, too. The maximum value gets more interesting and is based on a combination of public records for customer information breaches and the legal department's thinking. These values have been added to the table below (Table 8.11).

Table 8.11 Secondary Response and Fines and Judgment Costs

Loss Type	Minimum	Most Likely	Maximum	Confidence
Sec response	$2500	$11,500	$7,000,000	Moderate
Sec fines & judgments	$0	$0	$2,000,000	Moderate

Reputation damage is generally not as impenetrable a problem as many people think it is. You just have to ask the right people on the business side of the house.

Before going any further on reputation damage, we have to remember how this form of loss typically materializes for a commercial company—reduced market share, reduced stock price (if publically traded), increased cost of capital, and increased cost of acquiring and retaining employees.

In order to determine market share exposure, you have to answer two key questions: (1) how much is a customer worth to the business, and (2) what percentage of customers would be expected to terminate their relationship with the business from an event like this? The answer to the first question is usually represented as the average profit the organization realizes from a customer over the life of the relationship. Believe it or not, many organizations have this figured out, and you might be surprised how low the number is in some industries. In our case, this average profit per customer over the lifetime of the relationship is $150. If you're incredibly lucky, your organization will have data on the second question too, based on previous incidents. Otherwise, you'll need to speak with the marketing or other business folks to get their estimate. For the company in this scenario, the estimate was 5%; in other words, approximately one in 20 customers would choose to terminate the relationship, which is multiplied by the per-customer value and the number of compromised records:

- Market share loss minimum: $0
- Market share loss most likely: $5\% \times \$150 \times 20 = \$150$
- Market share loss maximum: $5\% \times \$150 \times 500,000 = \$3,750,000$
- Confidence level: Moderate

It is important to remember that damage to market share is not constrained to the loss of existing customers. A damaged reputation can also make market share growth slower and more difficult. This also should be part of the conversation with your business colleagues in marketing and sales. They may be able to make decent estimates on that aspect of loss, as well based on previously planned growth targets versus post-event growth estimates.

The question of the effect on stock price is another interesting one, with a lot of different opinions depending on who you talk to. There is beginning to be some better data and research on the matter, but it's still crucial to engage subject matter experts from the business. Their perception of the organization's stock price volatility is likely to be much better than any broad research out there today—or at least that is likely to be their opinion (which matters greatly). In this organization, the executive vice president of business strategy felt that even in a major event, any reduction in stock price would not exceed normal variances and would have a relatively short duration. For those reasons, we considered stock price exposure to be $0. Likewise, the executives did not expect there to be a meaningful change in the cost of capital or the cost of hiring or retaining employees.

The results of this analysis on reputation damage are shown below (Table 8.12).

Table 8.12 Secondary Loss Estimates Involving Reputation Damage

Loss Type	Minimum	Most Likely	Maximum	Confidence
Sec response	$2500	$11,500	$7,000,000	Moderate
Sec fines & judgments	$0	$0	$2,000,000	Moderate
Sec reputation	$0	$150	$3,750,000	Moderate

We hope you've noticed that most of the estimates related to secondary loss come from subject matter experts in the business rather than from us. This should always be the case. That said, many of these numbers are reusable across a variety of scenarios, which means you don't have to pester your business colleagues regularly in order to complete analyses. They truly appreciate this fact.

We're done acquiring numbers. It's time to plug them in and see what the results of the analysis are. The screenshot in Figure 8.1 shows our estimates entered into the FAIR application.

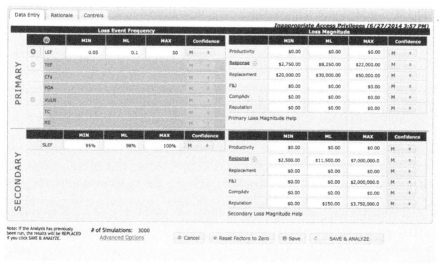

FIGURE 8.1

FAIR risk factors for inappropriate access privileges.

The screenshot in Figure 8.2 shows us the output of the analysis. Let's spend some time reviewing these results so that we can effectively communicate them to our stakeholders.

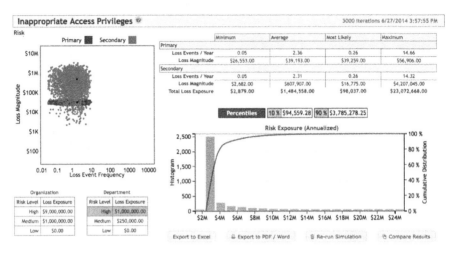

FIGURE 8.2

FAIR risk analysis for inappropriate access privileges.

The very first thing we always do when looking at the results is apply a mental litmus test—i.e., do the results appear credible? Always do this, especially when you're new to FAIR analyses. If the results look funky, begin troubleshooting your assumptions and data. With this in mind, the first place we're going to focus is on the "total loss exposure" line at the bottom of the table in the top-right corner of the screen. Of particular interest is the "most likely" value, which in this case is $98,037. (Going forward, we'll refer to these results as rounded numbers. It's a good habit to get into.) We focus here because if something's funky with the analysis, this is where it tends to be the most obvious. In this case, the most likely value doesn't surprise or worry us in any way regarding analysis credibility.

After the Most Likely value, our focus will depend somewhat on the question the analysis is trying to answer. Recalling that this analysis is all about gauging the level of risk from this audit finding, we can look in the lower left corner of the screen to see that this scenario qualifies as medium risk based on thresholds the organization has set. This value is determined by comparing the Total Loss Exposure Average value against those thresholds.

Other values we often find useful are the 10th and 90th percentiles. In some organizations, decisions regarding remediation efforts will be based off the 80th or 90th percentiles rather than the average. In this case, the 90th percentile value of just under $4M still falls within the organization's medium range. Another important number is the single loss event (SLE) magnitude value, which in this case is a little over $4M. This lets us know what the worst-case outcome turned out to be.

In this analysis, the other information on the screen is of less interest. You'll find that different parts of the results will serve different purposes based on the reason for the analysis and sometimes even who the information is going to be provided to.

There is one last thing to point out regarding these results, and that's the Total Loss Exposure Maximum value, which is a pretty big number—roughly $23M. However, there is something important to recognize about this value in this scenario; it's driven in large part from the maximum primary loss event number, which is 14. This means that in order to experience this amount of loss an organization would have to experience all 14 of those loss events. Some people looking at this would say, "After the first event we'd make whatever changes are necessary to prevent the other 13." That's a great idea assuming you're even aware that the first event took place. Keep in mind that these events can take place without anyone knowing about it for a long time, which means Bob the nefarious customer account representative could conceivably perform 14 malicious acts before anyone noticed. Think about it this way—every time one of those events takes place without anyone noticing, the organization essentially writes a check to cover those losses. Nobody knows the check was written yet when the events come to light, you can bet that any outstanding checks will be cashed. So yes, it is possible for the organization to experience the effects of 14 loss events in this scenario.

Now that we have the results, let's spend a little time talking about control opportunities. The obvious one is to improve access privilege management because it's obviously not working as well as it should. Think about it. If that control were improved such that only half as many users had inappropriate access, the loss exposure would be cut in half as well. The cost involved in improving a process is usually not that big, but the return on that investment can be a significant reduction in risk.

Another control opportunity is to limit how many customer accounts each user has access to. This might be easy if the organization has some logical distribution of responsibilities, perhaps by geographic region, etc. If this were implemented and instead of all 500,000 customers each user only had access to, for example, 25,000, the maximum values used in the loss magnitude estimates would come way down, which would also strongly affect the maximum and average level of risk. Note that this kind of change would not only play a role in the risk associated with this scenario, but also every other scenario involving malicious acts against this application, which could be a huge payback in terms of risk reduction.

Yet another control opportunity is related to logging. This one may be a bit more complicated and expensive to implement, but it's worth thinking about because like the one above, it is relevant to a broader set of scenarios. If the application's logging could establish normal values for the number of customer records each user accessed, it could flag instances where user access varied significantly. This would help in two ways: (1) it would provide early warning if Bob accessed 50 accounts in one day when his normal value was 20, suggesting that Bob either had an extra few doses of caffeine or he was up to something, and (2) if Bob's normal activity was 20 and all of a sudden it dropped to 0, it might suggest that his access still existed but he was not doing this work anymore—i.e., the access privilege management process might have failed. Of course, he might have gone on vacation too, so there would probably need to be logic in the flagging equation that only sets a warning if the drop-off persisted for more than a certain length of time.

The analysis of this scenario is complete. As we said earlier, sometimes all you'll need to complete is one analysis in your scenario table. If the results of this analysis had fallen into the high range, there might be no reason to do another analysis. Fortunately, at least from our perspective in writing this book, the results suggest the need to analyze the next scenario.

CYBER CRIMINAL/MALICIOUS/CONFIDENTIALITY

The good news is that parts of this analysis will go much more quickly than the last one because we'll be able to use a lot of the same data.

LOSS EVENT FREQUENCY

Determining loss event frequency for this scenario will be interesting because it will demonstrate considerations and approaches that will be useful repeatedly when dealing with cyber criminal scenarios.

To begin with, we have to be clear on the one key requirement that determines when cyber criminals are a relevant threat community relative to this audit finding—the system compromised by a cyber criminal has to be one that's used by an employee who has inappropriate access privileges. As we learned in the previous analysis, there are 30 of these users. This means we have a relatively small "attack surface area," which is a good thing. An analysis that included all 200 employees with access to this application would have almost seven times as much surface area and thus nearly seven times the exposure. Depending on how this analysis turns out, it might be worthwhile to evaluate that broader scenario. We won't do it in this book, but you're encouraged to try it at home.

The first question we always ask when estimating LEF directly is, "Do we have any known history of this event occurring?" In this case, we learned that the organization did not have any evidence that cyber criminals had ever gained access to customer information by compromising the workstation of an employee with inappropriate access privileges on this application. Nor, in fact, had this occurred within the broader population of users with access to this application. That being the case, we wanted to find out how frequently cyber criminals gained and leveraged this kind of control over systems used by the organization's entire user population. For this, we turned to our colleagues in security operations who wrestle cyber criminals and malware every day. Data from the organization's anti-malware security tools suggested that infections of user systems were relatively low in general, and that infections where this kind of remote access would exist were quite a bit lower—on the order of once per month—and responded to rapidly. The reliability of this information was considered pretty good given the advanced anti-malware solutions the organization had in place (it was not relying simply on antivirus). Of course, no security tool or even combination of security tools is perfect, but this provided a decent reference from which to base our estimates.

Given that the general user population of 10,000 people had roughly 12 infections per year, the frequency of infection for our 30 users would be 0.036 times per year, which is a little less than once every 25 years. We'll use that as the basis for our LEF estimates, but we have to document a key assumption that goes along with it—that every infection of this type on these systems results in a compromise of the application. In other words, we are ignoring the fact that a cyber criminal might gain control of one of these systems and not attack the underlying application. Our decision to ignore this possibility is a conservative approach (i.e., slightly paranoid), which increases the LEF estimate. Stakeholders or other interested parties can push back on this assumption if they like. Whenever we decide to take a conservative approach like this, we make sure we document in the rationale that we've done so. Based on the rationale above, our LEF estimates are shown in the following table (Table 8.13):

Table 8.13 LEF Calculations for Anti-malware Security Tools

LEF Minimum	LEF Most Likely	LEF Maximum	Confidence
0.03	0.04	0.1	Moderate

We used the data from our security operations colleagues (rounded up) for the most likely value and then subtracted and added to that for the minimum and maximum values (still applying the equivalent bet approach to arrive at 90% confidence for the range). For our most likely value, we set our confidence level to moderate based on the quality of information we were working from.

LOSS MAGNITUDE

Estimating loss magnitude for this scenario is going to be much easier than in the earlier scenario because we're going to leverage a lot of that earlier data, particularly for secondary losses. Think about it. The minimum and maximum values should be exactly the same for most of the loss forms—i.e., the best case is that only a single customer record is compromised, and the worst-case is that all 500,000 get stolen, so all of the estimates that are sensitive to those values will remain the same. Therefore, the only value that might change for most of the estimates is the most likely value.

Our primary loss estimates will vary a bit, though. For one thing, we almost certainly won't be terminating the employee whose workstation was compromised, so that loss form goes away. Offsetting that a bit, however, is the fact that we will definitely be doing forensics in order to be as certain as possible of what transpired. Rather than depend solely on our internal forensics capabilities for an event like this, we might bring in external forensic experts, which can cost a bundle. Our forensic estimates came to:

- Forensic costs minimum: $0 (we rely completely on internal resources)
- Forensic costs most likely: $50,000
- Forensic costs maximum: $200,000
- Confidence level: Moderate

We'll add the cost of forensics to the primary response cost estimates we used in the previous analysis. These values are shown in the table below (Table 8.14).

Table 8.14 Primary Response and Replacement Cost Estimates for Forensic Analysis

Loss Type	Minimum	Most Likely	Maximum	Confidence
Prim response	$2750	$58,250	$222,000	Moderate
Prim replacement	$0	$0	$0	

SECONDARY LOSS

Secondary loss event frequency doesn't change at all. We still anticipate having to deal with secondary stakeholders almost every time an event like this takes place (Table 8.15).

Table 8.15 SLEF Estimations

SLEF Minimum	LEF Most Likely	LEF Maximum	Confidence
95%	98%	100%	Moderate

As we mentioned above, the most likely values are likely to be the only things that change in many of the secondary loss estimates. The reason these values might change is because we assume the cyber criminal is going to try to take as many records as possible, whereas the privileged insider was considered more likely to take a smaller volume. In order to decide whether a change is necessary, we have to consider how much time the cyber criminal has from the moment they compromise the workstation until they figure out the kind of access they have and can leverage it. This is where our anti-malware tool's ability to rapidly detect a compromise comes into play—at least as long as the response function is also timely. Detection is of far less value if response is slow. The good news is that the average response time for our security operations team on these types of events is pretty good given everything they deal with—just under 8 hours. This means the cyber criminal usually has less than 8 hours to realize they are sitting on a gold mine of customer information and pilfer the goods. With this in mind, our estimates for the most likely number of compromised records will increase, but not dramatically. We will, however lower our confidence rating for the most likely value because we aren't sure how rapidly these threat agents could take information off of the application in that time span.

- Compromised records minimum: 1
- Compromised records most likely: 500
- Compromised records maximum: 500,000
- Confidence level: Low

Customer notification costs change in step with the changes to compromised records:

- Customer notification cost minimum: $3 \times 1 = \$3$
- Customer notification cost most likely: $\$3 \times 500 = \$1500$
- Customer notification cost maximum: $\$3 \times 500{,}000 = \$1.5M$
- Confidence level: Low

Customer support costs change in a similar manner:

- Customer support costs minimum: $0
- Customer support costs most likely: $10\% \times \$10 \times 500 = \$500$
- Customer support costs maximum: $10\% \times \$10 \times 500{,}000 = \$500{,}000$
- Confidence level: Low

As do credit monitoring costs:

- Credit monitoring costs minimum: $0
- Credit monitoring costs most likely: $10\% \times \$25 \times 500 = \$1250$
- Credit monitoring costs maximum: $10\% \times \$25 \times 500{,}000 = \$1{,}250{,}000$
- Confidence level: Low

Person-hours costs for time spent in meetings are not as directly associated with the number of compromised records; however, we will increase the most likely value because the nature of those meetings may change, because the threat community was a cyber criminal versus an insider.

- Person-hours minimum: $20 \times \$125 = \$2500$
- Person-hours most likely: $50 \times \$125 = \$10{,}000$
- Person-hours maximum: $400 \times \$125 = \$50{,}000$
- Confidence level: Low

The most likely estimate for legal costs is increased due to an expectation that regulators will take a greater interest in this type of event. It's one thing to have a privileged insider to go rogue, it's another to have your perimeter breached by a cyber criminal.

- Legal costs minimum: $0
- Legal costs most likely: $50,000
- Legal costs maximum: $500,000
- Confidence level: Low

Although PR costs also tend to be highly sensitive to the size of a breach, a compromise of 500 records was not expected to generate any measurable increase, so those values remain the same.

- PR costs minimum: $0
- PR costs most likely: $0
- PR costs maximum: $3,000,000
- Confidence level: Low

The table below shows the breakdown of our new estimates for secondary response costs (Table 8.16):

Table 8.16 Breakdown of New Estimates for Secondary Response Costs

	Minimum	Most Likely	Maximum	Confidence
Notification	$3	$1500	$1,500,000	Low
Customer support	$0	$500	$500,000	Low
Credit monitoring	$0	$1250	$1,250,000	Low
Meetings	$2500	$10,000	$50,000	Low
Legal	$0	$50,000	$500,000	Low
PR	$0	$0	$3,000,000	Low
Total	$2500	$65,000	$7,000,000	Low

Our legal colleagues suggested increasing the estimated fines and judgments most likely value, based on an expectation that one or more state Attorney General would want their pound of flesh, even with a relatively small compromise of 500 records. Their suggestion was to use $10,000 as an estimate. The fact that our confidence level would be set to low on this value eased their concerns about how reliable that most likely value was (Table 8.17).

Table 8.17 SLEF Estimates with Respect to Attorney Generals' Expectation

Loss Type	Minimum	Most Likely	Maximum	Confidence
Sec response	$2500	$65,000	$7,000,000	Low
Sec fines & judgments	$0	$10,000	$2,000,000	Low

The most likely value for reputation damage changed in lockstep with the change in our compromised records most likely value.

- Market share loss minimum: $0
- Market share loss most likely: $5\% \times \$150 \times 500 = \$3750$
- Market share loss maximum: $5\% \times \$150 \times 500,000 = \$3,750,000$
- Confidence level: Low

All of these changes are summarized in the secondary loss table below (Table 8.18):

Table 8.18 SLEF Estimates Involving Reputation

Loss Type	Minimum	Most Likely	Maximum	Confidence
Sec response	$2500	$65,000	$7,000,000	Low
Sec fines & judgments	$0	$10,000	$2,000,000	Low
Sec reputation	$0	$3750	$3,750,000	Low

As you can see, this second estimate gathering effort takes much less time than the first, which becomes more common as you do more analyses.

The screenshot in Figure 8.3 shows our input values in the FAIR application.

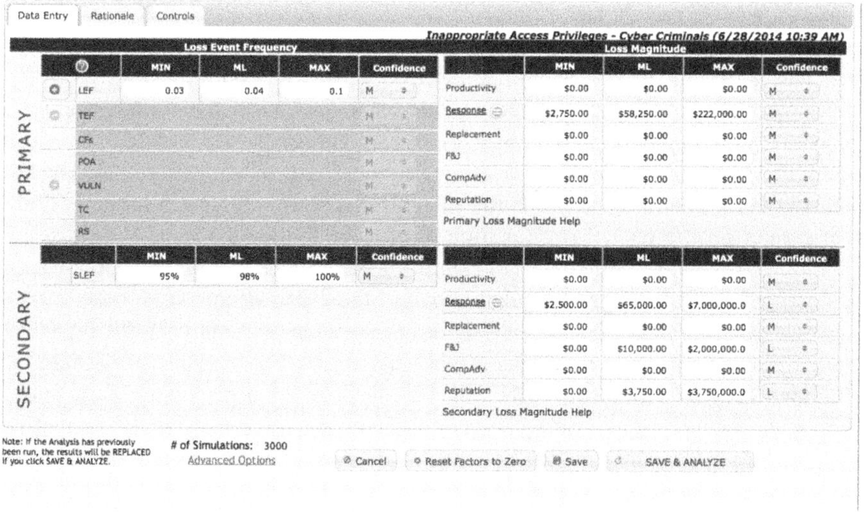

FIGURE 8.3

FAIR risk factors for cyber criminal—malicious—confidentiality.

The screenshot in Figure 8.4 shows the results when we crunch the numbers:

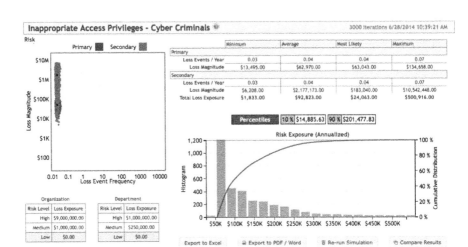

FIGURE 8.4

FAIR risk analysis of cyber criminal—malicious—confidentiality.

Here again, a quick mental litmus test of the results leaves us comfortable that we can stand up and defend the analysis. There are a few things worth pointing out about the results, though.

As you would expect, the lower LEF results in a lower total loss exposure. Of particular note is the much lower maximum value, which is not surprising given our inputs. We also see that the qualitative rating for this scenario is low (in the bottom-left corner), which reflects the much lower total loss exposure average. The SLE values, however, are somewhat higher than in the privileged insider scenario. The last thing to point out on this screen is the shape of the green histogram in the bottom-right corner. This fatter tail is a function of the low confidence levels we chose for our most likely value estimates. This simply means there is a higher potential for incidents to have loss magnitudes in that part of the distribution.

A last point to make on this analysis has to do with its reliance on the organization's advanced anti-malware management capabilities. For example, if we had the same anti-malware solution in place but were terrible about responding in a timely manner, the analysis results would be very different. As you can see in the screenshot in Figure 8.5, simply changing the loss magnitude most likely values to reflect the fact that the cyber criminal has more time to find and exfiltrate customer data increases the loss exposure significantly.

We would have similar results if we didn't have advanced anti-malware at all.

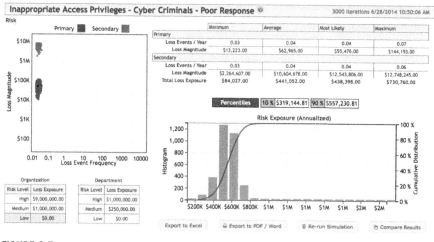

FIGURE 8.5

FAIR risk analysis of cyber criminal—malicious—confidentiality with bad response.

ANALYSIS WRAP UP

Having analyzed these two scenarios, we didn't feel the need to analyze the privileged insider/malicious/integrity scenario. The primary consideration driving that decision was that the act of changing data is much more likely to be identified than simply stealing data, which means it brings higher risk to the perpetrator. Higher risk drives a lower TEF. Based on this, we felt the risk associated with the integrity scenario was incremental relative to the two we already analyzed. These are the kinds of questions you need to ask and answer in order to decide whether you've done enough analysis. When you first start performing FAIR analyses, it will be harder for you to know when to call it quits, so you'll be more likely to analyze more scenarios than you probably need to. This is not a bad thing, because besides providing even better information for decision making, you'll also be calibrating your understanding of risk. Over time, you'll be better able to comfortably (and appropriately) decide when to pull the plug on an analysis.

As a result of these analyses, we're comfortable setting the severity of this audit finding as medium so that it can be appropriately prioritized among the many other issues and opportunities the organization faces.

By the way, you probably have invested more time in reading this example analysis than you'll spend in performing many analyses. Especially after you've done this for a while, you'll be surprised how quick you can become at it and how much of the data is reusable.

TALKING ABOUT RISK

After you've performed a couple of analyses on inappropriate access privilege scenarios, the process of performing additional similar analyses becomes much faster. In fact, after a few of these, you may not feel the need to perform additional analyses in many cases, because you'll have a body of previous work to which you can refer. You'll also have a more calibrated sense of these scenarios and their factors, which will make your own wet finger in the air more reliable—but never infallible, of course.

UNENCRYPTED INTERNAL NETWORK TRAFFIC

NOTE: As you do analyses, you will find that your rationale can be (and should be in most cases) concise. There is a balance to be struck between the value in documenting the reasoning that underlies an analysis and the level of effort spent in documentation. In practice, documented rationale for an analysis sometimes doesn't even fill a page of text. Other times it might be several pages. Most of the documented rationale we generate is shorter rather than longer and very often some of it is borrowed from analyses we've done previously. In very unusual circumstances documentation might run a dozen pages or more. These are pretty rare however, and when you're faced with one of these it's typically because the problem is believed to be a big deal, in which case it's time well spent.

You may notice that some of the rationale and descriptions in the scenarios below are similar (and in some cases identical) to the Inappropriate Access Privileges example. This is intentional for two reasons:(1) we are not assuming that you have already read the earlier example and would hate for you to miss out on some of the important points we made, and (2) it's important to reinforce foundational components for those that are new to FAIR. There are, of course, some important differences in this example that make it worth reading, even if you've committed the previous example to memory.

PURPOSE

Determine the level of risk associated with unencrypted sensitive information flowing across the organization's internal network. The reason for this analysis is to inform a decision regarding whether to deploy encryption on the organization's internal network.

BACKGROUND

The annual information security audit performed by a global security consulting organization identified that sensitive customer information is flowing unencrypted over the organization's internal network. They are recommending that network encryption be deployed internally.

ASSET(S) AT RISK

Because this organization is a financial services provider, the sensitive information in question is a combination of credit card numbers, customer financial information, and personal private information (e.g., name, address, date of birth, and social security number). This organization services roughly five million customers.

TCOM(S)

Threat communities include privileged and nonprivileged insiders, as well as cyber criminals who might penetrate the external network perimeter.

THREAT TYPE(S)

The primary threat type is considered to be malicious in nature; however, an argument has been presented that encrypting network traffic would also prevent unintentional viewing by network professionals during the course of their duties.

THREAT EFFECT(S)

Confidentiality is the threat effect of interest. Availability and integrity are not considered relevant to the question of whether to encrypt or not. An argument was made that integrity could be relevant to the question of encryption, but the team considered that to be unlikely enough to not even include it in the initial scoping table.

SCOPE

Based on the considerations above, our scope table at this point looks like this (Table 8.19):

Table 8.19 Scope Table for Levels of Risk Associated with Unencrypted Sensitive Information

Asset at Risk	Threat Community	Threat Type	Effect
Customer information	Privileged insiders	Malicious	Confidentiality
Customer information	Privileged insiders	Accidental	Confidentiality
Customer information	Nonprivileged insiders	Malicious	Confidentiality
Customer information	Cyber criminals	Malicious	Confidentiality

A scoping table with only four scenarios is not that intimidating. Nonetheless, we always want to be as efficient as possible in our analysis efforts, so we'll spend a few minutes thinking about each of these to see if there are good reasons to exclude any of them.

Recall that the anticipated frequency and magnitude of a scenario are the main reasons for it being included or excluded in scope, particularly when comparing one scenario to another. Therefore, you want to ask yourself whether any of these scenarios are significantly more (or less) likely to occur than the others, and whether any of them are likely to result in significantly more (or less) damage.

In this analysis, the privileged insider/accidental scenario jumps immediately to mind as a candidate for exclusion. This is primarily due to the fact there is likely to be no loss associated with their access to the information. Consequently, it's decided to exclude that scenario, leaving us with just three scenarios (Table 8.20):

Table 8.20 Slimmed Scope Table

Asset at Risk	Threat Community	Threat Type	Effect
Customer information	Privileged insiders	Malicious	Confidentiality
Customer information	Nonprivileged insiders	Malicious	Confidentiality
Customer information	Cyber criminals	Malicious	Confidentiality

Of the remaining three scenarios, it could be argued that the privileged insiders are less likely to capture and illicitly use as much data, which would equate to lower most likely loss magnitude estimates. They are, however, considered the most likely threat agent due to their access, so that scenario will stay in scope.

Loss magnitude for the nonprivileged insiders and cyber criminals is expected to be the same based on an assumption that since both have to go to some lengths to perpetrate the theft, they will most likely maximize their reward by taking as much data as they can. The frequency of attacks is expected to be higher for nonprivileged insiders than cyber criminals, though, because it's an easier attack for them to perform due to the fact that there are more of them and they already are in a position to attack the network. For now, scenarios will remain in scope, although the decision is made to analyze the nonprivileged insider scenario before the cyber criminal scenario. This is because if the nonprivileged insider results were low enough, there would be no reason to analyze the cyber criminal scenario, which should be even lower.

The question was raised as to the possibility of a physical attack against a network transmission line. Although that scenario is a possibility, the probability was considered so remote that the decision was made to exclude it from the analysis. If it had been considered worth analyzing, it would represent a different attack vector than the other scenarios, which would add another column (attack vector) to our scope table and potentially another several scenarios. As you can imagine, for some scenarios where multiple attack vectors are possible, this can add up quickly. In those cases, you want to be especially diligent in thinking through which scenarios should remain in scope.

ANALYSIS

In some cases, there is no obvious reason to choose one scenario over another to start with. In this case, we believe the privileged insider attack is the most likely of the three but potentially with a lower impact. As we noted above, though, we've decided to do the nonprivileged insider scenario before the cyber criminal scenario. We flipped a coin and decided to start with the privileged insider.

PRIVILEGED INSIDER/CONFIDENTIALITY

Because this is a privileged insider scenario, we already know we're 100% vulnerable to a threat event. As a result, we'll operate at the LEF level of the ontology for this analysis.

LOSS EVENT FREQUENCY

As always, the first question is whether the organization has had any known loss events of this type. The answer, as it often is in these types of scenarios, is no, which means we're left to make those more speculative estimates none of us prefers. The absurd estimates below are what we often start with anytime we're dealing with privileged insiders and no history to work from:

- Minimum: once every 1000 years
- Maximum: a million times a year

At this point, we start identifying factors that help to guide or limit our ability to narrow the range. We invariably want to know the size of the threat community, whether there has been any history of disgruntled or criminal behavior in the population, what the hiring and management practices are like, etc. We also want to consider the likelihood of a compromise by someone in this threat community going undetected. Based on the information we get from our inquiries, we begin to narrow the range until we get to our point of indifference between betting on our range versus the wheel.

In this hypothetical scenario, we'll say our threat population is comprised of between 10 and 15 people, all of whom have impeccable work histories and no criminal backgrounds. Given little else to work from, we end up with the minimum and maximum values below:

- Minimum: once every 20 years
- Maximum: five times per year

A question commonly comes up about an estimate like our maximum. Are we saying it couldn't happen more than five times per year? No, of course not. We're just placing a bet that there's less than a 5% chance of that happening, given the information we're working from. The process of making calibrated estimates doesn't guarantee accuracy; it only improves the odds. If we feel the need for absolute certainty, we can keep our range at the absurd values or at whatever point we remain 100% confident— which still doesn't guarantee accuracy. The problem then is whether the estimate has a useful degree of precision.

NOTE: In all seriousness, if someone is just too uncomfortable making calibrated estimates about these kinds of values, they should perhaps look for another line of work. Risk analysis may not be for them. That's not a disability; there are probably things they excel at that someone comfortable with making range estimates would be uncomfortable with. We've worked with these people, and it can be viscerally uncomfortable for them.

For a most likely value, we are going to choose a value toward the lower end of the scale. This was chosen based on our experience and beliefs regarding these professionals. Our confidence level in this most likely value will be low however, due to the absence of data (Table 8.21).

Table 8.21 LEF Calculations

LEF Minimum	LEF Most Likely	LEF Maximum	Confidence
0.05	0.07	5	Low

Now that the frequency side of the equation is taken care of, it's time to think about loss magnitude—i.e., when/if this happens, how badly is it going to hurt?

LOSS MAGNITUDE

The first thing we have to do is determine which of the six loss forms are likely to materialize as the *primary* loss from this type of event.

Productivity loss

We are quite certain that there would be no operational disruption in revenue generation from this event, nor would there be any reason for personnel to sit idle. As a result, productivity loss is not a factor in this event.

Response costs

There would certainly be time spent investigating and dealing with the event, so response costs are a factor.

Replacement costs

Likewise, we would clearly terminate a perpetrator so there would be replacement costs associated with hiring a replacement (unless the organization decided to not backfill the position).

As with most scenarios, competitive advantage, fines and judgments, and reputation loss are not relevant as forms of primary loss.

Primary response costs for an incident like this tends to fall into three categories: (1) person-hours spent in meetings regarding the incident, (2) investigation into what transpired, and (3) dealing with law enforcement. The magnitude of these costs will depend to some degree on how much information we have about the event and how easy it is to get the information. If the perpetrator confesses and it's easy to know the extent of the compromise, the amount of effort spent in investigation will be smaller. Law enforcement might also have information that helps with the investigation. If we have to bring in external forensic expertise to determine what went on, the dollars start stacking up fast.

As usual, we are going to make the following absurd starting estimate for primary person-hours:

- Minimum: 1 hour
- Maximum: one million hours

After talking with colleagues from HR and with people who have been with the organization a long time, we learned that there is no known history of insider confidentiality breaches in the company. This is, of course, a good thing from an organizational point of view, but a disadvantage from the perspective of making loss estimates. When faced with this situation, we begin asking questions of the CIRT coordinator. Have they run any practice drills for incidents of this nature, either table-top exercises or something more realistic? In this case, the response is that they have not run anything quite like this but they have taken the time to identify who all the stakeholders would be in such an event. They have, however, had to deal with other confidentiality breach events (mismailings of monthly statements, etc.) and were able to provide some rough numbers. Our expectation is that an event like our scenario would probably involve a heftier response than the incidents their numbers came from, but it gives us something to work from. We begin whittling down our range until we reach our point of indecision on our range versus the wheel, which is shown below:

- Minimum: 80 hours
- Maximum: 500 hours

In the absence of any reason to the contrary, we chose to split the difference for our most likely values (290 hours). We elected to use a low confidence setting for our most likely value because our lack of data or rationale to do otherwise.

We then multiplied these values times the organization's average loaded employee hourly rate of $50 to come up with the following primary response cost estimates (Table 8.22):

Table 8.22 Primary Response Estimates

Loss Type	Minimum	Most Likely	Maximum	Confidence
Primary response	$4000	$14,500	$25,000	Low

Replacement costs for a terminated employee are very easy to come by because, unfortunately, there's so much data. Our HR colleagues suggested the following values for replacement costs for a person terminated from this type of position (Table 8.23):

Table 8.23 Primary Response and Replacement Estimates

Loss Type	Minimum	Most Likely	Maximum	Confidence
Primary response	$4000	$14,500	$25,000	Low
Primary replacement	$40,000	$50,000	$80,000	Moderate

That's it for primary loss, which just leaves secondary loss.

SECONDARY LOSS

The first thing you need to do when thinking about secondary loss is identify the relevant secondary stakeholders. When dealing with customer information, two jump immediately to mind: the customers themselves, and regulators. Once you have the secondary stakeholders identified, you need to identify which forms of secondary loss you would expect to materialize. With that in mind:

Response
In an incident involving sensitive customer information, your response costs almost always include:

- The cost of notifying customers, and perhaps regulators
- The cost associated with increased volumes of customer support calls
- The cost of credit monitoring
- The cost of having people in meetings to strategize how to handle customers and regulators
- If the number of records is large enough, you're also likely to have legal costs and PR costs

NOTE: Every time you have secondary loss of any form, you have response costs of some sort. Every time. If one person picks up a phone to answer a customer's call regarding the event, that cost is considered secondary response. If one meeting is held to strategize on how to notify or deal with the secondary stakeholders, those person-hours represent a secondary response cost.

Fines & Judgments
There is always the potential for fines, judgments, or sanctions of some sort when dealing with sensitive customer information compromises.

Reputation
Reputation damage is also a potential outcome from any breach of sensitive customer information.

Productivity and competitive advantage losses do not typically result from these types of incidents. In fact, productivity loss rarely materializes as secondary loss. If you're surprised about competitive advantage being excluded, you might want to refer to the chapter on Common Problems. In that chapter, we explain why competitive advantage is so commonly misused. Secondary replacement costs usually only apply when the organization has to compensate for a secondary stakeholder's losses (e.g., replacing stolen funds from a bank account).

Having established the relevant secondary loss forms, we can start estimating secondary loss event frequency (SLEF). Because SLEF is a percentage (i.e., the percentage of primary events that have secondary effects) your absurd starting points are always 0% and 100%. However, the good news (analytically) when dealing with sensitive customer information scenarios is that you almost always have to engage the customer if their private information has been breached (at least in the United States). This makes SLEF nearly 100%. We say nearly because there can be situations where notification is not required. Consequently, we used a minimum of 95% and a maximum of 100% for the ends of our distribution, and 98% for the most likely value. When a range is this narrow, we don't worry much about our choice of confidence level, and just leave it at moderate (Table 8.24).

Table 8.24 Secondary LEF Calculations

SLEF Minimum	LEF Most Likely	LEF Maximum	Confidence
95%	98%	100%	Moderate

As we noted above, secondary response costs take various forms, each of which need to be evaluated separately.

In a customer information compromise analysis, you want to answer the question of the number of compromised records. The best case in these types of scenarios is that a single customer record is compromised. The worst case is that they're all compromised. At the beginning of the analysis, we learned that this organization has a total of five million customer records. That said, only four million of them are active customers whose data might be flying across the network. As a result, our maximum will be set to four million records. Have you noticed that our best-case condition (one record) and worst-case condition (4 million records) are not only the ends of our range, but also the absurd starting point? Unfortunately, in these scenarios we often don't have an opportunity to narrow the range off of our starting point. The range is the range.

The most likely value was estimated to be toward the low end of the range, because the expectation is that most insiders are intent on minimizing their chances of being detected and don't want to try to fence four million records. They're also more likely to be trying to satisfy a relatively marginal financial need. As a result, the most likely value was set at 50 records. The confidence level was set to moderate because although there is significant uncertainty regarding how many records a perpetrator might compromise, not all of the customer records (even the active ones) transit the network regularly. If we had selected low confidence, we would capture more samples from the high end of the distribution than is likely to be reasonable.

- Compromised records minimum: one
- Compromised records most likely: 50
- Compromised records maximum: 4,000,000
- Confidence level: Moderate

Customer notification costs are pretty easy to pin down, particularly if an organization has had to do it before, which most have (at least any that have been around a while and have a large number of customers). You'll want to get these numbers from your privacy office (if your organization has one) or whoever is responsible for notification. In this organization, notification costs were pretty well established for customers at $3 each. The organization has a boilerplate notification document already created, so there's very little effort required in customizing it. Note that this is the cost per notified customer and thus has to be multiplied by the number of affected customers.

- Customer notification cost minimum: $3 \times 1 = \$3$
- Customer notification cost most likely: $3 \times 50 = \$150$
- Customer notification cost maximum: $3 \times 4,000,000 = \$12M$
- Confidence level: Moderate

Customer support calls resulting from an incident are also sometimes included as a response cost. That said, some organizations choose to consider those a sunk cost in all but a worst-case scenario. After speaking with customer support management, we decided to include this cost in the analysis and use estimates they provided regarding the percentage of affected customers who would call and the average cost of each of those calls. Their numbers were 10% of the customers at $10 per call. Note that they opted to not provide a range but instead gave us discrete values. We can work with that.

- Customer support costs minimum: $0
- Customer support costs most likely: $10\% \times \$10 \times 50 = \$50$
- Customer support costs maximum: $10\% \times \$10 \times 4{,}000{,}000 = \$4{,}000{,}000$
- Confidence level: Moderate

Credit monitoring costs are also well established in many organizations. For this organization, the privacy group provided two values for us to work with—the percentage of customers who would use the offer of credit monitoring, and the cost each of those would represent. Those numbers were 10% and $25, respectively.

- Credit monitoring costs minimum: $0
- Credit monitoring costs most likely: $10\% \times \$25 \times 50 = \$125$
- Credit monitoring costs maximum: $10\% \times \$25 \times 4{,}000{,}000 = \$10{,}000{,}000$
- Confidence level: Moderate

The person-hours involved in meetings also can be pretty sensitive to the number of compromised records. Based on the previous events as well as other related events the organization has had that involved customer information disclosures, the estimate ranges were establish as a minimum of 20 hours, maximum of 400 hours, and a most likely of 50 hours. Note that we followed the calibration process for getting these estimates from management. The hourly rate for these meetings was estimated to be higher than what was estimated for primary response losses because there would be more executive involvement. As a result, it was set at $125 per hour.

- Person-hours minimum: $20 \times \$125 = \$2500$
- Person-hours most likely: $50 \times \$125 = \$6250$
- Person-hours maximum: $400 \times \$125 = \$50{,}000$
- Confidence level: Moderate

The legal cost estimates our legal department provided varied widely based on the number of compromised records. The best-case minimum of course is $0. The maximum, assuming all 4,000,000 records were compromised, was estimated to be $2,000,000. The most likely value of $15,000 was aligned with the estimated most likely number of compromised records cited earlier (50 records).

- Legal costs minimum: $0
- Legal costs most likely: $15,000
- Legal costs maximum: $4,000,000
- Confidence level: Moderate

Public relations (PR) costs are also highly sensitive to the number of affected customers. The best case is always $0. The worst-case, when all customers are affected, can be quite large. The number provided by business management and marketing for a worst-case event of this sort was $10,000,000. The most likely value was $0 based on an expectation that a compromise of 50 records would not result in any PR costs.

- PR costs minimum: $0
- PR costs most likely: $0
- PR costs maximum: $10,000,000
- Confidence level: Moderate

If you haven't noticed, determining secondary response costs can be a lot of work. The good news is that the information is highly reusable from analysis to analysis, so it gets much easier quickly. With the work we've done above, the response costs come together as shown below (Table 8.25):

Table 8.25 SLEF Estimates for Incidents Involving Sensitive Information of Customers

	Minimum	Most Likely	Maximum	Confidence
Notification	$3	$150	$12,000,000	Moderate
Customer support	$0	$50	$4,000,000	Moderate
Credit monitoring	$0	$125	$10,000,000	Moderate
Meetings	$2500	$6250	$50,000	Moderate
Legal	$0	$15,000	$4,000,000	Moderate
PR	$0	$0	$10,000,000	Moderate

These secondary response costs are totaled (and rounded) in the table below (Table 8.26).

Table 8.26 Secondary Response Estimates

Loss Type	Minimum	Most Likely	Maximum	Confidence
Secondary response	$2500	$22,000	$40,000,000	Moderate

Note that the confidence level in these estimates tracks with the confidence level set for the number of compromised records.

Because this scenario includes the potential compromise of customer credit cards, there is the potential for secondary replacement costs to be incurred. The first question you want to ask is whether all of the compromised records will likely include credit card numbers. To understand that, you have to understand the data flows across the network. In this case, a majority of customer data flowing across the network would include credit card numbers, so we decided to make a conservative (paranoid) assumption that all compromised records would include credit card numbers. Making this type of conservative assumption is fine, but you want to make sure you document it in your assumptions and the reasons why. Using data from the publicized compromises in the industry as well as internal sources, the per-card replacement cost was set to $5.

- Per-card replacement minimum: $0
- Per-card replacement most likely: $50 \times \$5 = \$250$
- Per-card replacement maximum: $4,000,000 \times \$5 = \$20,000,000$
- Confidence level: Moderate (Table 8.27)

Table 8.27 Secondary Response and Replacement Estimates

Loss Type	Minimum	Most Likely	Maximum	Confidence
Secondary response	$2500	$22,000	$40,000,000	Moderate
Secondary replacement	$0	$250	$20,000,000	Moderate

Fines and judgment loss estimates come straight from the organization's legal department, and are actually relatively straightforward, or at least the minimum and most likely values are. The minimum value is $0, reflecting an expectation that in a best-case scenario where one record is compromised, there's a very real possibility there would be no fines or judgments. In fact, even with 50 affected customers (the most likely number of compromised records), the legal folks expected no fines or judgments. There could be some, of course, but they didn't anticipate any, so this value is $0, too. The maximum value gets more interesting and is based on a combination of public records for customer information breaches and the legal department's thinking. These values have been added to the table below (Table 8.28).

Table 8.28 Secondary Cost Estimates with Fines and Judgments

Loss Type	Minimum	Most Likely	Maximum	Confidence
Secondary response	$2500	$22,000	$40,000,000	Moderate
Secondary replacement	$0	$250	$20,000,000	Moderate
Secondary fines & judgments	$0	$0	$10,000,000	Moderate

Reputation damage is generally not as impenetrable a problem, as many people think it is. You just have to ask the right people on the business side of the house.

Before going any further on reputation damage, we have to remember how this form of loss materializes for a commercial company—reduced market share, reduced stock price (if publically traded), increased cost of capital, and increased cost of acquiring and retaining employees.

In order to determine market share exposure you have to answer two key questions: (1) how much is a customer worth to the business, and (2) what percentage of customers would be expected to terminate their relationship with the business from an event like this? The answer to the first question is usually represented as the average profit the organization realizes from a customer over the life of the relationship. Believe it or not, many organizations have this figured out, and you might be surprised how low the number is in some industries. In our case, this average profit per customer over the lifetime of the relationship is $200. If you're incredibly lucky, your organization will have data on the second question too, based on previous incidents. Otherwise, you'll need to speak with the marketing or other business folks to get their estimate. For the company in this scenario, the estimate was 10%; in other words, approximately one in 50 customers would choose to terminate the relationship, which is multiplied by the per-customer value and the number of compromised records:

- Market share loss minimum: $0
- Market share loss most likely: $10\% \times \$200 \times 50 = \$1000$
- Market share loss maximum: $10\% \times \$200 \times 4,000,000 = \$80,000,000$
- Confidence level: Moderate

The question of the effect on stock price is another interesting one, with a lot of different opinions depending on who you talk to. There is beginning to be some better data and research on the matter, but it's still crucial to engage subject matter experts from the business. Their perception of the organization's stock price volatility is likely to be much better than any broad research out there today—or at least that is likely to be their opinion (which matters greatly). In this organization, executives felt a 2% drop in market capitalization would represent the worst-case, which represents $1,000,000.

Even a compromise of 4,000,000 records was not expected to affect the company's cost of capital based on other market and business factors. The results of this analysis on reputation damage are shown below (Table 8.29).

Table 8.29 Secondary Cost Estimates Involving Reputation

Loss Type	Minimum	Most Likely	Maximum	Confidence
Secondary response	$2500	$22,000	$40,000,000	Moderate
Secondary replacement	$0	$250	$20,000,000	Moderate
Secondary fines & judgments	$0	$0	$10,000,000	Moderate
Secondary reputation	$0	$1000	$81,000,000	Moderate

We hope you've noticed that most of the estimates related to secondary loss come from subject matter experts in the business rather than from us. This should always be the case. That said, many of these numbers are reusable across a variety of scenarios, which means you don't have to pester your business colleagues regularly in order to complete analyses. They truly appreciate this fact.

We're done acquiring numbers. It's time to plug them in and see what the results of the analysis are. The screenshot in Figure 8.6 shows our estimates entered into the FAIR application.

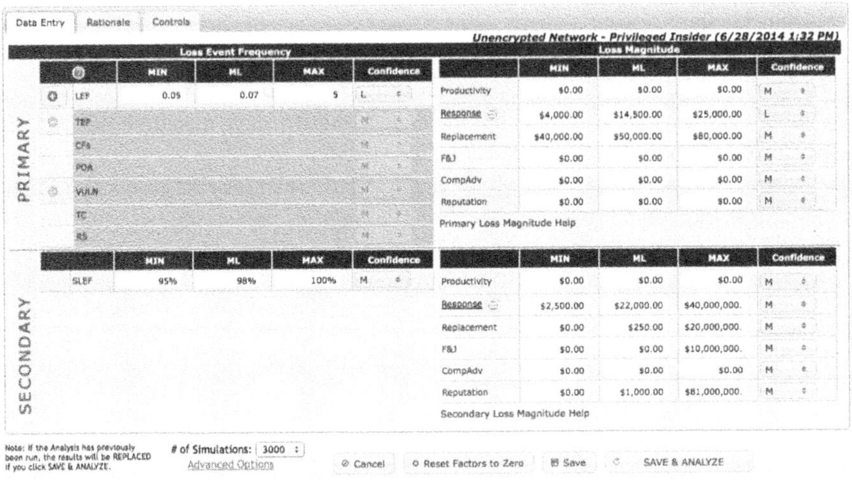

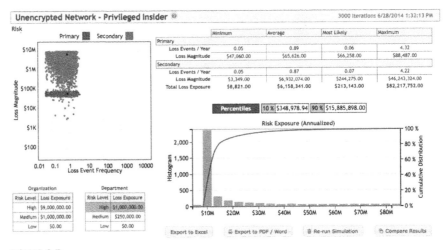

FIGURE 8.6

FAIR risk factors for malicious insiders—confidentiality.

The screenshot in Figure 8.7 shows us the output of the analysis. Let's spend some time reviewing these results so that we can effectively communicate them to our stakeholders.

FIGURE 8.7

FAIR risk analysis of malicious insiders—confidentiality.

The very first thing we always do when looking at the results is apply a mental litmus test—i.e., do the results appear credible? Always do this, especially when you're new to FAIR analyses. If the results look funky, begin troubleshooting your assumptions and data. With this in mind, the first place we're going to focus is on the total loss exposure line at the bottom of the table in the top-right corner of the screen. Of particular interest is the most likely value, which in this case is $213,143. (Going forward, we'll refer to these results as rounded numbers. It's a good habit to get into.) We focus here because if something's funky with the analysis this is where it tends to be most obvious. In this case, the most likely value doesn't surprise or worry us in any way regarding analysis credibility.

After the most likely value, our focus will depend somewhat on the question the analysis is trying to answer. Recalling that this analysis is all about gauging the level of risk from this audit finding, we can look in the lower left corner of the screen to see that this scenario qualifies as medium risk based on thresholds the organization has set. This value is determined by comparing the total loss exposure average value against those thresholds.

Other values we often find useful are the 10th and 90th percentiles. In some organizations, decisions regarding remediation level efforts will be based off of the 80th or 90th percentiles rather than the average. In this case, the 90th percentile value of roughly $16M falls in the organization's high range. In some organizations, this would be enough to have the scenario treated as a high-risk condition. Another important number is the single loss event (SLE) magnitude value, which in this case is just over $45M. This lets us know what the worst-case outcome turned out to be. A number that big tends to get management's attention. It's worth noting that this is still quite a bit smaller than if we simply added up all the maximum values used as inputs. This is a concern voiced by some people regarding this sort of analysis. To cover that end of the spectrum, some people simply add up the input maximums and report that as the analysis maximum instead of the computed value. This is a conservative approach, which may make sense in your organization. If we had chosen low or very low confidence for our most likely values, the odds are good that the tail would be better represented. Keep in mind, though, that we chose the moderate setting for a reason, so don't be too quick to toss the calculated values into the wind.

In this analysis, the other information on the screen is of less interest. You'll find that different parts of the results will serve different purposes based on the reason for the analysis, and sometimes even who the information is going to be provided to.

There is one last thing to point out regarding these results, and that's the total loss exposure maximum value, which is a pretty big number—roughly $82M. However, there is something important to recognize about this value in this scenario: it's driven by the maximum primary loss event frequency value, which is roughly four events. This means that in order to experience this amount of loss, an organization would have to experience all four of those loss events. Some people looking at this would say, "After the first event, we'd make whatever changes are necessary to prevent the other three." That's a great idea, assuming you're even aware that the first event took place. Keep in mind that these events can take place without anyone knowing about it, which means Bob the nefarious network engineer could conceivably perform more than one malicious acts before anyone noticed. Think about it this way: every time one of those events takes place without anyone noticing, the organization essentially writes a check to cover those losses. Nobody knows the check was written, and the check has not yet been cashed. But it's has most definitely been written, and when the event does (or events do) come to light, you can bet any outstanding checks will be cashed. So yes, it is possible for the organization to experience the effects of four loss events in this scenario.

Now that we have the results, let's spend a little time talking about control opportunities other than the proposed encryption. Two come to mind: (1) a data loss prevention tool (DLP), and (2) logging.

The DLP tool is not likely to be very effective against someone with the skills these actors would have, so we discount that right off the bat. Logging could potentially be effective as a deterrent, provided the logs would capture this type of illicit activity and were stored somewhere where someone with these skills and access could not manipulate them. Regardless, it would make their efforts more difficult, which might have some marginal deterrent effect, but the frequency is already low, so it was decided not to present logging as a viable alternative to encryption.

The analysis of this scenario is complete. Based on these results, the choice to deploy encryption may be obvious, depending of course on the cost and pain associated with encryption. If the decision regarding encryption still can't be made, we may need to analyze another scenario. By the way, whenever you're consider encryption as a control against privileged insider acts, you need to be very sure that it would in fact present an obstacle for them. There are many cases where privileged insiders like network engineers or database administrators will still be able to access the data in an unencrypted form.

NONPRIVILEGED INSIDER/MALICIOUS

The good news is that parts of this analysis should go more quickly than the last one because we'll be able to use some of the same data.

LOSS EVENT FREQUENCY

Unlike the privileged insider analysis, this threat community doesn't have privileged access to the data. As a result, we need to consider whether we should operate at a lower level of abstraction in the ontology. In order to make that decision, we need to consider two things: (1) Do we have loss event data that lets us make an estimate at that level? (2) Are we 100% vulnerable to the attack? Thus, an estimate of TEF is the same thing as estimating LEF. This is an interesting scenario, because even these actors aren't privileged. They don't necessarily have to overcome a set of resistive controls in order to carry out their attack. They could, of course, choose to try to break into one of the network switches through brute force, guessing passwords, or leveraging an exploit that gives them access and control over the device. Much more likely, however, they'll simply try to sniff network traffic by using some form of Address Resolution Protocol (ARP) poisoning attack. For those of you who are not familiar with that kind of thing, it simply boils down to them tricking the network into sending them data they aren't supposed to have access to. It's a technical attack, which somewhat limits the number of people who would give that a shot. Still, tools are available today that make it fairly easy. The bottom line for our analysis is that a conservative approach would say we are 100% vulnerable to this type of attack by these actors. As a result, we're still going to make our analysis at the LEF level of abstraction.

The good news is that due to the technical nature of the attack, and the potential for the attack itself to be recognized and the perpetrator caught, the LEF should be pretty low. With these considerations, we work through the process of making a calibrated estimate and come up with the following range and most likely values (Table 8.30):

Table 8.30 LEF Estimates for Technical Attacks

LEF Minimum	LEF Most Likely	LEF Maximum	Confidence
0.03	0.05	0.3	Low

At this point, some newcomers to this type of analysis might argue that insider malicious acts are much more common than this. They're right. The difference is that this estimate does not reflect the frequency of insider actions in general. These estimates are particular to this specific target and vector.

LOSS MAGNITUDE

Estimating loss magnitude for this scenario is going to be much easier than in the earlier scenario because we're going to leverage a lot of that earlier data, particularly for secondary losses. Think about it. The minimum and maximum values should be exactly the same for most of the loss forms—i.e., the best case is that only a single customer record is compromised, and the worst-case is that all 4,000,000 get stolen, so all of the estimates that are sensitive to those values will remain the same. Therefore, the only value that might change for most of the estimates is the most likely value.

We do not anticipate a need to make the primary loss estimates any different in this scenario from the analysis above. We'll still be terminating the perpetrator, assuming we can identify them (Table 8.31).

Table 8.31 Primary Response and Replacement Estimates

Loss Type	Minimum	Most Likely	Maximum	Confidence
Primary response	$4000	$14,500	$25,000	Low
Primary replacement	$40,000	$50,000	$80,000	Moderate

SECONDARY LOSS

Secondary loss event frequency does not change at all. We still anticipate having to deal with secondary stakeholders almost every time an event like this takes place (Table 8.32).

Table 8.32 SLEF Estimations

SLEF Minimum	LEF Most Likely	LEF Maximum	Confidence
95%	98%	100%	Moderate

As we mentioned above, the most likely values are likely to be the only things that change in many of the secondary loss estimates. The reason these values might change is because we assume the perpetrator is going to try to take as many records as possible, whereas the privileged insider was considered more likely to take a smaller volume. In order to decide whether a change is necessary, we have to consider how much time the perpetrator has to perform the act, as well as the volume of information they might capture in that time frame. After working with our network experts to come up with a calibrated range, we ended up with the following estimates:

- Compromised records minimum: one
- Compromised records most likely: 500,000
- Compromised records maximum: 2,000,000
- Confidence level: Low

If you're asking why the maximum is less than 4,000,000, it is because nobody could come up with a rational description of how someone using that attack vector could capture more than 2,000,000 records based on traffic flow. These considerations also affected the most likely estimate. Another consideration was the fact that the organization's ability to detect these kinds of attacks on the internal network is limited. If the organization had more effective network monitoring internally, it would increase the odds of intervening in the attack before it could be completed, or at least response might be timely enough to limit further the number of compromised records.

Customer notification costs change in step with the changes to compromised records:

- Customer notification cost minimum: $3 \times 1 = \$3$
- Customer notification cost most likely: $3 \times 500{,}000 = \$1{,}500{,}000$
- Customer notification cost maximum: $3 \times 2{,}000{,}000 = \$6M$
- Confidence level: Low

Customer support costs change in a similar manner:

- Customer support costs minimum: $0
- Customer support costs most likely: $10\% \times \$10 \times 500,000 = \$500,000$
- Customer support costs maximum: $10\% \times \$10 \times 2,000,000 = \$2,000,000$
- Confidence level: Low

As do credit monitoring costs:

- Credit monitoring costs minimum: $0
- Credit monitoring costs most likely: $10\% \times \$25 \times 500,000 = \$1,250,000$
- Credit monitoring costs maximum: $10\% \times \$25 \times 2,000,000 = \$5,000,000$
- Confidence level: Low

Person-hours costs for time spent in meetings are not as directly associated with the number of compromised records, but we will increase the most likely value because the nature of those meetings may change, because the threat community was a cyber criminal versus an insider.

- Person-hours minimum: $20 \times \$125 = \$2500$
- Person-hours most likely: $50 \times \$125 = \$6250$
- Person-hours maximum: $400 \times \$125 = \$50,000$
- Confidence level: Moderate

Note that these values are much smaller than many of the other forms of loss this type of event would generate. As a result, it is not worthwhile to work on these numbers too vigorously.

The most likely estimate for legal costs increases due to an expectation that regulators will take a greater interest in this type of event. It's one thing to have a privileged insider to go rogue, it's another to have your network sniffed by an insider. The maximum value drops a bit due to the lower maximum number of compromised records.

- Legal costs minimum: $0
- Legal costs most likely: $500,000
- Legal costs maximum: $2,000,000
- Confidence level: Moderate

PR costs also tend to be highly sensitive to the size of a breach. A compromise of 500,000 records was expected to be significant, and a compromise of 2,000,000 records was expected to generate roughly the same reaction as a compromise of 4,000,000.

- PR costs minimum: $0
- PR costs most likely: $2,000,000
- PR costs maximum: $10,000,000
- Confidence level: Moderate

The table below shows the breakdown of our new estimates for secondary response costs (Table 8.33):

Table 8.33 Breakdown of New Estimates for Secondary Response Costs

	Minimum	Most Likely	Maximum	Confidence
Notification	$3	$1,500,000	$6,000,000	Moderate
Customer support	$0	$500,000	$2,000,000	Moderate
Credit monitoring	$0	$1,250,000	$5,000,000	Moderate
Meetings	$2500	$10,000	$50,000	Moderate
Legal	$0	$500,000	$2,000,000	Moderate
PR	$0	$2,000,000	$10,000,000	Moderate
Total	$2500	$6,000,000	$25,000,000	Moderate

Secondary costs for credit card replacement increased for the most likely value, but fell for the maximum value due to the differences in the number of compromised cards.

- Per-card replacement minimum: $0
- Per-card replacement most likely: $500,000 \times \$5 = \$2,500,000$
- Per-card replacement maximum: $2,000,000 \times \$5 = \$10,000,000$
- Confidence level: Moderate (Table 8.34)

Table 8.34 Secondary Costs for Credit Card Replacement

Loss Type	Minimum	Most Likely	Maximum	Confidence
Sec response	$2500	$6,000,000	$25,000,000	Moderate
Sec replacement	$0	$2,500,000	$10,000,000	Moderate

Our legal colleagues suggested setting the estimated Fines and Judgments most likely value at $2M based on the data they had found through their contacts in the industry for a compromise of 500,000 records. Their suggestion was to use $5,000,000 as an estimate for the maximum. The fact that our confidence level would be set to low on this value eased their concerns about how reliable that most likely value was (Table 8.35).

Table 8.35 Secondary Costs with Fines and Judgment Estimates

Loss Type	Minimum	Most Likely	Maximum	Confidence
Sec response	$2500	$6,000,000	$25,000,000	Moderate
Sec replacement	$0	$2,500,000	$10,000,000	Moderate
Sec fines & judgments	$0	$2,000,000	$5,000,000	Moderate

The most likely value for reputation damage changed in lockstep with the change in our compromised records most likely value.

- Market share loss minimum: $0
- Market share loss most likely: $10\% \times \$200 \times 500{,}000 = \$10{,}000{,}000$
- Market share loss maximum: $10\% \times \$200 \times 2{,}000{,}000 = \$40{,}000{,}000$
- Confidence level: Low

All of these changes are summarized in the secondary loss table below (Table 8.36):

Table 8.36 SLEF Estimates Involving Reputation

Loss Type	Minimum	Most Likely	Maximum	Confidence
Sec response	$2500	$6,000,000	$25,000,000	Moderate
Sec replacement	$0	$2,500,000	$10,000,000	Moderate
Sec fines & judgments	$0	$2,000,000	$5,000,000	Moderate
Sec reputation	$0	$10,000,000	$40,000,000	Moderate

As you can see, this second estimate gathering effort takes much less time than the first, which becomes more common as you do more analyses.

The screenshot in Figure 8.8 shows our input values in the FAIR application.

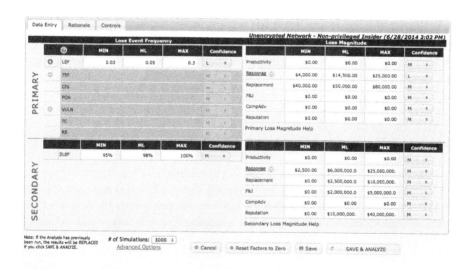

FIGURE 8.8

FAIR risk factors for malicious nonprivileged insiders—confidentiality.

The screenshot in Figure 8.9 shows the results when we crunch the numbers:

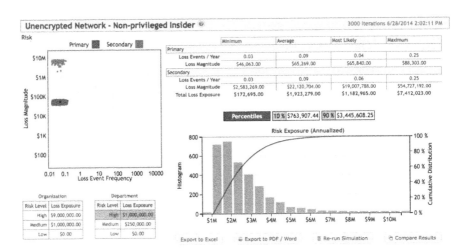

FIGURE 8.9

FAIR risk analysis of malicious nonprivileged insiders—confidentiality.

Here again, a quick mental litmus test of the results leaves us comfortable that we can stand up and defend the analysis. There are a few things worth pointing out about the results, though.

As you would expect, the primary loss magnitudes for this scenario are very similar to the previous one. This is because the inputs were identical. The lower primary LEF is evident, particularly the maximum value. This affects the total loss exposure line. Overall, the key differences appear to boil down to a lower maximum, a higher most likely, and a lower average (because of the lower maximum). All of this tracks nicely with the differences between the two scenarios in the number of compromised records. The qualitative rating for this scenario is medium (in the bottom-left corner). The most likely SLE value is higher in this scenario than the first, but the maximum SLE is similar.

Although the two scenarios both came out as medium risk based on the organization thresholds, there is an important difference. The LEF frequency estimates for the first scenario are quite a bit higher than the second, particularly the average, most likely, and maximum values. As you can see, comparisons between two scenarios can be made on several different parameters. The advantage to the total loss exposure line is that it provides a normalized point of comparison. The disadvantage is that it can't convey some of the subtle but important differences between scenarios. It's for that reason that the interpretation and communication of results is an important role for the analyst.

For this example, we'll go ahead and analyze the third scenario in our scope—the cyber criminal scenario.

CYBER CRIMINAL/MALICIOUS

As with the last scenario, parts of this analysis should go more quickly because we'll be able to use some of the same data.

LOSS EVENT FREQUENCY

Similar to the nonprivileged insider analysis, this threat community does not have privileged access to the data. In fact, in order to be able to attack the network, this threat community first has to breach the perimeter, which means this will be a two-layer analysis.

In a multilayer analysis, there has to be a threat event against the first layer (in this case, the network perimeter). That threat event has to become a loss event (i.e., the attacker has to have been successful at getting past the perimeter) before there can be a threat event at the second layer (the internal network the unencrypted data is flowing over). Our first task, then, is to determine the LEF at that first layer.

Network perimeter loss event frequency

There are multiple vectors through which a cyber criminal might pierce the perimeter —a compromised user desktop or laptop, a third party network connection, a compromised web application, a wireless network access point, etc. Rather than evaluate all of these, we will focus on just one for this analysis. Note: scenarios where you're trying to understand how easy or difficult it is to break into your network can benefit strongly from a well-scoped and performed attack-and-penetration exercise. It will give you a much clearer picture of just how porous the perimeter is. For this analysis, we'll assume that we've recently had that kind of exercise performed, and it identified that the easiest way into the network, by far, was through a compromised user workstation—but you knew that already, didn't you?

In arriving at a decent estimate for compromises on user systems, it helps tremendously if the organization has an advanced anti-malware product rather than just a run-of-the-mill antivirus product. In this scenario, we'll assume that isn't the case. Advanced anti-malware is in next year's budget (perhaps until we do an analysis that demonstrates a strong enough cost/benefit ratio to move it up in priority). Without that source of threat intelligence, we do the best we can—we leverage our antivirus data and the organization's experiences in investigating compromises.

The security operations team has some decent data on how often they're called on to perform clean up and perform forensics on user systems that have been compromised. Over the past year, they have had to clean up six such systems. In all six cases, the systems had been compromised by malware that antivirus could not handle. Fortunately, in all six cases none of the compromises had resulted in further network penetration. In other words, the threat agents had not leveraged their foothold. In two of the events, it was clear that they had rummaged around on the user's system, but that was it. That's useful data, but it only tells us what we know. It does not help us at all with what we don't know. In order to get a better sense for what we might be missing, we reach out to a couple of organizations in our industry that do have advanced anti-malware products. They graciously review their experiences with what the anti-malware product is catching that antivirus is not, as well as their data regarding the percentage of compromises that progress to deeper network penetration.

Based on their information, we make a calibrated estimate that our network will have a penetration beyond the perimeter with the following frequency:

Perimeter LEF minimum: 0.3 (once every 3 years)
Perimeter LEF most likely: 0.5 (once every 2 years)
Perimeter LEF maximum: 3 (three times per year)
Confidence level: Low

Definitely not good news, and this will be good fodder for additional analyses to build that business case for advanced anti-malware and intrusion detection for the internal network (Table 8.37).

Table 8.37 LEF Analysis for Advanced Anti-malware and Intrusion Detection for the Internal Network

LEF Minimum	LEF Most Likely	LEF Maximum	Confidence
0.3	0.5	3	Low

The next step is to try to estimate the likelihood of an actor who gets past the perimeter and tries to execute an attack against data flowing across the internal network. Clearly, the organization has no data on such an event. You hear stories about it happening, but it seems to be infrequent. To gain a better understanding, we have a conversation with the consultants we used to conduct the latest attack-and-penetration test. Their position on the matter is that if they were in the cyber criminal's shoes, they wouldn't bother attacking a relatively difficult target like a switch; they'd go after workstations, network shares, databases, and applications, which tend to be softer targets. They might take a poke at the network elements to see if they were highly vulnerable, but their focus wouldn't begin there. If they managed to compromise a network administrator's workstation, well, that was another thing altogether. With that in mind, we helped them make a calibrated estimate that ended up with the following percentages:

Onward penetration % minimum: 5%
Onward penetration % most likely: 10%
Onward penetration % maximum: 20%
Confidence level: Low

In other words, they believed that at most two out of 10 of attackers who made it past the perimeter would make a serious effort to attack a switch on the internal network. Based on those estimates, our TEF estimate for cyber criminals against data flowing across our network came to:

TEF minimum: 0.015
TEF most likely: 0.05
TEF maximum: 0.6
Confidence level: Low

Keeping in mind that this represents TEF versus LEF; we still have to estimate the internal network's vulnerability if one of these threat agents chose to attack it. The options are to estimate vulnerability directly or derive vulnerability by estimating threat capability and resistance strength. We chose to estimate vulnerability directly.

One thing to keep in mind in a multilayer scenario is that each layer acts as a filter. Each successive layer tends to filter out the less capable threat agents, which means the most capable ones are more likely to make it to the inside. The good news, if you want to call it that, is that user workstations on the network perimeter are not exactly a strong filter. It doesn't take a rocket scientist to get someone to click on a malicious URL in e-mail. We did consider, though, that these actors wouldn't even make a serious attempt at compromising a switch unless they thought they had the skills to pull it off. Given those considerations, we estimated that between 70 and 90% of the attackers would be able to successfully complete the attack, which leaves us with an LEF of (Table 8.38):

Table 8.38 LEF Estimates for Attack Percentage

LEF Minimum	LEF Most Likely	LEF Maximum	Confidence
0.01	0.04	0.54	Low

LOSS MAGNITUDE

Estimating loss magnitude for this scenario is going to go very quickly because it will use many of the same numbers we used earlier. There will only be two key differences: (1) there will not be anyone to fire because it isn't an insider act, and (2) we'll assume that we will have to bring in external forensic expertise to help with event management. This cost will be added to the primary response cost. All of the other loss magnitude numbers from the nonprivileged insider scenario will apply (Table 8.39).

Table 8.39 Primary Response and Replacement Cost

Loss Type	Minimum	Most Likely	Maximum	Confidence
Prim response	$4000	$150,000	$300,000	Moderate
Prim replacement	$0	$0	$0	Moderate

SECONDARY LOSS

Secondary loss event frequency does not change at all. We still anticipate having to deal with secondary stakeholders almost every time an event like this takes place (Table 8.40).

Table 8.40 SLEF Calculations

SLEF Minimum	LEF Most Likely	LEF Maximum	Confidence
95%	98%	100%	Moderate

Secondary loss magnitude numbers do not change either (Table 8.41).

Table 8.41 Secondary Loss Magnitude Estimates

Loss Type	Minimum	Most Likely	Maximum	Confidence
Sec response	$2500	$6,000,000	$25,000,000	Moderate
Sec replacement	$0	$2,500,000	$10,000,000	Moderate
Sec fines & judgments	$0	$2,000,000	$5,000,000	Moderate
Sec reputation	$0	$10,000,000	$40,000,000	Moderate

The screenshot in Figure 8.10 shows our input values in the FAIR application.

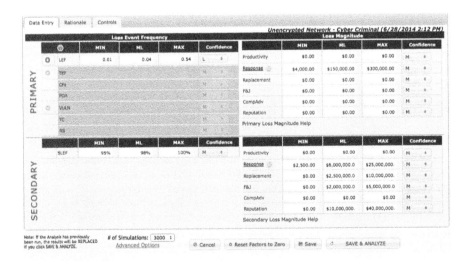

FIGURE 8.10

FAIR risk factors for cyber-criminals network perimeter attack.

The screenshot in Figure 8.11 shows the results when we crunch the numbers:

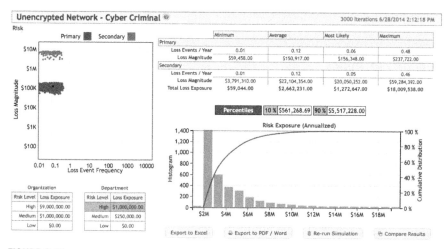

FIGURE 8.11

FAIR risk analysis of cyber-criminals network perimeter attack.

ANALYSIS WRAP UP

Based on these analyses, a recommendation to deploy encryption might be reasonable depending, of course, on the cost associated with that effort.

A question we sometimes hear is, "Where do I plug in the remediation costs?" In other words, people want to know where they would put in the costs associated with implementing encryption after an event has occurred. The simple answer is, you don't. Gap closing expenses after an incident don't go into this model. They should absolutely be included when you present your analysis to management for a decision, but they don't go into the FAIR equation (at least today) because those costs would be multiplied times the number of events. In other words, if you included the cost of implementing encryption in the analyses above, those costs would be multiplied times the number of events, such that if you had two breaches, the cost of implementing encryption would be represented twice.

WEBSITE DENIAL OF SERVICE
PURPOSE

Determine the level of risk associated with a denial of service attack against the organization's main Internet website.

BACKGROUND

Executive management has asked whether the organization is prepared to handle a denial of service attack against its main Internet website, and if not, how much they should worry.

ASSET(S) AT RISK

This web application provides online transactional services for a large part of the organization's customer base. As a result, a prolonged outage is believed to represent significant potential for lost revenue and reputation damage.

TCOM(S)

The relevant threat communities for this analysis could include cyber criminals, the general hacking community, and hacktivists. The question was raised regarding whether competitors should be added as a threat community in this scenario. After discussion, it was agreed that it would be very unlikely for a competitor in this industry to launch or contract for a denial of service (DoS) attack due to the potential for significant reputation and legal damages if the act was discovered.

THREAT TYPE(S)

The threat type is malicious.

THREAT EFFECT(S)

The relevant threat effect is "availability."

SCOPE

Based on the considerations above, our scope table at this point looks like this (Table 8.42):

Table 8.42 Scope Table for Denial of Service Attack Against the Organization's Main Internet Web Site

Asset at Risk	Threat Community	Threat Type	Effect
Customer transactions	Cyber criminals	Malicious	Availability
Customer transactions	Hacktivists	Malicious	Availability
Customer transactions	General hackers	Malicious	Availability

Do any of the scenarios seem like they can be eliminated based on frequency or magnitude considerations? Or can we just combine them into a single scenario? The frequency and sophistication of their attacks may be different. With that in mind, it was decided to alter the approach and instead create two virtual threat communities based on the sophistication of the attack: (1) a highly sophisticated attack we'll label "sophisticated attackers," and (2) a more run-of-the-mill attack we'll refer to as "basic attackers."

Here is what the scope table looks like now (Table 8.43):

Table 8.43 Altered Scope Table

Asset at Risk	Threat Community	Threat Type	Effect
Customer transactions	Sophisticated attackers	Malicious	Availability
Customer transactions	Basic attackers	Malicious	Availability

By the way—sometimes when you do this sort of consolidation, you realize later on in the course of performing the analysis that consolidation was a bad idea. Maybe some aspect of one threat community turns out to be materially different after all. For example, if we had simply consolidated all three of the original threat communities into a single aggregate threat community, we might very well have found it difficult describe a threat capability distribution for the aggregate community because it would have been so diffuse, maybe even bimodal. When this kind of realization happens in an analysis, it isn't a big deal. You just have to refine the definition and assumptions of the scenario you're in the midst of and create additional scenarios that reflect the expanded scope. Then you *must* go back and review any estimates you made in the scenario up to that point to make sure they don't need to change based on the new scope. Always remember to document any changes in scope and rationale.

ANALYSIS
SOPHISTICATED ATTACKER/AVAILABILITY
Loss event frequency

As always, we start out by asking whether the organization has any history with denial of service (DoS) attacks of this sort against this website and, if so, whether there's enough history to support making our estimates at the LEF level of abstraction. In this case, the organization suffered one DoS attack about five years ago. We weren't there at the time, but we were told it went on sporadically for 3 days and was a fairly painful experience for the information security and network teams. Before we base an estimate off of that data point, there are three questions that need to be answered: (1) how likely is this data point from the past to reflect future reality, (2) was that a sophisticated attack, and (3) what is a loss event in this instance?

Sometimes past data (or the lack thereof) can be reasonably reflective of the future, and other times not so much. We know that DoS attacks are on the rise, so we would probably want to reflect that fact in our estimate and cite any supporting data or rationale. The bottom line here is that, right or wrong, past data is the only kind of data there is. Sometimes it's more a matter of how far from the past the data comes

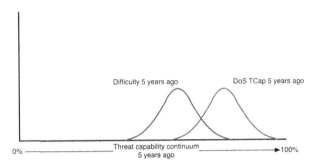

FIGURE 8.12

Denial of service Tcap 5 years ago.

from. Therefore, we have to leverage it intelligently, which means a certain amount of rational skepticism and critical thinking is important. This leads us to our second question—how sophisticated was that previous event?

In years past, DoS attacks were a bit different than they are today. Back then, the effectiveness of those attacks had more to do with the number of systems throwing packets at you. These days, some of the more sophisticated attacks are able to generate a higher number of packets per second and may have other characteristics that complicate dealing with the event. By today's standards, that attack 5 years ago was pretty rudimentary. At the time, though, it was bad enough. The point is that threat capabilities evolve over time. In Figure 8.12, we show where that attack might have been plotted along the threat capability continuum 5 years ago. We also show that our resistance to such an attack at the time was deficient relative to that kind of attack, thus the pain it caused.

TALKING ABOUT RISK

The threat capability continuum is a percentile scale used to represent the relative capabilities of a threat community (TCap) or the sophistication of a particular attack. More capable threat communities and more sophisticated attacks reside farther to the right along the continuum.

We also use this scale to estimate Difficulty (formally called Resistive Strength or RS) of our controls. By using the same scale for both TCap and Difficulty, we are able to compare the two values. We use distributions to reflect the inherent uncertainty in these estimates, and so we can use Monte Carlo to randomly sample from each distribution and determine the percentage of time that a sampled TCap was greater than a sampled Difficulty—i.e., our vulnerability.

The vertical axis on the chart simply provides a way to represent expectations of greater or lesser probabilities within the distribution—i.e., the peak of the distribution is our way of saying we believe this is where most of the members of the threat community exist capability-wise, or is the most likely effectiveness of our controls. In most cases, these are very fuzzy estimates, and the results of Monte Carlo sampling can be highly sensitive to the shape of the distributions (more or less sharply peaked). These are a couple of reasons why we advocate selective use of this process for determining vulnerability. With additional research and data, this sort of analysis will become much more effective and reliable. In the meantime, it can still be effective if done carefully. If nothing else, the concept is very useful for thinking through and explaining the question of vulnerability.

If we were to estimate the TCap of that DoS attack from 5 years ago, it would register lower on the threat capability continuum (see Figure 8.13). If, over the 5 years,

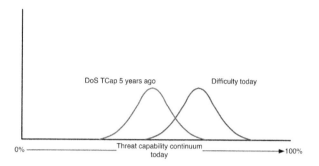

FIGURE 8.13

Denial of service Tcap 5 years ago—resistive strength today.

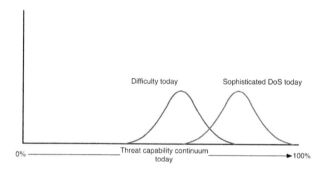

FIGURE 8.14

Denial of service Tcap & resistive strength today.

our RS (Resistance Strength is synonymous with Difficulty in this case) had evolved to keep apace of changes in the capabilities of the broader threat landscape (i.e., we maintain our position along the continuum), then we would be in much better shape to withstand that older attack. In fact, it might have no practical effect on our website.

However, this scenario is focused on the sophisticated attack. Figure 8.14 reflects the fact that the organization has put improvements in place over the past 5 years, and an expectation that these improvements have kept us roughly apace of the threat landscape. The problem, however, is that a sophisticated attack today would still be a real problem.

That's a long way of explaining some of the considerations that help us figure out whether we can leverage that past data point to estimate the frequency of a sophisticated attack going forward. In the long run, although that past data point may be somewhat informative, we are probably going to base our estimate more strongly on current threat intelligence.

The third question above—what is a loss event—may seem odd, but there's a reason for asking it. When a DoS attack takes place, it's not as though the lights simply go off on the website. Sometimes that's what happens, but very often it's a matter of service degradation rather than being completely down, and because degradation runs the continuum between "just a little slow" to "lights out," we have to draw a line that distinguishes what we're going to consider a loss event versus a threat event. There are two reasons this clarity is important: (1) it helps us decide whether to estimate LEF directly or derive it from TEF and vulnerability, and (2) as we'll see shortly, it helps us with our loss estimates.

If we choose to define a loss event as a complete outage, then anything less than that is a threat event, and we would take the time to either estimate vulnerability directly or derive it from estimates of TCap and RS. If we consider a loss event to include any trace of degradation, then it probably makes more sense to simplify the analysis and consider all DoS attacks to be loss events.

TALKING ABOUT RISK

Some critics will claim this analysis is a perfect example of useless navel gazing—that our time would be better spent on fixing problems. They may have a point. It would be much easier to simply answer the executive's question by saying something like, "We think there's medium (or whatever) risk associated with a DoS attack against our website" and then go about our duties. There's absolutely nothing wrong with that in some cases, and it might be the choice we would make, depending on whatever else might be on our plates and our understanding of what the executives are really looking for. If they are looking for a rough pass at how worried they should be, a simple high, medium, or low answer based on our instincts might be just the ticket. If, however, we're trying to build a business case for spending a bunch of money on improved defenses, then that may not be enough. Regardless, the examples in this chapter are simply intended to illustrate the process of performing a real analysis when the situation calls for it. As we've said elsewhere in this book, we are not advocating deep analysis at every turn. There is a time and a place for it, though, and it has been an incredibly valuable tool in our kit.

For the purposes of this scenario, we are going to consider any highly sophisticated DoS attack to represent a loss event under the assumption that our resistive capability is not going to protect some customers from having experiencing the outage. This being the case, we will estimate LEF directly rather than derive it from TEF and vulnerability. (Don't worry, though. In the next scenario we'll derive LEF instead of estimate it directly.)

Primarily given the available threat intelligence regarding DoS trends in our industry, we make the following calibrated LEF estimate (Table 8.44):

Table 8.44 LEF Values

LEF Minimum	LEF Most Likely	LEF Maximum	Confidence
0.2	0.3	1	Moderate

(NOTE: Because we've already provided examples of how to leverage absurd first estimates and the equivalent bet process, we won't continue to include that in our description of the analysis.)

Now that the frequency side of the equation is taken care of, it's time to think about loss magnitude— i.e., when/if this happens, how badly is it going to hurt?

LOSS MAGNITUDE

As always, the first thing we have to do is determine which of the six loss forms are likely to materialize as the *primary* loss from this type of event.

Productivity loss

By the very definition of our loss event, we anticipate that productivity loss is a reasonable possibility.

Response costs

There would certainly be time spent investigating and dealing with the event, so response costs are a factor.

Replacement costs

No systems or data are expected to require replacement, so this form of loss is not relevant in this scenario.

As with most scenarios, competitive advantage, fines and judgments, and reputation loss are not relevant as forms of primary loss.

There are two keys to estimating productivity loss (lost profit) in any outage scenario: (1) the potential duration of an outage, and (2) the amount of profit generated per time period (usually per hour). Why profit and not revenue? Generally, that's what management cares most about. That may not be true in all organizations, though, so you may want to find out from your stakeholders what you're approach should be.

So far, we haven't specified the industry our organization is part of or the service it provides. For this analysis, let's say the organization is a software as a service (SaaS) provider. Our customers subscribe to the service on a monthly or annual basis. This being the case, an outage of our website may not represent an immediate and direct loss of significant revenue. We would need to speak with colleagues from the business side of the house to see how many new subscriptions occur per hour and the value of those subscriptions. We'd also need an estimate from them regarding the percentage of new want-to-be subscribers that would wait for the outage to be resolved and subscribe later. This will depend in large part on how strong the competition is. We might, if we're lucky, even have data to help us with this. There is no doubt that the organization has had outages before—it happens. Therefore, we might have data that shows us whether there's a jump in subscriptions following a lengthy outage that suggests a percentage of subscribers that wait it out. Working with our business colleagues, we arrived at the following productivity loss estimate (Table 8.45):

Table 8.45 Primary Productivity Loss Estimate

Loss type	Minimum	Most Likely	Maximum	Confidence
Primary productivity	$0	$10,000	$100,000	Moderate

The minimum value represents a best-case scenario where the outage is short in duration and any affected new subscribers simply wait it out. The worst-case represents a week-long outage, or serious degradation, where a larger percentage of potential subscribers get tired of waiting and move on to the competition. The most likely value reflects the most common duration experienced by these kinds of attacks.

Primary response costs for an incident like this tends to boil down to person-hours spent dealing with the incident. Based on data we glean from organizations that have suffered these attacks recently, plus our own experiences in dealing with outages in general, we come up with the following person-hour estimates:

- Minimum: 40 person-hours
- Maximum: 400 person-hours

For most the likely value, we split the difference (220 hours).

We then multiplied these values times the organization's average loaded employee hourly rate of $50 to come up with the following primary response cost estimates (Table 8.46):

Table 8.46 Primary Productivity and Response Estimates

Loss Type	Minimum	Most Likely	Maximum	Confidence
Primary productivity	$0	$10,000	$100,000	Moderate
Primary response	$2000	$11,000	$20,000	Moderate

That's it for primary loss, which just leaves secondary loss.

SECONDARY LOSS

The first thing you need to do when thinking about secondary loss is identify the relevant secondary stakeholders. In this scenario, there are two: (1) customers, and (2) business partners who advertise on our website. Once you have the secondary stakeholders identified, you need to identify which forms of secondary loss you would expect to materialize. With that in mind:

Response

In an incident involving sensitive customer information, your response costs almost always include:

- The cost of notifying business partners
- The costs associated with increased customer support volume
- The cost of having people in meetings to strategize how to handle customers and regulators
- PR costs

NOTE: Every time you have secondary loss of any form, you have response costs of some sort. Every time. If one person picks up a phone to answer a customer's call regarding the event, that cost is considered secondary response. If one meeting is held to strategize on how to notify or deal with the secondary stakeholders, those person-hours represent a secondary response cost.

Fines & Judgments

This will depend largely on the terms of our business partner contracts. If contracts don't exclude this type of event from service level agreements, there might be some liability to estimate. For this example, we'll assume our contracts exclude liability for this type of event.

Reputation

Reputation damage is a potential outcome any time secondary stakeholders are negatively affected.

Productivity and competitive advantage losses don't typically result from these types of incidents. In fact, productivity loss rarely materializes as secondary loss. If you're surprised about competitive advantage being excluded, you might want to refer to the chapter on Common Problems. In that chapter, we explain why competitive advantage is so commonly misused. Secondary replacement costs usually only apply when the organization has to compensate for a secondary stakeholder's losses (e.g., replacing stolen funds from a bank account), which is not relevant in this instance.

Having established the relevant secondary loss forms, we can start estimating secondary loss event frequency (SLEF). Because SLEF is a percentage (i.e., the percentage of primary events that have secondary effects) your absurd starting points are always 0% and 100%. However, the good news (analytically) when dealing with a scenario invariably affects customers is that your SLEF is always 100%. We'll set the minimum value to 99% so our Monte Carlo function has a range to take random samples from (Table 8.47).

Table 8.47 SLEF Estimation

SLEF Minimum	LEF Most Likely	LEF Maximum	Confidence
99%	100%	100%	Moderate

As we noted above, secondary response costs take various forms, each of which needs to be evaluated separately.

In this case, our business colleagues decide that the costs associated with business partner notification are too nominal to even bother estimating.

Because of the nature of our business, we don't provide telephone customer support. In the case of an event like this, we would expect to have an increased volume of e-mails to respond to, but those would be answered with a boilerplate response, so that's a nominal expense as well. We would, however, anticipate the need to deal with a much higher load of Twitter and other social media dialogue and complaints. Combining those person-hour estimates with person-hour estimates related to meetings came to the following:

- Minimum: 50 person-hours
- Maximum: 200 person-hours

For most the likely value, we split the difference (125 hours). At a loaded hourly rate of $50, this came to initial secondary response costs of (Table 8.48):

Table 8.48 Secondary Response Cost Estimates

Loss Type	Minimum	Most Likely	Maximum	Confidence
Sec response	$2500	$6250	$10,000	Moderate

We also worked with our business colleagues to estimate PR costs that might occur from this kind of event. In a best-case event, there would be no anticipated PR costs. Likewise, for the most likely event, they felt the costs would be nominal as it would simply entail some concentrated social media time, which they felt should just be considered a sunk cost. In a worst-case scenario, however, they thought the costs could run as high as $250,000. So our secondary response costs ended up as follows (Table 8.49):

Table 8.49 Secondary Response Estimates for Worst-Case Scenario

Loss Type	Minimum	Most Likely	Maximum	Confidence
Sec response	$2500	$6250	$260,000	Moderate

Because our business is not publically traded and is already well financed, stock price and cost of capital aren't considered relevant to the question of reputation damage. Market share, however, is.

In order to determine market share exposure, you have to answer two key questions: (1) How much is a customer worth to the business? (2) What percentage of customers would be expected to terminate their relationship with the business after an event like this? The answer to the first question is usually represented as the average profit the organization realizes from a customer over the life of the relationship. Believe it or not, many organizations have this figured out, and you might be surprised how low the number is in some industries. In our case, this average profit per customer over the lifetime of the relationship is $100. If you're incredibly lucky, your organization will have data on the second question, too, based on previous incidents. Otherwise, you'll need to speak with the marketing or other business folks to get their estimate. In this scenario, the best-case estimate was 0% (no customers) and the worst-case was 20%. The most likely value was estimated to be 2%. Given a customer base of 50,000, this comes out to the following estimates:

- Market share loss minimum: $0
- Market share loss most likely: $2\% \times 50,000 \times \$100 = \$100,000$
- Market share loss maximum: $20\% \times 50,000 \times \$100 = \$1,000,000$
- Confidence level: Moderate

The results of this analysis on reputation damage are shown below (Table 8.50).

Table 8.50 Results of the Analysis on Reputation Damage

Loss Type	Minimum	Most Likely	Maximum	Confidence
Sec response	$2500	$6250	$260,000	Moderate
Sec reputation	$0	$100,000	$1,000,000	Moderate

We're done acquiring numbers. It's time to plug them in and see what the results of the analysis are. The screenshot in Figure 8.15 shows our estimates entered into the FAIR application.

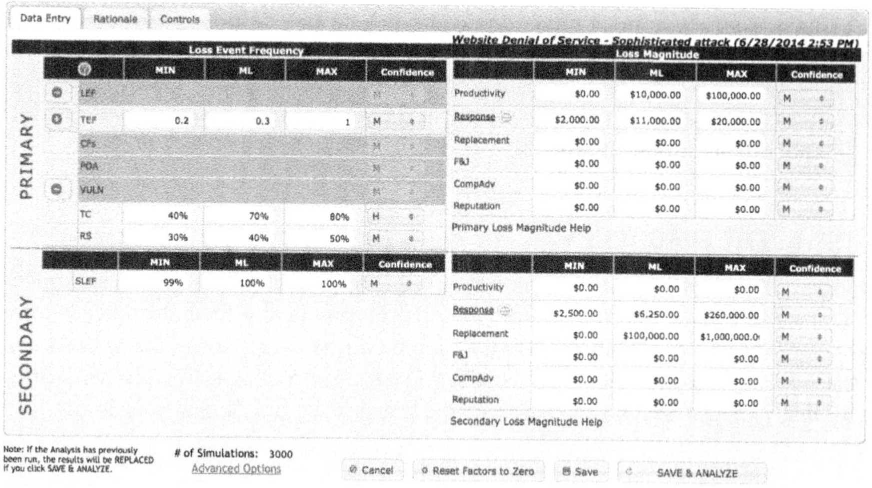

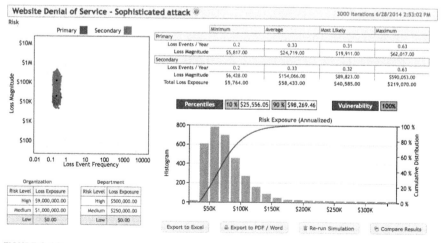

FIGURE 8.15

FAIR risk factors for denial of service attack.

When we crunch the numbers, we get the results shown in Figure 8.16:

FIGURE 8.16

FAIR risk analysis of denial of service attack.

We can see that the annualized numbers are not too bad. The SLE is fairly substantial, though. Based on this, we might suggest cyber insurance to help cover some of the losses.

BASIC ATTACKER/AVAILABILITY

By now you know what to anticipate with a subsequent analysis—some of the work has already been done in the analysis above. In this scenario, however, we'll derive LEF rather than estimate it directly.

LOSS EVENT FREQUENCY

Because this event is characterized by a less sophisticated attack, we anticipate that at least some of the time there would be no practical effects. In other words, not every threat event will necessarily become a loss event—or at least that's our expectation going into the analysis. That doesn't mean analysis results will align with that expectation, which is one of the reasons we do the analysis in the first place.

If we're going to derive LEF, then we first have to estimate TEF. Here again, we go back to the threat intelligence sources we used above. According to those sources, the frequency of less sophisticated attacks is higher than the sophisticated attacks, but is still expected to be relatively low against an organization like ours. Our calibrated TEF estimates were established as (Table 8.51):

Table 8.51 Calibrated TEF Estimates

TEF Minimum	LEF Most Likely	LEF Maximum	Confidence
0.2	0.5	2	Moderate

Now the question is whether we want to estimate vulnerability directly or derive it by estimating TCap and Difficulty. We'll do both in this analysis to demonstrate the process for each approach.

Estimating vulnerability directly simply involves estimating the percentage of times a threat event would become a loss event. Because this is a percentage value, the absurd estimate is 0% and 100%. Very often, the next step we'll take is to change our range estimate to 50% and 100%, essentially forcing the question of whether we're at least 95% confident that half or more of these events will become loss events. Given our understanding of our technology infrastructure and the capabilities of our Internet service provider, we are not at least 95% sure that half of the attacks would result in noticeable effects. That being the case, we ask the same question, but this time set the minimum value at 25%. We are comfortable that at least one out of four attacks would result in loss of some sort, so our new range looks like this:

- Minimum: 25%
- Maximum: 100%

We do the same thing for the high end of the range and continue to work the calibration process until we reach that point where we can't decide between our range and spinning the wheel, which left us at:

- Minimum: 30%
- Maximum: 80%

In other words, between 30 and 80% of these attacks should result in tangible loss—i.e., customer activities are affected. We put the most likely value at 50%. The nice thing about estimating vulnerability directly is it's the kind of thing that you could get data to support (or not). Certainly if the organization was unfortunate enough to experience a series of these events you'd find out whether the estimate was good or not. Another option would be to engage a consultant to throw some DoS attacks at you and see the percentage of time the website is affected. The second option probably is not feasible though, or worthwhile.

That's the easy way to set vulnerability. If you want to, however, you can derive vulnerability by estimating TCap and Difficulty. As we've said before, this is not our preferred approach in most cases. Let's walk through the process, though, so at least you'll have seen it and can try to use it if you feel the need.

The first thing to keep in mind is that estimates for both TCap and Difficulty are made against the threat capability continuum we discussed earlier. They have to be measured using the same scale in order to be compared to each other. Another thing to keep in mind is that this is a percentile scale. Before we make any estimates, though, we need to provide some labels for the two threat communities we're going to be talking about:

1. We will refer to threat community under analysis for this scenario that would be throwing the basic DoS attack at us as TComB (for basic).
2. We will refer to the broader threat community that includes anyone who might engage in DoS activities as TComAll.

In some scenarios, TComAll is the threat community under analysis. In those cases your TCap estimates simply reflect the entire continuum (minimum 0th percentile, most likely 50th percentile, and maximum 100th percentile). However, let's say the threat community you're analyzing (TComB) is made up of a distinct subset of the overall community (TComAll). In that case, your estimate might look as follows:

- Minimum: 30th percentile
- Most likely: 50th percentile
- Maximum: 80th percentile

With these estimates, you're actually saying that the lamest actor in TComB (the minimum value) is better than all but three out of 10 in TComAll. You're also saying that the most capable actor in TComB (represented by the maximum value) is good enough that only two out of 10 in TComAll are better. The 50th percentile estimate is your way of saying that most of the actors in TComB are average compared TComAll. Viewed graphically, it looks something like Figure 8.17:

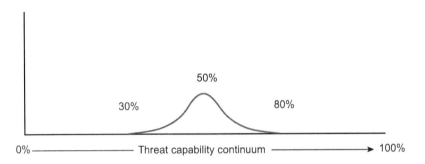

FIGURE 8.17

Denial of service attack—TCom analysis.

For Difficulty the questions are a little bit different. Let's use different values for Difficulty than we used above to hopefully reduce confusion:

- Minimum: 60th percentile
- Most likely: 75th percentile
- Maximum: 90th percentile

The most important thing to keep in mind when making estimates for Difficulty is that you are always estimating against TComAll. The threat community in this scenario, TcomB, needs to be forgotten about for this part of the exercise. This is where a lot of people go wrong with this approach to deriving vulnerability. They estimate Difficulty against TComB rather than TComAll, which is essentially the same thing as estimating vulnerability directly. So forget about TComB when estimating Difficulty.

With the Difficulty estimates above, we're saying that in order to defeat our control, a threat actor has to be at the 60th percentile (the minimum value)—anybody below that in capability has no prayer of successfully denying service to the website. We're also saying that anyone above the 90th percentile (the maximum value) is absolutely certain to defeat the control, every time. It's uncertain whether anyone between those two values will be successful at generating a loss event. The most likely value is an estimate of what we believe is the most likely level of efficacy for the resistive controls—i.e., most of the time the controls are effective up to the 75th percentile, but the odds are less likely that they'll be effective above that in the scale.

Having made these estimates for TComB and Difficulty, we can display the values graphically (Figure 8.18):

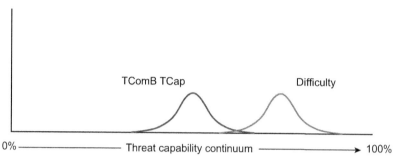

FIGURE 8.18

Denial of service attack attack—TCom analysis for TComB.

The first thing we should notice is that when you take random samples from each of these distributions, very infrequently will a sample from TComB's TCap be greater than a random sample from Difficulty. If you take thousands of random samples from each distribution and compare them, only a relative few times will TCap be greater than Difficulty. This means your vulnerability is low. If the distribution positions on the continuum were reversed, and TCap was higher than Difficulty, then your vulnerability would be much higher. If the distributions were exactly the same shape and on the same points on the continuum (superimposed over one another), then each random sample has a 50/50 chance of Difficulty being lower or higher than TCap, and your vulnerability is then 50%.

As you can see, this process takes more time. That said, there are times when it can be very helpful. The trick to getting it right is to ensure that your Difficulty estimate is made against TComAll. Something else to think about—when you estimate vulnerability directly, aren't you essentially doing this exact same process in your head?

LOSS MAGNITUDE

This will be easy. The first step is to ask yourself whether the losses from this event are likely to be any different than the previous one. If not, your work is done. If there are factors that are likely to be different, you simply make those changes and call it a day. In this case, we believe both the maximum and most likely values are likely to be lower, but we aren't sure enough about a difference in the maximum values to change those. We'll reduce the most likely values based on an assumption that the event will be easier and faster to mitigate. Our Internet service provider expert agreed with that assumption. Consequently, the resulting primary loss estimates ended up as follows (Table 8.52):

Table 8.52 Primary Loss Estimates

Loss Type	Minimum	Most Likely	Maximum	Confidence
Primary productivity	$0	$5000	$100,000	Moderate
Primary response	$2000	$5000	$20,000	Moderate

That's it for primary loss, which just leaves secondary loss.

SECONDARY LOSS

Based on our definition of what constitutes a loss event, we will leave the SLEF as before (Table 8.53).

Table 8.53 SLEF Estimation

SLEF Minimum	LEF Most Likely	LEF Maximum	Confidence
99%	100%	100%	Moderate

As we did above, we'll cut the most likely values roughly in half, which gives us (Table 8.54):

Table 8.54 Secondary Response and Reputation Estimates

Loss Type	Minimum	Most Likely	Maximum	Confidence
Sec response	$2500	$3000	$260,000	Moderate
Sec reputation	$0	$50,000	$1,000,000	Moderate

We're done acquiring numbers. It's time to plug them in and see what the results of the analysis are. The screenshot in Figure 8.19 shows our estimates entered into the FAIR application.

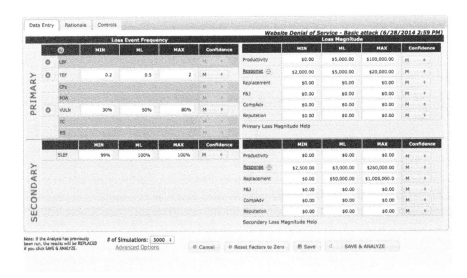

FIGURE 8.19

FAIR risk factors for basic attacker—availability.

When we crunch the numbers, we get the following (Figure 8.20):

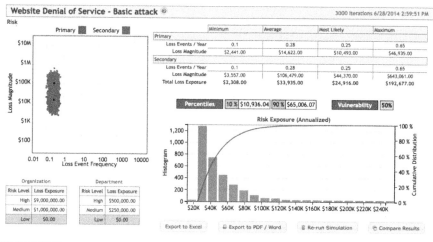

FIGURE 8.20

FAIR risk analysis of basic attacker—availability.

We can see that the results are lower than the first analysis. The worst-case SLE is still fairly substantial, though.

ANALYSIS WRAP UP

Having done these analyses, we may or may not be in a position to make a strong business case to improve our capabilities to resist these kinds of attacks or buy cyber insurance to cover some of the costs. However, at least the decision-makers will be able to make a better-informed decision. Performing these analyses also makes other website availability analyses (e.g., infrastructure outages, etc.) easier to complete because some of the loss information will be reusable.

Thinking about Risk Scenarios Using FAIR

In this chapter, we examine some common or contemporary scenarios or situations through what we refer to as "a FAIR frame of mind." We hope that by sharing our thinking on these topics, you can glean one or more benefits; you may discover some additional solutions for control options, identify a fresh approach to analyzing a risk scenario, or find ways of applying FAIR within your organization.

Viewing information security problems (or any other risk-related problem) through a FAIR lens tends to boil down to just a couple of things:

- Maintaining risk as the context, versus simply the condition of a control, a threat community, or the potential impact of an event. It is the combination of all three of these factors that matters, rather than just one or two.
- Thinking critically about the problem rather than reacting emotionally.

As you go through this chapter, you may very well realize that your organization, or you personally, already approach risk scenarios in a FAIR-like manner. If that's the case, then integrating FAIR concepts and terms should come easily, and FAIR might simply represent a handy reference for how you approach challenges going forward. Regardless, we encourage you to keep in mind that FAIR is first and foremost a framework for critical thinking, which means that it can act as a guide to help you mentally parse whatever problem you're faced with and examine it more thoroughly.

TALKING ABOUT RISK

One of the authors had an opportunity to help an information security team out of a jam a few years ago. The members of the security team were split in their opinion of whether each laptop in the organization should be encrypted with its own key, or whether a common key for all laptops was the better choice. Apparently, the debate had been going on for weeks and had stopped progress on the laptop encryption project. They thought performing a quantitative FAIR analysis on the question might clarify things. As it turned out, they were mistaken. A full-fledged analysis wasn't necessary.

We began the process by identifying the threat communities and scenarios in which laptop encryption would be a relevant control. Within about 20 minutes of high-level discussion regarding the scope of the analysis, it became apparent to everyone on the security team that a common encryption key was the right answer. We never got to a point in the discussion where we needed to deal with quantitative values. Simply approaching the conversation in a structured manner provided enough clarity for everyone to agree on the better choice for that organization.

If your experience in using FAIR is anything like ours, you will be surprised at how often this happens. You start the process of a formal analysis only to have the answer become clear before you even get to the point of using numbers. Sometimes you'll still want or need to complete the analysis because you are building a business case for funding, providing a baseline for later analyses, establishing a big picture of the organization's loss exposure for management, or for other reasons, but it is important to know that you don't always have to go into "full quant" mode.

THE BOYFRIEND

We thought we'd start off with an example that isn't typically part of the information security problem space, because we've been told that using FAIR to evaluate noninformation security problems helps many people better assimilate FAIR principles.

Imagine that you have a teenage daughter and that she has for the first time (gasp) a teenage boy in her life. For fathers especially, this is a nightmare scenario exceeding anything they will encounter at work related to fighting cyber criminals. The obvious solutions are not legal, so we have to come up with ideas for managing the risk associated with this that do not result in the need to flee to a nonextradition country. In desperation, you turn to FAIR.

Your mind jumps immediately to vulnerability (Vuln). Your daughter is sweet and not physically imposing (low-difficulty/resistance strength (RS)), and the boy is a brute by thirteen-year-old standards (high threat capability (TCap)), at least as seen through the eyes of a daughter's parent. Mental note: you really need to enroll her in those martial arts classes you've been thinking about. This doesn't help you today, though, so you continue your search for other options.

Loss magnitude (LM) is too terrible to contemplate. The parent's prerogative, however, is to assume the worst-case outcome. You know you will be there for her if anything does go awry, like if he dumps her for her best friend. So at least you are trying to be mentally prepared and have a rough incident response plan in place. With LM control options somewhat limited in nature, you decide to explore the loss event frequency side of the equation further.

Short of moving, the options for eliminating contact between Romeo and Juliet are limited because they attend the same school and have some of the same friends. You might, however, be able to reduce contact frequency outside of controlled circumstances. This is a twofer control opportunity because not only do you reduce contact frequency, but also the controlled circumstances reduce the probability of illicit actions on the part of Romeo when contact does occur. It never crosses your mind of course, that Juliet might have her own illicit actions in mind (incomplete information is inevitably a part of risk management). Regardless, you institute new rules regarding where she can go and in what circumstances. Her questions regarding why she is being grounded are answered by explaining that she isn't grounded; you just want to be more involved in her life. She mutters something unpleasant under her breath.

Because you can't personally accompany your daughter 24 hours a day and a private security detail is not in the budget, you realize that there are likely to be circumstances when the two of them will be together in uncontrolled circumstances. With that prospect staring you in the face, you resort to the age-old tradition of using thinly veiled threats to reduce the probability of action—you know, like cleaning your shotgun on the porch as they leave to go have pizza with friends (the shotgun you purchased that morning just for this purpose). You might even pull Romeo aside and show him those martial arts trophies from 20 years ago.

These steps (plus the online criminal background check you had done on the boy and his parents—i.e., threat intelligence) help you to feel better that you haven't overlooked any important control opportunities. There remains some amount of residual risk, but you realize that this is the nature of parenthood.

Clearly, most parents are not going to feel the need to examine a scenario like this using FAIR. It can, however, be helpful for dealing with many domestic questions like whether or not to buy an emergency generator for the home, whether to have firearms in the home, how much and what kind of insurance to buy, and what sorts of locks, windows, or landscaping to install.

SECURITY VULNERABILITIES

NOTE: Use of the word "vulnerabilities" in this section is aligned with common use in the industry, which is contrary to how FAIR defines the word. We chose to use the common term in this section because its a convenient collective noun for the output of the scanners. We aren't pedantic about terms like this; however if you are using them in risk analysis your usage should be consistent with our earlier definitions.

As part of security reviews and due diligence activities, there is often some automated scanning done of the systems and applications. The results of these scans can often be voluminous, and most organizations struggle to remediate the huge volume of vulnerabilities in a timely fashion. Adding to the challenge, as we have mentioned elsewhere in the book, is that very often the severity ratings given to these vulnerabilities are inaccurate and inflated. For example, we've reviewed scan results where as few as 5% of the "critical" and "high risk" results were accurate once the threat and asset considerations were taken into account. This low signal to noise ratio means that organizations are faced with a choice. If they choose to assume the scan severity ratings are accurate, they can:

- Be very aggressive in their remediation practices, which introduces risk associated with the remediation process itself breaking business applications and disrupting business processes
- Set very long remediation timelines, which means those few vulnerabilities that are truly severe may go unmitigated for longer periods of time
- Not worry about hitting remediation timelines defined in policy, which introduces risk associated with poor audit and regulator reviews, as well as creates an indefensible due diligence position if a significant loss event were to occur.

Another option is to assume the scan results can't be relied on and apply sufficient resources to review and validate each and every scan result. This is impractical for most organizations. Yet another option is to apply a rudimentary risk-based filter to triage the scan results.

This kind of filter begins by differentiating systems of higher value (and/or liability) from those of lower value/liability. Keep in mind, however, the fact that systems have intrinsic value/liability (based on their criticality to business processing or the sensitivity of information involved) as well as inherited value/liability (based on the criticality or sensitivity of assets those systems may provide access to). An example of a system that might have limited intrinsic value but a high inherited value/liability proposition is a network administrator's laptop. It might have very little information of value stored on it, but it provides access to critical network infrastructure. This process of differentiation can be (and probably should be) established in how the scanner is set up. In other words, configure separate scans for high value versus medium value versus low value systems.

Another important differentiating factor is threat event frequency (TEF). Some organizations we've seen simply carve the threat landscape into two halves—those systems that are Internet-facing (with its higher TEF) versus those systems that are not directly in the line of fire from the Internet. You can be even more granular if you like, for example differentiating those systems that are subject to direct attacks from the Internet (e.g., web applications, servers, network devices, etc.) from those that are exposed through user actions (e.g., desktops and laptops). Here again, you can use this approach to further simplify your evaluation and remediation by creating different scans based on system value/liability and threat landscape (Table 9.1). For example:

Table 9.1 Direct versus Indirect Threat Landscapes Based on Liability

Scan	System Value	Threat Landscape
1	High	Directly internet-facing
2	High	Indirectly internet-facing
3	High	Internal
4	Low	Directly internet-facing
5	Low	Indirectly internet-facing
6	Low	Internal

As you can see, you can be as granular as you like in carving up the scans. There is an investment in time required in order to identify system value and threat landscape, but the benefits in terms of more meaningful results and thus more cost-effective remediation efforts should more than make up for that investment.

A final filter that we've seen applied to good effect is to essentially ignore any scan result of three or lower on a scale of 1–5 (with five being the most severe). The reason being that the vast majority of findings with a rating of three and below are not worth the trouble of tackling through a specific remediation effort. Let the normal upgrade and patching cycle on systems and applications resolve those findings. Are there exceptions? Certainly, but you have to draw the line somewhere. If your organization is more comfortable with including 3's in the remediation mix, have at it. Alternatively, you can remediate 4's and 5's to start with, and if your organization has remaining bandwidth to deal with 3's, it can do so.

With this approach, you can define remediation time frames that match the triaged severity (Table 9.2), for example:

Table 9.2 Defining Remediation Time Frames Matched with the Severity of Threats and System Values

Scan Severity Rating	System Value	Threat Landscape	Remediation Time-Frame
5	High	Directly internet-facing	24 hours
4	High	Directly internet-facing	7 days
5	High	Indirectly internet-facing	7 days
4	High	Indirectly internet-facing	30 days
5	High	Internal	30 days
4	High	Internal	60 days
5	Low	Directly internet-facing	90 days
4	Low	Directly internet-facing	120 days
5	Low	Indirectly internet-facing	120 days
4	Low	Indirectly internet-facing	180 days
5	Low	Internal	180 days
4	Low	Internal	360 days

Please note that we aren't recommending the time frames above, as they're there for illustration purposes. Your organization needs to decide its time frames based on the combination of its tolerance for risk versus the level of effort involved in meeting a timeline.

Clearly, this approach still assumes that the severity ratings provided by the scanners are accurate in terms of how vulnerable a system is likely to be. It also uses qualitative ratings and all the pros and cons that come with that. An approach that can help refine your remediation efforts further, but at the cost of time and energy, is to do FAIR analyses on findings that fall in the top two rows of the table above to validate their relevance. The good news is that in many organizations there would not be that many of those findings to deal with. Once you get into the Indirectly Internet-facing systems though, the numbers of those findings can mount more quickly simply due to the larger number of systems involved.

As you can see, we've applied FAIR principles in this example without using a single PERT distribution or Monte Carlo function. In doing so we've set the organization up to more cost-effectively and consistently manage the risk associated with Vuln scanner results. Of course, your organization might decide that it prefers one of the options we described earlier in this section: aggressive remediation regardless of the effect on business processes, establish long remediation timelines, or simply to live with a lot of missed remediation deadlines.

WEB APPLICATION RISK

Web application vulnerability is a special case of the previous section. There are some unique aspects about it, however, that warrant a short section unto itself.

Similar to vulnerability scanner results in general, we very often see results from web application scanners that don't stand up to even superficial review. Consequently, organizations are faced with the same choices we mentioned before—aggressive remediation regardless of the cost, setting long remediation timelines, or a lot of missed remediation deadlines. Aggressive remediation of web application vulnerabilities—especially for applications written in-house by the organization—potentially has a more direct effect on the organization's ability to grow and evolve as a business. Specifically, very often the programmers who are tasked with fixing vulnerable conditions are the same ones who should be developing new business-enabling web application capabilities and features. As a result, the time spent fixing bugs equates to lost business opportunity. This can create a pretty strong tension between the security team and the development team, as the security team is focused on protecting the organization and the development team is focused on growing the business. It also makes it especially important to only fix bugs that really need to be fixed. Ideally, organizations avoid this problem by writing secure code to begin with, but this is sometimes easier said than done given the complexity of some applications, the inevitable variability in developer skills, and the evolution of threat capabilities.

Some important considerations that can help you triage the findings (we'll call the findings "deficiencies") that come out of many web application vulnerability scanners include:

- Is the web application Internet-facing? If it isn't, then the TEF should be considerably lower, unless an organization has a pretty unusual internal threat landscape.
- Is the deficiency directly accessible or does the attacker have to authenticate to the application first? Obviously, if a deficiency requires authentication, then it is far less likely to be discovered and leveraged through simple means. In other words, the TCap of the threat community is going to have to be higher, and almost any time you raise the TCap, you lower the TEF. There are simply fewer highly skilled and motivated threat agents than there are run-of-the-mill, opportunistic threat agents. When you're talking about an authenticated attack, you are also talking about a targeted attack, which again lowers the TEF. By the way, if your web application has good logging in place, you might actually be able to acquire decent data regarding the volume of illicit activity that takes place by threat agents who have authenticated to the application. Illicit activity tends to have patterns that, once recognized, can alert you to an account that has been compromised, or that the threat agent set up specifically for malicious purposes.

- Speaking of TEF—not all deficiencies experience the same rate of attack, either because they are lower value from the threat agent's perspective, they are harder to execute successfully, or both. Working with experts in web security threat intelligence, you can have some pretty substantial differentiations in TEF between different deficiencies, which can make prioritization much easier.
- Does the deficiency enable the threat agent to compromise a single user account at a time, or the entire customer base? In most cases, you should care much more about any deficiency that enables the threat agent to siphon off the entire contents of the database because of the LM implications. Most of the really damaging web application compromises we've heard of are of this latter variety.
- Does the deficiency enable the threat agent to gain control over the system the application is running on? These can be very dangerous deficiencies; however, the good news is that many of them are more difficult to execute (higher required TCap, lower TEF).

Just using these criteria can help an organization prioritize its web application deficiencies far more effectively than what natively comes out of the scanner. We've also found it very helpful to engage one or more representatives from the development team in performing this kind of triage. It not only helps each team educate the other, but the outcome is (or should be) a jointly agreed upon prioritization. Besides more cost-effective risk management, this also can significantly reduce the tension between the two teams.

We would be remiss if we didn't point out that doing full-fledged FAIR analyses on web application deficiencies enables an organization to make comparisons between the loss exposure a deficiency represents and the cost in person-hours (and perhaps opportunity costs) involved in remediating the deficiency. When an organization is able to do that, it is more explicitly making risk-informed business decisions. At least one web application scanning provider is in the process of integrating FAIR into their product, which will be able to provide automated quantitative loss exposure and cost-to-remediate results for deficiencies they uncover.

On a separate but related topic, we want to state that we're advocates of continuous (or at least high frequency) scanning for Internet-facing web applications versus monthly, quarterly, biannual, or annual scanning. As you will learn in the Controls chapter that follows, the time it takes to discover a deficiency can play a huge role in how much vulnerability a deficiency actually represents, particularly in high TEF environments. Furthermore, we also believe strongly in scanning applications in production rather than just in a test environment. There was a time in the past where scanning methods posed real danger to the stability of web applications, but some scanning providers have a proven track record of being benign.

Note that web application security is a specialty unto itself, and we highly recommend that organizations either hire, engage, or train-up expertise in this area, even if an organization outsources web application development and doesn't develop its own.

CONTRACTORS

If your organization has engaged, or plans to engage, contract workers in or from another country, then the question of additional controls governing their access will come up. Very often, these questions warrant doing a full-fledged FAIR analysis to understand the amount of risk a particular situation represents and which controls are likely to be most cost-effective. The risk associated with offshore contract workers, tends to boil down to an "us versus them" problem. Usual risk scenarios of this category seek to ask questions like, "Should we allow contractors to use their mobile devices to get the email we send them?" or "Is it safe to let the offshore contractors connect to our network using their company's laptops?" We like to take a cynical view of this by calling it a xenophobic risk analysis. This tongue-in-cheek characterization highlights the real question up for consideration: "How much more (or less) likely are contractors from another country to do malicious things than employees or contractors who are native to your country?" This is a TEF question, so much of your thinking should revolve around factors that affect, or could affect, TEF.

Although we believe it's safe to say that people in most countries are not inherently more treacherous or malicious than people in other countries, there are often differences in hiring practices (e.g., background checks), law enforcement practices, and culture that can raise or lower the risk associated with doing business in one country versus another. If you examine those factors you might find cause for greater or lesser concern. However, if there is no reason to believe there are hiring, law enforcement, or cultural differences that would increase TEF, then it may be reasonable to expect that the frequency of malicious acts by the offshore workers would not exceed that of a similar population of the organization's onshore workforce. Another factor that affects TEF is the population of contractors because, all else being equal, a higher population of people means a higher probability of a bad actor. This can be a useful consideration when faced with prioritizing a risk issue that applies to both a larger offshore provider and a smaller one. Regardless of the intrinsic factors that drive TEF, if you can implement controls that are deterrent in nature—e.g., strong monitoring and significant consequences to the contract organization, for example, you have the opportunity to drive a lower likelihood of threat events.

Sometimes, though, the contractors might be innocent of any malicious intent, but instead become unwitting pathways for cyber criminals or nation state actors into your organization's landscape. In fact, the odds may be greater of this sort of compromise than a compromise resulting from a malicious contractor. When considering this angle from a TEF perspective, you need to gain an understanding of the contractor's control environment. We touch on third-party risk briefly again in a later chapter, but it is obviously a major consideration.

Even though the question underlying offshore contractor risk is largely about TEF, it's not the only consideration. If we're to maintain a risk-based focus, we also have to consider LM. When it comes to contractor risk (domestic or offshore), LM usually boils down to three primary factors: (1) the volume/value/liability of data assets the contractors would have access to, (2) the depth and breadth of connectivity they would have into the organization's infrastructure, and (3) the level of administrative or privileged control they would have on critical infrastructure elements (e.g., servers, databases, network, etc.).

Secondary stakeholders are also an important consideration. Sometimes your organization's hand will be forced by prevailing negative perceptions in the industry regarding offshore contractors. In some cases, there is an expectation that a compromise involving offshore contractors would be poorly tolerated by secondary stakeholders, meaning a particularly severe legal and/or regulatory backlash if an event occurred. In other cases regulators, external auditors, or business partners may define specific control requirements the organization feels compelled to comply with regardless of how much risk actually exists. The bottom line is that, given those control expectations, the organization can be assured of harsh reactions from those stakeholders if a loss event occurs. When this is the case, there may be little need for analysis. An organization may decide not to engage offshore contractors based solely on this consideration, or it may implement highly stringent controls on the offshore contractors that it does engage.

From a risk reporting perspective, if your organization has a large number of overseas contractor relationships it may be worthwhile to distinguish contractors from one country versus another. This can be due to the differences mentioned above regarding hiring practices, etc., or perhaps due to the fact that there may be a much larger number of contractors from one country than another, which suggests a greater potential for threat events (all other things being equal). In some circumstances it might even be worthwhile to distinguish between contract organizations if there are significant differences in terms of size, the factors mentioned above, or the type of assets they would have access to. Very often the need to distinguish between countries or contractor organizations comes from questions management has posed regarding which contract relationships represent the most risk.

It's also useful to keep in mind that overseas contract work more often results in loss to an organization through unfulfilled expectations and dissatisfied customers than malicious acts. At least that's been our experience. This is largely attributable to differences in culture and communications, and tends to improve over time as both parties learn how to communicate with each other better in order to understand expectations as well as requirements. Regardless, this represents loss to an organization and perhaps should be part of any analysis (formal or informal) regarding the risk associated with offshore contract work.

A last question worth considering in these scenarios is less about how much stronger an organization's controls should be for offshore personnel but rather why controls for its own employees should be relatively weaker. For example, if the organization has deployed a more secure remote access architecture for its contract workforce, why shouldn't its employees be required to leverage that same architecture since the organization has put the time, money, and energy into building it. It's a very different argument to impose additional controls on employees when you don't already have the controls in place, but once you implement it for the contractors it makes it much more difficult to argue that everyone should not leverage the more secure architecture.

PRODUCTION DATA IN TEST ENVIRONMENTS

You might occasionally (ahem) run into an organization that uses production data, very often sensitive customer data, in test environments. The concern, of course, is that controls in test environments rarely are as strong as those in production environments, which raises the question of how much risk this practice represents. The common options organizations have in this situation are usually not easy or cheap. They can create nonproduction data with sufficient realism that they no longer need to use production data. Sometimes this involves obfuscating (desensitizing) production data so that it no longer represents liability if compromised. (At the time this is being written, obfuscation technologies are becoming more cost-effective, which is a very good thing.) Another option is to implement and maintain production-level security controls in the organization's test environment, which can be challenging in a number of ways. Very often, the situation is complicated by the fact that some organizations don't have a completely independent test environment—i.e., some production systems are required during the course of testing.

Over the years we've encountered another option that some organizations have found to be a good solution, at least until they are in a position to implement one of the options above. This option takes into consideration an aspect of secondary loss that, at least as it has played out to-date in the United States, helps an organization limit its loss exposure to an acceptable level. The suitability of this approach may, of course, vary based on the type of information at risk, the laws in your country, and how the actions of government regulators evolve over time. Our point is that you need to understand the current state of enforcement before proposing this solution where you work. We've included it in this chapter because it might in fact be a useful solution for some organizations, but more importantly because it demonstrates how to leverage FAIR concepts and principles in approaching this sort of problem. With all of those caveats taken care of, let's look at what we're talking about.

The magnitude of loss an organization experiences from the compromise of sensitive customer information is very often highly correlated to the volume of sensitive records involved. For example, a compromise of 10 customer records is far less likely to warrant the wrath of regulatory bodies in the same way a compromise of a million customer records might. Furthermore, the level of media attention and reputation damage from a smaller breach, particularly when there have been some absolutely huge compromises for comparison, will be much less severe. For example, regulators and the media historically haven't gotten too wound up about compromises of fewer than 1000 records. Therefore, if an organization can limit sensitive customer information in its test environment to a smaller volume and only what is absolutely required in order to complete testing, then it is reducing the number of customers placed at risk and its own liability. The key to making this work, of course, is putting into place a process that manages when and how much production data goes into a test environment.

This approach does not affect TEF, at least not significantly. An argument might be made that a smaller volume of sensitive data represents a less attractive target. That said, we find it difficult to materially adjust any TEF estimate based on that argument.

PASSWORD SECURITY

How long should a password be? This is one of the common questions regarding passwords faced by information security teams. On one side of the debate might be an information security professional who wants the minimum password length to be 14 characters, and in the other corner is the business user or customer who uses their cat's name ("Mittens") as their password for everything. In yet another corner of the ring might be a security professional who believes it's a moot question because in their view passwords are useless artifacts of the distant past.

As with so many questions related to information security and risk management, a question regarding the "right" password length or other password attribute is open-ended—i.e., there is no indisputable best answer. That said, some answers make more sense than others in a given circumstance and FAIR can help us find those more sensible answers.

The most common password attributes that we deal with are:

1. Length
2. Composition/complexity
3. Failed attempts before the account is locked out
4. Expiration
5. History/reuse

Each of these has its specific purpose from a security perspective. Length, complexity, and failed attempt limits are intended to make guessing and brute force attacks less likely to succeed. Expiration is intended to limit the useful lifetime of a compromised password and/or limit the available time brute force attacks have before the password changes and the effort has to start all over again. Password reuse limitations are intended to make password guessing more difficult, assuming the attacker has some knowledge of previous passwords. Each of these attributes, however, also makes life a little bit tougher on the user and, users being people, they find ways to compensate whenever life becomes difficult. When it comes to passwords, this means doing things like writing them down on sticky notes, using very simple passwords and simply tacking a number on the end, or virtually reusing passwords by making trivial changes from expiration to expiration (e.g., changing the number at the end of the password from month to month).

TALKING ABOUT RISK

Expiration and history might not contribute to the prevention of guessing quite as much as is hoped. In a 2010 paper by Zhang, Monrose, and Reiter[1], they performed original research that helped explain how effective expiration was to password security. The authors documented previous research indicating that most users adopt some sort of pattern or method for choosing new passwords when their current password expires. Because of this, the authors were able to devise an algorithm that guessed the new password based on an existing password (they had a data set of passwords and password histories). Effectively, it means that their algorithm did really well at guessing the next password you would choose, once it knew your existing password in an offline attack (63% success). They then simulated an online attack and it was successful 17% of the time. Even those that use clever "leetspeak" (the structured substitution of numbers and characters for letters that is commonly used by hackers) signal to attackers that you will use a series of predefined substitutions in up to 75% of accounts, which can limit the effectiveness of an expanded key space.

[1]Zhang, Y., Monrose, F., & Reiter, M. (2010). *The security of modern password expiration: An algorithmic framework and empirical analysis.* In proceedings of the 17th ACM conference on computers and communications. New York: ACM (pp. 176–186). Retrieved 11 Feb 2014 from ACM Digital Library.

In FAIR training, we'll sometimes ask the class to analyze the risk associated with someone using a simple dictionary word for their Internet banking account. Very often, the class begins the analysis with their minds already made up that this scenario represents a lot of risk. After all, conventional wisdom tells us that dictionary words are incredibly easy to crack. But as the class begins thinking through the problem a threat agent faces in attacking online banking accounts, the picture becomes a little clearer, and the question of scenario scope definition becomes more important.

First, of course, a threat agent has to find out, figure out, or guess the account holder username they will be attacking. If it's a blind attack—i.e., they have no specific user account in mind and are just blindly attacking the bank's online interface— then the threat agent has to not only guess the password, they also have to guess account usernames. In many cases, that's a fools errand, especially if the bank's web application recognizes that the login attempt is coming from a different computer than usual, and thus asks some additional security questions. And it is unlikely that truly capable threat agents will waste their time on that approach. This suggests two things regarding this type of attack from an analysis perspective: (1) TEF may not be as high as initially feared, and (2) TCap may be relatively low.

If it isn't a blind attack and the threat agent is going after one or more specific accounts, then they're still faced with finding out or guessing the username. If they have taken the time to find out the username, it suggests either a certain level of threat agent motivation and capability, or that the threat agent is close to the target—i.e., knows them personally. From an analytic perspective this likely means a couple of things: (1) you are dealing with a smaller population of threat agents, and (2) these are more capable actors. Note that a threat agent who is personally close to their target is inherently more capable than one who isn't because of their greater knowledge of the target—knowledge being one aspect of TCap. These threat agents are also more likely to be in a position to learn the password through conversation or observation. The good news is that the population of motivated, personally close threat agents should be very small for most people. A threat agent that isn't close to their target but has the capability and motivation to find out the target's username is probably skillful enough to realize that brute force password guessing against an online banking website is more likely to result in a locked out account than a successful compromise. For these threat agents, there are likely to be better options.

So if blind attacks against the online banking application represent a relatively low loss event frequency because TEF and TCap are low, and if nonblind attacks against specific online bank accounts represent a relatively low loss event frequency because the threat community is so small, then what's left? In today's risk landscape, the most common attacks against online bank accounts are through malware that infects a victim's computer through a fake banking website the victim is redirected to, or some other social engineering approach. When this happens the victim's username and password are captured or given away, which eliminates the need for the threat agent to guess anything. The password could be 20 random characters and it wouldn't matter. Likewise, an attack against the target's data transmission—perhaps by compromising a weak SSL implementation—means the threat agent is able to capture rather than guess the password.

From a LM perspective, most financial institutions have been pretty good about covering losses their account holders incur from online banking attacks. Consequently, at least from a loss of funds perspective, the victim's LM is pretty low. There may, of course, be other secondary loss magnitude (SLM) issues associated with things like bounced checks that try to clear after the threat agent has siphoned off all of the victim's money.

By thinking through the question of weak online banking passwords in this manner, we come up with a clearer understanding of the different scenarios and their relative riskiness. The same sort of approach is useful with any question related to authentication. You have to think through the threat communities, the different vectors of attack, the factors and considerations that affect TEF and TCap within each vector, and the efficacy of the authentication attributes within those vectors. You also have to keep in mind that the more stringent the password attribute settings, the more likely it will be that users will find ways to simplify their password-related challenges. Usually, these methods of simplification create other opportunities for threat agents (e.g., passwords written on sticky notes). The point is, the appropriate balance between security and productivity can be easier to figure out through some structured thinking.

TALKING ABOUT RISK

We are familiar with an organization that took the time to do a thorough risk-based analysis of its authentication attribute options. For the conditions within that organization, the analysis suggested there was little practical difference in terms of risk mitigation between a six or eight character password of moderate complexity. Its optimum password expiration was determined to be 90 days, failed login attempts before lockout was five, and password history/reuse limitation was five. Your organization's mileage may vary, but the business side of this organization appreciated what they perceived to be a more reasonable set of requirements. The organization also was well positioned to provide a clear set of rationale to anyone who had questions about why they set their password attributes the way they did.

BASIC RISK ANALYSIS

In the absence of doing a quantitative risk analysis, you can always do what might be referred to as a quasi-quantitative analysis. This involves using a set of predefined quantitative ranges that have been labeled using qualitative terms, and then leveraging a set of matrices based on the FAIR ontology. If you read the original white paper on FAIR from 2005, you might recognize this as the BRAG (Basic Risk Analysis Guide) process. We've included an updated version of it here because we've gotten feedback that people found it to be useful. Before using this assessment guide, there are a few things to keep in mind:

- Using this guide effectively requires a solid understanding of FAIR concepts and methods
- The fidelity you get from scales like these is not very high
- Sometimes it's difficult to decide between one scale versus another (e.g., "high" versus "medium") because the actual value might straddle the two ranges. In this case, you can choose the more conservative ("paranoid") or less conservative value based on whatever rationale you feel you can defend. Alternatively, you can do the analysis twice—once using each of the two scale values in question. You might find that the results of the analysis are not affected by the choice. If the results are different between the two values, you can report both results to management, explaining the reason for the difference.
- The LM scale described in this section is adjusted for a specific organizational size and risk capacity. Labels used in the scale (e.g., "very high", "low," etc.) may need to be adjusted when analyzing organizations of different sizes

  Basic FAIR analysis is comprised of 12 steps in four stages:
  Stage 1—Identify scenario components

1. Identify the asset at risk
2. Identify the threat community under consideration

   Stage 2—Evaluate Loss Event Frequency (LEF)

3. Estimate the probable TEF
4. Estimate TCap
5. Estimate Difficulty
6. Derive Vuln
7. Derive primary loss event frequency (PLEF)
8. Derive secondary loss event frequency (SLEF)

   Stage 3—Evaluate LM

9. Estimate probable loss magnitude (PLM)
10. Estimate SLM

    Stage 4—Derive and articulate Risk

11. Derive and articulate primary and secondary risk
12. Derive and articulate overall risk

   You will note as you read the process description that follows that we have included example choices and derived values based on those choices.

STAGE 1—IDENTIFY SCENARIO COMPONENTS

Step 1—Identify the asset(s) at risk

In order to estimate the control and value characteristics within a risk analysis, the analyst must first identify the asset (object) under evaluation.

Asset(s) at risk: _____

Step 2—Identify the threat community

In order to estimate TEF and TCap, a specific threat community must first be identified. At minimum, when evaluating the risk associated with malicious acts, the analyst has to decide whether the threat community is human or malware, internal or external, etc. In many circumstances, it's helpful to define the threat community more specifically—e.g., network engineers, cleaning crew, etc., and characterize the expected nature of the community.

Threat community: _____

Description	

STAGE 2—EVALUATE LOSS EVENT FREQUENCY

Step 3—TEF

Using the scale below, estimate the TEF for the threat community under analysis against the asset under analysis (Table 9.3).

Contributing factors: Contact frequency, probability of action.

Table 9.3 Scale Used to Estimate Amount of Threat and Times Per Year

Rating	✔	Description
Very high (VH)		>100 times per year
High (H)		Between 10 and 100 times per year
Moderate (M)	X	Between 1 and 10 times per year
Low (L)		Between 0.1 and 1 times per year
Very low (VL)		<0.1 times per year (less than once every 10 years)

Rationale	

Step 4—TCap

Using the scale below, estimate the capability of the threat community under analysis (Table 9.4).

Contributing factors: Skill, resources.

Table 9.4 Scale Used to Estimate the Skills and Capabilities of the Threat Community Under Analysis

Rating	✔	Description
Very high (VH)		Top 2% when compared against the overall threat population
High (H)		Top 16% when compared against the overall threat population
Moderate (M)	X	Average skill and resources (between bottom 16% and top 16%)
Low (L)		Bottom 16% when compared against the overall threat population
Very low (VL)		Bottom 2% when compared against the overall threat population

Rationale	

Step 5—Difficulty

Contributing factors: Strength, variance over time (Table 9.5).

Table 9.5 Scale Measuring Degree of Strength Variance Over Time

Rating	✔	Description
Very high (VH)		Protects against all but the top 2% of an avg. threat population
High (H)		Protects against all but the top 16% of an avg. threat population
Moderate (M)	X	Protects against the average threat agent
Low (L)		Only protects against bottom 16% of an avg. threat population
Very low (VL)		Only protects against bottom 2% of an avg. threat population

Rationale	

Step 6—Vuln

In this step, you plot the Difficulty and TCap values from the previous steps against the matrix in Figure 9.1 to derive Vuln.

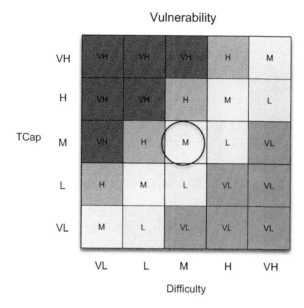

FIGURE 9.1

Deriving venerability.

    TCap (from Step 4): _M___
    Difficulty (from Step 5): __M__
    Vuln (from matrix above): __M__

Step 7—PLEF

Plot the TEF value from Step 3 and the Vuln value from Step 6 against the matrix in Figure 9.2 to arrive at the PLEF for the scenario.
    TEF (from Step 3): __M__
    Vuln (from Step 6): __M__
    PLEF (from matrix above): __M__

Step 8—SLEF

Using the percentage ranges in the table below, estimate the percentage of time that secondary losses would result from primary events (note that you can skip this step if secondary losses are not possible or are extremely unlikely). We'll refer to this as secondary loss event % (SLE%).

Using the estimated SLE% from the task above, and the PLEF from Step 7, use the matrix in Figure 9.3 to derive the SLEF (Table 9.6).

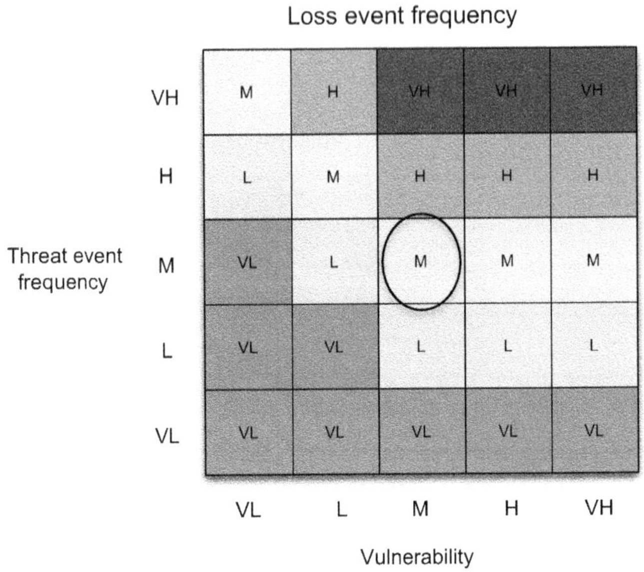

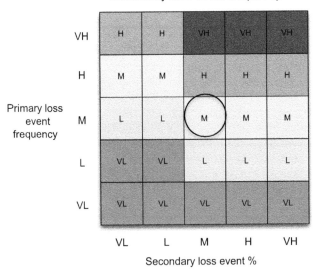

FIGURE 9.2

Deriving loss event frequency.

FIGURE 9.3

Deriving secondary loss event frequency.

Table 9.6 Percentage Ranges Used to Estimate Secondary Loss Event %, or SLE %

Frequency		Range Low End	Range High End
Very high (VH)		90%	100%
High (H)		70%	90%
Moderate (M)	X	30%	70%
Low (L)		10%	30%
Very low (VL)		0	10%

Rationale	

PLEF (from Step 7): __M___
SLE % (from the table above): __M___
SLEF (from the matrix above): __M___

STAGE 3—EVALUATE PROBABLE LOSS MAGNITUDE (PLM)

Step 9—Estimate PLM

Using the scale below (Table 9.7), estimate the LM for each form of loss that might result from the loss event being analyzed. As demonstrated below, put those estimates in the appropriate columns in the table that follows (Table 9.8). Note that your estimate can reflect either the most likely magnitude of loss, the worst-case loss, or best-case loss. We typically recommend using the most likely loss value. You can do a separate analysis using worst-case values if you believe that would be helpful.

Table 9.7 Scale Used to Measure or Evaluate Probable Loss Magnitude (PLM)

Magnitude	Range Low End	Range High End
Very high (VH)	$1M	–
High (H)	$100K	$1M
Moderate (M)	$10K	$100K
Low (L)	$1K	$10K
Very low (VL)	$0	$1K

Table 9.8 Overall Probable Loss Magnitude (PLM) Derived from the Loss Event

Productivity	Response	Replacement	Fines & Judgments	Competitive Advantage	Reputation
	Moderate	Low			

Having entered values for each loss form, you simply "sum" them to arrive at an overall PLM. In the example above, we might assume that the replacement losses added to the Response losses would not be sufficiently large to make the overall PLM high, thus the overall PLM would remain moderate.

Overall PLM (from the scale/table above): __M__

Step 10—Estimate secondary loss magnitude (SLM)

You estimate SLM (Table 9.9 and 9.10) in the same way you did with PLM in Step 9.

Table 9.9 Scale Used to Estimate Secondary Loss Magnitude (SLM)

Magnitude	Range Low End	Range High End
Very high (VH)	$1M	–
High (H)	$100K	$1M
Moderate (M)	$10K	$100K
Low (L)	$1K	$10K
Very low (VL)	$0	$1K

Table 9.10 Values in Response to Scale Used to Estimate Secondary Loss Value

Productivity	Response	Replacement	Fines & Judgments	Competitive Advantage	Reputation
	Moderate		Low		Low

Depending on the scenario we might take the values in the table above and decide that the overall secondary loss is High.

Overall SLM (from the scale/table above): __H__

STAGE 4—DERIVE AND ARTICULATE RISK

Step 11—Derive and articulate primary and secondary risk

At this point you simply plot both the primary and secondary risk values on the matrix in Figure 9.4.

Primary LEF: ____M_____ (from Step 7)
Secondary LEF: _____M____ (from Step 8)
Primary PLM: _____M____ (from Step 9)
Secondary PLM: _____H____(from Step 10)
Primary risk (from the matrix above): __M___
Secondary risk (from the matrix above): __H___

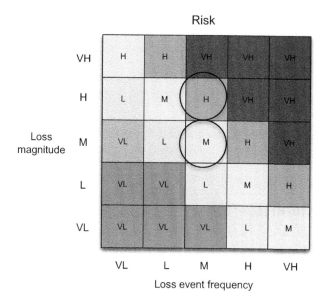

FIGURE 9.4

Deriving risk.

Step 12—Derive and articulate overall risk

Using the values from Step 11 and the matrix in Figure 9.5 you can derive the overall risk for the analysis.

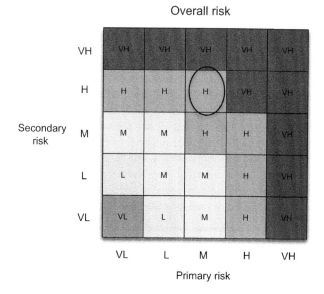

FIGURE 9.5

Deriving overall risk.

Primary risk (from Step 11): __M__
Secondary risk (from Step 11): __H__
Overall risk (from the matrix above): __H__

SECTION SUMMARY

Having read this far in the book, you undoubtedly see the numerous inherent limitations of an approach like BRAG. Nonetheless, sometimes quick-and-dirty is good enough.

PROJECT PRIORITIZATION

NOTE: You might find it useful to read the Controls and Risk Management chapters before reading this section. We won't assume you've done that, though, and have tried to provide sufficient context so that what follows is not confusing.

At least once per year, most information security organizations have to prioritize the areas for improvement they will go to battle for in the annual budget wars. Very often, this process takes the form of getting key people from the information security team together for a couple of days to discuss, debate, and sometimes furiously argue their different perspectives. In the end, perhaps majority rules. Or perhaps the CISO (or equivalent) simply pulls rank. Regardless, although there is usually very good dialogue in those discussions, the dialogue usually isn't structured in a way that enables clear comparisons to be made. As a result, when pressed, people who take part in those discussions often can't confidently assert that the most important issues facing the organization are being addressed. Even when they are initially confident, that confidence will often break down if they're asked to explain in depth why one project was chosen and another wasn't. The explanation might boil down to, "That's what most of the people in the room felt was most important." Of course, the group opinion might be spot-on. Or at least they might be in the right ballpark. Or not. Unfortunately, the process doesn't lend itself to much assurance in that regard.

Part of the problem is that these discussions tend to be controls-focused rather than risk-focused. For example, an audit or security review may have identified control deficiencies and labeled them as high risk, but that is very different than asking the question, "Where does the greatest amount of risk exist in the organization (and why), and which control improvements will have the greatest positive effect?" Until you answer this question, improving controls is a bit of a shot in the dark. Not entirely, of course, because information security and audit personnel bring experience and intelligence to the table, but it increases the odds of missing something important.

TALKING ABOUT RISK

Speaking of audit professionals, it isn't unusual to see them take a risk-focused view of the world. They often logically differentiate the organization's business processes (e.g., finance, HR, etc.) and then identify different "inherent risks" that could occur within each business process (e.g., financial misstatement within the finance process). These inherent risks are events that would be expected to go wrong *in the absence of any control*. They might then assign each of those inherent risk events a rating (high, medium, low, etc.) to reflect the damage that would be expected if the event occurred. Supposedly then, the business processes that have high inherent risks would warrant the greatest amount of risk management attention. On the surface, this seems logical. In practical application, though, not so much. Allow us to provide an illustration.

Consider a bank. The bank has numerous processes that handle money and certainly in the *absence of any controls* there is a distinct possibility that the money would go missing from any of these processes. These "inherent risk" events would probably be labeled high-risk under the assumption that money is important to the bank. Some folks might jump in and say, "Wait a minute. Not all of the bank's processes handle the same amount of money. Therefore some processes would have a higher level of inherent risk than others." Our answer to that is, "What keeps one process from handling more or less money than another?" It seems that one obvious answer would be, controls do.

But what about some of the other processes in a bank? HR perhaps? What kind of inherent risk events does it have and how severe could they be? Well, in the *absence of any controls* it is entirely possible that the bank would hire a convicted serial killer like Hannibal Lecter as its CEO—or perhaps worse—as head chef for the dining hall. Or both. We are talking about *no HR controls*, after all. There also would be inherent HR risk events related to inappropriate conduct of various severe sorts that we will leave undescribed here. The prospect of no controls for HR seems to suggest that the inherent risk level for HR is also high. How about the dining hall? What risk events are inherent there? In the absence of any controls related to food storage or preparation—sick and dead people all over the place, which suggests that the dining hall also has high inherent risk. Our point is simply that in the absence of any controls we have a really hard time coming up with a business process that isn't high risk. A big part of the problem is that most people we've talked with aren't actually thinking of NO controls when they're estimating inherent risk. In most cases, they're thinking about the absence of some controls (maybe the most obvious ones) and often haven't explicitly considered exactly what they're including or excluding.

Notionally, inherent risk sounds good, but it seems to fall apart pretty fast under any sort of examination. The primary problem is its reliance on that concept of "absence of any control." We believe a much more realistic and useful approach is to consider inherent risk to be the current risk levels given the existing set of controls rather than the hypothetical notion of an absence of any controls. Residual risk would then be whatever risk levels remain after additional controls are applied. Another option is to measure residual risk using FAIR and then subtract the effect of specific controls to arrive at inherent risk. In this approach, inherent risk wouldn't reflect a "no controls whatsoever" condition, but rather a situation absent of specific controls, which is much more realistic.

In order to be consistently effective at prioritizing information security projects, you have to first prioritize the risk-related challenges the organization faces, and then select the most cost-effective solutions for those most important problems. From our perspective, this cries out for quantitative analysis for at least two reasons: (1) it makes it much easier to differentiate and prioritize the problems and potential solutions, and (2) it articulates project value proposition in terms that can even the playing field in those budget wars. That said, maybe your organization hasn't decided to do quantitative analysis just yet or hasn't acquired the tools to do so. Not wanting to leave you high and dry on this score, we will give you some ideas on how to tackle the problem without resorting to numbers.

PRIORITIZING THE PROBLEMS

There are several high-level questions an organization needs to consider when evaluating its risk landscape: (1) how much risk exists currently, (2) where is it concentrated, (3) what control deficiencies are most contributing to those areas of high concentration, and (4) how is the organization positioned to manage risk over time?

Of these four questions, the last three can be answered to some degree without quantitative analysis, which is what we will cover in the sections below.

TALKING ABOUT RISK

There are those in the industry who believe that prioritization should boil down to those issues, management is most interested in dealing with rather than issues that represent the most risk to the organization. We concede to their argument if, and only if, no analysis has been done to determine which issues represent the most risk. In that case, of course, it boils down to whatever bur is in management's saddle at the time (e.g., which media report or scary story they've most recently heard). In our experience, however, management tends to be most interested in dealing with the stuff that represents the most risk to the organization. We just have to be able to identify which issues those are and help the decision-makers wrap their heads around the issues and their severity. The only way to do that is through some form of analysis and communication of the results in terms they understand.

Risk concentration

There are several ways to approach the question of identifying where risk is concentrated in an organization. You can structure your analysis with a business process focus, a technology focus, or a combination of the two. A business process focus is similar to how we described audit's approach above (minus the use of inherent risk for obvious reasons). You identify the primary business processes in the organization and evaluate the current level of risk in each. Taking a technology-focused approach involves carving the organization's landscape into chunks that might look something like the following:

- Internet-facing web applications
- Internet-facing servers
- Internet-facing network devices
- Internal web applications
- Legacy applications
- Network devices
- Personal systems (desktops and laptops)
- Mobile devices
- Databases
- Unmanaged databases

The granularity of how you carve up your world can be as coarse or fine as you like. Finer granularity provides higher precision but at the expense of more work. We suggest that you start with relatively coarse granularity and evolve to higher granularity as need and resources dictate.

A combined approach involves carving up the risk landscape by business process and then within each business process adding another layer of coarse technology-focused differentiation. It might look something like this:

- Online banking business process
  - Web applications
  - Servers
  - Databases

When carving up the landscape in this manner, the question often comes up regarding "shared services and systems" like those provided by the IT organization. We've found it usually works well to define a separate business process referred to as "IT shared services" (or something like that) to encompass those parts of the technology infrastructure that aren't easy to associate solely with one of the other business functions. If your organization has affiliates, subsidiaries, or very distinct lines of business, you can add another layer of abstraction over the top of the business process. The point is, you can carve up your landscape in any way that is logical and useful.

Regardless of how you carve up the landscape, the next step is to begin a high-level risk analysis of each element. The process for doing this should be reminiscent of the analyses we discussed earlier in this chapter. You should consider the value and liability of the assets at risk, the threats against those assets, and the existing control conditions that protect the assets. You can accomplish this by applying the BRAG process we covered earlier. You can also just apply qualitative values to each scenario in a scoping table like the one shown below for the Internet Banking web application (Table 9.11):

You will notice that we added columns for TEF, LM, controls, and risk. Here again, since this is intended to be quick-and-dirty, we aren't going very deep analysis-wise, but it's still likely to be better than the approach most organizations use today. You will need to establish some definitions for the different ratings in each column. For example, loss values of "H" mean that there is potential for significant impact if a loss event occurs. For control efficacy, perhaps an "H" rating means that the controls are believed to be well designed and variance in their condition is low (and yes, we cringe a bit every time we use qualitative ratings, but they still serve a useful purpose. You just have to understand and accept their limitations.)

You can expand or contract the scoping table as you see fit. As we mentioned above, greater granularity provides higher precision but at cost in terms of the time required to complete the table. You will learn pretty quickly the level of granularity that best fits your needs. It's another example of the trade-offs that are part-and-parcel of risk management.

After you've evaluated the risk associated with each element in your risk landscape, you should have a better idea of which parts of the landscape represent the most risk to the organization—i.e., where risk is concentrated.

Asset control deficiencies

After identifying where risk is concentrated in your organization, you will need to examine the control conditions that are contributing to those higher concentrations of risk. Before we go any further, though, we need to make a distinction that is covered in-depth in the Controls chapter. When we're talking about controls in this section we are referring to controls that directly affect loss exposure at the asset level. In other words, these controls play a role in one or more branches of the FAIR ontology that we covered in Chapter 3; for example, passwords and other authentication controls that affect an asset's Difficulty, backup and recovery controls that affect LM when an

Table 9.11 High-Level Risk Analysis by Considering Value/Liability, Threats, and Control Conditions

Asset at Risk	Threat Community	Threat Type	Effect	Internet Banking Process			
				Loss	Threat Event Frequency (TEF)	Control Efficacy	Risk Rating
Web app	Priv insiders	Malicious	Confidentiality	H	L	M	M
Web app	Priv insiders	Malicious	Availability	M	L	M	L
Web app	Priv insiders	Malicious	Integrity	M	L	M	L
Web app	Priv insiders	Error	Confidentiality	M	L	M	L
Web app	Priv insiders	Error	Availability	M	M	M	L
Web app	Priv insiders	Error	Integrity	M	L	L	L
Web app	Cyber criminals	Malicious	Confidentiality	H	H	H	M
Web app	Cyber criminals	Malicious	Availability	M	L	H	L
Web app	Cyber criminals	Malicious	Integrity	M	L	M	L
Web app	Acts of god	Natural	Availability	H	L	H	L
Web app	Infrastructure	Failure	Availability	M	L	M	L

asset experiences an availability event, logging and monitoring controls that may act as a deterrent and thus reduce TEF from threat agents who might attack the asset, etc. In the next section, we'll discuss controls that affect risk indirectly. Examples of these controls include things like auditing, policies, risk analysis, asset inventories, etc.

Understanding that we are focusing on asset-level controls at this point in the process, you'll want to evaluate the condition of controls that are relevant within each branch of the risk ontology. For the asset you're evaluating, do control opportunities exist that can reduce TEF through reducing contact with threat agents (e.g., firewalls and other ways of creating a layer of defense in depth between a threat community and an asset) or reducing TEF through deterrence (e.g., improved logging and monitoring, or stronger consequences)? Are there opportunities to increase Difficulty through better authentication, access privilege management, or structural integrity (e.g., patching, configuration management, or more secure coding standards)? Likewise, are there opportunities for improvement in detection and response controls (e.g., logging, backups, recovery processes, incident and crisis management practices, etc.)? To a large degree, this is simply a deeper dive into the Control Efficacy column you might have used if you used a scoping table like the one above.

The most significant opportunities for improvement identified in this part of the process will become a large part of the focus when we discuss solution selection a little further on. By the way, there is a decent chance this process will identify opportunities for control improvements that are common across more than one asset and/or set of scenarios. These systemic opportunities are especially valuable to recognize and leverage.

Risk management

How much risk an organization has, where risk is concentrated, and the asset-level control deficiencies that contribute to those conditions are lagging indicators of the organization's ability to manage risk over time. In other words, the decisions made within an organization and the organization's ability to consistently execute against those decisions created those risk and deficient asset-level control conditions. We provide a lot more material on this in the following chapters, so we'll keep things relatively high-level in this section. For our purposes here, we will consider risk management to be a simple function of the organization's ability to make well-informed decisions and its ability to execute against those decisions over time. The bottom line is that you can reduce risk concentrations by improving asset-level controls until the cows come home, but if you haven't identified and remediated the causes for those conditions, you're just playing whack-a-mole.

Risk decision-making quality boils down to two things: (1) the quality of information decision makers are operating from, and (2) the decision-makers themselves. The second of these is (or should be) the simpler of the two—making sure decisions are made by people who are authorized to make those decisions and are held accountable for those decisions. This is straightforward enough that we don't need to discuss it further here. The information quality component of risk decision-making is also relatively basic in concept. That said, it tends to be more problematic in practice.

In our experience, there are generally two components to information quality that are substantially broken in many organizations: (1) risk landscape visibility, and (2) the quality of risk analyses. The first component, risk landscape visibility, seems to be a significant problem in most organizations of any size or complexity. It is a rare thing for us to encounter an organization that has strong visibility into all of the following: the organization's assets, the threat landscape those assets exist in, and the control conditions surrounding those assets. For that matter, it's relatively uncommon for us to encounter organizations that have good visibility into even one of those elements. Without reasonably good visibility into all three of those aspects of the risk landscape, it's pretty difficult to argue that an organization is managing risk well.

TALKING ABOUT RISK

There may be some readers who rejoice at that last sentence and will say something to the effect of, "See! We've said all along that risk management isn't possible because you can never know all of the assets, all of the threats, or the condition of all of the controls!" These people are half right. Perfect knowledge of those elements is not possible, but risk management isn't about perfect knowledge. Good risk management is about making the most of the information you do have and continually improving your information over time; and just so we are clear—people who say they don't do risk management are fooling themselves. Every decision a thinking animal makes has a risk component to it, whether it's consciously recognized as such or not. Animals that hope to survive make choices that are intended to balance reward with an acceptable level of risk, and they never have perfect information to support those decisions. This is risk management, whether you choose to call it that or not.

We describe visibility in more detail in a later chapter and share an approach that can help an organization make significant improvements. Until then, simply recognize that visibility plays a major role in whether an organization is making well-informed risk decisions.

Regardless of how good or bad an organization's visibility might be, if analysis of the available data is bad, then decisions are going to be poorly informed. If analysis consistently inflates risk ratings, then decision-makers are faced with a low signal to noise ratio—i.e., they won't be able to discern the truly important stuff. The means they're more likely to spend resources on issues that should not be a priority and overlook things that should be a priority. This leaves the organization with more risk than it would like and wastes resources that could be applied to other objectives.

Remember that earlier section where we discussed a process for identifying risk concentrations? Well, keep in mind that your ability to do that process well is inherently affected by the visibility limitations your organization currently has, as well as the quality of analysis performed. This isn't intended to discount the value of the work you've done to identify risk concentrations, it's simply intended to point out that you should view that work as a first pass and that it will undoubtedly be refined as your visibility and analysis quality improve. You have to start somewhere.

Now that we understand the risk management elements that need to be evaluated, we need to discuss how to go about it. The simplest approach is simply to ask yourself whether your organization has good visibility in all three elements and whether it benefits from good analysis. If your organization is like most, the answers to these two questions are, "no" and "no," which means you can add them to the organization's list of really important risk-related problems that need to be resolved. If you want to go a little further with the analysis (and you should), you can leverage the landscape definition used in the risk concentration process. If you defined a technology-focused landscape, then your table might look something like the one below (Table 9.12):

Table 9.12 Risk Management Scale for a Technology-Focused Landscape

Technology	Asset Visibility	Threat Visibility	Control Visibility
Internet-facing web applications	H	M	M
Legacy applications	H	H	H
Network devices	H	L	M
Personal systems	M	L	L
Mobile devices	L	L	L
Databases	M	M	M
Unmanaged databases	L	L	L

A similar table can be developed if a business process-focused (or combination business and technology-focused) definition was used for the risk landscape.

As you can see, visibility is likely to vary across the risk landscape. By combining some initial analysis regarding where visibility is particularly weak and the level of risk each element is believed to represent (as identified in the risk concentration process), you can prioritize your visibility improvement efforts.

Prioritizing the challenges an organization has with poor risk analysis has two dimensions: (1) the analysis method being used, and (2) where to apply more mature analyses versus less mature analyses. We assume you can guess which method we favor, which just leaves the question of where to apply more versus less mature methods. To a very large degree, the answer depends on a combination of the level of effort required, the resources that are available, and the gravity of the decision. The good news is that the newest generation of FAIR-based software has vastly simplified the process, which makes it far more feasible to apply FAIR broadly. This will continue to improve as the tools evolve. Nonetheless, broad data integration with security and GRC tools will not happen over night, which means the question of when to do mature analysis will still be relevant for a while. There also will be some parts of the risk decision-making landscape that can never be automated.

As you can probably imagine, there is no single rule of thumb for when to apply more mature risk analysis methods versus not. That said, there are a few situations where we believe it is either necessary or generally worthwhile to perform fully quantified analyses:

- Building business cases for expensive or burdensome risk mitigation initiatives
- Communicating the significance of particularly nasty risk conditions to management, especially if the conditions themselves are difficult for non-security people to grasp
- Establishing an organization's information security risk appetite
- Measuring and communicating where an organization stands relative to its risk appetite
- Prioritizing significant risk issues that defy differentiation using qualitative methods

Having gotten this far in the book, we suspect you've already begun to develop a sense of where FAIR can be applied quantitatively versus qualitatively in your organization. As you read the following chapters, your perspective on this is likely to become more refined and clearer.

SOLUTION SELECTION

Once an organization has identified its most critical risk related challenges, there are almost always more than one way to mitigate those challenges. There are cheap fixes, quick-and-dirty fixes, expensive fixes, systemic fixes, and sophisticated fixes for almost any problem you can think of. Some remedies will be relatively painless to the business, whereas others will be anything but painless. We can leverage FAIR to help us think through the options and determine which is the best choice in any given circumstance.

Before going any further, we need to recognize that not every organization agonizes much over which solution they prefer. Sometimes they have a favorite vendor. Other times they simply don't want to think that hard about it and prefer to just go with their gut. Regardless, the information below is simply a proposed alternative for those who do prefer to exercise a more structured approach to this type of decision.

Selecting the most appropriate solution for a particular problem is often simpler than prioritizing which problem to solve in the first place. For example, let's imagine that you followed the prioritization approach we described earlier and decided your organization's highest priority was to reduce the risk associated with its Internet-facing web applications. In this case, all of the solution options will serve one primary purpose—reducing the frequency and/or magnitude of loss associated with internet-facing web applications. As a result, comparing your options is relatively straightforward. Which solution provides the most risk reduction at the lowest cost and burden to the business? Sometimes there will need to be another variable related to how quickly a solution can be put into place. This will depend in large part on the expected frequency of threat events. If TEF is very low relative to the time it will take to implement the mitigation solution, then implementation timeliness may be less important.

TALKING ABOUT RISK

There are those in the industry who advocate that political considerations—i.e., what management and other stakeholders are most comfortable with—should be the prevailing factor in choosing risk mitigation solutions. We know full well that politics can play an important role in risk management, but we would never base our recommendation on politics, because in our view that is disingenuous and represents an abdication of our responsibility as professionals. Our responsibility is to help management make well-informed decisions. If their decisions run contrary to our advice, that is fine—even if their decisions are politically motivated. At least we've given them a legitimate opportunity to make a well-informed decision.

Going back to our example, where Internet-facing web applications are considered to be the most important issue, there could be several mitigation options to consider:

- Training in secure programing practices for the software developers
- Implementation of a web application firewall (WAF)
- Implementation of continuous web application Vuln scanning
- Improved web application logging and monitoring

There would likely be other options as well (we can think of a few), but this will do for illustration purposes.

To begin the comparison process, you first need to identify the manner in which each option affects the frequency and/or magnitude of loss. We'll map these affects against elements in the FAIR taxonomy, and (because we aren't doing the quant approach in this example) we'll use an ordinal scale (with five being highly effective) to express our beliefs about the efficacy of each solution. The table below illustrates this approach (Table 9.13):

Table 9.13 Threat Scale for Training, WAF, Scanning, and Logging

Solution	Threat Event Frequency (TEF)	Vulnerability (Vuln)	Primary Loss Mag	Secondary Loss Mag	Cost	Burden
Training		2			Moderate	Low
WAF	4				Moderate	Moderate
Scanning		4*			Moderate	Low
Logging		1**	2	1	Moderate	Low

Don't take the ratings shown in this table seriously. They are there for illustration purposes and may or may not be accurate for your organization. Some things to note about our table:

- We didn't include a column for timeliness, because it was assumed going into the analysis that all of the options could be implemented in relatively short order. Why include a column for comparison when all of the options are expected to be roughly the same?
- The cost column ended up being roughly equal, but it was included because we didn't go into the analysis expecting that to be the case. Because all of the options turned out to be equal on that score, it became irrelevant as a variable for comparison.
- The asterisk for scanning denotes a dependency or caveat of some sort. In this case, the caveat has to do with scanning being just one piece of the puzzle. Continuous vulnerability scanning can have a profound effect on an organization's ability to detect deficient conditions rapidly, but if the ratings that come out of a scanner aren't accurate (as we discussed earlier) or if the organization is slow to remediate deficiencies, then scanning's efficacy in reducing risk is not going to be realized. Consequently, when evaluating specific scanning solutions, it's necessary to evaluate the solution's ability to accurately rate the deficiencies it finds. By the way, the ability to rate deficiencies effectively also strongly affects the organization's ability to remediate deficiencies in a timely fashion. If the ratings are accurate, there are almost certainly going to be fewer "critical" or "high risk" findings, and thus organizations are much more likely to treat them seriously.
- Logging is an interesting entry because it appears to affect risk in more than one way. If illicit activity captured in the log is recognized and reported quickly enough, an organization can make changes that could interrupt an attack while it's in progress and before its had a chance to be successful. That reduces vulnerability. It is dependent, however, on timely recognition and reporting of the illicit activity (i.e., monitoring), which is why that entry has asterisks. Absent timely recognition and reporting this control has no effect on vulnerability. Logging's effect on PLM has to do with a reduction in investigation efforts, which can be relatively substantial if logging is poor. Likewise, good logging can potentially reduce secondary loss if, for example, an organization is able to confidently determine the breadth and depth of a compromise, which can avoid unnecessary notification and other secondary costs.
- Some of you may be wondering why the WAF effect was rated in the TEF column versus the Vuln column. The reason is this—firewalls shield the assets behind them. In other words, the web application never experiences the exploits (the threat events) that are blocked by the WAF—i.e., there is a reduction in TEF at the web application layer of abstraction. The vulnerability of the web application itself hasn't changed, but the organization has deployed defense-in-depth that results in a reduction in loss exposure.

- The burden column is just a way to express how much reduction in productivity the organization is expected to realize. In this example, perhaps there's an expectation that keeping the WAF rules in tune with web application changes might impose a reduction in how quickly the organization can deploy new releases. Note that we aren't suggesting this is necessarily true. This is just for illustration purposes.

Also, you will want to provide some sort of definition for each ordinal scale value (e.g., 1 = "Expected to reduced loss exposure by less than some percentage," etc.) and the qualitative labels (e.g., "Moderate cost is between $x and $y dollars in annual TCO"). Yes, we know, as soon as you do that it begins to feel like you are half way to doing quantitative analysis. You can choose to go fully qualitative if you prefer, and just use qualitative descriptions for each ordinal or qualitative value. Keep in mind that we are talking quick-and-dirty here.

At the end of the exercise, one solution or another will hopefully stand out from the others, making the choice more clear. If none of the options stand out, then make the decision recognizing that you at least took the time to think through the choices and can explain that there wasn't a clear winner based on the criteria you used, or maybe you will consider yet another criteria (e.g., whether an option closes a compliance gap) that will swing the decision. You may also find that the best option (if you can afford them) is to implement more than one of the solutions.

A final note on this section; the example we showed above involved solutions that affect frequency or magnitude of loss directly (asset-level controls). Not all controls do this. For example, doing better risk analysis (which is a decision-making control) affects risk but does so by improving the organization's ability to know which problems are most severe and which solutions are likely to be most cost-effective. You will learn more about this in the Controls chapter. The point is that it is relatively easy to compare two or more controls that affect risk directly. It is also relatively easy to compare two or more controls that affect risk indirectly. It is much more challenging, however, to compare a control that affects risk directly with one that does not. The good news is that you shouldn't have to face that challenge because these different types of controls solve different problems.

SMART COMPLIANCE

Compliance with government regulations or industry standards like the Payment Card Industry's Data Security Standard is a choice. We know some people will consider this to be a controversial or even an outrageous statement, but it is true nonetheless. Please understand that we are not advocating noncompliance; we're just pointing out that the decision to comply is yet another of the many risk decisions an organization has to make. Having said this, it is also true that many organizations would prefer to comply and avoid the pain that can accompany noncompliance—sanctions, damaged reputation, reduced business opportunities, and in some cases, fines or even criminal prosecution. Still, there are a number of laws, regulations, standards, and contracts that many organizations find themselves not complying with on a daily basis. We worked with a retail establishment on one occasion that revealed it constantly found itself in some state of violation of law simply due to the volume of federal, state, county, and local municipal laws under which it operated. The organization's leadership actively decided that it far simpler to pay (some) of the fines associated with noncompliance than it was to manage the necessary program and staff to ensure 100% compliance. This may outrage some of you, although we suspect you aren't altogether unsurprised. This is one of those situations where leadership in the organization has taken a higher-level view of the risk posed by noncompliance and found it preferable to the expenses required to bring noncompliant systems into compliance.

RISK ASSOCIATED WITH NONCOMPLIANCE

We have encountered people who don't initially recognize that "noncompliance risk" can be analyzed just like any other risk scenario. It still comes down to a question of the frequency (or likelihood) of a noncompliant condition being identified and the losses that result from such an event. In fact, we have had the opportunity to use FAIR to help organizations understand the amount of noncompliance risk they have. There are primarily three types of noncompliance scenarios, the differences boiling down to how the threat event materializes.

The first scenario type is when an auditor or regulator initiates a review of an organization's compliance. In these scenarios, the threat community is the auditor, regulator or other party who would evaluate the organization, potentially identify noncompliant conditions and perhaps be the catalyst for losses. Generally, TEF is simply the frequency of examinations the organization is subject to and Vuln boils down to the probability that a noncompliant condition will be identified and losses result. It really is fundamentally no different than any other risk analysis. The only difference worth noting is that any fines or judgments levied by the auditor or regulator, and the costs associated with defending against those losses, would be considered primary loss instead of the more usual situation where those types of losses are secondary. These losses become primary losses because the primary threat community in the scenario (the regulator), rather than a secondary stakeholder, inflicts them.

The second scenario type occurs when a compromise occurs that stimulates regulator actions against the organization. For example, a healthcare organization that experiences a compromise of patient information is likely to have a visit from its friendly neighborhood regulator. In this case, the scenario is really just part of the secondary loss component of the breach analysis, and losses associated with the regulator fall into the secondary loss category. At its core, this type of risk analyses will be based upon how likely you think the organization is to experience a breach event.

TALKING ABOUT RISK

Our suspicion is that the plethora of regulations that continue to evolve related to information security risk management exist at least to some degree because regulators have little faith in industry or organizational ability to manage information security risk effectively. Clearly, the track record supports this skeptical perspective. Perhaps as the information security profession matures, the situation will improve and regulators will become more comfortable. Or perhaps, regulators will simply raise the bar. It wouldn't hurt our feelings if regulators looked upon some of the content in this book as fodder for raising the bar.

Assuming that an organization has chosen to be as compliant as possible, the focus for the organization then should become how to be cost-effective in its compliance efforts. We like to think of this as "smart compliance." Following the processes we discussed earlier, FAIR can be used to help organizations prioritize the noncompliant conditions they almost invariably have. It can also be used to identify the most cost-effective solutions for achieving and maintaining compliance. A last point is that when you're faced with discussing or defending compliance efforts it can be extremely helpful if you are able to describe the rigor behind your choices. Our experience has been that regulators and auditors are rational professionals who tend to be very supportive when they see evidence that an organization is being rigorous in its risk management efforts.

TALKING ABOUT RISK

We submit that the notion of "being compliant" is a bit of a misnomer (or pipe dream, take your pick). We have yet to see (or even imagine there being) an organization that is 100% compliant across its entire risk landscape, at least with regulations or standards that have any depth or complexity. If we're right, the question isn't whether an organization is compliant or not but rather how noncompliant an organization is. The notion that PCI compliance has any relevance in terms of protection from secondary stakeholder reactions following a compromise is probably naïve. Every credit card compromise we are familiar with occurred due to a condition that was not compliant with the PCI DSS despite the fact that the organization had been deemed compliant in the last review. Again, this shouldn't be surprising if we understand that 100% compliance is not realistic. It might be helpful if everyone openly admitted that "being compliant" is a relative term so that more realistic expectations could be set.

GOING INTO BUSINESS

For the final example in this chapter, we wanted to provide another demonstration of how you can apply FAIR principles to help with noninformation security problems.

Whether or not to leave corporate or government employment and go into business for yourself is certainly one of the more daunting questions a professional can face in their career. There are many ways self-employment can go badly, which means it is a target rich environment from a risk analysis and risk management perspective. And based on the failure rate statistics for start-ups it appears as though there is room for improvement in how people approach the problem. Clearly, we can't cover the problem comprehensively in just one small section of one chapter, but the purpose here is simply to demonstrate the breadth of FAIR's utility.

RISK ANALYSIS

Starting out in this sort of analysis involves taking an inventory of the major negative outcomes that potentially arise from starting a business. A partial list might include:

- Failure of the business
- Family problems arising from business-related stress
- Loss of personal finances applied to the business
- Health issues associated with business-related stress
- Personal legal liability

We can map these pretty effectively to how FAIR approaches loss:

- Business failure typically results from resources running out, or at least running so low that founders decide to pull the ripcord before they meet terra firma. In other words, more events occurred that drained resources (operational costs and losses) than events that provided resources (revenue).
- Family problems can arise due to financial strain or simply the stress associated with long hours and the emotional roller coaster that often comes with starting a business. In either case, you can consider family members to be secondary stakeholders who react negatively to the events that affect the founders.
- Loss of personal finances falls squarely in the replacement loss category.
- Health issues that reduce the availability of the founder can result in productivity loss and potentially reputation.
- And of course there is always the potential for a founder to be exposed to personal liability based on poor decisions or sloppy execution.

But these are outcomes. What are the events that result in these outcomes, and the threats, control deficiencies, and loss considerations that create those events? A few come straight to mind:

- Legal actions against the startup. These might include actions brought by; competitors for violating intellectual property, customers for broken contracts or sloppy work, employees for various HR related issues, or regulators for violating one law or another. Deficient controls that create these circumstances might include poor contractual reviews, poor HR practices, inadequate reviews of existing patents and copyrights, quality problems associated with manufacturing or services, or inadequate attention to legal compliance.
- Inefficient use of capital and other resources. Yes, when capital or resources are spent inefficiently it should be considered a loss event. This can result from poor prioritization or from choosing the wrong solutions when trying to solve various business problems. By the way, this should be another good reminder of why it is so important to be cost-effective in managing information security and other forms of risk.
- Operational outages due to weather, equipment failure, operator error, etc. This can result from things like inadequate controls related to design, construction, selection, and operational practices.

- Malicious events perpetrated by insiders or outsiders of various sorts, including; the compromise of sensitive information, theft of tangible assets, vandalism, corrupted information, etc.

Evaluating each of these would undoubtedly involve the development of scope tables that describe the assets at risk, relevant threat agents or threat communities, the type of event, and the effects. These contents of the tables might be a little bit different than what we commonly use for information security analysis, but that's okay. The point is simply to include the key factors and support a critical thinking approach. Having defined those scope tables you could then apply formal quantitative analysis to the scenarios or perhaps something less formal like what we covered earlier in the chapter. Either way, you certainly can't expect to consistently and effectively manage what you haven't measured, so it makes sense to do some form of analysis on at least those scenarios that are anticipated to be most relevant.

Another option is to develop the scoping tables and perform some high-level analyses before starting the business. It would then be easier to refine and refresh the status of key metrics as the business chugs along. That would be the proactive thing to do.

RISK MANAGEMENT

It also is crucial to examine the risk management parts of the equation: decision-making and execution. There are myriad decisions involved in starting a business, and we know that in order for an organization of any size to consistently make good decisions those decisions have to be made by the right people operating from good information. The good news is that the question of who the decision-makers should be in startup businesses is pretty straightforward—it's the founders. The bad news is that although founders might be experts in their profession, very often they are not experts (or even very knowledgeable) in business matters, which makes the quality of information they operate from especially important. The information has to be timely, accurate, and in terms they understand and can easily assimilate into their decisions (sound familiar?). However, there are at least two different categories of information to think about: (1) general information about the ins and outs of running a business, and (2) information that is specific to how the business is operating at any given moment. In order to make sense of the second type of information, you need to have the context provided by the first type. This makes a great argument for founders to partner with someone who has experience in building and running a startup.

In the absence of partnering with an experienced business professional, there are a lot of good references and resources that provide general information for startups. Too often, though, founders don't take advantage of those resources or simply do not have the bandwidth to leverage them. As a result, even good information about the specific conditions of a business is not as likely to be interpreted effectively.

Information quality still boils down to visibility and analysis. In a startup, this might include visibility into market conditions and direction, customer needs, financing options, human resources, the competition, to name just a few. Here again, very often founders in a startup will have limited visibility, either because they don't know how to gain that visibility or simply due to resource limitations. Regardless of the cause, poor visibility will equate to poorly informed decisions and an increased chance of failure. On a similar note, even good visibility would not help if analysis and interpretation of the information is badly flawed.

The bottom line is that good decision-making in a startup requires decision-makers who have good quality information and who sufficiently understand the business context. We are personally familiar with people who have started and failed at startups because these criteria were not met.

On the surface, execution in a startup would seem to be simpler. There are fewer people in the organization so there should be fewer layers of bureaucracy to impede clear communication. Although this is true, too often we have seen (and experienced) where clear communication is believed to have taken place, but did not. In a small, fast-moving organization, these instances of unclear communication can have significant impacts very quickly. The other challenge is that in a small startup, resources (including key skill sets, like marketing) can be scarce. This means that despite good strategic or operational decision-making an organization may not be able to execute effectively against those decisions.

It doesn't take too much imagination to picture how weaknesses in decision-making and execution drive the risk scenarios and outcomes we discussed in the risk analysis section. We feel this does a nice job of illustrating the relationship between risk management capabilities and the risk that later exists in an organization. Using FAIR to think through these problems logically should help manage this overall risk landscape.

CHAPTER SUMMARY

In a later chapter on risk management, we will introduce the notion of implicit risk management versus explicit risk management. Boiled down, the difference is that *explicit* risk management involves setting specific and measurable risk objectives and then managing to those objectives over time. Using FAIR in the manner we've described the examples in this chapter represents *implicit* risk management because there is no explicit measurement of risk or comparison against a defined risk management objective. These examples simply represent doing a better job of implicit risk management by leveraging FAIR principles and some critical thinking. This can be an important first step along the path toward higher risk management maturity.

As you apply FAIR on a day-to-day basis, you will most likely find yourself performing informal analyses more often than the formal, quantitative analyses. That said, formal quantitative analysis is usually necessary in order to build business cases for security funding that can be compared on equal footing with funding requests from other parts of the organization. It also provides an entirely different level of maturity to the problems of prioritization and optimized solution selection. Lastly, quantitative analysis becomes inherently more necessary as an organization moves up the risk management maturity continuum.

Common Mistakes

10

For some people, the hardest part of learning FAIR is having to overcome bad habits. Okay, maybe "bad habits" isn't the right phrase. Maybe "old habits" is better, or "preconceived ideas." What it boils down to though, is that for most people, FAIR represents a recalibration of your mental model about what risk is and how it works. This recalibration is more substantial for some people than for others.

This chapter will cover some of the newbie mistakes we observe in others and made ourselves at one point or another (yes—we have had our own recalibrations to deal with). The hope is that by highlighting these common stumbling blocks you are more likely to recognize, avoid, or deal with them. It's also critical for you to know these if you intend to instruct others in performing FAIR analyses, or if you will be reviewing analyses performed by others. As you read through this chapter, you will undoubtedly notice that some of the context was mentioned in earlier chapters. This is intentional so that people do not have to go rummaging around if later they just want a quick review of common mistakes and troubleshooting.

MISTAKE CATEGORIES

We tend to boil down these common mistakes into five high-level categories:

- Checking results
- Scoping
- Data
- Variable confusion
- Vulnerability analysis

We're going to start our discussion with checking results because it is often the first clue that one or more of the other mistakes were made in the analysis. If you don't check your results, you may miss the opportunity to identify your other mistakes.

CHECKING RESULTS

We like to think of this as a "litmus test" for your results. Do the results make sense? More importantly, would you feel comfortable presenting (and defending) them in front of stakeholders whose opinion matters to you?

Very often, when we're training a new set of FAIR analysts, the first analyses they perform in groups (without our intervention) have results that are outlandish. In fact, it's not uncommon for these first analyses to end up with loss exposure results that exceed the value of the organization the analysis is intended to represent. We love it when this happens because it is a first opportunity for us to teach them how to recognize and diagnose analysis problems. We intentionally let them make these mistakes even when we spot them doing it in mid-analysis because there is nothing like learning from your own mistakes.

The bottom line is that when you finish an analysis you should *always* look at the results with a critical eye. Push back on it mentally. Challenge it. Have someone else review it. Poke it with the skeptics stick. Whatever. Just do not blindly accept it. If you sense any problem with it, go back and review your scope, assumptions, and data to find potential problems. After a while (and it doesn't take long), you learn to recognize and avoid the problems you seem to be most prone to. Odds are good that the problems you encounter are those we cover below.

As we mentioned in an earlier chapter (but will repeat here anyway), it is at this point the skeptics in the crowd may ask a very legitimate question. Are we advocating that you should look at your results and, if you don't like them, tweak the analysis until you like the results? Yes. That is exactly right. The key, however, is your intent. If you are revising the analysis so you are confident that it represents the most accurate and unbiased view of risk possible, then go forth and tweak. If, however, you're tweaking it so that it gives you results that promote a position, belief, or agenda (e.g., making the results scarier so that you can get management to act), then you are the human equivalent of a monkey with a hammer: a very dangerous thing.

FAIR is no different than any other analytic method. You can absolutely game it to serve your personal agenda, and, unfortunately, we have seen it used that way. With that being said, gaming is very dangerous to your credibility and harder to pull off using FAIR than you think. Harder, in fact, than the qualitative methods we've encountered. You see, the minute you have to put numbers to a variable you open the prospect of those numbers being challenged. Our experience has been that the process of using numbers encourages examination; particularly when results don't align with people's sense of reality. If you have gamed those numbers and have stupid rationale behind them, you are going to look foolish. Guaranteed.

SCOPING

Scoping analyses is where most people struggle at first. For many people, it's the first time they have had to actually think very rigorously about what they are applying a risk rating to. For example, if someone is asked to rate the risk associated with Internet cloud services, they often will briefly reach into their mental grab bag of first-hand experience (if any), media reports, conference presentations they've attended, and personal beliefs and say "high," "medium," or "low." What they probably have not done is think very hard about things like:

- The type of event in question—confidentiality, integrity, and/or availability.
- The threat community (TCom) in question—insiders, hackers, nation state actors, etc.
- The vector of attack—web application, server, user, endpoint, etc.
- Which controls are relevant given the above considerations.

The point we're trying to make is that the process of formally scoping an analysis is new to many people, so it's where the steepest learning curve is and it is where people tend to make the most mistakes at first.

Within the scoping category we see several common subcategories of problems:

- Analysis depth
- Analysis breadth
- Misalignment with purpose
- Shifting scope in mid-analysis

ANALYSIS DEPTH

The FAIR ontology goes relatively deep in its layers of abstraction. That is both a good thing and a bad thing. It's good because the deeper levels of abstraction provide mental prompts regarding the factors at deeper levels that influence factors at higher levels (e.g., that random, regular, and intentional contact are different from each other and that all three influence contact frequency, threat event frequency (TEF), and loss event frequency (LEF)) and it allows you to "go deep" when you need to. It's "bad" whenever someone decides to try to perform an analysis at deeper layers of abstraction than is necessary (because it is a waste of time) or at layers where estimates are just too hard to make.

The rule of thumb is simply to not go any deeper in your analysis than you have to. In fact, we now teach new analysts to start at the top of the ontology (at LEF) and ask themselves whether they can simply make their estimates there rather than trying to estimate TEF and vulnerability to derive LEF. A great example is weather-related scenarios. Why on earth would I try to estimate TEF and vulnerability for weather-related outages when there is probably good data regarding the frequency of these events? Besides, imagine how difficult it is to define what represents a relevant weather threat event. Would that rain shower last week count as a threat event? This is very tough to do. Say that you do find a way to reasonably define which weather events count as threat events, how are you going to determine vulnerability? You would either back into it based on history regarding how often outages occurred relative to the TEF you defined (in which case you're just doing busy-work because you're using LEF to back into vulnerability), or, worse, you try to estimate mother nature's TCap and your Difficulty. Good luck with that.

ANALYSIS BREADTH

One of the best clues that you may have scoped an analysis too broadly is if you are having significant difficulty making estimates for your variables. For example, if you are trying to estimate vulnerability and the minimum value is extremely low and the maximum value is extremely high (e.g., 1–99%), then there is a decent chance that you need to narrow the TComs in scope for the analysis. Maybe you have included privileged insiders (against whom you are always highly vulnerable to) with non-privileged insiders (against whom you should have a much lower vulnerability to).

The most common trouble spots from an analysis breadth perspective are:

- Not differentiating between very different TComs. Your vulnerability can be much different depending on the TCom. Furthermore, your TEF can be much different as well. These differences make estimates much harder to pin down, which prolongs the analysis and makes the results less precise and less actionable (because mitigation options may be significantly different).
- Not differentiating between loss event types. Under no circumstances should you try to glom together an analysis that tries to account for an availability event and a confidentiality event (likewise integrity). These different events usually have very different frequencies, and the form and magnitude of loss is often very different. Oh, you might have some availability effects from some types of confidentiality events (a stole laptop, for example), but that would be an unintended artifact of the confidentiality event and, thus, not affect the frequency estimate.
- Not differentiating between assets at risk. For example, estimating loss magnitude (LM) values for database-related risk is going to be problematic if the database population varies significantly in terms of the volume, sensitivity, and/or criticality of data and purpose. Likewise, estimating vulnerability is going to be much tougher if you lump managed databases in with unmanaged (so-called shadow information technology) databases that may have very different security applied to them.

MISALIGNMENT WITH PURPOSE

What we mean here is that it isn't unusual to see new analysts start off trying to answer the question of how much risk is associated with one type of event only to end up scoping and analyzing something different. For example, if the question to which we want an answer is "How much availability risk is associated with disgruntled insiders?" but we've included in our numbers accidental outages because of operator error, then we have a misalignment between purpose and outcome.

The key to avoiding a problem like this is twofold:

- Very clearly define the question you are trying to answer up-front, and
- Check yourself at each point in the analysis to ensure that the values you are entering are aligned with the question at hand.

SHIFTING SCOPE IN MID-ANALYSIS

It's very common that you will be in the midst of an analysis only to discover that the original scope needs to be narrowed (e.g., carving one analysis into two in order to differentiate between assets, threats, etc.). This redefinition of scope is usually a good thing because it means that you understand the problem better now, your results are likely to be more precise and actionable, and the estimates are probably going to be easier to make. The only problem is if you don't revisit and potentially adjust any estimates you made earlier in the analysis, before the re-scoping. We see this one regularly, so stay alert to this!

DATA

Yes, garbage-in, garbage-out is an unavoidable fact of any analysis, FAIR included. The most common mistakes we see of this nature include:

- Not getting LM data from reliable sources
- Not challenging your assumptions
- Not calibrating your inputs

The last two of these are pretty straightforward, and if you paid attention when we covered calibration (and particularly if you have been trained in making calibrated estimates and/or read Douglas Hubbard's book *How to Measure Anything*), this shouldn't be a problem. The first one though, getting LM data from reliable sources, is something we feel compelled to emphasize here.

The bottom line is that information security professionals should, in most cases, be the last people in the world to provide LM estimates. We simply do not have the necessary background, expertise, or insight into the business. From what we've seen, information security professionals will almost always overestimate LM. As a result, whenever possible (and it should almost always be possible), get LM numbers from people in the business who are experts in that part of the business (or industry sources, where they are available). Go to the lawyers for estimates on legal defense costs. Go to business operations and/or sales for numbers related to revenue losses, etc.

VARIABLE CONFUSION

Second to scoping, this category is perhaps the next most common problem for new analysts. What it boils down to is making estimates for one variable but plugging those values into a different FAIR variable. A common example is to estimate vulnerability but put those numbers into the RS variable.

The list below provides the most common points of variable confusion that we run into:

- Mistaking contact frequency for TEF
- Mistaking TEF for LEF
- Mistaking response losses for productivity loss

- Confusing secondary loss with primary loss
- Confusing reputation damage with competitive advantage (CA) loss

When in doubt, particularly in your early days of using FAIR, regularly refer back to the definitions for each of these variables when you are performing analyses.

MISTAKING CONTACT FREQUENCY FOR TEF

This mistake occurs primarily when people are trying to estimate something like the TEF for attacks against an Internet-facing system or web application. Very often, we will see people use an incredibly large TEF estimate because, after all, these systems are on the Internet and everybody knows attacks happen every few seconds on the Internet (or so the thinking goes). Multiply an attack every few seconds by the number of minutes in a day and 365 days in a year and you get a really big TEF. Even if they estimated their vulnerability to be very low—something under 1%—you still end up with a huge LEF that suggests the organization should have gone out of business a long time ago. So, what's wrong? Well, to a large degree it boils down to their interpretation of what constitutes a threat event.

By our way of thinking, if a threat event occurs and you are vulnerable to it, a loss event immediately occurs. Yet much of the activity we see on the Internet is better described as contact (i.e., somebody is scanning and poking around looking for things that qualify as particularly interesting by their standards). Very often when those scans encounter your systems and applications, they are looking for evidence of weakness but they aren't going to necessarily leverage those points of weakness immediately. They'll report it back to the mother ship, which may or may not result in additional probing and an actual attack later. Yes, we know there is a lot of gray in this area and some scans are more maliciously inclined than others. Nonetheless, when we actually examine Internet logs we see a much smaller number of events that we would qualify as actual threat events.

MISTAKING TEF FOR LEF

This seems to be a more common mistake on the examination than it is in the trenches. We aren't sure why. Regardless, there are times when people estimate LEF directly (as we encourage you to do whenever possible), but their estimate is based on how often threat events (e.g., attacks) are occurring rather than how often loss events occur. The difference is pretty straightforward. Loss materializes when a loss event occurs (thus the name). Loss does not occur for threat events. Just keep that in mind if you are doing an analysis and you aren't sure whether your estimate reflects TEF or LEF.

MISTAKING RESPONSE LOSS FOR PRODUCTIVITY LOSS

We see this one a lot. When people are thinking through the activity that occurs when a loss event takes place—the meetings, the disruption, the investigation, etc.—they tend to associate this with a reduction in productivity. Although that makes a certain amount of sense, there is actually still a lot of productivity taking place, it just isn't the normal kind of productivity. People are working hard trying to deal with the event, and this is productive in the sense that it's helping the organization survive. The way to think about it is, when organizations want to capture the soft dollar costs associated with people *responding* to an event, those costs should fall into the *response* loss bucket.

CONFUSING SECONDARY LOSS WITH PRIMARY LOSS

We see this a lot too. Where people seem to go astray is that they forget a basic tenet of secondary loss—any loss or cost that is incurred in anticipation of or as a result of secondary stakeholder reaction to an event, qualifies as secondary loss. If someone answers a telephone call from a customer who couldn't check his or her bank balance online because the system is down, that is a form of secondary response loss. If an organization has to replace a customer's stolen credit card, that is secondary replacement loss. If a meeting is called to figure out whether breach notification laws are relevant to a compromise the organization has experienced, the involved person-hours are a secondary response cost.

CONFUSING REPUTATION DAMAGE WITH COMPETITIVE ADVANTAGE LOSS

This is a fun one because the manner in which loss materializes is *almost* identical between these two. What we mean is that whether it's due to reputation damage or a change in competitive position, the outcome is very often the same—lower market share, lower stock price (if the organization is publically traded), higher cost of capital, and higher employee retention costs. Looking at it from another perspective might make it clearer. If someone came to us and said that an organization's market share and stock price fell, and their cost of capital and employee retention costs went up, there is literally no way we could guess whether the cause was reputation damage or damaged CA any better than if we flipped a coin.

Besides the difficulty this fundamental similarity presents, people very often also believe that an organization's good reputation provides CA. Therefore, if reputation is damaged then CA is damaged. On the surface, this appears to make sense, but it falls apart when you look at it closely and here is how: With that line of thinking there is no difference between reputation and competitive position. They are, in fact, the same thing. In both cases, it boils down to external stakeholder beliefs regarding the value and/or liability of the organization, its leadership, and/or its products and services. Of course, those stakeholder beliefs are mirrored in market share, stock price, etc. Therefore, because they are the same thing, there should be no surprise that when reputation is damaged so is competitive position.

From our perspective, practically speaking, competitive advantage mostly boils down to one thing—lower operational costs than the competition. For example, if our organization has the ability to operate at a lower run rate than our competition because of better technology, better processes, better geographic access to market, etc., that is competitive advantage. Just about anything else about an organization that we have been able to come up with more appropriately belongs in reputation.

VULNERABILITY ANALYSIS

This isn't so much a category of mistake as it is a point in the analysis where people commonly make mistakes. In fact, it is really a special case of variable confusion, which we covered above. We feel the need to highlight it though because people seem to struggle with it so much.

Before we go any further, let us reinforce something we have touched on a couple of times already—do not go any deeper in the ontology than you have to when doing an analysis. If you can estimate vulnerability directly, do it. Don't mess around trying to derive it from TCap and Difficulty if you don't have to, and you usually do not have to. With that advice given, let's examine why TCap and Difficulty seem to create so much havoc.

The first problem is that most people are not used to thinking in these terms. The terms themselves are new and the notion of actually estimating TCap and Difficulty has probably never crossed their mind. For that matter, it is relatively unusual to find people who are used to thinking about vulnerability as a percentage. When most people use the term vulnerability they're using it as a label for some control condition that is perceived to be deficient in some manner, as in "That six character password is a vulnerability." The fact that FAIR is tweaking the meaning of one term, introducing two new ones, and then deriving a value for the changed term from some sort of interaction between the two new ones—well, it shouldn't be a surprise that people get confused.

What commonly happens when people make a mistake with this is they confuse either TCap with vulnerability, Difficulty with vulnerability, or both. What seems to help is to actually draw two identical TCap continuum graphs (we covered this in the Ontology chapter). The first graph will be used to estimate Difficulty, and the second graph will be used to estimate TCap. It is very important that these graphs be on a different piece of paper or on a different part of a whiteboard, if you're using a whiteboard.

Using the first graph, estimate the Difficulty for the asset under analysis. Recall that Difficulty is an estimate of effectiveness against all of the threat actors that make up the continuum and not the TCom that is in scope for this analysis. Forget about that TCom for now. Once you have estimated the Difficulty values and written them down somewhere, burn, shred, erase, or somehow dispose of the graph you used for that estimate.

Using the second graph, estimate the TCap of the TCom that is in scope for this analysis. Don't think about the asset's controls or the Difficulty you came up with in the previous paragraph. Block those from your mind. All you are interested in is estimating where along that TCap continuum this TCom exists. Once you have established that estimate and recorded those values, you can dispose of the second graph in a similar fashion to the first.

Now, enter your Difficulty values in the Difficulty fields for whatever tool you are using. Likewise, enter the TCap values in the appropriate fields. You're done. The key is to evaluate these values as independently of each other as possible because if aren't not very deliberate in your thinking you stand a much greater chance of getting it wrong. Of course, the easier thing to do is just estimate vulnerability directly, but you knew that already.

Controls

OVERVIEW

Control frameworks abound: Control Objectives for Information and Related Technology, National Institute of Standards and Technology, Payment Card Industry (PCI), and International Organization for Standardization (ISO) all provide their own taxonomies and lists of controls. In each case, the framework provides a list or description of recommended controls and/or the control objectives. Sometimes, the description is specific (e.g., what constitutes acceptable encryption), whereas in other cases, the descriptions are more general (e.g., thou shalt do risk assessments). This is all useful stuff that can help an organization understand whether it's on the right path, more or less, from a controls perspective. What these frameworks do not tend to do, however, is describe the nature of controls, the relationship between controls, or how to measure/estimate the effectiveness of controls within a risk analysis. Because of this, we believe a deeper understanding of controls is crucial if we want to maximize our risk management effectiveness.

In this chapter, we'll introduce a set of ontologies for controls that enable us to be more effective in control evaluation and measurement and as a way to help people simply understand controls at a deeper level. We'll also describe how to think about controls within the context of performing FAIR analyses because not all controls affect risk in the same way. This may seem like an obvious point, but we think you'll be surprised by where we've taken controls analysis. It's likely a different perspective than you have encountered before, and we think it sheds light on some previously dark corners of the risk analysis problem.

TALKING ABOUT RISK

By the way, if you haven't noticed, we love mind maps (well, one of us does). If you aren't already familiar with them, we highly recommend them. They are a marvelous tool for organizing thoughts and illustrating ideas. Truthfully, were it not for mind mapping, FAIR probably would never have been created without them.

HIGH-LEVEL CONTROL CATEGORIES

From our perspective, there are three high-level categories of controls:

- Asset-level controls: Controls applied directly to manage the frequency and/or magnitude of loss from events that can affect assets (e.g., system configuration and patching, passwords, access privileges, logging, backup and recovery tools and processes, door locks, and HVAC systems). The thing to keep in mind is that loss occurs when threats negatively affect assets, so from that perspective, these controls are the most direct link to managing loss exposure.

- Variance controls: Controls intended to minimize the variance of asset-level controls over time (e.g., policies, standards, education and awareness training, well-defined processes, automation, auditing and testing, and remediation). As we'll discuss further on, although asset-level controls are the most direct link to loss exposure, managing variance is the key to asset-level control effectiveness over time. In fact, we believe the condition of variance controls is often the best measure of an organization's overall risk posture.

- Decision-making controls: Those elements that help stakeholders define, adjust, and enforce expectations, and allocate resources to achieve risk management objectives (e.g., organization objectives, laws and regulations, risk tolerance definitions, metrics, reporting, and risk analyses). Another way of thinking about these controls is that they're intended to prevent, detect, and respond to bad risk management decisions.

We'll discuss each of these categories and how they work together, beginning with asset-level controls. Before we discuss these categories, we need to introduce the concept of control relationships.

TALKING ABOUT RISK

In the early days of FAIR, the Resistive Strength factor within the ontology was called Control Strength. Unfortunately, it was soon apparent that people were including all kinds of controls in their estimate of "Control Strength," including things that should be accounted for elsewhere in the model (e.g., backup processes that affect loss magnitude but not vulnerability). As a result, their Control Strength estimates were sometimes inaccurate. When I (J.J.) realized this, I also realized that I hadn't thought through the controls aspect of the ontology as thoroughly as I needed to. This led me down a long path of trying to understand—really understand—controls. The results of this understanding are presented within this chapter.

CONTROL RELATIONSHIPS

Not surprisingly, controls have relationships between each other. For example, some controls depend on the existence of other controls to be effective. To illustrate this point, let's start simple. Imagine that there are only three categories of asset-level controls: preventative, detective, and responsive (Figure 11.1). Preventative controls affect the likelihood of a loss event occurring, detective controls enable us to recognize when a loss event has occurred, and responsive controls allow us to minimize the loss event's effect on the organization. (We'll go deeper soon, but for now we just need to make a couple of key points regarding the relationship between controls of varying types.)

Imagine that it's possible to have controls that are perfect (i.e., they are 100% effective) (Figure 11.2). (Yes, we know there is no such thing as a perfect control, but bear with us while we make a point.) With perfect *preventative* controls, we wouldn't need detective or responsive controls, because there would be no loss events to detect

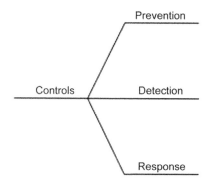

FIGURE 11.1

Basic control ontology.

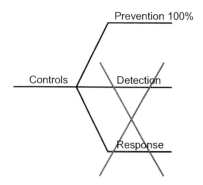

FIGURE 11.2

Controls in a perfect world.

or respond to. Example: Suppose there were such a thing as unbreakable encryption, both in terms of key strength and how it's used. With perfect encryption, we wouldn't need to worry about detecting when someone has broken the encryption, nor would we need to have an incident response capability to manage such an event. (This whole concept of control perfection has got to be driving some of you nuts… Hang in there.)

Conversely, with perfect detective and responsive controls, there would be no need for preventative controls (i.e., instantaneous detection and response capabilities that eliminate the materialization of loss even when preventative controls fail) (Figure 11.3). Example: Assume someone breaks our encryption. We would detect it instantaneously, and our response would eliminate any potential for loss to materialize.

To eliminate the need for preventative controls, however, we need to have both perfect detection *and* perfect response. If either of these is imperfect, then our need for preventative controls returns.

The point of this fantasy is to illustrate that control relationships take either of two forms: *and* or *or*. Those of you with engineering backgrounds or other exposure

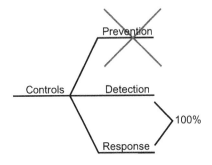

FIGURE 11.3

Alternate version of controls in a perfect world.

to Boolean logic may have already recognized this. Preventative controls have an *or* relationship with the combination of detection and response controls, whereas detection and response have an *and* relationship between each other. In other words, we can have preventative controls *or* detection *and* response controls.

TALKING ABOUT RISK

For those of you who aren't familiar with Boolean concepts, simply think of it this way: when an *and* relationship exists between two controls, *both* have to be effective for their benefit to be realized. For example, you can have the best detection capability in the world, but if your response capabilities are badly broken, then the overall capability is broken. With an *or* relationship, if *either* of two controls is effective, then the overall benefit is realized.

Now let's set fantasy aside. Suppose our preventative controls are only 90% effective. In other words, when threat agents act in a manner that could result in loss, 90% of the time their actions are thwarted (e.g., only 10% of fraud attempts are successful at gaining access to money). This means that 10% of the time we have to detect that a loss event has occurred and respond to it. Therefore, if our detection and response controls are, in combination, 90% effective against that 10% of events (e.g., we are able to recover 90% of the money the fraudsters tried to run off with), then the combined preventative, detective, and responsive control effectiveness is 99% (Figure 11.4).

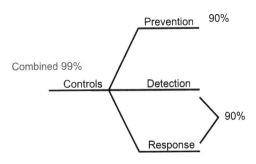

FIGURE 11.4

Combined effectiveness.

Being able to recognize the relationships and dependencies between different controls enables us to more effectively recognize where gaps exists, and prevent gaps in the first place. It also enables us to do a better job of gauging the efficacy of combinations of controls.

ASSET-LEVEL CONTROLS
AN ONTOLOGY FOR ASSET-LEVEL CONTROLS

As you can see in Figure 11.5, our controls ontology takes a different approach than most. We've found this logical breakdown and additional detail to be extremely helpful in controls analysis and selection. At the first layer of abstraction in this ontology, we have the traditional categories of prevention, detection, and response. Unfortunately, this is about as far as many people tend to go in terms of characterizing the role of different controls. The problem with not going any deeper is that we lose the ability to explicitly evaluate and consider the relationships between controls. This level of abstraction is specific to loss events

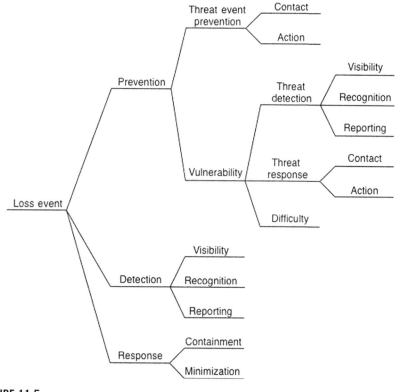

FIGURE 11.5

Asset-level control ontology.

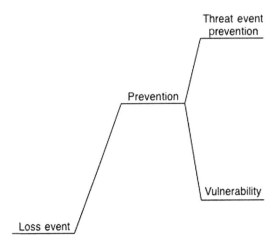

FIGURE 11.6

Prevention control ontology.

(i.e., preventing loss events, or detecting and responding to loss events). The reason for this distinction will become clear as we describe the rest of the ontology. At the next layer of abstraction, under prevention, it begins to get a little more interesting (Figure 11.6). Here, we have two branches: Threat Event Prevention and Vulnerability.

THREAT EVENT PREVENTION

There are two approaches to preventing threat events: (1) minimizing contact between the threat agent and the asset, and (2) reducing the probability of action on the part of the threat agent (Figure 11.7). For example, if we don't hike in a part of the wilderness where grizzly bears are active, we reduce the frequency of contact (which reduces the frequency of attacks and, thus, the frequency of losses). Or, we can wear a "bear bell" (these really exist) while hiking, which alerts the bear of our approach and allows the bear to vacate the area. In this case, contact has occurred (i.e., the threat agent is aware of the asset and in a position to attack but chooses not to because they aren't surprised by the hiker and, thus, have time to get away). These two control functions have an *or* relationship (i.e., they aren't dependent on each other, and if either of them was "perfect," you wouldn't need the other).

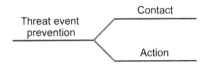

FIGURE 11.7

Prevention Threat Event Frequency control ontology.

Other examples of minimizing contact frequency would include the following:

- Introducing layers of defense between the asset and the threat agent (e.g., employment screening processes and firewalls)
- Reducing the number of threat agents (e.g., good hiring and personnel management processes)
- Reducing the asset surface area (e.g., reducing the number of assets)
- Other examples of reducing threat agent probability of action include the following:
  - Hardening the target (or making it appear to be hardened)
  - Reducing the threat agent's perception of asset value
  - Increasing the threat agent's perception of risk (e.g., introducing effective and secure logging/monitoring capabilities and enforcement practices)

VULNERABILITY

The Vulnerability branch (Figure 11.8) refers to controls that determine the likelihood that a threat event will result in a loss event.

THREAT EVENT DETECTION

Threat event detection has three components to it: visibility, recognition, and reporting. Visibility is simply a matter of having data that will contain evidence of a threat event if it occurs. One example would be closed circuit television cameras on the outside of a building. Properly aimed (and turned on), these devices provide visibility into activities at potential points of attack. Recognition is a matter of being able to discern that a threat event is underway (e.g., Hey! Someone's attempting to pick the lock on the door!). This may be a matter of simply having someone (or something) watching the monitor/logs and who is capable of discerning anomalous activity. Reporting consists of engaging a response function to intervene in the threat event, ideally before it becomes a loss event (e.g., notifying the guard force). This timeliness consideration highlights the fact that it isn't enough to just have visibility, recognition, and

FIGURE 11.8

Vulnerability control ontology.

reporting. These elements also have to be timely. These three elements are also a great example of an *and* relationship. It doesn't matter how perfect any two of these are. If any one of them is deficient, the entire detection function isn't going to be effective.

THREAT EVENT RESPONSE

When a threat event is in progress, there can sometimes be an opportunity to intervene before loss actually materializes. Of course, for that to happen, the threat event has to be detected and reported in a timely enough manner to engage a response capability. You may have noticed that the two elements under Threat event response are the same as those under Threat event prevention. In this case, contact refers to the process of breaking contact with the threat agent (e.g., running away, or blocking the IP address of an attacker). Action refers to terminating the threat agent's actions before they're completed (e.g., terminating the threat agent (choose your own definition for "terminating") or increasing the threat agent's perception of risk (e.g., setting off alarm bells)).

TALKING ABOUT RISK

When you map Threat Event Detection and Response controls against the FAIR taxonomy, where do they apply? When asking that question in training classes, the most common reply is "Resistance Strength/Difficulty." Actually, however, these two elements affect "Threat Capability." Here's why: if we think about the factors that make up Threat Capability, they include skills and resources. Resources are a function of time and materials. If we're able to limit the amount of time a threat agent has to complete their action, then we have reduced their capability. It's subtle; however, we like to use this as an example of where the ontology can help us think more clearly and deeply on our control opportunities when needed.

DIFFICULTY

Difficulty is simply any control that directly obstructs a threat agent's ability to inflict harm. Common examples within an information security context include passwords, access privileges, hardened system configurations, encryption, and secure application coding practices. Examples (usually) outside of an information security context include bars on windows, bulletproof glass, and armor.

CASE STUDY

While working an engagement as a consultant to a bank, the bank's information security team lamented that they had purchased a technology to help manage data leakage, but bank management wouldn't let them deploy it fully. Specifically, the technology was capable of blocking the ability to write sensitive information to USB ports, but management would only let them turn on the technology's logging and notification function. In other words, whenever someone would try to move sensitive information onto a USB device, the technology would pop up a warning that the action was being logged and reported, and that it was against policy. In the information security team's view, this was next to useless.

The information security team was asked whether most USB drive use was malicious or simply a shortcut people were taking to make getting their jobs done more easily. They concluded that, by far, the most common use-case was simply as a shortcut. They were then asked what percentage of bank employees, when presented with the technology's warning message, would complete the act of moving sensitive data to the USB drive. Their estimate was that less than 5% (1 of 20) would complete the act. In other words, even in its "degraded" state, this control was estimated to be approximately 95% effective in terminating this specific (and by far most frequent) threat agent activity, which translates ultimately into a lower loss event frequency. Of course, its effectiveness against a more determined malicious actor would probably be significantly less. Regardless, it was anything but useless.

This may be a good time to point out that, as illustrated in the previous example, controls often provide value in more than one element of the ontology. The data leakage technology's blocking function would be an example of Difficulty, whereas its logging, reporting, and notification functions played a role in threat event prevention (by deterring action), threat event detection and response, and loss event management, as we will see later. As you think about the various controls you use, it's important to consider where they fit in the ontology.

TALKING ABOUT RISK

What role would camouflage play as a control? How about network segmentation? At this point, you should begin asking yourself these kinds of questions. Also, start to think about the *and/or* relationship between combinations of controls.

By the way, one of our pet peeves is the claim that, "Security by obscurity is no security at all." Really? If that's the case, then we had better alert our military and intelligence organizations to forget about cover stories and camouflage. Sure, you may not want to depend solely on obscurity, but it has its place as a control and in some circumstances can be quite effective.

LOSS EVENT DETECTION

When threat event prevention and vulnerability management fail, we end up with a loss event that we need to detect and respond to (Figure 11.9).

The first observation to make is that we have the same visibility, recognition, and reporting elements herein as we did in vulnerability management/detection. And, in fact, in some cases, the same people, technologies, and processes that should or

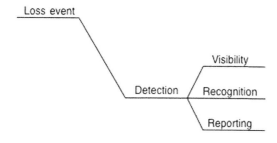

FIGURE 11.9

Loss event detection control ontology.

could play a role in vulnerability management/detection actually only play a role here because they aren't timely enough to enable effective intervention into a threat event before it becomes a loss event.

Examples of loss event detection controls include the following:

- Financial audits
- Data leakage technologies (not in a blocking mode)
- Burglar alarms

LOSS EVENT RESPONSE

Once a loss event has been detected, response controls kick in (Figure 11.10).

The containment branch contains the same two sub-branches we saw in the threat event/response branch previously described—contact and action—and the descriptions are the same. We still need to either break contact with the threat agent or terminate the threat agent's actions.

Examples would include the following:

- Removing belongings from a flooded building (contact)
- Blocking an attacker's IP address after they'd already breached the network (contact)
- Firing an employee who acted maliciously (contact)
- Threatening or retaliating against an attacker (action)
- Applying an antidote that blocks the effect of a poison (action)

The minimization branch is all about limiting the damage that results from a threat agent's actions on an asset. Examples include the following:

- Restoring normal operations
- Replacing lost or damaged resources

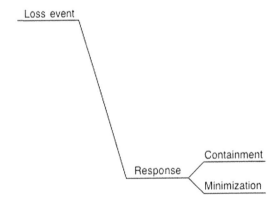

FIGURE 11.10

Loss event response control ontology.

- Performing legal or other actions to recover property from perpetrators
- Limiting negative secondary stakeholder reactions (e.g., credit monitoring for customers whose information was compromised, public relations campaign for investors, and voters)

ASSET-LEVEL CONTROL EFFECTIVENESS

There are a couple of things to keep in mind if you want to estimate the effectiveness of controls using this ontology. First, effectiveness should always be estimated as a percentage (e.g., 50% effective). Second, this percentage must be evaluated within the context of the control's purpose. If it's a control that affects threat event frequency, then the control's effectiveness would be estimated in terms of a percentage reduction in threat event frequency (as illustrated in our earlier case study). If the control's effect is on vulnerability (i.e., the percentage of time a threat event becomes a loss event), then you would estimate its effect as a percentage reduction in vulnerability. Finally, if a control affects the magnitude of loss from an event, then its effectiveness would be estimated as a percentage reduction in loss magnitude.

The good news is that, in many cases, you can actually measure these effects. Take the banking case study, for example. The organization could, if it chose to, use the data leakage solution for a period of time without the user notification turned on to establish a baseline of questionable activity. It could then turn on notification and see its effect. We've done this in the past with data leakage (and other) technologies, and the effect was remarkable, which made it incredibly easy to communicate the technology's value proposition to management.

TALKING ABOUT RISK

When we use discrete numeric values in our examples, like "50% effective," in actual practice, we would almost always make our estimates using distributions (e.g., minimum, 30%; maximum, 50%; most likely, 40%). The reason for this is twofold: (1) it allows us to represent the inevitable uncertainty in our estimates, and (2) it enables us to use Monte Carlo functions in our analyses.

DEFENSE IN-DEPTH

One of the interesting uses of this ontology is that we can model the effect of defense in-depth (Figure 11.11). To do this, you have to keep in mind that this is an asset-level ontology and that it would apply to each asset in a "chain" of assets. For example, let's say we have two levels of defense: a safe that resides within a locked room. The full ontology applies to each of these assets (yes, the locked room is considered an asset because, in addition to its own value, it inherits the value/liability proposition of the assets it contains).

The controls in the "outer" layer (the room) help to manage the threat levels faced by the "inner" layer (the safe). We know this probably seems painfully obvious, but the ontology can be remarkably useful when thinking through different

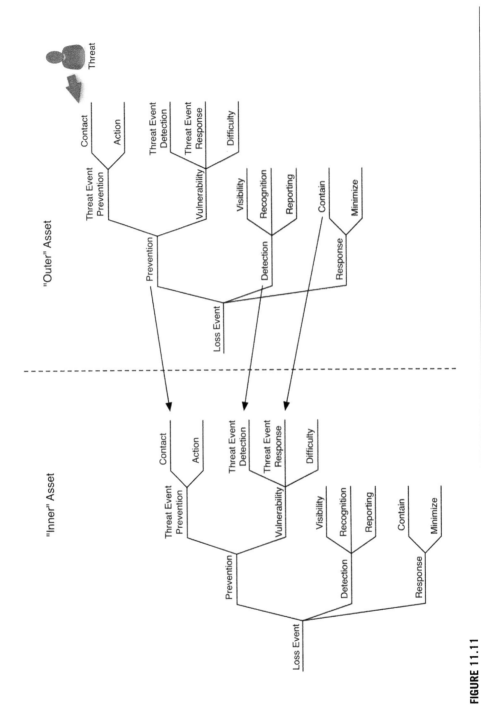

FIGURE 11.11

Defense in-depth analysis.

combinations of controls in a defense in-depth analysis. By the way, this asset-level controls ontology has also (unfortunately?) proven to be helpful while dealing with a breach, because it enables you to be exceptionally thorough in identifying control opportunities that help manage a breach more effectively.

VARIANCE CONTROLS

Edwards Deming had it right. From a risk management perspective, exceptional variance from an intended state/condition is the true enemy from a quality perspective. And after all, it's the quality of security (or lack thereof) that gets organizations into trouble. Ask yourself how many loss events you are familiar with that occurred when all of the controls were operating as intended. Few, if any, coming to mind? The bottom line is that it's unusual for information security losses to occur when controls are operating in the way they're designed. This statement should resonate strongly with compliance-minded folks who sometimes claim that the only reasonable/responsible approach to security is to simply ensure that control requirements are being adhered to. They are half right. Of course, the only way to figure out what the appropriate control requirements should be, from a business perspective, is through decisions made by organization stakeholders who are risk informed. Furthermore, it's only by understanding the relevance of variance (from a loss exposure perspective) that management can appropriately prioritize their reactions when variance is discovered.

So, how does variance affect risk? Imagine that the horizontal axis in Figure 11.12 represents the continuum of capability for a population of threat agents. In other words, the continuum runs from the least capable actor (at the far left) to the most capable actor (at the far right) in a population. Assume the bell-shaped curve represents the distribution of capabilities for the threat agent population, and the vertical axis represents the number of threat agents in the population who exist at each level of capability. Yes, we know. The actual distribution of capabilities within a threat population may not be bell shaped. This is simply for illustration purposes.

When we define control expectations through policies or standards (e.g., password parameters), we are essentially choosing a point to operate at along this continuum

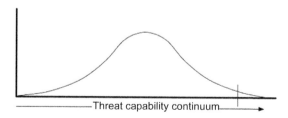

FIGURE 11.12

Threat Capability continuum.

(represented by the small vertical line). Hypothetically, any threat agent with capabilities greater than our control's effectiveness will be successful. Any less capable threat agent will not be successful.

Looking at this illustration, it is apparent that there are far fewer threat agents in the population who can defeat an asset whose controls match policy expectations. This inherently limits the frequency/likelihood of a loss event (unless the only actors coming after you are the hot-shots, in which case your control policies had better be farther to the right).

Now, assume we're concerned with the control state of a population of assets and/or the control state of a single asset over time. In a perfect world, we could test the control state(s) over time and find perfectly consistent compliance (as represented in Figure 11.13 by the stacked lines over the policy line, each line representing the results of a compliance review). In this condition, our vulnerability is exactly what it should be—at least as defined by policy. (We'll discuss policy adequacy in the section on decision-making controls.)

Unfortunately, perfect world and real world rarely coincide. What we are more likely to find through testing over time is some amount of variance (particularly for a population of assets or a highly dynamic single asset). This variance can, depending on the frequency and degree of variance, dramatically increase the odds of threat capability exceeding control effectiveness.

Consequently, the policy, process, and technology controls that we design and advocate to prevent, detect, and resolve asset-level control variance are at least as important as the asset-level controls themselves. In many cases, excellent variance management of weaker asset-level controls should be more effective than weak variance management on particularly strong asset-level controls. To illustrate this point, compare the diagram in Figure 11.14, which, let us assume, represents a case where a strong control is called for by policy, but there is a significant degree of variance in the control over a population of assets and/or over time.

Conversely, Figure 11.15 illustrates the case where a somewhat weaker control is called for by policy, but variance is much better managed. Clearly, this results in less vulnerability.

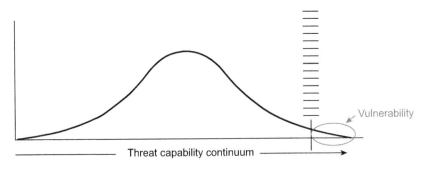

FIGURE 11.13

Threat Capability over time.

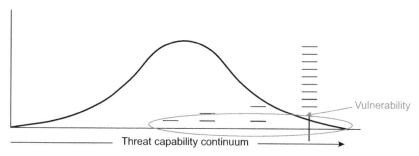

FIGURE 11.14

Strong asset level control, but weak variance management.

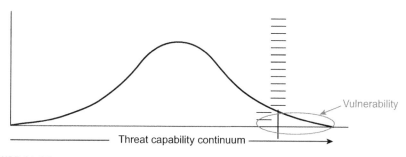

FIGURE 11.15

Weaker control, strong variance management.

TALKING ABOUT RISK

You'll also hear people talk about "assurance" or "compliance," which, similar to managing variance, is just the other side of the coin from a nomenclature perspective. The reason we prefer the term "variance" is twofold: (1) it is more readily associated with measurement methods and metrics, and (2) it allows us to use the prevent, detect, and respond nomenclature (after all, you wouldn't want to "prevent assurance"). There is another reason variance is the better term, too, which we will cover shortly.

So, if the key to asset-level control effectiveness over time is managing variance, what does that entail? Well, the good news is that many of the processes and technologies that risk management professionals regularly advocate are focused on minimizing variance. A couple of key examples are policies and awareness training. Policies set the bar and define the intended state. Without this, large degrees of variance are almost ensured. Likewise, those who are expected to comply with control expectations need to be made aware of those expectations through one form or another. Without that awareness, again, greater degrees of variance should be expected. Finally, you can have clear policies and standards, and personnel can be aware of these policies and standards, but if they aren't capable of complying motivated to comply, then you will still end up with an undesirable degree of variance.

VARIANCE CONTROLS ONTOLOGY

If you're wondering whether there's an ontology for variance management controls like there is for asset-level controls, of course there is, and parts of it should look familiar (Figure 11.16):

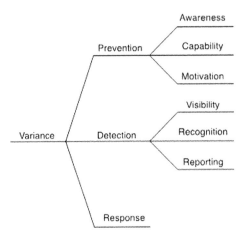

FIGURE 11.16

Variance control ontology.

VARIANCE PREVENTION

Preventing variance boils down to the three things mentioned earlier: awareness of expectations, the capability to comply, and the motivation to comply. Of course, if expectations (i.e., policies and standards) aren't defined, then people have nothing of which to be aware. This is one of the key links between variance management and decision making. This is also, by the way, another classic case of a Boolean relationship between controls because a deficiency in any one of the awareness, capability, or motivation elements will result in variance regardless of the strength of the other two elements. We'll discuss this more when we cover root cause analysis in a later chapter, and you may (or may not) be surprised at which of these three elements tends to be the most common cause of variance at the organizations in which we have done root cause analyses.

VARIANCE DETECTION

Detecting variance is the next branch in this ontology, and it looks and behaves exactly like the detection branches in asset-level controls. You first have to have visibility because you can't deal with variances if they aren't within view. Examples of things that provide visibility into control variance include the following:

- Auditing
- Control self-assessments

- Second line of defense reviews
- Policy compliance reviews
- System configuration scanning
- Change management processes
- Personnel

This last one might raise your eyebrows, but think about it. If you have personnel in place where controls exist, then you inherently have some degree of visibility. That said, unless people are aware of what the control expectations are, there is little chance that you will have effective recognition—the second element in the detection branch. With that in mind, what would you suppose the relationship is between visibility and recognition? If you said "and," congratulations!

Recognition, of course, boils down to being able to distinguish that a variant condition exists ("Hey, that's not supposed to be unlocked!"). Then, having recognized a variant condition, the next all-too-obvious element is reporting (i.e., getting the information about a variant condition into the hands of the people/processes that are geared to do something about it, in a timely manner).

Guess what happens without effective variance reporting? Nothing. You can have great visibility and marvelous recognition, but if the reporting function is broken, you're in trouble. Consequently, this means we have another *and* relationship and each element in this branch is dependent on the other two for the detection branch to be effective at all. Unfortunately, it is remarkable how often deficient control conditions are seen and recognized but not reported. "It's not my job," "I didn't know who to report it to," or "I didn't want to get anyone in trouble," are all too common explanations. This is yet another opportunity for awareness and motivation.

TALKING ABOUT RISK

Did you notice the recursive nature of what was just described? Reporting on control variance is itself a control and, as such, the same variance ontology applies (i.e., "How much variance exists in the reporting of control variance?"). It can get a little mind bending but it's logical once you have wrapped your head around it. We'll talk about this again a little further on in the chapter.

VARIANCE RESPONSE

After a variant condition has been reported, there obviously needs to be some sort of response function in place to deal with it. In large part, response boils down to implementing, in a timely manner, whatever remediation decision has been made by the appropriate stakeholder(s). These remediations may, of course, be predefined through policies, standards, and/or guidelines.

TALKING ABOUT RISK

In our experience, it's common to see control frameworks that include elements regarding prevention, detection, and response, but not clearly differentiate whether these elements are intended to prevent, detect, and respond to control problems (variance) or loss events. The fact is these are different parts of the risk problem-space, and differentiation is critical for effectively defining and using metrics, as well as communicating the significance of issues. Terminology and models are not just semantics. They matter in a real sense.

We strongly encourage you to examine whether the organization you work for differentiates between "incidents" that are loss events (e.g., the unauthorized disclosure of sensitive information) and those that are threat events (e.g., an attempted compromise of a web server) and those that are variance events (e.g., a system that isn't configured properly from a security perspective). These are fundamentally different types of events, and your metrics need to recognize that fact. Too often, we see organizations whose metrics don't differentiate, which means that decisions driven by these metrics are misinformed.

WHERE AND WHEN VARIANCE OCCURS

So, significant variance is a "bad thing." Fairly obvious, but when and where does variance raise its ugly head? We'll bet 9 of 10 of you (or more) can list most of the obvious ones (during design and implementation, when changes occur to the asset, etc.). That said, we are now going to throw you a curve ball. There is another point at which variance occurs on asset-level controls that probably few of you would guess. And here is the pitch—it has nothing *directly* to do with the control condition. Allow us to explain.

As we discussed earlier, control expectations/requirements are (or should be) set to achieve a desired state of risk. As we have been talking about, when asset-level controls are implemented incorrectly or changes to controls occur, we end up with an unintended (and usually undesirable) level of vulnerability. But what if, instead of changes to controls, we experience an increase in threat capability? Same outcome—increased vulnerability (and thus, risk), which is a variance from the intended level of risk. Consequently, when we say we are "managing variance," we are actually managing variance in the amount of risk we face, which can be based on control conditions *or* threat capability.

An all-too-common practical example from the information security discipline is when a new exploit is identified in a computer operating system. In this case, the controls haven't changed, but we nonetheless have an increased level of vulnerability—a level of vulnerability that varies from the intended state. Consequently, when we are defining, implementing, and maintaining controls to manage variance, we also have to include the means of detecting and resolving when threat capability changes. This is why it is so critically important to stay on top of changes in the threat landscape. In our experience, by far, the best way to achieve this is through the use of threat intelligence providers. Few organizations invest the necessary resources to generate truly good threat intelligence on their own.

When threat capability changes occur, we have to engage a response function so that we can make changes to our control conditions and bring the level of vulnerability back to our desired state (e.g., apply a new patch to the system). As we'll see in an upcoming section, the timeliness of variance detection and response is often critical to the overall effectiveness of variance management.

TALKING ABOUT RISK

Sometimes, we'll run into someone who will claim that a system was vulnerable even before the new exploit was discovered. After all, the flaw existed all along. The problem with that argument is that threat capability is composed of a threat agent's skills and resources. However, without a threat agent's knowledge of the flaw (knowledge being a threat resource), the capability to exploit the flaw did not exist and, thus, the vulnerability associated with that flaw did not exist.

EXPOSURE WINDOWS AND THREAT EVENT COLLISIONS

Unfortunately, despite our best efforts, "stuff" (variance) happens and, thus, we have what we refer to as "windows of exposure." And, this is where it gets kind of interesting. In the illustration below, assume the horizontal axis represents time, and the vertical axis represents the degree of a system's vulnerability. Furthermore, let's assume that when we put an asset into production, we have designed, built, and implemented the asset in compliance with control-related policies and standards. As depicted in Figure 11.17, in a perfect world, the level of vulnerability never varies from the intended state (we are allowed to dream, are we not?).

In reality, changes in vulnerability are likely to occur at various times throughout the lifetime of the asset. These changes may, as we pointed out earlier, occur as a result of changes to the asset's controls or changes in threat community capabilities. Regardless, when these changes occur, the asset is operating at an unintended level of vulnerability until the variance is identified and remedied (Figure 11.18).

FIGURE 11.17

Vulnerability over time (Shangri-La version).

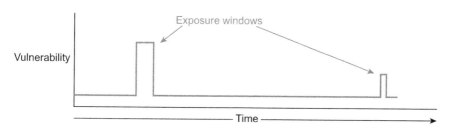

FIGURE 11.18

Vulnerability over time (real version).

The frequency and duration of these increased exposure windows, and the degree of change in vulnerability during these windows, are major components of what drives the risk proposition of an asset over time. But they aren't the only component.

Figure 11.19 shows an asset's exposure window characteristics over time relative to a threat event (the red vertical line along the time axis). If threat events don't happen often, then the probability of a "collision" between the threat event and an increased level of vulnerability in an exposure window is relatively low. Heck, if the threat event frequency is low enough, then we may be able to tolerate relatively wide and/or frequent exposure windows (depending, of course, on what the loss magnitude of such an event might be).

If, however, as depicted in Figure 11.20, threat event frequency is higher, then we must be highly proficient at preventing, detecting, and responding to variance to minimize the probability of collisions between threat events and exposure windows.

What this tells us is that to manage variance effectively (and the risk it introduces), we have to understand both an asset's window of exposure characteristics and the threat event frequency it faces, and then put into place the appropriate variance management capabilities to minimize collisions. Keep in mind, though, that even when an asset's vulnerability is at the intended level, it still has some amount of vulnerability. As a result, a threat event by a capable enough threat can still result in a loss event at any point along the timeline. The good news is that organizations often have at their disposal (but rarely use) good data on windows of exposure and threat event frequency, which makes this an important area of improvement for most organizations.

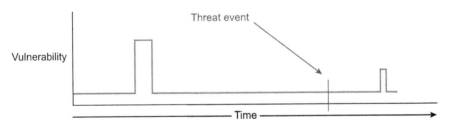

FIGURE 11.19

Threat events and vulnerability windows over time.

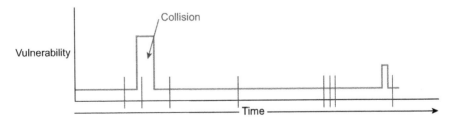

FIGURE 11.20

Threat events and vulnerability collision.

TALKING ABOUT RISK

We just read two reports on Internet web security written by two separate information security companies. Both of these reports offered lots of data and statistics about web security: one company[1] focusing on the number of vulnerabilities it observed in the thousands of customer websites it provides security for, and the other company[2] focusing on data associated with attacks against the customer websites with which it works. The report on vulnerabilities stated that 86% of all websites they tested had at least one serious vulnerability, and that the average window of exposure was 193 days. The report on website attacks stated that, on average, websites were subject to high severity attacks once every 15 days.

What's wrong with this picture? Both of these companies are highly reputable, seem to have access to solid data, and seem to use reasonable statistical methods. Still, something is just not right. These reports would seem to imply that nearly all of those websites with "serious vulnerabilities" should have been compromised, at least given our premise on the relationship between exposure windows and threat event frequency. Of course, maybe they have been compromised. The report doesn't provide that information.

Here's our take on the problem. Given that the analyses underlying the reports were done separately and independently, there was no effort to correlate the frequencies of specific vulnerabilities against specific attacks (e.g., the probability of an Structured Query Language (SQL) injection attack hitting a site that has an SQL injection vulnerability). Furthermore, as a chief information security officer (CISO) for three organizations, I (J.J.) have become familiar with the odd situation where an application thought to have a specific vulnerability is subjected to attack but isn't compromised. Sometimes, this is because the vulnerability is a false positive or there are compensating conditions that keep it from being truly exploited. Other times, it's because the attack didn't find that vulnerability among all the web pages and variables on those web pages. Often, the vulnerabilities exist behind an authentication layer and weren't really accessible to most attacks. And, other times, what someone calls a "Serious Vulnerability" or a "Serious Attack" has to be taken with a grain of salt. Regardless, the point is that we have to exercise a lot more critical thinking and go deeper in our analyses before we can really gain clear and meaningful intelligence from these kinds of data. Don't get us wrong, though: there was a ton of useful information in both of these reports, and we believe they are absolutely headed in the right direction.

[1]Whitehat Security Website Security Statistics Report—May 2013.
[2]Imperva Web Application Attack Report—July 2013.

BEYOND ASSET-LEVEL CONTROLS

So far, we've been focused on managing variance in asset-level controls. In large part, this is because that's where threat events and loss occur, but it isn't the only place where managing variance is important.

As alluded to earlier, the controls used to manage variance (e.g., policies, audits and testing, reporting, and remediation processes) are subject to their own variance-related problems. For example, an organization may have defined a policy or standard regarding the timeliness of remediation activities (a variance control) because it considered that activity to be important from a risk management perspective. If, however, the actual remediation time frame varied significantly from this expectation, then the organization would have larger windows of exposure than it wants and, thus, would not be maintaining its intended risk posture. As you might guess, the same variance management ontology would apply here as it does to asset-level controls. We want to prevent variability in variance controls as much as possible through awareness, capability, and motivation; detect it in a timely manner through good visibility, recognition, and reporting; and respond to it in a timely manner by making the appropriate decision makers aware, providing them good information regarding the significance of the variance, and following their direction in resolving the broken variance control.

By now, you're probably noticing a trend. Variance management seems to apply to almost everything (well, everything that we might call a control). With this in mind, then, it should be no surprise that variance management principles apply to decision-making controls as well, which will be covered further on in this chapter. The bottom line is that variance management is "where it's at" in terms of effectively dealing with risk. That said, variance management is never going to be effective if the organization's risk management decision making is broken. More on that in a minute…

VARIANCE METRICS

We're going to cover metrics in detail in a later chapter. In our opinion, metrics regarding variance are potentially the most important metrics when it comes to understanding not only the current risk posture of an organization but its ability to manage risk over time. There are three reasons for this:

- As we discussed earlier, variance in asset-level controls is usually the greatest factor when it comes to how much risk an organization has at any given moment.
- Control checklists containing things like, "Do you have a password policy that requires passwords of at least 8 characters in length and a mix of uppercase, lowercase, and numbers?" may tell us the intended state of controls for an organization, but it tells us squat about the actual state of controls. It tells us even less about how much risk the organization is likely to have a year from now.
- As we'll review in the next section, how much variance an organization has can also be a solid indicator of trouble in an organization's variance management and decision making.

Consequently, if you can only measure one thing about an organization's risk posture (your organization or someone else's), our suggestion is that you focus on variance. It speaks volumes.

DECISION-MAKING CONTROLS

Here again, Deming had it right: the problem almost always boils down to management. More specifically in the risk management realm, we would submit that it boils down to management decision making. This should *not*, however, be interpreted as a blanket indictment of people in management positions. Not by a long shot. Many times, they are making the best decisions they can, but they're hamstrung by bad or missing information, the wrong person is making the decision, or they have insufficient/scarce resources with which to manage the problem.

In this section, we'll describe a decision-making ontology and how we categorize decision making. We'll also touch on how this all fits into a systems view of risk management. By the way, if any of the examples we give sound suspiciously like they come right out of your organization, it's simply a reflection of the pervasive nature of some of these problems.

COMMON PROBLEMS

It might be helpful to start out by providing a short list of the problems we've commonly seen that are related to suboptimal risk management decision making. As you read this list, ask yourself whether any of them might apply to your organization:

- Routine noncompliance with policies
- Inconsistent policy enforcement
- Lack of clarity regarding accountability
- Lack of clarity regarding authority
- Frequent changes in risk management focus and direction
- Loss events involving assets that no one seemed to know existed
- Audit findings that come as a complete surprise

These are all symptoms of the kinds of organizational decision-making problems that the controls in this section can help manage. Because this may be a less familiar "control territory" for some of you, we're going to be a bit more explicit in our descriptions of the problems and controls than we were in the asset-level and variance control sections.

TALKING ABOUT RISK

Soapbox warning!! Within the information security discipline, there is a too-common belief that executives don't care about risk, are willing to accept any amount of risk to meet their business objectives, and just fundamentally do not "get" information security risk. This hasn't been our experience at all, not even remotely. Our experience has been that if we have done a good job of thinking through and describing meaningful risk conditions and cost-effective risk management options, we have had zero, zilch, nada problems in gaining appropriate levels of executive management attention and support. We used two words in that last sentence, though, that are key: meaningful and appropriate.

Regarding being meaningful: recognize that the risk issues we bring before management are just one slice of a much larger pie of things they have to deal with. They have to focus on and prioritize not only the risk stuff we take them but decisions related to business opportunities, operational issues, and other forms of risk the organization inevitably wrestles with. Consequently, we need to ensure that we only put problems and solutions before them that are truly relevant, and that we convey this information in terms that are meaningful to *them*. Usually, this means expressing risk in monetary or mission-related terms and developing cost-benefit analyses for the solutions we recommend, which is one of the reasons why FAIR has worked so well for us.

Regarding being appropriate: we may do an outstanding job of risk analysis and business case development, and may even convey this information in terms that make executives stand up and cheer. At the end of the day, though, because of that bigger pie they have to deal with, they may not give us the resources we've asked for. And you know what? That is just fine. An "appropriate level of support" is relative to that larger pie and has nothing at all to do with our personal views on whatever the issue was.

DECISION CATEGORIES

Before we get into the decision-making controls ontology, we need to recognize that there are decisions and then there are *decisions*. At the end of the day, we view the decision-making landscape as being composed of three main categories:

- Strategic decisions,
- Operational decisions, and
- Incident management decisions

Strategic decisions are those that set objectives and expectations for the organization. Operational decisions are those that manage the people, processes, and technologies in an effort to achieve the organization's objectives. A lot of this has to do with managing variance. Last, incident decisions are those that deal with events and crises that represent immediate potential for loss.

Who makes the decisions in each of these decision categories will vary from organization to organization, as well as from situation to situation. As a general rule, however, executive management will be responsible for setting objectives and expectations, and middle management will be responsible for most of the operational decisions. Incident management decision making is less cut-and-dry.

TALKING ABOUT RISK

Much of what we're talking about in this next section might be referred to as "governance" by others. The truth is that risk-related decision making takes place at all levels of an organization, and the concepts and principles we are talking about in this section apply to them all. Thus, we believe the term "decision making" is more generic and less likely to be misinterpreted than "governance."

DECISION-MAKING CONTROLS ONTOLOGY

The general structure of this ontology (Figure 11.21) should by now begin to look familiar, but with a twist. Instead of prevention as the top branch of the first level of abstraction, we have enablement.

Enablement

We chose to use the term enablement rather than prevention because it seemed unnatural to have an ontology related to decisions where one of the control branches could be mistakenly interpreted to mean, "preventing decisions." Clearly, the intent would be to prevent bad decisions, but we opted to place the focus on enabling good decisions (kind of a glass half full point of view). We're hopeful this was a good decision on our part.

Information

The information branch is all about ensuring that decision makers are provided the best possible information from which to base their decisions. As you might guess, we believe this is an area where huge improvement opportunities exist in information security.

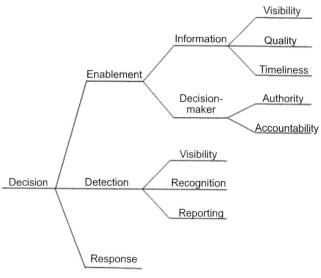

FIGURE 11.21

Decision ontology.

Visibility. This is one of the most significant problems in the risk management programs we encounter. First, the simple fact is that no organization can rationally make the claim that it is managing risk effectively (let alone cost-effectively) if it has poor visibility into its risk landscape. Whether it's inadequate asset management, an incomplete and out-of-date understanding of control conditions, or a limited understanding of the threat landscape (or all three in many cases), an organization's ability to make risk-informed business decisions is often a long shot at best.

It would be interesting to do a study on the percentage of loss events that occur in organizations where management had poor visibility into the portion of their risk landscape where the loss event occurred. It might be that the asset at risk wasn't being managed by the usual personnel or processes, that the deficient control conditions surrounding the asset were unrecognized, or that the threat was one the organization hadn't really spent any time or effort to consider or address (or perhaps a combination of these). On the other hand, what percentage of the time, we wonder, had the condition(s) that contributed to the event been known by decision makers and simply accepted or were on the schedule for remediation at a later date? And, if the conditions were known, how effectively had the associated loss exposure been analyzed and communicated (i.e., how well informed were the decision makers)?

Regardless, controls related to risk landscape visibility involve ensuring that decision makers have a reasonable level of understanding in the following three areas of the risk landscape:

- *Assets*: We want to know where they are, and their value/liability characteristics (i.e., how much we should care about them). Classification schemes are a commonly discussed, but rarely effectively applied, approach to setting asset value/liability. Keep in mind, though, the second of these two characteristics—liability. This implies that you also need to understand the external factors that affect loss magnitude, like regulations, contractual agreements, and barriers to customer exit. Controls that can help with this include the following: asset inventory management, classification, and change management. Hey, wait a minute! Isn't change management a variance control? Why yes it is, but it plays a role here as well. At a strategic level, this information should be high level (e.g., percentage of assets that have been classified, significant changes to the regulatory environment, and significant growth or shrinkage of the asset inventory).

- *Controls*: Okay, congratulations! Assume that you have great visibility into your assets. You're still in trouble, though, if you don't know the asset-level, variance, and decision-making control conditions that exist to protect those assets. Controls that can help with this include audits and various control testing processes. Here again, those controls play a role in managing variance but also provide visibility in the broader sense. At a strategic level, this information might include things like significant areas of variance and progress against new control initiatives.

- *Threats*: Plain and simple—you can't make good risk decisions if you don't understand what you're up against. You need information regarding the frequency of threat events and, in the information security arena at least, you also need intelligence regarding threat capability. For organizations concerned about weather and natural disasters, there are readily available sources of threat intelligence. For physical security, there are always law enforcement agencies. For information security, there are several threat intelligence providers out there; it would be difficult to be a good CISO without engaging one (or at least a happy CISO). At a strategic level, this information might include significant changes in the threat landscape, or projected changes based on threat intelligence sources.

We wouldn't be surprised if some readers are concerned about the level of effort required to evaluate the visibility of these elements. It isn't as bad as you think. In the metrics chapter, we'll share an approach to visibility analysis that we believe can be helpful and practical.

Information quality. The second most common problem with the information decision makers rely on is that far too often it seems like little to no critical thinking goes into the risk ratings put before management. Let's give you an example.

I (J.J.) attended a meeting in an organization I was working with where the CISO was briefing leadership on a dire circumstance. Specifically, the information security team had just finished running a web application security scanner against one of the company's key web applications and found hundreds of "critical and high-risk vulnerabilities." You could almost see the blood drain from the faces of these executives, and immediately the conversation turned to how quickly the vulnerabilities could be fixed (at the expense of meeting several key business development initiatives). Before things went too far, though, I asked a few questions:

- Was this a new application or had it been on the Internet for a while? (Answer: It had been online for years.)
- Were the vulnerabilities new or had they likely been there a while? (Answer: Many were believed to have been there for months or years.)
- Was the application subject to threat events with any regularity? (Answer: Yes, it was constantly under attack.)
- Given the above, how come the company is still in business? (Answer: Blank stare)
- Had the organization regularly engaged consultants to test the security of the application? (Answer: Yes)
- Had they ever compromised the application? (Answer: No)
- Were they hiring qualified consultants? (Answer: Yes)

Clearly, something was wrong. Were we to believe the application scan results or the consultants? Or neither? Regardless, the tone in the room changed immediately from one of "Heaven help us!" to "Let's dig into this and get some better information." A little digging and analysis revealed the following: (1) there were only a handful of truly significant vulnerabilities, (2) the frequency of threat events was much lower than believed, and (3) they hadn't been scoping the consultant work to be very thorough. On the basis of this revised information, management aggressively tackled the most important deficiencies and developed longer-term remediation plans for the rest. They also budgeted for better consultant work.

Here is a quick question for you to see if you've been paying attention. Given the previous example, which controls ontology applies? If you said "asset-level controls," you get a silver star. Yes, the weaknesses within the application represented asset-level deficiencies (variances from the desired state) that indicated higher levels of vulnerability and, thus, risk. If you also said, "variance controls," you get a gold star. The existence of deficiencies in the application represented room for improvement in the organization's ability to prevent variant conditions. You get a platinum star if you also said "decision making" because they were operating with visibility deficiency in terms of good information about control conditions and threat landscape, and an information quality problem in terms of the scan result accuracy.

TALKING ABOUT RISK

In both the asset-level and variance control ontologies, there were elements labeled "reporting" in the detection branches. Well, reporting to whom? Decision makers, that's who. And, thus, we have linkages between those ontologies and the decision-making ontology. The reporting branches in these ontologies are the sources of information that will be consumed by the decision-making processes, be they strategic, operational, or incident management related.

We will cover this more specifically in the risk management and metrics chapters, but it is worth pointing out now that the three control ontologies that make up risk management (asset level, variance, and decision making) represent a system of interrelated parts. As a system, what goes on in one can affect the others profoundly, which means the overall risk condition of an organization is fundamentally driven by this system. The problem in our experience is that few organizations explicitly recognize and focus on this systemic/feedback point of view. Oh, there may be tacit recognition at a superficial level, and everybody talks about metrics, but almost nobody really understands the details or manages the system through meaningful data and analysis. It is generally off-the-cuff and highly reliant on the experience and intuition of the people within the organization—talk about variance!

That said, many organizations may feel they just don't have the resources required to really dive in and optimize their risk management system. We get that. We do believe, however, that by explicitly defining and describing how this system works we are enabling organizations to more easily recognize where they can make incremental improvements in this regard.

It's a bit harder to identify specific controls regarding information quality. About the closest thing we commonly encounter is when an organization stipulates that its information security personnel have certain certifications (e.g., certified information systems security professional, certified information security manager, and certified in risk and information systems control). The assumption being that certified professionals will provide better quality information to their stakeholders. Although this is true in some respects, as of this writing, none of these certifications (other than the Open Group FAIR certification) cover risk analysis and measurement effectively. This, combined with the prevailing poor risk measurement practices in the information security industry, leaves us believing that the quality of risk information being given to decision makers represents a major opportunity for improvement in risk management overall. Improvements that organizations should consider include the following:

- Having people trained and certified in FAIR (or at least have them read this book)
- Implement a process for risk analysis peer reviews
- Requiring periodic third-party reviews of the risk information provided to decision makers

Another information quality control in which we strongly believe is to have someone (usually the CISO or equivalent) sign his or her name to any risk report being used to drive key decisions (e.g., policy exceptions). This isn't a signature making him or her directly responsible for the decision being made, but rather his or her signature attests that the risk conditions described in the report are accurate given the information that was available at the time of the report. In other words, although CISOs shouldn't be held directly responsible for the decisions being made by the business, they should be held accountable for the quality of information used to guide those decisions. As a CISO, I (J.J.) have always implemented this control for two reasons: (1) to differentiate my accountability from those of the decision makers, and (2) to motivate me, and thus my team, to provide the best information we can given our resources. This control has saved my bacon on a couple of occasions when the risk report had indicated significant risk existed, management decided to accept the risk, and a loss event subsequently occurred. In both cases, I wasn't held accountable for the decision. In conclusion, managing risk effectively requires good information about risk. If that's broken, then everything else has to be strongly suspect.

TALKING ABOUT RISK

Some people's response to this attestation of risk information quality control is, "Maybe I ought to call everything high risk so that my backside is always covered." First, that's the coward's way out. Second, they are every bit as likely to lose their job by being overly conservative as not because most business executives will see through that ruse in relatively short order. Look, if someone wants to lead an information security organization, he or she had better get used to the fact that he or she is accountable (formally or not) for helping the organization manage risk as *cost-effectively* as possible. The only way to do this is to have a solid understanding of risk, risk measurement, and risk management, and be able to communicate information effectively to decision makers. It isn't a simple job, and it takes a certain amount of intestinal fortitude. In using FAIR, we have been far more comfortable in our ability to meet these requirements.

Information timeliness. Okay, so we have (hopefully) made our point about visibility and information quality, but even the best visibility and highest quality information is of limited use if it gets to the decision makers too late. From a controls perspective, this is a little bit easier to wrap our arms around. An organization can establish policies and processes that will help ensure timely reporting for each of the three decision types. For strategic decisions, maybe it's quarterly and year-end reporting. For operational decisions, maybe it is weekly and monthly reporting via metrics and dashboards. For critical deficiencies and loss event management, maybe it is a service-level agreement stating that conditions of certain severities are reported within a certain number of hours. The good news is that we haven't usually seen as many problems with timeliness as we have with visibility and information quality.

Decision maker

Great information about the risk landscape is for naught if the wrong people are making decisions. Over the years, we have seen what we believe is gradual improvement on this score in information security. For a long time, it seemed the prevailing mind set was that the CISO should be making policy and other major risk management decisions in organizations. Thankfully, we see more and more recognition that these are ultimately business decisions that need to be made by business executives. There is still room for improvement, to be sure, but at least things seem to be on the right path.

Regardless of the gradual improvement we think we see, this is still an opportunity for improvement in many organizations. In our experience, it boils down to two key points: (1) ensuring that decision maker(s) have the authority to make decisions, and (2) ensuring that they will be held accountable for their decisions.

Decision-making authority. Ensuring decision-maker authority is critical. Far too often, we have seen mid-level management making risk decisions that should be made at a much higher level within the organization. What makes someone authorized to make a decision? Two things come straight to mind, depending on the nature of the decision: (1) having the resources to support the decision and/or (2) having the means to enforce compliance. A great (horrible?) example of "authority gone wrong" is when information security leadership defines the information security policy and doesn't have it truly vetted and approved by executive management. In this (all too common) example, personnel outside of the information security team often recognize that there are no real teeth behind the policies, so they feel free to ignore them. What's unfortunate is that some risk professionals will argue tooth and nail that executive business management can't make these decisions intelligently and should cede policy setting to information security leadership. First, executive management didn't get where they are by being slow witted. Second, the resources to get things done and the ability to apply consequences come from the business, not information security. As we have said before, it is incumbent on risk professionals to make sure they communicate the issues clearly to executives so that they are making good decisions. If executives don't "get it," the blame is on the risk professional, pure and simple.

So, what kind of controls can we apply to help ensure that decisions are made by the right people? There are three that we like a lot:

- Clearly defined roles and responsibilities
- ARCI (Accountable, Responsible, Consulted, Informed) chart, which is also sometimes referred to as a RACI chart
- Another is similar to an ARCI chart, but it specifically lays out what level of management is authorized to make risk decisions based on the magnitude of risk and the scope of risk (i.e., whether the risk issue only affects a department, or the entire organization). In some organizations, this is referred to as a Delegation of Authority document.

Accountability. Accountability is pretty closely related to authority—or at least you would think so. The problem is that when the wrong person is making a risk decision, he or she can often duck accountability by claiming he or she didn't know they did not have authority. This is a reasonably legitimate argument if an organization has not clearly defined authority levels. Another common accountability problem is "decision by committee." When everyone is responsible, nobody's accountable. A third problem from an accountability perspective is simply the often informal nature of decision documentation (i.e., if someone doesn't have to sign his or her name to a document, they tend to feel less accountable).

The best accountability control we've seen (assuming authority is well defined) is requiring decision makers to sign a statement that explicitly acknowledges their accountability. Most commonly, we see this on risk acceptance documentation and change management approvals. Of course, when an organization is first starting to enforce this as a requirement, there may be resistance by some decision makers. As a result, it's important that this requirement come from high up in the organization. When this is done right, it is remarkable how much more deliberate and risk averse many decision makers become. They will still take risk, of course, but odds are better that it will be more appropriate risk taking.

Detection

For the feedback system to be complete, we also need to have the means of detecting when suboptimal risk decisions are being, or have been, made. The structure of this part of the ontology is likely to be familiar and probably obvious to you.

Visibility

Visibility into risk decision making in general has begun to improve in recent years because an increasing number of organizations implement more formal processes surrounding policy making, policy exceptions, change management, and information security strategy approvals. This is also one area where governance, risk, and compliance products have sometimes been helpful. However, these aren't the only, or even necessarily the best, points of visibility into suboptimal decisions. Other great sources include the following:

- Internal and external audits
- Regulatory examinations
- Security testing
- Loss events

The first three of these are often explicitly focused on identifying decisions that have (in someone's opinion) gone awry. For example, findings about inadequate policies and processes are essentially opinions about the decisions that drove those conditions. We won't debate here whether those opinions (and the decisions that helped to inform them) are all that well informed themselves. Nonetheless, the process of examining the decisions an organization makes provides visibility. Loss events can also be a great (if unfortunate) source of visibility into decisions that were poorly informed or made by the wrong person.

Although all four of these sources of visibility exist in most organizations to some degree, our experience has been that it is rare for an organization to explicitly recognize them as an opportunity to identify decision-related problems. This boils down to, again, being explicit in your approach to risk management.

Recognition

We alluded to this previously, but all the visibility in the world is useless if we do not take the time and effort to examine decisions with an eye toward improvement. Was this audit finding due to suboptimal decision making at a policy, process, or other level? Was the information that guided this decision flawed in some material way? Did the right person make the decision? These are the types of questions we must ask if we hope to recognize opportunities for improvement. Absent this, we are stuck in risk management groundhog day—seeing the same decision-making problems repeatedly.

Controls to support the recognition of decision-making problems can include things like building root cause analyses questions into audit management and incident management processes. Other opportunities include things like performing periodic reviews of risk analyses being used to guide decisions. After all, there is no reason to wait for an incident or an audit finding to identify a problem.

Reporting

Here again, this is straightforward. The good news is (or should be) that the conditions resulting from bad decisions are often reported as a natural part of the process.

That said, unless decision improvement is an explicit goal, there is a decent chance that identified problems may not be reported. This can be particularly problematic in some cases because the people making suboptimal decisions may be relatively senior in the organization. Consequently, political awareness can be important. Each organization will be different in this regard, but in particularly touchy cases, we will speak directly and confidentially with the decision maker. More often than not though, the fundamental problem is simply that they were operating from bad information.

Response

Fundamentally, response boils down to correcting both whatever causative factors contributed to poor decision making and improving any formal documentation of those suboptimal decisions (e.g., changing bad policies). A significant source of poor information that drives bad decisions is the information security policies themselves. It has to do with the verbiage used in policies and standards. Bottom line—many of the policies and standards we have encountered are nearly unreadable, and people cannot or will not take the time to decipher them. In one organization where I (J.J.) was CISO, I was so appalled at the policy verbiage that I brought in a language expert to evaluate the policies. His verdict—they were written for someone at the grade 23 level; I had no idea there was a literacy level that high! His recommendation was to rewrite them for a sixth grader. We compromised and wrote them at the ninth grade level, which made the information much more accessible.

In addition to grade-level considerations, another problem we are all-too-familiar with is a lack of conciseness. Some organizations (you know who you are) have policies that are pages and pages long, often filled with boilerplate filler that personnel have to dig through to find out what is actually expected of them. Many people simply will not invest the time to do this, which means the policies are next to useless as a means to support decision making. Perhaps the worst example we have ever seen of this was the encryption policy in a financial institution. This policy was more than 60 pages long, filled with all kinds of completely useless information from a variance management perspective. There is virtually no chance that people were going to actually dig through this thing to figure out what the requirements were. We went through this thing with a proverbial hatchet and cut it down to a page and a half.

A possible control to deal with this is to have communications professionals review policies and standards for readability and conciseness. Alternatively, ask yourself whether the average ninth grader would be able to read and understand what is expected of them. If not, there is work to do.

CONTROL WRAP UP

And there you have it: controls. If you are feeling overwhelmed by what we covered here, the good news is that the risk management and metrics chapters will reinforce much of what we've covered. We think you'll find these concepts become pretty easy to digest and apply as you work with them.

Risk Management

12

"Human beings, who are almost unique in having the ability to learn from the experience of others, are also remarkable for their apparent disinclination to do so."
Douglas Adams

Your organization already manages risk. That is a given. The question, however, is whether your organization is doing it implicitly or explicitly. For example, your organization might have aligned its information security policies with ISO and it might have an ISO-based enterprise risk assessment performed annually. People in the organization probably prioritize and work hard to fix the findings from that assessment, and they respond to the information-security curveballs that invariably are thrown at the organization throughout the year. That is most definitely a form of risk management. However, it isn't explicit. It isn't explicit because where the organization ends-up risk-wise is a by-product of those efforts. In order to be explicit, there would need to be a specific target that is actively being managed to. To get our point across, let's change gears from managing information security risk to managing your finances.

An implicit approach to managing your finances would involve things like reading money management journals, earning money in some manner, putting money in the bank, and spending money (mostly) on things you need. These are all very good and important things to do, and an implicit outcome of such an approach is likely to be a better financial position than if you were not doing those things. That said, in order for you to *explicitly* manage your financial position, you have to set a financially-defined objective, continually measure yourself against that objective (e.g., balancing your checkbook), and make measured adjustments to help achieve and maintain that objective (e.g., spend less and earn more, or maybe even spend more!).

Some folks might respond to this by saying, "But my organization does measure itself on risk! We check ourselves against best practice, we have a GRC product chock-full of "risks," and we have an information security balanced scorecard. Management has even defined the organization's risk appetite as "moderate to low." So if that's the case, where does the organization stand currently relative to that risk appetite? When you find discrepancies from best practice how much additional risk is that driving into your organization? Of the remediation initiatives you fired-up based on the last risk assessment, how much risk are they taking out of the organization? Let us reiterate: we are not saying that an implicit approach to risk management is bad. It just means you have less control of the outcome, in large part because the outcome isn't clearly defined and your measurements are typically only loosely associated with risk. Another thing to keep in mind is that, much like objectivity and subjectivity, this notion of implicit and explicit risk management is a continuum rather than two exclusive binary states. As a result, the objective is to evolve your organization's risk management practices to a point along that continuum that strikes the right balance.

In this chapter, we will begin by sharing the most common questions we hear from executive management with regard to information security. By explicitly recognizing what the executives are looking for when they ask these questions, we improve the odds of answering them effectively. We'll also spend some time defining what "explicit risk management" means and looks like from our perspective, so that we can differentiate between the more common implicit practices and opportunities to be more explicit. Some of the more common risk management decisions that come with the territory will also be discussed. We'll categorize these decisions and then share some examples of implicit and explicit ways to support them. To wrap up the chapter, we'll provide a description of the risk landscape elements and their relationships to each other. This is critical to understand in order to treat the landscape as a system of interrelated parts, which allows us to make rational measured adjustments that support an explicit approach. This will set things up nicely for the metrics chapter that follows.

COMMON QUESTIONS

The most common questions we encounter from executive management regarding information security include:

- Are we spending enough (or too much) on security?
- What are the most important concerns, and are we on top of them?
- What are our best-bang-for-the-buck risk management options?
- Are we keeping up with the evolving threats?

All of these questions are asked within the broader business management context that executives have to deal with. In other words, underlying these questions are two concerns:

1. How worried do they need to be, and
2. Do they have a need or opportunity to reallocate resources (usually as a result of number 1)?

The answers to these questions will be compared against a very similar set of questions and answers being asked of the other parts of the organization (e.g., sales, production, etc.) in order to drive who gets what resources, and when. The problem is, for most organizations the honest answer to these questions will fall somewhere between, "We think so," "We're not sure," and "We have no earthly clue."

TALKING ABOUT RISK

There is another question we commonly get from executive management that is not listed above—"How do we rate relative to our peers?"

The simple fact is that humans like to compare themselves against others. It's reassuring to know that you haven't strayed too far from the herd, and as a species, we do tend to be herd animals in some respects. We worry, though, that when organizations focus on comparing themselves to their peers they forsake their opportunity (and their obligation to stakeholders) to look for ways to optimize their risk management efforts.

We believe that a significant contributing factor to the interest in benchmarking has been the absence of more meaningful metrics regarding where the organization stands, risk-wise. If executives had access to risk metrics that helped them to better understand where the organization stood from a loss exposure and risk management perspective, the importance of comparisons as an aid in decision-making would diminish. Today, however, very few organizations seem to have a solid understanding of their risk position, so all that's left for them is to follow the herd. Moo.

The rest of this chapter will lay a foundation that, combined with what's covered in the rest of this book, should help organizations more confidently and accurately answer these questions, and much more.

WHAT WE MEAN BY "RISK MANAGEMENT"

Based on what we discussed above you might be able to put together a definition for risk management that would be close to ours, but we're going to save you the trouble and share our definition anyway. Why is a definition necessary? Well, like much of the rest of the nomenclature we encounter in this profession, we see a fair amount of variability in how people use the term "risk management." Besides, we'd like to deconstruct our definition a bit, so that we can drive some points home.

From our perspective, risk management can be defined as:

The combination of personnel, policies, processes, and technologies that enable an organization to cost-effectively achieve and maintain an acceptable level of loss exposure.

This is probably not too far off what you thought we'd come up with. So now that we've provided this as a starting point, let's break it apart and dig into it a bit to make it real.

COST-EFFECTIVELY

We believe our profession has been sorely remiss on the topic of cost-effectiveness. Our responsibility as mature professionals is *not* simply to help our organizations manage risk. Our responsibility is to help our organizations manage risk cost-effectively. You can't achieve this through the box checking and "regression toward the mean" practices that permeate the profession today. Yes, we are familiar with the arguments in favor of common practices and benchmarking, and some of these arguments make sense for some organizations. There is definitely a continuum for risk management maturity and just above the low end of that continuum (the low end being no program at all) blindly following common practices is a decent place to start. If an organization wants to evolve beyond that base level of maturity though, it has to exercise the critical thinking skills and more mature approaches that are not part of what pass as common practices today.

One of the arguments we often hear for common practices and benchmarking is that many security organizations don't have the resources to do more than that. Underlying this argument is the assumption that it costs more to be more mature, which isn't necessarily true. If an information security organization is able to prioritize better and choose more cost-effective solutions, it's pretty hard to imagine how this automatically equates to higher cost. In fact, it could result in less cost. Yes, a more mature organization may spend resources in ways they aren't today (e.g., doing risk analysis) and in some cases they may end up having a bigger budget, but better analysis should result in more appropriate use of resources, and a bigger budget might result because management better understands its risk landscape. *Organizations compete on many levels, and if an organization is able to manage risk more cost-effectively than its competition, then it wins on that level.*

Another argument we hear is that there is safety in numbers—i.e., "you can't get fired for following common practices." This is a "herd mentality" belief that might be accurate to a certain extent in terms of CYA, but when common practices are as immature as they are today in the industry it doesn't take much imagination to see how this can be a bad thing for an organization's ability to manage risk cost-effectively (the word "lemmings" comes to mind when thinking about this).

ACHIEVING AND MAINTAINING

This part of the definition is yet another area where we believe our profession has significant room for improvement, as we will learn more about further into this chapter and in the chapter on metrics. The "achieving" component of the definition suggests that an objective exists. We'll talk more about this shortly when we discuss the "acceptable level of risk" part of the definition. For now, we're going to focus on the part about "maintaining."

The risk landscape is dynamic, as are the needs of an organization and even the personnel who run the organization. Very simply, this means that managing these evolving and changing elements requires monitoring and feedback. *Metrics are that feedback.* However, in order to leverage metrics effectively they have to be meaningful, and in order for them to be meaningful we have to understand the risk landscape as a system of interrelated parts and they have to apply to a meaningful context— business risk management, in our case. We'll cover this further very shortly, but that in a nutshell is what the FAIR ontologies are all about.

In the metrics chapter, we'll discuss the problems our profession has struggled with regarding metrics, and offer approaches that we believe can significantly improve the situation. Suffice it to say for now that in order to achieve and maintain any objective over time (risk or otherwise) requires the ability to measure and compare.

AN ACCEPTABLE LEVEL OF LOSS EXPOSURE

Okay, it's three for three. By that we mean this is the third of three straight elements in our definition for risk management where our profession hasn't hit the mark historically. We've encountered very few organizations where "an acceptable level of loss exposure" has been clearly defined. Why? A host of reasons, really, the first being our profession's challenges with measuring risk. It's pretty tough to define an acceptable level of loss exposure when you haven't (until FAIR came along) been able to measure loss exposure in meaningful terms.

As a result, what organizations have tended to do is adopt (or develop) a risk assessment framework (à la PCI, NIST, ISO 27000, etc.) as well as a set of "common practices," and implicitly operate as though compliance with that framework and associated policies will achieve an acceptable level of risk. On the surface, this seems much simpler than a risk measurement approach. That said, there are concerns underlying this approach:

- It assumes that the organization's management has explicitly chosen to comply with that framework—which necessarily implies there is commensurate levels of funding, resources, and political capital funneled into said compliance. This is rarely the case when a security organization chooses the framework and begins comparing the organization to it without getting executive support first.
- It assumes the framework adequately covers the scope of that organization's risk landscape. The good news is that these frameworks tend to be relatively comprehensive. In fact, some of them have literally hundreds of boxes to check. That said, gaps exist in some of these frameworks, at least when we check their coverage against the FAIR control ontologies.
- It assumes the framework does not over or under control the organization's risk landscape. Without measuring control efficacy against both cost and explicit risk-based objectives, it's less clear whether an organization is applying the right level of control.
- Checklist frameworks do not engender an analytic or systemic approach to managing risk. In other words, the relationships between risk management elements are not well understood or managed. We have already beaten this drum pretty hard, but we'll discuss this in even more detail later and examine why this leads to what we refer to as "risk management groundhog day."

The bottom line with adopting a predefined checklist and set of common practices is that an organization is making an awful lot of assumptions regarding what it is getting. This isn't inherently bad; it's just a form of implicitly managing risk. Then again, as we said earlier, organizations have to start somewhere and these frameworks and practices can provide a reasonable place to start for organizations putting a risk management program in place for the first time, or that are upgrading a home-grown program that is completely screwed up.

Explicitly managing risk requires that one or more risk-based objectives exist. By "risk-based" we mean based on loss exposure levels, not "let's reduce audit issues by 50%." Targets related to control conditions are still implicit and do not enable you to effectively answer the questions we discussed at the beginning of this chapter.

TALKING ABOUT RISK

But information security is different from the rest of the business, right? Well, let's see…

Business decisions generally boil down to benefit versus cost versus risk. Should the organization fund that new marketing campaign? It depends. How is it going to help us meet our objectives, at what cost, and how much risk is involved? Should the organization spend the money to acquire that small competitor? It depends. How is it going to help us meet our objectives, at what cost, and how much risk is involved? Should the organization implement that new information security technology? It depends. How is it going to help us meet our objectives, at what cost, and how much risk is involved? Oh, wait a minute. That is entirely different. The first two scenarios have an up-side, usually in terms of increased revenue, but the information security scenario is pure down-side, or so some people would argue. They're mistaken.

To see this more clearly, it helps to imagine what would happen if an organization removed its information security policies, people, processes, and technology. Sure, in the short term (maybe very short term) all of the resources that were tied-up in infosec could be allocated toward achieving other organizational objectives, and all of the "drag" information security places on business productivity would be gone (woo-hoo, no more passwords!). However most organizations wouldn't survive very long in that condition. Significant losses of various forms would occur. So the up-side to information security is that the organization reduces its loss exposure and improves its odds of achieving its objectives, or at least its overall survival. There is no logical reason the up-side can't be defined as a reduction in loss and an improvement in survival odds. So what's the downside? Just as with the marketing campaign and the acquisition, there are at least a couple of downsides to investing in information security:

- The invested resources aren't available to leverage for other initiatives that may in fact represent better value.
- Whatever is being invested in security may introduce loss. It might be the "drag" placed on business productivity or even outright broken business processes (been there, done that). Then again, marketing sometimes results in negative public reactions, and acquisitions sometimes result in negative shareholder reactions or unforeseen legal liability.

Of course, as with every investment, there is the potential for the expected benefits to not materialize. Imagine a marketing campaign that doesn't quite pan out, an acquisition that fails to generate the projected value, or an information security investment that doesn't really affect risk much. So no, information security is not different. Unfortunately, what has tended to be different is that the information security profession has been unable to express its value proposition meaningfully.

THE RISK MANAGEMENT STACK

Having defined risk management, we need to go a step further. We have put together a set of building blocks we call the "risk management stack," all of which form the foundation for what is required to achieve and maintain effective risk management. It is the very simple structure shown in Figure 12.1, comprised of five elements.

The "well-informed decisions" element is fairly obvious, so we won't bore you with a long description for it. The "effective comparisons" layer would seem to be obvious too, but we're going to discuss it anyway because there is room for clarification. Specifically, every decision involves a choice, and in order for those choices to be well informed, the decision-maker has to be able to reasonably compare the options before them. If, for example, the decision involves choosing between funding the mitigation of a weaknesses in a web application and funding a new marketing campaign, wouldn't it be nice if the comparison could be more apples-to-apples versus apples-to-oranges? Unfortunately, with the way risk is "measured" in information

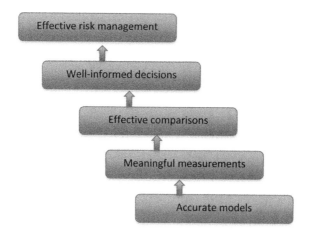

FIGURE 12.1

Risk management stack.

security today, these types of comparisons are pretty tough to make. After all, if that defective web application is rated "high risk" and the marketing campaign is forecasted to increase revenue by 5%, it's hard to argue that the decision is well informed.

Given our discussion regarding effective comparisons, it's probably pretty obvious what we're aiming for with the "meaningful measurements" element, so we don't feel the need to elaborate too much. We will point out, however, that FAIR's genesis was all about finding a way to provide meaningful measurements so that we could satisfy management's desire to make effective comparisons and well-informed decisions.

The last element is fundamentally what FAIR's ontologies provide. They are, first and foremost, intended to be reasonably accurate models of risk and risk management, which enable (for the first time, we would argue) everything else in the stack. You will see us refer to this stack again as we progress through the rest of this chapter and in the metrics chapter.

DECISIONS, DECISIONS

Managing risk boils down to the ongoing process of decisions and actions. In this section, we'll discuss the implicit nature of how these decisions are commonly approached, as well as how they can be approached more explicitly. In a later section, we will integrate a discussion about actions, i.e., execution within the context of those decisions.

DECISION CATEGORIES

You may recall that earlier in the book we said there were three broad decision categories: strategic, operational, and incident management. That was a bit of an oversimplification, which we're going to expand on here. You see, there is another layer of decision stratification that's important to recognize as well, which includes:

- Expectation setting (e.g., risk appetite, policies & standards, etc.)
- Prioritization (e.g., funding and resource allocation)
- Solution selection

You can probably come up with others. We have, but they either tend to be small potatoes, relatively speaking, or they fit into one of these three subcategories so we are going to resist the urge to get more granular. These decision subcategories apply to each of the main decision categories we discussed previously (strategic, operational, and incident management). We'll spend a little time describing each of these in the next section. The reason for framing the decision landscape like this is so that we can begin to identify opportunities to be more explicit in our risk management efforts. This also helps us determine which metrics are likely to be most useful for the different decisions at each level.

TALKING ABOUT RISK

By the way, if you're wondering whether all the "frameworking" and "ontoligizing" we've been describing is going to result in a risk management practice that is over complicated, unwieldy and impractical, the simple answer is no. These are mostly just background concepts that are intended to explain the how and why of risk and risk management. You can choose how formal you want to be in applying these things. We could easily have put together a checklist and set of "best practices" and asked you to simply trust us…but you already have checklists and best practices galore, and there would be little reason to switch to a FAIR approach unless you knew us personally and thought we had a clue. In addition, by documenting this stuff we're putting it out there to be poked, prodded, and undoubtedly improved upon over time. In fact, we believe there are a lot of Masters and Ph.D. research opportunities could spring from what we've covered. No doubt checklists and maturity models will come in due time.

As we wrap up this book, you should begin to see that being more explicit in how you manage risk is not out of reach. It's simply a matter of realizing that it is an option and having enough insight into it that you can find your own sweet spot along the continuum. For that matter, you may realize that your organization already is being more explicit than not. If that's the case, then you now have the opportunity to more explicitly brag about it.

Expectation setting

Expectations set at the strategic level generally take three forms: (1) risk appetite, (2) policies, and (3) intended outcomes from strategic initiatives (e.g., major upgrades to identity and access management capabilities). Expectations at the operational level are what you probably would expect; standards that support the policies, and outcomes from more tactically focused initiatives (e.g., a project to simplify the information security policy verbiage). Within incident management, expectation-setting is extremely tactical and often moment-by-moment. Within this section, we are going to focus mostly on the strategic decision category, expecting that you will be able to extrapolate the discussion into operational and incident management decisions.

Risk appetite setting

Let's start with the hard one and get it out of the way. "Risk appetite" and "risk tolerance" are another great example of concepts and terms commonly recognized and discussed in the industry, but where clear and consistent usage are rare. Yes, pick a glossary in one of the common references and you are likely to find definitions, but ask professionals on the street or, better yet, see how it's being applied (if it is being applied) in practice and we're betting you will see a lot of inconsistency.

Call it what you will, the topic boils down to the level of loss exposure executive management is willing to live with; at least that's the description that makes sense to us, and that description sets the stage for much of what follows in this chapter and the next. For brevity's sake, you will more often than not find us referring to it as "risk appetite" rather than "the level of loss exposure executive management is willing to live with." In order to explicitly manage risk, an organization has to (has to!) define its risk appetite. Otherwise, there is nothing to achieve and maintain. There is no "there" there. Lewis Carroll may have said it best in Alice's conversation with the Cheshire Cat in *Alice in Wonderland*:

> *Alice: Would you tell me, please, which way I ought to go from here?*
>
> *Cat: That depends a good deal on where you want to get to.*
>
> *Alice: I don't much care where…*
>
> *Cat: Then it doesn't matter which way you go.*
>
> *Alice: … so long as I get somewhere.*
>
> *Cat: Oh, you're sure to do that if you only walk long enough.*

That last comment by the Cheshire Cat pretty much hits the mark with information security. How many information security organizations do you know where the organization's risk appetite has been defined by (or even discussed with) executive management? Without that, explicit risk management is a pipe dream.

Earlier in the book we described how heat-maps could be used to help management roughly express their risk appetite. Think of this use of heat-maps as a step in the right direction. Farther along on the continuum is where an organization sets its information security risk appetite in a manner similar to how it's often done for credit or investment risk—as a monetary threshold. Skeptical? We'll spend more time with this in the Metrics chapter, and provide examples of how risk appetite like this can be done. For now, suffice it to say that this is an important step toward more explicit risk management.

Policies

Policies and standards are supposed to be the way in which management defines and documents its expectations regarding risk management activities. In fact, they are often thought of as an implicit representation of leadership's risk appetite. Given that perspective, defined acceptable levels of variance from those expectations might be viewed as representing the organization's risk tolerance. As an implicit approach to risk management, this isn't a bad way to go. The problem, of course, is that if nobody bothers to examine what the policies represent from a risk management perspective, or the drag they place on the business, it's more likely they will introduce excessive control and cost in some areas, and insufficient control in others. It's back to that explicit thing again.

In order to better align policies with executive management's risk appetite, they have to at least be evaluated at a high level for both their risk management value within the context of risk appetite and the burden they place on the business. For rough alignment, this evaluation does not have to be done in great and gory depth, but enough so that the executives have a sense for what they are signing up for, and why.

TALKING ABOUT RISK

As CISO for one organization, I (Jack Jones) had the all-too-rare opportunity to do a high-level review of each and every information security policy with the CEO. During this review, we discussed the high-level risk and business burden implications of each policy. During that discussion, he tightened some of the policies and loosened others. The outcome was that he thought of those policies as his (which he made very clear to his staff), and woe be it to anyone who skirted his policies.

This opportunity may not exist in many organizations. CEOs are just too busy. That might change if they understood the value it would bring to the organization. Besides, the odds are good they haven't been asked if they would be willing to make the time. If they agree to do this, you need to do at least two things: (1) make very sure the policies are clearly and concisely written beforehand so you don't have to wade through a bunch of useless goo in the course of the conversation, and (2) come to the table prepared to discuss, realistically, the risk implications and business burdens of the policies. Fear, uncertainty, and doubt have no place at this table, and you will not get a second chance if you come off as immature in your thinking on these matters.

If the CEO isn't available it is often feasible to review policies with executives below the CEO, especially if there is something like an information security governance council where you work, who can gain a sense of ownership and accountability for the policies. We have been fortunate enough to experience this as well, and although it's not as effective as having the CEO's personal stamp on the policies, it can still make a big difference.

When management doesn't feel a sense of policy ownership, they may not view the policies and standards as representative of their needs and thus may not consistently enforce or support them. This has a number of negative effects, not the least of which includes:

- The organization's culture adopts the view that policies and standards are optional, resulting in more frequent and severe control variance that may create far more risk than executive management would, in fact, be comfortable with
- Internal auditors and external stakeholders (e.g., regulators) constantly hammer the organization for poor compliance
- If a severe loss event does occur, the organization is faced with a higher level of liability due to a poor compliance record

For many organizations, the process for arriving at a "good" set of policies that aligns reasonably well with management's expectations happens over time. Very often, it starts with the security team defining a set of policies (or they hire a consultant to do it for them, or they download them from the Internet). What transpires over time is that one or more (usually more) of these policies prove problematic from a business activity perspective, resulting in policy exceptions (or policies that are skirted without going through an exception approval process). If the security organization is paying attention, it will be on the lookout for policies that consistently have approved exceptions or are skirted, and then work with business executives to adjust the policies to better align with how the business wants to behave. The challenge, of course, is that unless executives understand the risk implications of policies and behaviors, it is very easy for them to inadvertently accept levels of risk in the name of "business progress" that they would not accept if they clearly understood the level of exposure.

We'll take this opportunity to reinforce something we touched on in the chapter on controls—somewhat weaker policies that have less variance will almost invariably result in less risk than strong policies with high degrees of variance. Being able to identify and leverage this kind of trade-off is a great example of applying a more explicit risk management approach to policy making.

Initiatives

Including initiatives as part of expectation setting might seem odd. If so, that may be because our profession doesn't tend to look at them through that lens.

Organizations often invest significant resources in the name of information security. Why do they do that? Well, it's because there is a perception that the need exists. Implicit in that investment is an expectation that the concern will be addressed. It is unusual, however, to see an explicit effort to validate that the proposed value from that investment was realized. This is true even when the value proposition was to improve compliance or increase efficiency, which are both relatively easy to check. About the closest thing we've encountered is when internal or external audit checks to see if gaps were fixed. Even this, however, very often occurs at a much later date, perhaps during the next audit cycle. What this means is that organizations throw money into big, complex, initiatives that often place an operational burden on the organization—but don't consistently check to see if they realized the proposed benefits. This is yet another example of implicit risk management.

The value proposition for information security initiatives and activities, whether they are strategic, operational, or in response to an incident, always boils down to an effect on the frequency or magnitude of loss. This is true even for initiatives intended to increase efficiency because inefficiency is just another form of loss. Likewise, non-compliance with regulations and laws represents loss exposure, so initiatives to correct those conditions are reducing that exposure. In order to more explicitly manage risk, two things have to happen: (1) an initiative's value proposition needs to be described in risk-related terms, and (2) the results of the initiative need to be examined to see if they were realized. Yes, we know that can be difficult when we are talking about loss exposure. After all, how do you check a reduction in loss exposure for an event the organization may never have experienced in the first place? In those cases it's a matter of verifying through testing that the new or improved control is performing as designed. The assumption then is that it is providing the value it's designed for.

The bottom line is that there is, or should be, some expectation of benefit from these investments. Explicit risk management pays attention to this value proposition both in proposing the investment and in looking back on the outcome.

Prioritization

Risk management prioritization boils down to a problem of resource allocation based on where risk is concentrated within the organization (e.g., which business processes and/or technologies represent the most risk) and which conditions within the organization are most problematic (e.g., which threats or deficient control conditions contribute most to risk). This need to prioritize occurs within all three major decision categories, and the better able you're able to differentiate risk concentrations and causes, the better you will be at prioritization and the more cost-effective your organization will be.

At the strategic level, where executives are involved, there are usually two (by now familiar) dimensions to the question of funding:

- Is the organization spending the right amount on information security, and
- Where do information security problems stand relative to all of the other challenges and responsibilities executive management has to consider

In order to be explicit, the answer to the question of "enough" versus "too much" spending on information security has to be based on an assessment of the current aggregate level of risk relative to the organization's risk appetite. Most of the time, this question is answered with the equivalent of hand waving and comparisons against similar organizations in the industry, in other words,–implicitly.

Sometimes organizations will use heat-maps. Properly done, with quantitative analyses and loss scales that management has reviewed and vetted, heat-maps begin to look suspiciously like explicit risk management. Their use still begs lots of questions regarding things like how many "highs," etc. are acceptable, but at least it is risk-based. That is at least progress from the usual state of affairs.

TALKING ABOUT RISK

Some organizations try to answer the "enough" or "too much" questions by using industry metrics such as "security spend as a percentage of IT budget." There are many problems with this approach, not the least of which is the underlying assumption that an organization's peers are spending the right amount. Wisdom of the masses, right?

Many of the risk management personnel we have encountered, particularly in the information security profession, will argue tooth-and-nail that their organization is underspending on risk management. If it's true that many organizations are underspending on risk management, and if that "deficient" level of funding is being used as an industry baseline for the "are we spending enough" comparison, then organizations using this as a gauge for their spending are almost by default going to underspend. Again, assuming one believes the numbers to be meaningful. We believe they are not.

If that wasn't reason enough to call into question industry funding comparisons, here are three additional things to think about:

- If an organization is underspending compared to the average, that fact alone is not likely to increase budget materially in the absence of other compelling rationale. It might add to the argument but it is unlikely to stand on its own unless the difference is profound
- If an organization is spending the same amount as the industry average it can make getting additional funding more difficult, even in light of real need, and
- If an organization is spending more than the industry average, it may make additional funding especially difficult to attain, and inevitably introduces the question of whether the organization should cut back on funding

In other words, in two out of three situations, comparisons will hurt your chances of getting more funding, and in one instance, it might actually result in a reduction in funding. Now, the idea of a change in funding from current levels based on comparisons would be fine if we had any real confidence that the baseline was a reasonably accurate gauge of an organization's funding needs. Our experience, however, does not leave us with any comfort in that regard. Reasons why we lack that confidence include:

- As we have already discussed, the level of risk being reported to executives is often inaccurate.
- Organizations at different levels of risk management maturity are quite likely to have different spending needs. Therefore, if my organization is less mature than "average", it might very well need to spend more than average, at least in the short term. See our second point, above, regarding how this can complicate the funding discussion.
- Organizations vary widely regarding what is included in the risk management budget. Some organizations include costs surrounding firewall management, identity and access management, etc., while others consider these to be operational network and help-desk expenses. Some of the surveys we've encountered appear to try to normalize the scope of what falls into the risk management bucket, which can help; we've seen some pretty lame efforts, too.
- Risk tolerances can vary from one organization to another. As a result, deciding whether your organization is spending enough based on what other organizations are spending may lead you to over or under spend relative to your stakeholder's needs.

We understand that executives like to compare themselves against their peers. Its part of being human, and these people tend to be highly competitive. However, the question of "enough" or "too much" spending simply can't be answered through comparison until the industry has matured a long way from where it is today. Besides that, what's more important is whether the organization is spending wisely.

Earlier, we discussed being able to explicitly understand, describe, and check the value proposition for information security initiatives from an expectation-setting perspective. Having that clear value proposition also makes it possible to compare and prioritize potential investments in information security versus the other needs and wants of the organization. Providing meaningful risk-based metrics to describe information risk management concerns and proposals makes this much easier. For example, if you can describe the loss exposure for the top three (or however many) information security concerns in monetary terms, it makes it much easier for the executives to compare those concerns against the other forms of risk the organization faces and the growth opportunities it's pursuing. This is particularly true if the expected level of risk reduction can be put into the context of the organization's current risk position and risk appetite.

At an operational level, there are two primary resource allocation problems to solve:

- What are the priorities today and in the foreseeable future that form the basis for funding requests presented to executive management, and
- How to recognize when there is a need to reprioritize and reallocate to address tactical concerns

Most of the time, we see organizations simply carve up their "risks" into high, medium, and low buckets. Done well, this is better than nothing. The whole approach does beg some tough questions, though, including:

- What are the criteria for something to be assigned to a particular bucket?
- Which of the "risks" within the high bucket are highest?

- How much difference is there between the lowest high-risk issue and the highest medium-risk issue?
- How many "mediums" equal a "high?"

Often, people avoid turning over these rocks because of what they're likely to find:

- Nobody defined clear criteria for the different buckets (and no, using qualitative terms to define qualitative risk rating labels—e.g., "High risk exists when there is a high potential for high impact" —does not rise to the level of clear criteria)
- Nobody took the time to really figure out which of the "risks" in a particular bucket was highest
- It is anybody's guess whether there is a meaningful difference between the lowest high and highest medium, and
- You can't aggregate qualitative values.

A highly experienced professional with a decent mental model of risk may be able to do a reasonably good job of identifying, off-the-cuff, those issues that represent the most risk to the organization. We've heard impassioned arguments that nothing more than that is required. In fact, that any time spent on real analysis is wasted. The problem with this argument is that the underlying mental models many people operate from have been biased by media reports, vendors, common misperceptions, as well an inevitable set of cognitive biases. As a result, the ability for many people to effectively prioritize off-the-cuff is questionable. If all you feel you're capable of analysis-wise is shooting from the hip, then leveraging a framework like FAIR to calibrate your mental model should improve the odds of getting it right. In the chapter on implementation, we provide another example of how an organization can exercise a combination of different levels of analysis—including both quick and dirty and more thorough analyses—to prioritize a set of issues without wasting a bunch of time or effort. It's about balance. Well, balance and a decent model.

SOLUTION SELECTION

There is almost always more than one way to skin a cat, and this is certainly true when it comes to choosing solutions for risk-related concerns. One of the options is, of course, to do whatever is considered common practice, or best practice. Sometimes, this is exactly the right thing to do. In fact, sometimes this is even the most cost-effective thing to do. What's important though, is being able to figure that out because a significant portion of our value proposition as professionals is (or should be) our ability to determine which solutions are most appropriate given the situation.

In strategic decisions, you are often dealing with bigger, more expensive, and potentially more burdensome risk issues and their solutions. When this is the case, making a cost-effective choice is especially important. The good news is that you typically have (or should have) more time to identify and weigh your options. In operational decisions, the importance of cost-effectiveness can be a mixed bag—sometimes it's still a very important consideration, and other times it is less so. Sometimes you can take the time to do a solid evaluation, and sometimes you can't. However, even when time and resources are constrained, simply recognizing that cost-effectiveness is a consideration is likely to help calibrate your decision. As you get into incident management decisions, very often the most important thing is to simply get a solution in place. The focus is to minimize damage to the organization. Survive. Worry about cost-effectiveness later.

TALKING ABOUT RISK

We are familiar with one CISO who was faced with a PCI audit that had identified the absence of data-at-rest encryption on his organization's primary business databases. These systems contained massive volumes of credit card and other sensitive information. Unfortunately, when brought in to pitch their solutions the encryption vendors all admitted that (1) their products hadn't been applied to databases of that size/architecture before and they could not guarantee that there wouldn't be problems, and (2) any implementation was going to require significant changes to the business applications. The cost implications ran into the millions of dollars, with an implementation timeline of at least 18 months and an expectation of some amount of business disruption during the process.

The CISO used FAIR to evaluate and compare the current state of loss exposure, the loss exposure reduction expected to result from data-at-rest encryption, and the loss exposure reduction expected from an alternative set of controls. These alternative controls included, but were not limited to:

- Internal network segmentation
- Hard token authentication controls for system, application, database, and network personnel
- Improved logging and detection controls, and
- Improved processes for ensuring that hard drives would be wiped before leaving controlled areas

At the end of the analyses, the CISO was able to show that the alternative controls provided better risk reduction than encrypting data-at-rest. Better yet, these alternative controls required no changes to applications, no business disruption, a much faster time to implement, and costs under $500,000. When presented with these analyses, the PCI QSA had no problem signing off on the solution. Another example of explicit, cost-effective risk management in action.

We hope that you've begun to get a better sense for what it means to explicitly manage risk. Simply recognizing the difference between implicit and explicit risk management can make a big difference, as it allows you to consciously choose your approach on an instance by instance basis. Sometimes, despite what you would like to do, you'll have little choice but to make an implicit choice. That's okay—at least you made a choice. Over time you should find that the more you are able to take the explicit path, the easier it will become. By the way, this can also become a question when you are considering moving to a new employer. Ask them questions that will let you know how they operate from a risk management perspective and their level of interest in maturing.

A SYSTEMS VIEW OF RISK MANAGEMENT

In this section, we'll build a picture of the risk management landscape element-by-element and describe how these elements work together as a feedback system. It will also become readily apparent where and how risk analysis fits into the system and why it is so important in order for the system to function properly. This also sets us up nicely for the Metrics chapter that follows.

Our profession has talked about being proactive for years. In order to do this, we first have to understand the risk landscape as a system. Before we get into the details though, we need to level set on a basic concept regarding the relationship between risk and risk management. This concept is simply that *the amount of risk an organization has today is a lagging indicator of how it managed risk in the past.* In other words, the decisions made in the past and the organization's execution against those decisions resulted in its current level of loss exposure. This being the case, if we understand the factors that drive effective (or not so effective) risk management, then we can do some powerful root-cause analyses to understand what brought us to where we are from a loss exposure perspective. There is also a corollary to the first concept. If we understand our current risk management capabilities and how they affect loss exposure over time, we can infer what our future risk position is likely to be. Essentially, we can turn the coin around and evaluate our current risk management capabilities to get some idea of what our future risk posture is likely to be—unless we make changes.

THE RISK MANAGEMENT SYSTEM

Having laid the foundation above, let's start understanding the system. The first two elements in the landscape are Risk and Risk Management. The risk component of the landscape is a function of the threats, assets, controls, and impact factors (e.g., laws, etc.) that drive loss exposure. The controls we are referring to within this part of the risk landscape are the asset-level controls we discussed in the chapter on controls. In other words, these are the controls that directly affect the frequency and/or magnitude of loss (e.g., passwords, backups, logging, etc.).

The risk management element is comprised of decisions and execution (see Figure 12.2). Those decisions drive the personnel, policies, processes, and technologies that an organization chooses to implement, all of which are (at least implicitly) intended to achieve risk objectives, regardless of whether those objectives are clearly defined or not. Although decisions in the form of policies, processes, and technologies represent an intended level of control, what an organization actually gets in terms of risk is a function of execution within the context of those decisions.

In order for decisions to have a reasonable shot at being the right decisions, the decision-makers must have good information regarding the value proposition of those decisions (the up-side), the organization's risk appetite, how much risk is involved in the decision, the policy, process and/or technology options, and the organization's ability to execute consistently and effectively against the decision. In order for execution to take place consistently and effectively, the people responsible for execution have to be aware of the expectations, have the capability to execute (in terms of skills and resources), and be motivated to execute, all of which are dependent on the communication, support, and enforcement applied to those decisions.

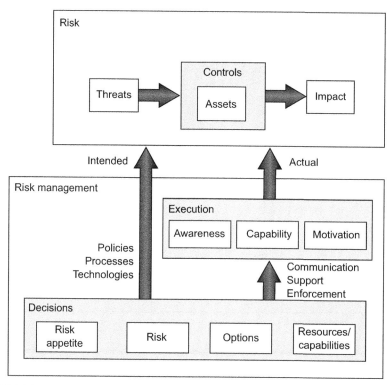

FIGURE 12.2

Basic model of risk and risk management.

In order for this model to be a system, it needs a feedback loop. We should include feedback about the condition of asset-level controls (e.g., passwords, compliance levels, etc.). Additionally, we should include metrics that cover threat intelligence and losses. The addition of these pieces of information is helpful to the decision making process, as it allows for a more fully informed decision maker.

Even though risk assessments include information about noncompliant control conditions through the controls feedback loop, we rarely see organizations go to the trouble of also determining *why* the controls aren't compliant. As a result, we need to add another feedback loop to our system. In this case, metrics regarding the things that affect execution (e.g., awareness, capabilities) and root-cause analysis data that informs us as to why execution failure created those variances. Something that goes well beyond the superficial, "Our awareness program isn't strong enough." Figure 12.3 shows a completed feedback system, where the conditions contributing to execution failure are also communicated to decision-makers. Only with this feedback in place can they recognize and respond to the things that drive variance, and thus risk, into the landscape.

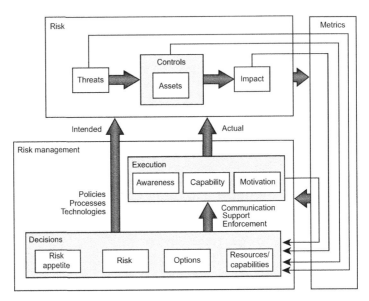

FIGURE 12.3

Risk management system.

TALKING ABOUT RISK

Remember we mentioned something we called Groundhog Day? If you're familiar with the Bill Murray movie of the same name, you'll remember that his character relived the same day over and over again until he finally, through long trial and error, eventually figured out the changes he needed to make as a person to win the heart of his beloved. In the context of risk management, Groundhog Day (GHD) represents the phenomena of experiencing the same risk management challenges time after time. You know your organization is stuck in GHD if you find yourself regularly uttering phrases such as, "Dude, again? Really?" regarding audit findings and security deficiencies.

The absence of information regarding why control variance exists is the main contributing factor behind the Groundhog Day phenomena. We see organizations fix controls. We rarely see them fix the reasons for repeated control failures. Oh sure, if the control is important enough and if it is noncompliant often enough, then some draconian threats will often be made to "encourage" people to comply. Sometimes that's enough, at least for a while. Nevertheless, often it isn't effective over the long haul because the fundamental source of the problem is not being addressed. Breaking out of risk management GHD requires an effective use of feedback within the system.

For example, if a superficial assessment suggests that motivation is the reason that noncompliance is a problem for a particular control, go further. Evaluate whether motivation to comply is lacking because, just maybe, your risk management program hasn't informed executives that people don't view compliance as important. Maybe people don't view compliance as important because management doesn't enforce it. Maybe management isn't enforcing it because the policy in question is the wrong policy for the organization. Maybe it's the wrong policy because nobody has done a decent risk analysis to determine what the right policy might be. The process is similar to the "five whys" approach for root cause analysis, of which you may have heard. The bottom line is, if you get to the root of the problem, you have a much better chance of actually solving it and breaking out of GHD. We would much prefer to do a little extra digging to get to the root of the problem and solve it once and for all, rather than play whack-a-mole with the same issue repeatedly.

Managing anything inherently involves feedback loops, but it is unusual to see an organization's risk management program actually operate effectively as a feedback system. As a result, very often you'll see risk management programs that experience the same problems repeatedly, even when the program has checked all the requisite boxes in its risk management framework of choice. Very often this results from poor feedback loops and not treating the risk management landscape as a system.

One definition for insanity is doing the same things over and over again, expecting a different result. Given that definition and the lack of effective feedback loops, we would argue that many risk management programs are relatively insane. The various ontologies and concepts within FAIR, combined with a systems view of the risk landscape and an effective use of metrics, can drive more sanity into risk management.

Information Security Metrics

13

Would you believe us if we told you there was one metric, and only one, that would tell you everything you needed to know about an organization's information security risk posture? No, probably not, and you'd be right. That said, the number of metrics required to gain a meaningful understanding of an organization's risk posture is not hundreds, or even dozens. Not, at least, if you understand the key elements that drive risk into an organization.

A comprehensive coverage of metrics isn't possible in a single chapter. Therefore, our focus here is on understanding where and how metrics fit into an information security risk management program and how to leverage them effectively. To provide this understanding, we'll share a framework you can use for identifying meaningful metrics and figuring out their value proposition. Of course, we'll provide examples, both in this chapter and the next one. Our examples will not be exhaustive, though. If you're looking for exhaustive examples, there are a lot of books on the market dedicated to information security metrics.

Speaking of other books, if you're looking for a very good book dedicated to the subject of information security metrics, we really like *IT Security Metrics* by Lance Hayden. Hayden goes into significant detail on the nature of data, statistics, and analysis. For the data geeks in the crowd, we also really like another book entitled *Data-Driven Security: Analysis, Visualization, and Dashboards* by Jay Jacobs and Bob Rudis. We would like to think that the concepts and frameworks presented in this book, and especially this chapter, will allow you to better leverage the wealth of information in those books.

TALKING ABOUT RISK

The word "data" can take a plural or singular form (e.g., "data are" or "data is"). Scientists and other quants often prefer the plural form, while much of the rest of humanity seems to prefer the singular form. Fortunately, the word's meaning does not change based on the form that is used, nor is there confusion about what it means. For those reasons, we didn't sweat it. We hope you wouldn't either, at least while reading this book.

CURRENT STATE OF AFFAIRS

The use of metrics promises to take our profession from art to science (or at least to something less superficial and more science-like). In order to realize that promise, however, our profession has to solve a few fundamental problems first—problems we have beaten a drum about throughout this book. For example, without consistent and logical nomenclature, it becomes wickedly hard to normalize data or communicate effectively. After all, if one person's "threat" is another person's "risk" is another person's "vulnerability," it is extremely difficult to find common ground. How do you know what data you need in the first place, and how do you apply data to derive meaningful results if your "models" look anything like "Threat x Vulnerability/Controls," or are simply checklists? Finally, the only way your metrics become meaningful is if they support explicitly defined objectives that matter. In this chapter, we continue the process of tying together what has been covered in the earlier chapters—nomenclature, models, and objectives—so that you can leverage metrics more effectively.

TALKING ABOUT RISK

We have heard the statement on more than one occasion that an important criterion for a "good" metric is that the data should be easy to acquire. Yes, it's great when data acquisition is easy. but if you rely on that to drive which metrics you use, you may miss out on really important information. All we're saying is don't just rely on the easy stuff. Understand the decision you are trying to support and get the best information you can, given your time and resources.

TALKING ABOUT RISK

It's been our experience that information security organizations can often get away with having relatively useless (or worse, misleading) metrics. On numerous occasions, we have seen auditors, regulators, executives, and third-party assessors apparently attribute program maturity and effectiveness to a bunch of colorful charts and graphs, even when the metrics are either misleading or go entirely unused in decision-making.

METRIC VALUE PROPOSITION

Remember what we said in the Risk Management chapter; that risk management boils down to a series of decisions and the execution of those decisions? Well, this entire chapter could perhaps be entitled "Decision Support" because the only reason for generating metrics is to inform decisions. In fact, *if you're publishing metrics that aren't being actively used in decision-making, then you are wasting time and resources.* Because of this, we're going to come at metrics with a clear eye toward their role in decision support. Behind every decision there are one or more goals that an organization is driving toward. Before we go on, ask yourself what overarching goal might form the foundation for decisions within a risk management program. We'll answer the question shortly, but here is a hint—we discussed it in the Risk Management chapter.

Within the metrics world, you may have heard people talk about the "Goal, Question, Metric" (GQM) method for developing good metrics. We really like this approach because it helps people focus on and understand a metric's value proposition[1]. For example, the GQM approach might go about defining a metric in the following way:

- Goal: Reduce the number of network shares containing sensitive information
- Question: How much sensitive information resides on network shares?
- Metric: Volume of sensitive information on network shares

This is a clear and concise way to define that kind of metric. However, you have to be a bit careful to not put the cart before the horse. The above example suggests that a decision had already been made regarding a different question. Perhaps that different question was, "Do we need to reduce the volume of sensitive information on our network shares?" (Apparently, the answer was "yes"). There may have been a question before that; something like, "Do we have significant concentrations of risk associated with sensitive information?" (Again, apparently the answer was "yes"). Absent the context of those questions and their subsequent decisions, chasing a metric like the volume of sensitive information on network shares might not be a good use of time even given a great metric definition method like GQM. We have to define the big picture—those "macro goals"—first.

In keeping with our decision-based focus, we would like to make a fairly subtle but important observation about the question component of GQM. In the above example related to network shares, the original question was phrased as "how much," yet the implied questions that might have come before were phrased differently. The "Do we need...?" and "Do we have...?" phrasing is more explicitly aligned with decision-making because, depending on the answers, different actions may be required. The question of "how much" doesn't explicitly relate to a decision or goal. Implicitly, perhaps, but it's important that we understand the decision context for the metric as explicitly as possible.

Before we dive into the section on how to leverage GQM to make metrics meaningful, there is one more thing to point out—comparison. Specifically, metrics are fundamentally a means of making comparisons between, for example:

- Current conditions and desired future conditions
- Risk scenarios (prioritization)
- Mitigation options (selection)
- Past conditions and current conditions (efficacy of past decisions and actions)

You may have noticed that this also aligns with the risk management stack—meaningful measurements enable effective comparisons, which enable well-informed decisions. We love it when things come together like this.

BEGINNING WITH THE END IN MIND

So, did you come up with any ideas regarding our question about an overarching GQM-type goal for metrics? As you'll recall from the Risk Management chapter, our

---

[1] The IT Security Metrics book by Lance Hayden does a great job of discussing GQM.

definition for risk management includes the phrase, "…*cost-effectively achieve and maintain an acceptable level of loss exposure*." That sounds suspiciously like a goal to us, so you get a diamond encrusted platinum star if that's what you came up with. With that goal as our starting point, let's continue to break this down and apply the GQM approach for our metrics. We can begin by breaking our overarching goal into four subgoals:

- Being cost-effective
- Achieving alignment with the organization's risk appetite
- Maintaining alignment with the organization's risk appetite
- Defining the organization's risk appetite (that "acceptable level of loss exposure")

The next step is to break these down into more granular subgoals.

BREAKING IT DOWN

In this section, we'll begin to break down our overarching goal into layers of sub-goals, questions, and metrics. We'll wait to discuss these subgoals until a little further on though, because some of the discussion will be lengthy. For now, let's just cover the outline.

In the mind-map shown in Figure 13.1, we have broken out our four main sub-goals into another layer of granularity. Once you have a handle on this layer of abstraction, we think you will find it is pretty easy to figure out additional layers of subgoals, questions for these goals, and then the metrics that inform those questions and their associated decisions.

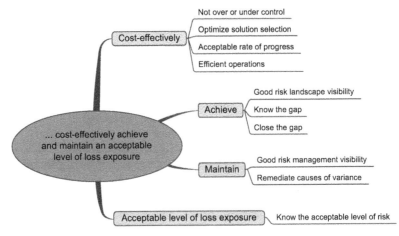

FIGURE 13.1

Mindmap of example risk management metric goals.

Before we move on, there are a few things we need to point out about the framework above:

- This framework may not be the only way to decompose the risk management goal. You may find that a different set of subgoals, questions, and metrics works better for you, or you might find that this framework provides most of what you need, only requiring a handful of your own tweaks.
- Efforts for achieving and maintaining will likely (should likely) run in parallel. If you aren't tackling the root causes for variance and unacceptable loss exposure (primarily a part of the "maintain" function) even as you are mitigating current exposure, then your progress in achieving an acceptable level of risk is likely to be much slower. This is because even as you fix things, bad risk management practices will be introducing risk elsewhere.
- Even if your organization achieves its desired level of risk, the dynamic nature of the risk landscape is undoubtedly going to throw occasional curveballs that take the organization out of that comfort zone. Also, keep in mind that in some cases, management's comfort zone may shift. Either way, you should view this as a never-ending process. However, that has always been a mantra of information security and risk management, right?

The bottom line is that the value of any metric should be defined within the context of a goal. When it comes to information security, that goal is to manage risk cost-effectively over time through better-informed decisions. Starting with that as the focus, the rest is easy; or at least easier.

MORE DETAILS

Okay, let's dig in and start to flesh this framework out a bit. As we do, you might very well identify questions and metrics (maybe even subgoals) that you would like to add. If so, go for it. This table (Table 13.1) is not intended to provide the final word on the topic or be entirely comprehensive. It's intended to demonstrate the approach and provide a good starting point. You will note, too, that some metrics will support more than one question or goal.

After this section, we'll discuss each of the subgoals in greater detail to help ensure clarity and because some of them are particularly challenging in nature (e.g., determining an organization's acceptable level of loss exposure).

One thing we hope you've noticed is that most of this is dependent on the ability to measure risk. We'll discuss this in greater detail further on, but we didn't want to miss the opportunity to drive home the point that effective risk management, particularly cost-effective risk management, is naturally dependent on risk measurement practices. If risk measurement isn't meaningful or is done poorly, then the odds of effectively managing risk go way down.

You may note that we didn't explicitly include examples related to reducing controls if, for example, an organization found it was overcontrolling loss exposure in some part of its risk landscape. Keep in mind though that the "close the gap" goal

Table 13.1 Example Goals, Subgoals, Questions, and Metrics

Goals	Subgoals	Questions	Metrics
Cost-effective	Not over or under control	Are we aligned with risk appetite?	Acceptable level of risk Current risk level
	Optimize solution selection	What is the most cost-effective solution?	Solution costs Solution benefits
	Acceptable rate of progress	Are we progressing toward objectives at the proper rate?	Milestones Current risk condition Previous risk condition Elapsed time Forecast risk condition
	Efficient operations	Are we focused on the most important things?	Areas of risk concentration Key control deficiencies
		Is the full cost-benefit of our resources being realized?	Resource utilization Resource cost
Achieve	Good risk landscape visibility	Do we have good visibility?	Threat intelligence Asset management Control conditions Impact factors
	Know the gap	How far away from alignment are we?	Acceptable level of risk Current risk level
	Close the gap	Where does risk exist?	Risk assessments Self-identified points of exposure Loss events
		What control deficiencies exist?	Risk assessments Self-identified deficiencies Loss events
Maintain	Good risk management visibility	Do we have good risk management visibility?	Asset visibility Threat visibility Controls visibility Impact factor visibility Decision visibility Execution visibility
	Remediate causes of variance	Which root causes are driving variance into the environment?	Variance data Root cause analysis results
Acceptable level of loss exposure	Know the acceptable level of loss exposure	What is the acceptable level of loss exposure?	Current risk level The organization's loss capacity Management's tolerance for loss

does not specifically say, "reduce risk." In some cases, closing the gap might mean, "increase risk." This is something to keep in mind because we have in our careers found numerous instances where controls (e.g., a lot of the common SOX controls, as an example) could be relaxed to significantly reduce the business burden and not result in a material increase in risk. As you might imagine, when you find these opportunities, management loves you for it.

In this next section, we will begin to examine our subgoals and metrics in more detail. For reasons that will become obvious, we'll cover them in a different order than we have presented them above.

TALKING ABOUT RISK

Since we brought it up... I (Jack Jones) have in the past been something of a nuisance to external and internal auditors on the subject of SOX controls. In one organization, I challenged them to describe the relevance of many of the common IT SOX controls outside of a science fiction loss scenario. For most of the controls in question, they couldn't. As a result, we worked together to review the SOX controls, ended up eliminating some, and demoting a significant percentage of the others to general IT controls status. This resulted in more accurate SOX-related risk reports for management, fewer wasted resources dealing with burdensome SOX processes on controls that didn't warrant it, and a very happy set of executives. Cost-effective risk management in action!

ACCEPTABLE LEVEL OF LOSS EXPOSURE

We need to tackle this goal first because the other goals are inherently dependent on this one. What we're talking about here is risk appetite, or tolerance, depending on who you're talking to (more on this later). Regardless of what you call it, what it boils down to is the level of loss exposure executive management is comfortable with. This is an aspect of risk management that information security organizations rarely tackle effectively, if at all.

Perhaps the most common approach we've seen (and we have approached it this way in the past) is to assume that an organization's information security policies are a tangible representation of management's risk appetite. Based on this assumption, measurements focus on variance from policies and standards. This approach is relatively straightforward and conceptually correct, but it is also inherently implicit and has a couple of fundamental flaws, at least as it is most commonly done:

- It is relatively unusual to encounter organizations whose policies and standards have actually been reviewed in a meaningful manner with executive management. More commonly, the information security team defined (or downloaded, or had a consultant define) the policies and standards and had management "sign-off" on them. Unfortunately, if the risk management value and cost implications of policies and standards aren't discussed with management, they won't know what they are signing-off on. As a result, the policies and standards may not actually set the stage for a level of risk, and cost, that management is okay with, which increases the probability of getting wrapped up in the Groundhog Day phenomena we mentioned earlier.

- Risk status reports based solely on compliance levels still aren't inherently meaningful to management. If the organization isn't complying effectively with one requirement or another, so what? How much should management care?

The bottom line is that if your organization operates on the assumption that policies and standards represent the organization's risk appetite then it is critical that you do as much as possible to make sure the assumption is accurate. As we described in the previous chapter, getting face time with executives to discuss policy risk and cost implications is a critical first step. Another critical requirement is to monitor policy exceptions and enforcement practices. If you see a lot of exceptions to a policy, or inconsistent enforcement of violations, it is a good sign that the policy doesn't match how management wants to operate (either that, or management has not been given the information they need to understand the risk implications). Finally, it is also important to ensure that when reports regarding noncompliance are taken to management, the "so what" question is answered through meaningful risk analysis. This enables more explicit risk management.

A more effective approach to defining risk appetite in many organizations is to define it in monetary terms. That's how it's done in the financially focused risk disciplines like credit risk and investment risk, and it is inherently more meaningful to executive management. Unfortunately, information security loss exposure has traditionally been expressed as a set of high, medium, and low conditions (usually related to control deficiencies versus loss event scenarios). It's a significant leap of faith to believe that high, medium, and low terms are really meaningful to an organization's executives. Besides, how many "highs" are too many? How many "mediums" equal a "high?" What do we mean by "high risk", anyway? What are the loss event scenarios to which those ratings are referring? This being the case, information security has been badly hamstrung in defining the most foundational element of its overall goal! Without that definition, the ability to leverage GQM in a truly meaningful manner is likewise hamstrung.

The information security discipline faces another challenge though, beyond measuring risk in meaningful terms. In credit risk, an organization is (or should be) able to keep reasonably good track of the credit it has given and taken, and define a threshold for the related loss exposure that it doesn't want to exceed. Unfortunately, in information security it is arguably impossible to have complete visibility into all the nooks and crannies where things can and do go wrong. This visibility problem makes it much more challenging to represent the complete picture of loss exposure an organization faces, and thus precisely define its acceptable loss exposure threshold. That said, the problem is not insurmountable as long as several points are kept in mind:

- Visibility needs to be an explicit element of your risk management metrics so that areas of poor visibility are recognized and improved on over time.
- The overall confidence in aggregate loss exposure measurements should be tempered by the organization's risk landscape visibility.
- We should not expect high degrees of precision in aggregate loss exposure measurements. Risk measurement and metrics is about getting better, more

useful information than the typical high, medium, and low ratings (which, keep in mind, suffer from the same visibility problem).

We'll spend a lot more time on this question of visibility later in the chapter.

TALKING ABOUT RISK

The terms "risk appetite" and its close cousin "risk tolerance" are often poorly understood, very rarely used to good effect, and commonly used interchangeably. Similar to the word "risk," you will sometimes get as many different definitions for these terms as people you ask. Potentially useful definitions we have seen include:

- Risk appetite: A target level of loss exposure that the organization views as acceptable, given business objectives and resources
- Risk tolerance: The degree of variance from the organization's risk appetite that the organization is willing to tolerate

Given these definitions, a simple analogy for appetite and tolerance would be speed on a highway. The department of transportation or other government entity sets a speed limit. This could be roughly thought of as analogous to risk appetite and reflects the decision-makers beliefs regarding an appropriate balance between traffic flow, highway and environmental wear-and-tear, and public safety (among other things). The people using the highway will usually travel at speeds greater or lesser than the speed limit as opposed to exactly at the speed limit, and the point at which law enforcement actually begins ticketing violators could be viewed as analogous to risk tolerance. Given normal weather and other conditions, it is extremely rare to see law enforcement enforce the speed exactly at the limit. Consequently, while risk appetite can be thought of as a line drawn in the sand that helps to set expectations, risk tolerance can be thought of as the variance from appetite that drives day-to-day decisions to operate differently in some manner. Note the operative word here—decisions.

Defining an acceptable level of loss exposure

If we want to define an acceptable level of loss exposure for an organization, how do we go about doing that? Our GQM framework tells us that we need three pieces of information: the organization's current level of risk, the organization's capacity for loss, and management's tolerance for loss. Of these three elements, information security can only provide one—the organization's current level of risk. The other two elements are pieces of the puzzle that executive management brings to the table and may not, in fact, state explicitly.

TALKING ABOUT RISK

Why do we need the organization's current level of risk when establishing risk appetite? Actually, we shouldn't need it. All we should need is the organization's capacity for loss and the executive management's personal views on risk. That said, there is a decent chance today that if you ask executives to give you a specific information security risk appetite value, they will say something like "less" and shrug—ironic, eh? Many of them simply haven't considered the possibility that information security risk can be quantified and aggregated because all they have ever seen are red, yellow, and green heatmaps. They may, of course, decide to reference a quantitative risk appetite definition that the organization uses for one of its financial risk domains, which is not a bad thing. Or, perhaps, to paraphrase Supreme Court Justice Potter Stewart's answer when he was asked why a particular motion picture did not qualify as obscene, an executive may respond with, "*I'll know it when I see it.*"

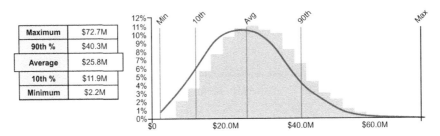

Maximum	$72.7M
90th %	$40.3M
Average	$25.8M
10th %	$11.9M
Minimum	$2.2M

FIGURE 13.2

Example aggregate risk distribution.

If the organization's current level of loss exposure is an important piece of information that's needed to set risk appetite, how do we go about measuring it? There are a couple of ways we have seen that work well.

One option is for an organization to perform a high-level triage of the results of its most recent security review or audit. Assuming the examination was comprehensive and identified the control conditions that were significantly different from what they were supposed to be (i.e., were variances), a quick, risk-based triage of those findings can be performed to identify which of those conditions and related scenarios appear to represent the greatest exposure. Having applied that filter, full-fledged factor analysis of information risk (FAIR) analyses can then performed on these scenarios. Now, to get the big picture you can't simply sum up the loss exposure from each of these analyses, as that would represent the loss exposure if all of moons aligned simultaneously (kind of an asteroid-strike view of the world). You have to apply Bernoulli and/or Poisson functions by using a spreadsheet, statistical tool, or (simpler still) a commercial FAIR application (see Figure 13.2).

This will give you a distribution of joint probabilities that provides a truer view of the aggregate exposure from those scenarios. It's only a partial view of the overall loss exposure of the organization, but if the security review/audit and analyses were done well, then the results should provide a good approximation of where the organization stands with loss exposure. It is certainly a great place to start. If you prefer a simpler approach (but one that is a couple of steps lower in terms of effectiveness and explicitness), you can plot the FAIR results on a heat-map.

TALKING ABOUT RISK

We have found the question of incomplete visibility and its effect on analysis results to be a great talking point with management. Specifically, if visibility into parts of the risk landscape is weak, and if that is believed to impact the quality of a risk analysis and leadership's ability to make better-informed decisions, then management is more likely to support visibility improvement efforts.

Senior executives who have had to deal with setting thresholds in other areas of risk should be able to look at this information and come to a reasonable conclusion about whether that amount of loss exposure is, in their eyes, acceptable for the organization. Is the analysis precise? Of course not. As we've discussed elsewhere, high levels of precision aren't the goal. The goal is more useful information than they've had before. We find it hard to believe that an executive would prefer a list containing five "high risk" issues, and 24 "medium risk" issues over the quantitative data above. Furthermore, with the approach above, you're also able to identify which scenarios, assets, and control deficiencies are contributing most to the overall level of risk, which can always be plotted on a heat-map to help with prioritization.

Another approach is to use something like CXOWARE's RiskCalibrator application, which significantly simplifies the process. Think of it as a TurboTax-like approach to performing an enterprise information security risk analysis that automatically provides the aggregate loss-exposure picture, as well as identifying where risk is concentrated, which threat communities are most problematic, and which control deficiencies are driving the most risk into the organization (and thus where the best bang-for-the-buck is from a remediation perspective). It also performs sensitivity analysis so that the organization knows where to focus on improving metrics quality, and where the organization is sensitive to changes in the risk landscape in either good or bad ways.

Imagine for a moment that you are incredibly fortunate (from our point of view) and you work for an organization that has established a quantitative statement of information security risk appetite. Congratulations! Now what? Even if you performed an analysis like we described above, you have at least one more important question to answer. Which part of the analysis results do you compare against the defined threshold? You see, the outcome of an aggregate risk analysis is not a discrete number (e.g., $X of loss exposure). No, the outcome is a distribution, like the one shown in Figure 13.3, of potential levels of loss exposure reflecting the imprecision and inevitable uncertainty in the analysis. So which number from within this distribution do you use for comparison against the defined risk appetite? The average? The maximum? One of the percentiles? Or do you use the single event worst-case? The unsatisfying answer to this question is, "It depends."

Suppose your organization defined its information security risk appetite as $30 million of annualized exposure. If we compare that value against the aggregate

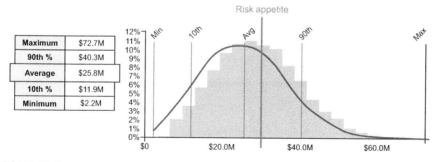

FIGURE 13.3

Risk appetite.

results shown in the chart above, it falls in between the average and the 90th percentile. So, does the organization's aggregate loss exposure fall within its defined appetite or not? Well, the answer is "yes" if the organization has chosen to reference against the average, and "no" if the organization has chosen to reference against the 90th percentile. The point is, an organization needs to establish an agreed upon expectation regarding which point of a loss exposure distribution will be used for such comparisons. Where on the distribution an organization settles also provides a hint regarding its risk tendencies. An organization that chooses to reference against the 90th percentile of the distribution can probably be thought of as more risk adverse than one that references against the average.

Another possibility is that management won't set a specific risk appetite value, but instead will look at the organization's current loss exposure and say something like, "What will it take to cut that in half in the next 24 months?" That's fine, too. It's specific, which enables explicit risk management to take place.

TALKING ABOUT RISK

If you are thinking about talking with your organization's senior executives about defining a quantitative information security risk appetite, you should be aware that they are very likely to ask the question, "Who else is already doing this?" and "Is there a benchmark we can compare ourselves against?" The unfortunate fact (at the time of this writing) is that the answers to these questions are, "almost nobody" and "no." FAIR has been plowing new ground regarding measuring information security risk for a dozen years now, and has gained recognition and use in tactical decision-making. Using quantitative risk analysis in the strategic management of information security risk is the next logical progression. We believe it's simply a matter of time before this gains widespread recognition and adoption.

An important thing to keep in mind regarding "an acceptable level of loss exposure" is that it is highly situational. Although an organization may in normal circumstances enforce relatively close alignment to its defined risk appetite, opportunities or constraints may create circumstances where organization leadership knowingly and willingly make decisions regarding risk that takes the organization outside of the defined threshold. This may take the form of additional risk-taking or reduced risk-taking. This is where the notion of risk tolerance could come into play, at least if you subscribe to the definition we mentioned earlier. An organization might define thresholds above and below its normal risk appetite, beyond which a careful examination and exceptional approvals might need to occur regarding risk decisions, policies, etc.

TALKING ABOUT RISK

There is something that strikes us as odd about the belief held by some information security professionals that executives have an almost unbounded appetite for information security risk. It's odd because studies show that when people are given a choice between potentially gaining something versus potentially losing something of similar value, they will choose to avoid the loss. As a species, humans are simply wired to be risk averse. In our evolutionary past, although the need to acquire food, water, mates, etc. was important to survival, we could (up to a point) continue to survive if we passed up on those opportunities. If, however, we failed to avoid a significant threat, then we died. Game over, plain and simple. As a result, we are wired to more highly prioritize loss avoidance. In order for people to choose the "gain" option, they have to believe that the potential for gain is meaningfully greater than the potential for loss. Consequently, if an information security professional's experience is that executives routinely disregard warnings of "high risk," then that suggests one or more of the following:

- Either the information security professional did not effectively communicate the loss exposure,
- The executives do not view the information as credible, or
- The risk information they are putting in front of the executives truly is not relevant when compared to the opportunities or competing risk issues the executives have to deal with

Our experience has been that when we present risk in terms that are meaningful, that we can defend, and that are truly significant, executives tend to exhibit more risk-averse tendencies.

ACHIEVING ALIGNMENT

With "an acceptable level of loss exposure" defined, we now have something to achieve alignment with. This subgoal is relatively straightforward, and has three subgoals of its own:

- Good risk landscape visibility
- Know the gap, and
- Close the gap

We will cover all three of these below, as well as some of the metrics that support them.

Good risk landscape visibility

We've already discussed visibility a bit, but here we'd like to make a not-so-subtle claim: it is impossible to achieve an acceptable level of loss exposure if your visibility into the risk landscape has gaping holes. Well, maybe not impossible, but it would be pure coincidence if an organization actually achieved alignment with its risk appetite while half blind. As a result, the first subgoal under achievement has to be to attain good visibility into its risk landscape, which requires metrics regarding assets, threats, controls, and impact factors.

Asset visibility

Common asset metrics tend to include how many assets there are, where they are located, what organization processes they support, who is responsible for them, etc. This includes system assets, network assets, application assets, data assets, and facilities, etc. Without this information, you can't accomplish some of the other key elements in risk management, like risk assessments and analysis, with nearly as much confidence. No organization will ever have perfect visibility, but if visibility isn't an explicit objective, there is a much higher probability of gaping holes. Organizations that have a decent handle on asset metrics tend to have mature asset management processes surrounding the introduction of new assets, changes to assets, and disposal of assets. Where this exists, it's often part of the business continuity program, which may include a configuration management database (CMDB) solution.

Threat visibility

Threat metrics should, unsurprisingly from a FAIR perspective, focus on threat event frequency (TEF) and threat capability. For some threat communities (e.g., insiders of one sort or another), you can also include a metric regarding the number of threat agents, because there is likely to be some correlation between the number of threat agents and the probability of threat events (malicious or not).

Very few organizations really seem to leverage threat metrics. Oh, you'll often see things about the number of viruses blocked, the number of scans against web systems, and such, but beyond that, organizations tend to underutilize what could be a rich source of intelligence. Later in the book we give SIEM providers a hard time for not leveraging their data very effectively. Today nobody is asking them to be very proficient because common practices regarding threat metrics are usually pretty superficial. If you adopt FAIR as a fundamental component of your organization's risk management practices, you will inherently evolve your approach to threat metrics.

Control visibility

Control metrics are going to be primarily about the frequency, severity, and duration of variance. As you will recall from the controls chapter, variance is the enemy because variance from an intended state of control, almost always exists when a significant event occurs. In the controls chapter, we discussed that variance duration is comprised of two elements: the time it takes to discover a variance, and the time it takes to remediate variance. Also recall from the controls chapter, this exposure window data can be combined with TEF data to help us understand how quickly we need to remediate weaknesses.

Impact factors

There are three categories of impact factor metrics: asset characteristics such as volume; sensitivity and criticality; organizational conditions like stock price, cost of capital, compliance requirements, etc.; and external conditions like regulatory penalties. For the most part, these metrics are used within risk analyses themselves, rather than as a separately reported metric.

Visibility analysis

An approach we've used to gauge and manage visibility involves carving up the risk landscape into logical categories and then estimating the level of visibility the organization has into each category. For example, we might carve the landscape into: servers, web applications, network devices, databases, etc. For each of these, we would estimate the current asset, threat, control, and impact visibility on a scale of 0–100%. In other words, we would estimate how much we think we know about each metric dimension (asset, threat, control, and impact) of each category. If we believe we have perfect visibility into the asset dimension of servers, for example, our estimate would be 100%. If we weren't sure whether we even had servers in our environment, or we suspected we did but had no idea where they were, our estimate would be 0%. Yes, we know, we're asking you to estimate what you don't know, which some people really struggle with conceptually. There are a few things that can help with this, though:

- Just as we did when performing risk analyses, use calibrated ranges—e.g., "between 80 and 90%."
- Think about the processes, technologies, and other aspects of your environment that would affect this estimate. For example, if your organization has a lot of unmanaged databases and other "shadow IT" in it, then your visibility into those parts of your risk landscape is likely to be much lower.
- Another way of thinking about it is if tomorrow you suddenly gained perfect visibility into a category (e.g., servers), how far off would today's visibility estimate be? Were you off by 10% (i.e., your current visibility is 90% of what was actually out there)?

The point here, though, is not to have a perfect estimate. The point is to force the organization to think about visibility explicitly and differently than it has before, and then put into place the processes, technologies, etc. that allows it to improve its visibility. For example, let's say we did this visibility estimation drill for the databases, servers, and web applications in our organization and charted the results in Excel (see Figure 13.4). What can we tell by simply looking at the charts?

The vertical axis represents the estimated percentage of visibility (higher is better). Vertical box length represents the level of uncertainty in the estimate (smaller boxes are better).

First, it's pretty clear that there is good visibility in every dimension of the web apps. This may be because in this organization it's a smaller and more closely managed part of the landscape. The organization also seems to have a reasonably decent handle on assets in every category, perhaps because it has good asset management practices and change management. Likewise, it appears to have good controls visibility, perhaps because it has strong controls testing practices and technologies that provide up-to-date information on control conditions. For databases and servers though, it's clear that threat visibility isn't great, and there appears to be a lot of uncertainty about the estimates themselves. Also, there seems to be questionable visibility regarding database impact, which suggests that the organization may not know as much as it should about the sensitivity, criticality, or both, of these assets.

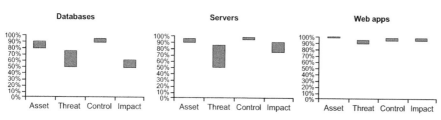

FIGURE 13.4

Visibility charts.

Having exercised this drill and come up with results like this, an organization can implement or improve processes and technologies that will improve and then maintain visibility. For example, maybe it needs to improve database and server logging and monitoring to improve threat visibility. Perhaps they need to review the purpose and content of databases to improve their understanding of sensitivity and criticality, and/or apply a classification scheme to them. Regardless, at least now they have a way to identify and address weaknesses in their visibility.

From a risk management perspective, an organization that has been through this exercise and acted to improve and maintain its visibility is obviously going to be much better positioned to achieve alignment with its risk appetite than an organization that hasn't.

Know the gap

You can't close a gap you aren't aware of. The good news, from a metrics perspective, is that we have already covered this one in the earlier discussion about establishing the organization's "acceptable level of loss exposure." Basically, the gap between the organization's current loss exposure and its acceptable level of loss exposure tells us how much further it has to go, which can drive the level of effort and resources an organization applies—i.e., the larger the gap, the more emphasis is going to be placed on closing it.

Close the gap

It probably goes without saying that achieving alignment with an organization's acceptable level of loss exposure most often involves risk reduction efforts. Certainly in some cases the coin will be turned and the organization will make decisions to increase exposure to loss, but this is the less common case in our experience. Regardless, there are two dimensions to this subgoal, and thus two questions the metrics need to help answer: "Where does risk exist?" and "What control deficiencies exist?"

From a level of effort perspective, the good news is that the same sources of data generally answer both questions. Risk assessments, self-identified reporting, and loss events are the three most common metric sources for this subgoal. Risk assessments and loss events are fairly obvious in terms of what they mean and the data they provide. Self-identified reporting, however, can take a couple of different forms, including personnel who notice that something is out of whack and report it, as well as tools or processes that are implemented specifically to identify and report on the condition of assets and controls (e.g., configuration monitoring tools, regular access privilege reviews, etc.). The process of closing the gap simply involves making changes in the people, policy, process, and/or technology that reduce the gap between the current state of loss exposure and the organization's risk appetite.

MAINTAINING ALIGNMENT

It doesn't matter whether we're talking about your bank account, your health, or the risk posture of your organization, maintaining the condition of anything over time boils down to preventing undesirable conditions, and then detecting and remediating undesirable conditions when they do occur. In order to accomplish this in risk management, you need to have visibility not only into the assets, threats, controls, and impact factors we discussed earlier, but also into the risk management elements (decision making and execution). When variance does occur, as it invariably will to some degree, you have to be able to figure out why it occurred so that you can address the root cause—particularly if it's a systemic problem.

We've already covered the first four metrics associated with this goal: asset, threat, control, and impact factor metrics, so we won't belabor them here. However the last two—decision visibility and execution visibility—warrant some discussion.

Decision visibility

Decision visibility metrics boil down to two subtypes; who is making decisions, and the information upon which they are basing their decisions. Data captured about decision-makers on their policy approvals, policy exceptions, change management approvals, etc. is important for two reasons: first, to be able to follow up on decisions that are questionable (either in who made them or why they were made), and second, to hold people accountable. The importance of this second point cannot be overstated. The level of scrutiny and caution many executives will put into a risk decision is different if there is a decent chance they'll have to explain their decision to someone up the food chain at a later date. Knowing which decision-makers are accepting the most risk, and thus which parts of the organization are introducing the most risk, can provide a useful picture of how risk is being managed.

Metrics regarding the quality of risk information are also important, and this is something about which very few organizations pay attention. Analyst training, qualification data, and metrics regarding analysis quality can be extremely useful. The table (Table 13.2) below provides a partial list of some of these metrics.

Table 13.2 Decision Visibility Metrics

Subcategory	Example Metrics
Analyses	Percentage of analysts certified in the organization's chosen risk analysis method
	Number of risk analyses performed
Analysis quality	Number of risk analysis reviews
	Number of risk analyses determined to be inaccurate
Decisions	Number of policy exception reviews
	Number of approved risk acceptances
	Number of high risk acceptances
Unauthorized decisions	Number of risk acceptance decisions by unauthorized personnel

TALKING ABOUT RISK

In one organization we've worked in, we managed to put a process in place that ensured information security was engaged to provide consulting and oversight for all IT projects. Just hard-wiring engagement like this into the IT project management process was considered a victory. At last, we would be able to really help ensure that the organization did not implement "risky stuff."

Based on our beliefs about previous project management practices and decision-making, we expected some percentage of projects to be slapped down by management for potentially introducing too much risk. What we encountered, however, was business as usual. Our infosec personnel would document their concerns during the course of projects and present their risk reports to management. Management would yawn and ask, "Where do I sign (to accept the risk)?" After a while, it became obvious that something wasn't right because a significant number of projects were being implemented where the level of security risk had been rated "high," and not one project had been rejected by management.

After digging into the metrics, we discovered that fully a third of the projects had been rated "high risk." This raised a concern because, as bad as we thought some common practices were, it seemed unlikely that the organization could have survived as long as it had if it was routinely implementing that much high risk into its technology landscape. A closer look at the specific findings behind those "high risk" ratings provided the answer—the majority of concerns that the information security personnel had been calling "high risk" did not pass the laugh test. For example, virtually any time a policy was being violated, it was automatically characterized as high risk. Surely, there are times when policy noncompliance represents high risk, but just as surely, this is not always the case. It's not even the case in most instances.

To resolve this problem, we first trained all of the personnel in a rudimentary form of FAIR analysis and gave them a simple process and set of matrices to use when determining the level of risk associated with any findings they might have. A few months later, we looked at the data again. The number of "high-risk" projects had dropped by more than two-thirds. In other words, fewer than 10% of projects now were labeled "high risk" (and there was still room for improvement, analysis-wise). At this point, we went to management, explained the new risk analysis approach, and advised them that if they saw a project labeled "high risk", they owed it to themselves to think long and hard about accepting the risk. A couple of months and a few more conversations later, executive management decreed that henceforth no projects would go into production with high risk unless acceptance was signed-off at the appropriate level; even then, there had to be a defined remediation plan with committed resources. In the following year, only one high-risk project went into production, and it had the appropriate approvals and remediation requirements.

Prior to doing decent risk analysis, management couldn't discern the important stuff from the "noise." Unfortunately, buried within that noise were conditions they did not want their signature next to—we just hadn't helped them recognize which conditions those were. After we improved our risk analysis methods, and could demonstrate it, their attitude changed and we finally started making a difference for the organization. Being able to use metrics regarding analyses and individual findings enabled us to recognize and address a critical problem that was affecting decision-making.

The bottom line is that if your organization doesn't at least occasionally examine the quality of the risk information being given to decision-makers, then you might be missing out on an important opportunity to improve decision-making. In a large organization especially, tracking the quality of analyses over time and across a population of personnel can help you identify analysts who need additional mentoring, or systemic problems in risk analysis and reporting.

Be particularly mindful of risk assessments performed by people outside of your organization. We regularly encounter third-party assessments that are embarrassingly bad in terms of how they rate risk. Left unchallenged, this informat ion at best creates unwarranted concerns. At worst, it could result in resources being redirected from more important objectives. We have regularly "sniff tested" third party findings (usually just the "highs" and "mediums") to see what percentage of them made sense and could be defended. It isn't unusual for us to find fewer than 50% that pass the sniff test.

TALKING ABOUT RISK

A few years ago I (Jack Jones) engaged a global security consulting practice to perform an attack-and-penetration exercise on the company I worked for as the CISO. Shortly into the engagement, the consultants approached me with some dire news. They had discovered several high-risk "vulnerabilities" in one of the most important corporate web applications, and were recommending aggressive remediation measures. I examined the findings and pushed back on the consultants. Yes, they had identified weaknesses, but had they considered the frequency of the kinds of attacks that would leverage those weaknesses? How about the frequency of any sort of attack against that application, and especially the part of the application where the weaknesses existed? How much skill was required to exploit those weaknesses? What kind of access to underlying sensitive data would be gained and/or what level of control over the underlying systems? After talking through these considerations, the consultants backpedaled and changed the "high severity" of their findings to "medium," and in several instances, to "low." As a result, my organization was able to appropriately prioritize its remediation efforts and avoid unnecessarily impacting key projects and business operations.

These consultants weren't stupid. On the contrary, they were simply following a script and using a method for rating risk that only looked at the control deficiency, and didn't think through the threat or impact aspects of the situation.

Execution visibility

These metrics help us to understand how the organization is doing in terms of managing the factors that affect execution. This usually includes things like policy and standards improvements (from a clarity, conciseness, and usability perspective), communications from management regarding expectations, awareness training, and enforcement (and rewards, if the organization is being smart about changing behaviors).

The table below (Table 13.3) provides some examples of execution visibility metrics that you might find useful.

Table 13.3 Execution Visibility Metrics

Example Metrics
Percentage of personnel who have had generic security awareness training
Percentage of personnel in specific roles who have received awareness training pertaining to their specific responsibilities
Number of personnel who were rewarded or commended for their security decisions and actions
Number of personnel who were reprimanded or fired for their security decisions and actions
The frequency of control reviews (broken out by technology, etc.)

Continued

Table 13.3 Execution Visibility Metrics—cont'd

Example Metrics

The percentage of assets where control reviews are taking place

The maximum, minimum, and mean time to discovery of a variance

The number or percentage of variances discovered through different sources (e.g., audit, security testing, self-reporting, third parties, incidents, etc.)

The maximum, minimum, and mean time to correction (may be broken out by control type, technology, department, etc.)

TALKING ABOUT RISK

In the past, we've had good success with leveraging metrics to generate healthy competition between business units related to audit findings, patching, and user awareness. Executives are often a competitive bunch, and this can drive focus and improved execution against key risk management objectives. It also can have a positive effect on the risk management culture of the organization. Like anything else, though, it shouldn't be overdone. Keep these competitions limited to issues that everyone agrees are important.

We also have set up processes to present individual awards to people (outside of information security) who demonstrated exceptional contributions to information security through their ideas for improvements or sharp attention to problems. People tended to take real pride in these awards.

REMEDIATE CAUSES OF VARIANCE

Where unintended variance exists, unintended risk exists. As a result, we need to be able to identify the existence of variance so that we can remediate it and, more importantly, with respect to maintaining a desired level of loss exposure, resolve the underlying causes of variance.

Variance data

Variance data come from the same sources we encountered for the close-the-gap goal: risk assessments, self-identified reporting, and loss events. From one perspective, the data are the same—they are the findings and deficiencies provided from those sources. From a metrics and decision-making perspective, however, the data take a different form. Instead of the "findings to be fixed" point of view in close-the-gap, variance metrics are intended to help us understand the frequency, severity, and duration of variance across the population of assets and controls. The difference boils down to the fact that the close-the-gap goal is all about, well, closing the gap, while the variance data is intended to help us manage risk over time by understanding and treating the sources of variance.

Examples of variance data are shown in Figure 13.5. In these charts, it appears that network systems are well managed, with little variance except for some patching. Databases and servers are struggling, however, particularly with patching (go figure).

You can (and usually should) get into much more detail with this kind of data, fleshing out things like time to discovery, time to remediate, severity levels, etc. For

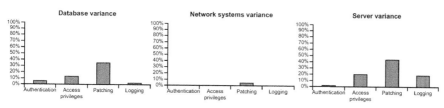

FIGURE 13.5

Variance charts.

example, even though databases may have a relatively high percentage of systems that aren't up-to-date with patches, the risk implications of those missing patches may not be as significant as another part of the environment that has a lower frequency of variance. The bottom line is, there is a lot of useful intelligence to be gained from these metrics about what is working and what is not working within your environment.

Root cause analysis

As we pointed out earlier, our profession is adept at identifying control deficiencies but not well practiced at figuring out why deficiencies come to exist, often repeatedly within an organization. In response to this problem, we developed a root cause analysis (RCA) process that some of you might think of as a prestructured "five why's" process for determining root cause. Not only does the process help identify the root cause for individual issues, it also can be used against a portfolio of issues to identify systemic sources of problems within the organization. Used in this way, very often an organization will discover that one or two fundamental problems are responsible for most of its control deficiencies. Resolving these systemic problems can have a significant positive effect on the organization's risk posture. We feel this topic warrants specific attention, so you'll find a detailed discussion regarding RCA in the next chapter.

TALKING ABOUT RISK

Deming had it right. If you aren't familiar with Edwards Deming, he is the engineering expert who helped the Japanese manufacturing industry evolve its practices and become the world's center of manufacturing quality excellence. A large part of Deming's focus was on managing variance in the manufacturing process and output. The result was better product reliability.

Well, information security is not that much different. As we've mentioned elsewhere in this book, bad things happen largely where variance exists. As a result, a significant part of our task in information security is to reduce the frequency, severity, and duration of variance. You can try to accomplish that by playing whack-a-mole and addressing each instance of variance individually, or you can seek out and resolve the fundamental sources of variance. We strongly prefer the latter.

Examples of the metrics that result from a root cause analysis are shown in Figure 13.6. As you can see from the first chart, the primary cause of variance was due to choices made by personnel. An analysis of those choices in the second

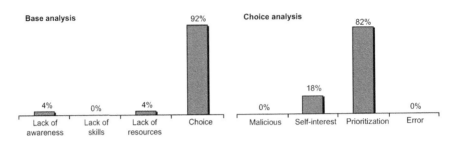

FIGURE 13.6

Rca metrics.

chart found that the vast majority was due to people prioritizing other business imperatives over information security. Additional analysis might find that these prioritizations were inappropriate and due to poor communication or enforcement by management, or because stronger incentives existed for the other choices (e.g., meeting deadlines and budgets).

COST-EFFECTIVENESS

We have said it before, but it bears repeating. Our responsibility as information security and risk management professionals is not to help our organizations manage risk. Our responsibility is to help our organizations manage risk cost-effectively. In many ways, the information security profession implicitly recognizes this and in large part tends to operate in ways that support this goal. In order to do this well, however, it needs to be an explicit goal with metrics that we actually pay attention to.

Not over or under control

Intuitively (or in some cases because business stakeholders have beaten this into our heads) we understand that there is a balance between risk, opportunity, and cost. Finding that balance inherently requires the ability to measure risk in a manner that allows us to compare, in like terms, where we are against where we want to be. We would not recite again the challenges our profession has faced to-date in this regard, but at least now we have models, tools, and methods that improve the odds of striking this balance. From a metrics perspective, we've already covered the two elements in this subgoal: an articulation of what constitutes an acceptable level of risk for the organization, and a means of measuring the organization's current level of risk.

Optimize solution selection

This is a sore point for us because we see relatively little attention paid to it in our profession, and it can be an opportunity to make a real difference for organizations. The archenemy of this opportunity is commonly known as "best practices." Don't get us wrong. There is a role for "best practices" in the industry as a point of reference, or if your organization is beginning from scratch and simply needs a place to

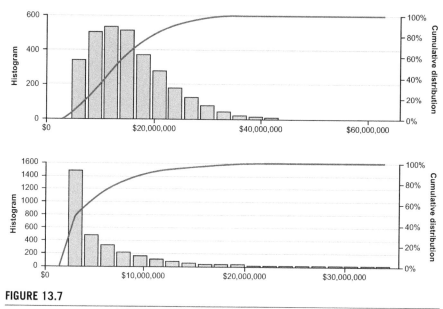

FIGURE 13.7

Loss exposure before and after controls.

start. What they should not be is a crutch, or a stick for beating management into doing what the information security organization, audit department, or regulators think it should do. Unfortunately, that is a common-use case.

TALKING ABOUT RISK

Sometimes you will hear people differentiate between "best practices" and "common practices." The differentiation is relatively common sense in that common practices (what the majority are doing) aren't necessarily the same thing as more advanced "best" practices. Very often however, the usage of these terms tends to get blurred. The bottom line is, if your organization wants to align with industry-adopted practices, it would be a good idea to decide whether it wants to align with common practices or best practices, or a mix in different parts of its risk landscape. Regardless of where and how it chooses to align, we strongly believe that those practices be considered guidelines, and that the organization should still exercise critical thinking to find "best fit" solutions whenever possible.

Being able to evaluate current state loss-exposure levels and the effect new or changed controls are likely to have on those levels can be incredibly powerful for guiding decisions. The charts in Figure 13.7 show the results of an analysis for current state loss exposure (top chart) and forecast loss exposure (bottom chart) after implementing a proposed control. This represents the benefit side of the cost-benefit equation. In order to do this, however, you have to be able to identify the control opportunities and estimate their effects. This is where FAIR and the controls ontologies can be leveraged to great effect. Also, the better your risk-related metrics, the more you can do in this regard.

The cost side of the equation is most commonly focused on the capital and operational costs of controls. Depending on the control, this may be all you need to focus on. In some cases, however, you also have to consider the opportunity costs to the organization—i.e., resources applied to information security can't be applied to other organizational objectives, and/or the drag on business processes that some controls introduce.

Acceptable rate of progress

This is another aspect of risk management that we see some attention paid to, but often not by information security—it's executive management throttling the rate of progress through its purse strings. Generally, information security is working to reduce risk as fast as its resources allow, and often complaining that it can't move fast enough due to a lack of resources. Well what is "fast enough?"

TALKING ABOUT RISK

Here again, it is important to keep in mind that executive management is faced with growing the business, managing operational expenses, and managing risk of various types, information security being just one of those types. It's also important to keep in mind that it is executive management's risk appetite and risk management pace that matters and not our own. If we're unhappy with the pace, then maybe we haven't done a good enough job of communicating risk to them so that their level of concern increases and the purse strings open up. Maybe it's simply a matter of them having even bigger fish to fry, of which we are not aware.

Having metrics related to the gap between the current level of risk and the organization's risk appetite, the progress that has been made since previous checkpoints, and the progress that's forecast for the next checkpoint can be huge in terms of gaining and keeping management support. It also provides a way to forecast the effects of risk management initiatives so that management can better understand the value proposition, and thus make better-informed investment decisions.

A visual representation like Figure 13.8 provides an at-a-glance view of past progress, current state, and forecasted progress, given current or planned resources. From this, management can better decide whether they want to pick up the pace, stay on pace, or even slow down. You can also break this down further into different dimensions of the risk landscape that are of particular interest or concern to management (e.g., online systems, SOX, etc.) so that the pace can be controlled more granularly. We've found that illustrating past progress is very helpful so that executive management can understand what they have gotten from their previous investments. Be aware though, that a postanalysis of previous risk management investments might show that they were not well chosen or executed, which could be disappointing news to your stakeholders.

Efficient operations

Operational efficiency has two primary questions associated with it. Both are important, but we would argue that if you only focus on one of these, focus on the first question.

- Is the organization focused on the most important issues and opportunities?
- Is the organization fully realizing the cost-benefit from its resources?

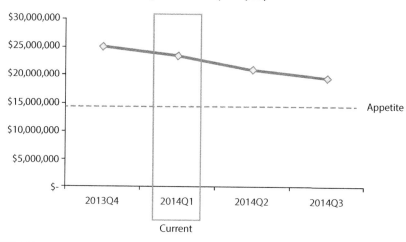

Loss exposure trend (80th pctl)

Appetite

2013Q4   2014Q1   2014Q2   2014Q3

Current

FIGURE 13.8

Loss exposure to tolerance over time.

Focusing on focus

You may have noticed that so far we haven't talked about prioritization. Identifying and fixing problems, yes, but not in what order. Your wait is over! This is, of course, one of the most important elements in risk management and a prime opportunity for metrics. Unfortunately, it's also where our profession has struggled mightily.

The focus question has two categories of metrics to it:

- Metrics that help us to understand where risk is concentrated, and
- Metrics that help us to prioritize the conditions that provide the best risk reduction and/or risk management bang-for-the buck

The first metric comes from examining the risk landscape and being able to measure the level of risk in each area of that landscape. Being able to do this, however, requires that we carve up the landscape in some logical manner. Maybe it makes sense in your organization to parse the landscape from a technology point of view—e.g., databases, servers, personal systems, applications, network systems, etc. We have seen this work well. We've also seen organizations carve the landscape up by business process—e.g., online retail, finance, HR, research and development, etc. Another option that we kind of like is a mixture. For example, an organization might identify a handful of key business processes as distinct analytic targets, and then carve the rest of the landscape up by technology category. From an analytic perspective, it doesn't matter that much. It's whatever fits best for your organization.

Performing a risk analysis on each of these landscape elements allows you to compare them and recognize where the organization has the most risk and thus should focus its efforts. Figure 13.9 shows partial results from one such analysis.

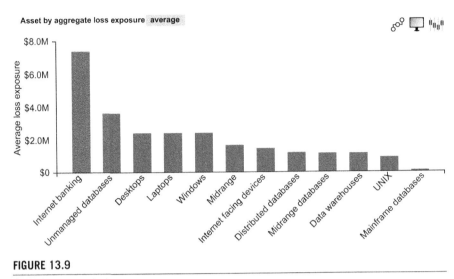

FIGURE 13.9

Asset by aggregate loss-exposure.

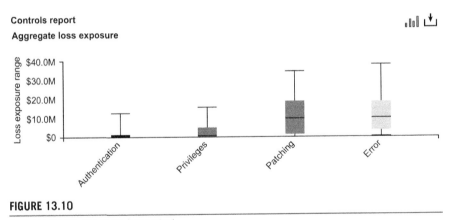

FIGURE 13.10

Aggregate loss-exposure by control.

The second metric (Figure 13.10) comes from examining the elements that are driving risk into the organization; typically, deficient controls. By understanding which controls are responsible for the most risk, particularly within the highest areas of risk concentration, you're able to manage risk much more cost-effectively.

By extending this analysis into the variance and decision-management controls, you're able to not only remediate risk cost-effectively, but also improve risk management functions cost-effectively. This type of analysis and reporting takes us much farther along the maturity continuum than where we've been with the standard risk assessment containing a list of "risks" that are really control deficiencies.

Leveraging resources

This last metric component is another underutilized opportunity in most organizations. The first part has to do with fully utilizing our personnel. Do we understand what their skills are, and are we effectively leveraging those skills? From a metrics perspective, we can survey our information security personnel for their backgrounds, skills, education, certifications, and even personal preferences. With this information, we can better place people where they will provide the most value to the organization and have the greatest likelihood of personal satisfaction and professional success.

TALKING ABOUT RISK

As a new leader in an organization, one of the first things we do is meet with each person in our organization to learn about their backgrounds, skills, work preferences, etc. Every time, this has resulted in significant changes to work assignments, and in some cases, the organization's structure. Every time, morale and productivity also improved significantly.

The second part of this metric component is maximizing the utility from tools the organization already has in place or chooses to deploy. It involves mapping the capabilities of tools against the controls ontologies so that organizations can more fully recognize and leverage the value of its investments. Once the capabilities are mapped, an organization can overlay that mapping against its risk landscape to identify where strengths and weaknesses exist.

TALKING ABOUT RISK

FAIR and the controls ontologies also can be a useful way of evaluating the value proposition of vendor products and services. In fact, in the past we've been asked by vendors to evaluate their products' value propositions so they can improve their marketing message. We've been happy to do this, but sometimes the results aren't what the vendor expects…

THE FEEDBACK PERSPECTIVE

Do you recall the diagram in Figure 13.11 from the chapter on risk management, and how in order to manage the risk landscape as a system, you need to use metrics as feedback?

Well, if we were to map each metrics defined from our GQM outline to this diagram, we would find that every element in the landscape is covered. What this means is that by following our GQM framework, an organization is naturally managing the risk landscape as a system.

MISSED OPPORTUNITIES

One of the things that baffles us is when people in our industry say, "We don't have enough data." In almost every case, this couldn't be further from the truth. In fact, with all the tools at our disposal these days, we are practically awash in data. As a profession,

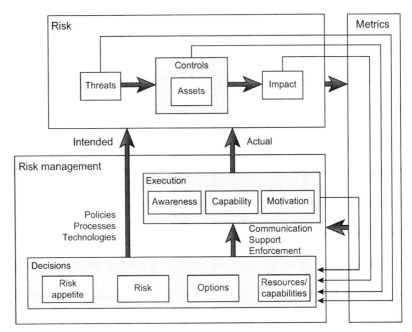

FIGURE 13.11

Risk management.

however, we haven't leveraged the available data effectively, in large part (we believe) because the profession hasn't had the models to tell us which data we needed to answer which questions. With the FAIR ontologies and the GQM framework discussed earlier, this shouldn't be nearly as significant a problem going forward. In other cases, we simply fail to recognize some of the metrics opportunities staring us in the face, and yet at other times, the data our tools provide us fall well short of their potential.

LOSS METRICS

The silver lining to loss events is that they can be a marvelous source of information to improve the quality of risk analyses and our understanding of the risk landscape. Unfortunately, we encounter very few organizations that fully leverage this data. As you review the information below, ask yourself these questions:

- How fully does your organization take advantage of its incident data?
- What would it need to do to improve in this manner?
- If your organization fully leveraged its incident data, how much would it help you when doing risk analysis?

The answers to these questions for most organizations are "*not very*," "*some relatively simple process and documentation changes*," and "*a lot.*" The point is that many loss metrics aren't difficult to acquire, and they can offer significant value in helping us understand our risk landscape.

There are several categories of loss metrics that we like to use:

- Incident counts, which tell us about loss frequency
- Loss magnitude data, which helps us understand incident impact
- Threat data, which tells us who or what caused the incidents (including motivation)
- Control data, which tells us what failed (and hopefully also what worked)

You'll notice that these metrics are more than just how often bad things happened and how bad they were. They also have to do with answering the question, "why?" The table below (Table 13.4) provides some examples of these metrics.

Most organizations capture a fraction of this information, yet it's all there to be had. Does it take additional work? Sure it does, but once capturing these variables becomes an inherent part of the incident management process, the relatively little additional work is well worthwhile.

FALLING SHORT

First of all, in the interest of full disclosure, we either currently or in the past have worked for vendors, so we've been as guilty as anyone else in the deficiencies we are about to describe. Hopefully, by discussing the weaknesses we see in vendor metrics, the bar will rise a bit and our profession will begin to see meaningful improvements.

If you work for an information security vendor, ask yourself whether your products or services can improve in their ability to provide meaningful metrics, particularly given what has been covered in this book. With this in mind, we're going to take this opportunity to use the SIEM vendors as an example and suggest that they are falling short of their potential from a metrics perspective. From what we've seen and experienced (and admittedly we haven't seen them all), these products and services largely focus on letting their clients know that a particular event is happening or nothing wrong with this. has happened. In other words, they're primarily an incident detection and reporting service. Sometimes they also include data regarding the types of vulnerabilities on systems they monitor. There's nothing wrong with this. It's very important data. What they aren't doing, however, is fully leveraging the treasure trove of data at their disposal.

For example, as a CISO we would love to know not just that web application X has been subjected to 20 attacks in the past month, but that 18 of those attacks also were directed against every other application on our network perimeter. Furthermore, of those 18 attacks, 15 of them were also thrown at other unrelated businesses on the Internet at roughly the same time. What does this tell us? It suggests that of the 20 attacks, five were targeted at our organization, and two of those were targeted specifically against application X.

Table 13.4 Loss Metrics

Category	Example Metrics	Discussion
Incident counts	Malware infections Phishing compromises Lost/stolen laptops, etc. Applications compromised	These metrics are important but do not require much explanation. The more interesting loss metrics have to do loss magnitude, threats, and controls.
Loss magnitude data	Number of records lost	How many sensitive records, if any, were compromised? This can, and should be, further broken out by type (e.g., social security numbers, credit card numbers, other PII, corporate sensitive information, etc.).
	Number of customers notified	This is relatively self-explanatory. If we also know the per-customer notification cost, then this information helps an organization pin down response costs from events.
	Credit monitoring offered	How many of the people whose information was compromised were offered credit monitoring?
	Credit monitoring accepted	How many of the people who were offered credit monitoring actually took advantage of the offer?
	Customer churn	If an event involved customers (or business partners for that matter), how many of them took their business elsewhere? This data is rarely documented or explored after an event, but it is there to be had and can really help an organization to understand the sensitivity of its customer base to events of various types. A related piece of information has to do with the lifetime value (in terms of profit) of customers who leave. Note that this does not have to only occur after a confidentiality breach, as severe outages or data integrity issues can also drive customers to leave.
	Fines and judgments	The good news is that most organizations do not have events that involve fines and judgments. But when they do, this is critical information to capture.
	Legal expenses incurred	Regardless of whether fines or judgments occur, it is not uncommon for organizations to engage internal or external legal expertise. When it is internal legal resources, these are "soft monetary" costs in terms of person-hours. For external legal resources, it is cold, hard cash.
	SLAs missed	Not only do we need to know whether a service level agreement was missed, but also the effect. Did the organization have to discount some invoice or refund some money?
	Public relations costs incurred	Following particularly nasty events, organizations may end up spending significant sums on managing their reputations. These costs should be captured when they occur.

Forensic expenses incurred	In many incidents, it is necessary to apply forensics to understand exactly what happened. When this occurs, whether using internal resources or external consultants, the costs should be captured.
Number of personnel affected	When there is an availability outage or significant degradation in system/application performance, it is important to capture the breadth and severity of the effect on personnel. Combined with an average, loaded hourly wage rate, this can help an organization gauge the productivity impact of events.
Person-hours expended in response	Response costs include the person-hours expended in dealing with an incident. Knowing how many people are involved, for how long, and at what loaded hourly wage, can help an organization to understand these costs.
System down-time	Self-explanatory.
Lost revenue	Sometimes when business processes are affected by outages, revenue loss occurs. A common practice is to use the length of an outage times the average revenue generated during that time of day and/or year to derive lost revenue. That often overlooks the fact that many times revenue is delayed rather than lost. In other words, depending on your business model, competition, etc., your customers may simply wait for the crisis to pass and then resume their business without an actual loss of revenue. Consequently, in order to get this metric right, you need to differentiate between lost versus delayed revenue.
Affect on stock price	Yes, we know this one is tough for a lot of reasons. Furthermore, few organizations to-date have had events been bad enough to demonstrate reputation damage as an effect on stock price. If your (publicly traded) organization suffers a significant event, however, you would be remiss to not pay very close attention to the effect on stock price. NOTE: A close cousin to stock price reduction is an increase in the cost of capital. There are now a few organizations with incidents so severe that they have started paying attention to this.
Insurance paid	With the increased use of cyber insurance, another metric worth paying attention to is how much (and what types) of the loss were covered by insurance.
Insurance costs	Assuming that your cyber insurance provider had to satisfy a claim your organization made, it would be good to know whether the insurance premium increased and, if so, by how much.
Fraud losses	Self-explanatory.
Fraud loss recovery	When fraud occurs, especially online fraud, there are often opportunities to recover the funds. This metric helps us to measure the efficacy of our recovery capabilities and thus our actual fraud losses.

Continued

Table 13.4 Loss Metrics—cont'd

Category	Example Metrics	Discussion
	Time to discovery	A critical piece of information is how long it took us to recognize that the loss event occurred. This not only informs us about the strengths and weaknesses of our detection capabilities, it also helps us to estimate the value proposition of improved detection capabilities — e.g., how much less loss would have occurred if we had detected the event sooner?
	Time to contain	After an event has occurred, how long did it take us to contain the event — e.g., bring up backup systems, kick the hacker off our systems, etc.?
	Time to resolve	How many hours, days, weeks, or months did it take us to resolve the event and return to "normal?" Normal often being defined as that state in which the event is no longer the topic of specific tracking and management attention. This can be anything from hours for simple outages to months (many months) for some catastrophic events.
	Remediation cost	Sometimes we have to implement additional technologies, policies, people, or processes in order to resolve an event. Documenting those costs is also important in order to understand the true effect of an event.
Threat data	Threat actors	Documenting who or what the actors were (or who were believed to be) helps us to understand what we are up against.
	Threat capability	Not all threat actors are created equal, nor do all compromises require rocket science to execute. By evaluating the level of expertise that was required to create a compromise, we implicitly gauge the efficacy of our controls. This can be incredibly informative in evaluating our loss exposure going forward and in making business cases for change.
	Threat intent	This is relatively straightforward. Was the actor looking for financial gain, to drive an ideological agenda, or just to hurt the organization (or was it Mother Nature simply acting out)? Of course, unless the actor is known, this may be somewhat speculative and based on inference given the type of event and the specific actions taken by the actor.
Control data	Control failure	This simply requires us to document what type of control (or controls) failed that resulted in the loss event materializing. Was a password compromised? Was a system not up-to-date on patching? did anti-malware fail to deal with a new virus? Did employment screening fail to detect a criminal history? Was someone untrained on how to recognize a phishing attempt? Did someone fail to label a network connection properly and as a result someone else disconnected the wrong cable?
	Control success	This is information helps us to understand which controls are helping us to limit the severity of loss events that occur. Unfortunately, this is commonly overlooked and undocumented. Did someone recognize that another employee was engaged in illicit activity? Did someone breach an account but was prevented from accessing sensitive information because access privileges were properly constrained, or because a system configuration setting limited access?

Going a step further, we would love to know more about the nature of those five attacks. How sophisticated did they appear to be—i.e., where did they fall along the threat capability continuum? Were they automated or manual? What types of weaknesses did they probe for? How persistent have they been—e.g., have they occurred in the past from the same source? Is that source focusing solely on our organization or do they also appear to be targeting our competitors? This kind of richer intelligence can be incredibly meaningful to an information security program that's paying attention. All of a sudden it's much easier to identify and respond to subtle changes that previously weren't discernible.

We also regularly encounter products that use significantly flawed models (yes, all models are inherently flawed to some degree, even FAIR) to drive both the data they collect and the analytics they apply to the data. In our experience, the products historically most challenged in this regard are vulnerability scanners. Very often, these tools use analytic functions that have relatively serious flaws, such as:

- Performing somewhat questionable math on ordinal scales
- Weighted values that don't appear to be substantiated in any clear fashion
- Variables applied to the wrong part of the equation, and
- Risk equations that are missing key variables

That said, some of the variables those tools capture can be extremely useful in our analytics, but we never rely on the risk scoring these tools provide because of our concerns. The good news is that two things are taking place as this book is being written: (1) a new version of CVSS is coming out, which we've been told has some important improvements; and (2) we're working with a vulnerability scanning vendor to improve their models and use of data. The results should be a much more highly refined and accurate output that will help their clients prioritize remediation much more effectively and efficiently.

The bottom line is, many security products seem to be missing the metrics boat to a greater or lesser degree. With any luck, some of what we've covered in this book will help.

KEY RISK INDICATORS AND KEY PERFORMANCE INDICATORS

Key Risk Indicators (KRIs) and Key Performance Indicators (KPIs) can play a critical role in managing risk effectively, or they can waste an organization's time and resources. Consequently, it's a good idea to get them right. Before we dive into the details though, we'd like to share some ground rules regarding KRIs and KPIs so that we're all on the same page:

- The word "key" is, well, key. The challenge, of course, is where to draw the line between those metrics that qualify as "key" versus those that don't. As far as we can tell, there is no clear, bright line to guide us, so each organization will have to make its own determination. Below, we'll discuss some of what, in our minds, are considerations that make a metric "key."

- "Risk indicators" should be metrics that inform us about how much loss exposure we have right now or how it's trending. The point is, KRIs are about *risk*. You know—threat conditions, asset-level control conditions, and the assets themselves.
- "Performance indicators" should be *execution and decision-making* metrics informing us about the risk management elements that contribute to our current level of risk and that affect our future level of risk.

Another consideration to keep in mind regarding KRIs and KPIs, is who the stakeholders are that will be using these metrics and what decisions are potentially going to be affected. For example, only a subset of the CISO's key metrics is going to be directly relevant to the Board of Directors and senior executives. In large part, the difference has to do with temporality and level of detail. The CISO will need to recognize specific risk or performance conditions that can have more immediate effects on loss exposure and that may require more immediate changes to processes, resource allocations, or technology (or the need to report something up the chain). Senior executives, on the other hand, tend to be more interested in whether things are or are not on track relative to earlier decisions and priorities, and whether they need to be particularly worried overall.

For that reason, we differentiate between what we refer to as strategic versus operational KRIs/KPIs. We'll spend most of our time discussing the operational KRIs/KPIs because they are often what feed the strategic ones. That being the case, you can assume the following sections are talking about operational metrics unless we specifically say otherwise.

Clues to "keyness"

KRIs and KPIs exist solely for the purpose of telling us that something important, from a risk or performance perspective, is either amiss or trending toward being amiss so that we can make adjustments and avoid unacceptable outcomes. This basic description tells us two things we need to do in order to recognize which metrics are key: (1) identify what's important to us, and (2) identify the variables that contribute to whether something has become, or is becoming, a problem.

Importance

Importance tends to differ between KRIs and KPIs. With KRIs, importance is based directly on asset value/liability—i.e., potential negative impact. Because KPIs are focused on decisions and execution that have some future affect on risk, importance is based on how quickly and profoundly that affect can take place. In either case, it boils down to assets at risk.

When considering assets at risk, identifying what is important should be relatively straightforward, at least conceptually. They are those things that represent the greatest potential for harm if negatively affected. In practice though, it can be a bit more challenging. One of the aspects that can make it more challenging is the notion of intrinsic asset value versus inherited asset value. For example, a bank safe has intrinsic value associated with how much it cost to purchase and install. The inherited value of the safe, however, includes the value of everything it protects. With that in mind, the more an asset contains, the more value it has. For example, the intrinsic value of a password is low, but the inherited value may be high depending on the types of information and system assets it protects. Likewise, an Internet-facing firewall may have nominal intrinsic value, but its inherited value tends to be extremely high because of everything it helps protect. (For the programmers in the audience, this resembles an object-oriented mode of thinking).

A last consideration regarding inherited value is that sometimes containment is not obvious. For example, if two servers have a trust relationship with one another from an authentication and access privilege perspective, each server inherits the value of the other because a breach of one represents a potential breach of the other. As you can see, this would become very complicated, very fast, if you tried to tackle it at a fine level of granularity. Fortunately, we can abstract the problem to a coarser level of granularity by essentially considering those two servers to be one "virtual" asset. This coarser granularity sometimes comes at the cost of precision in terms of estimates regarding control conditions, etc., but it should not affect accuracy, and it is very often a worthwhile tradeoff in terms of reduced complexity.

When trying to identify the importance of information, there are four primary considerations: (1) the value (or criticality, if you prefer) of the information in terms of helping the organization meets its objectives, (2) the potential liability associated with the information, (3) the volume of information, and (4) the cost associated with reconstructing the information if it is lost or corrupted. Note that confidentiality, availability, and integrity each can affect information differently.

When considering physical assets, importance boils down to two things: (1) the cost to replace the asset, and (2) the criticality of the asset in terms of its role in helping the organization meet its objectives.

A final thing to be aware of is that the "keyness" of some metrics may vary over time. Although most are likely to remain "key" indefinitely, others may come and go from the list of key metrics within an organization. For example, if an organization has historically struggled to comply with a specific policy expectation (e.g., access privilege management) *and* as a result represents a level of risk that has gained executive attention, then metrics regarding that condition may become key because it has been identified as something of particular interest to executives. Once the necessary improvements have been made and maintained long enough to demonstrate stability, these metrics may no longer qualify as key. Another example of a temporary key metric might be the achievement of project milestones on a large initiative that has executive leadership interest.

Condition factors

Having laid the groundwork for the "importance" aspect of KRI/KPI development, it's now time to consider the factors that contribute to whether the condition of important assets is acceptable or not.

More about KRIs and KPIs

In this section, we will provide some high-level examples of the kinds of metrics we focus on for KRIs and KPIs. We'll also discuss why we focus on these, and share some considerations that can help guide you in developing your own. Please keep in mind that your needs may be different, and thus your KRIs and KPIs may be very different from the ones presented here.

Digging into KRIs

We carve KRI metrics into four categories: loss metrics, TEF metrics, threat capability metrics, and control condition metrics. We'll discuss each of these below. Before we do, we'll reiterate that KRIs are about loss that has materialized or that the organization is exposed to.

Loss Loss metrics, particularly loss magnitude numbers, are often considered to be of more interest to senior executives than CISOs. That said, a significant jump in the frequency of loss events, even when loss magnitude is low, can reflect changes requiring immediate attention. For example, if an organization detects a significantly higher number of malware that have made it past perimeter defenses (these are loss events even if the loss magnitudes are often nominal), it may point to an increase in threat capability, a decrease in control efficacy, or both. Similarly, an increase in the frequency or severity of loss events associated with new software releases might indicate problems with developer skills, testing processes, or project deadlines. The good news is that loss events are a great source of risk intelligence. The bad news is that they are lagging indicators that suggest our leading indicators need some work. Even that is good news in a way, though, because at least we're in a position to recognize and deal with it.

Threat event frequency In order to qualify as "key," you will generally want these metrics to focus on especially sensitive or critical assets or locations within your landscape. Examples include critical websites, large data stores, and assets with high levels of inherited value (e.g., the network perimeter). At the time of this writing, threat agents are increasingly focused on attacking users and end-user systems, which means TEF metrics at those points of attack are becoming more important.

Once your organization has established what the "normal" level of threat activity looks like against these points of attack, what you are looking for is to be able to recognize significant changes in threat activity. We're less interested in the fact that we had 50 attacks against our key web applications than we are that this represents a 50% increase over the previous week. Unusually high levels of threat activity are of obvious importance and may drive the need to alter controls. Unusually low threat activity can be equally important and may mean a couple of things:

- Threat actors have shifted their focus to another part of your environment (or to some other organization entirely),

- Your detective controls are no longer working due to unintended changes in those controls, or threat capabilities have evolved in a manner that allows them to evade detection.

Trends regarding shifts in TEF can be considered operational or strategic, depending on time horizon. This is an example of where good threat intelligence, typically from outside the organization, can be especially helpful.

Threat capability It's important to recognize when significant changes occur in the sophistication of the threat landscape. With regard to malicious actors, we are first and foremost interested in changes in the sophistication of attacks being experienced by the organization or by other organizations in the same industry. Secondarily, we also want to know when capabilities have changed regarding important technologies used within the organization (e.g., new zero-day exploits against Oracle databases if the organization uses Oracle for key business processes or to manage particularly sensitive information). We do not, however, care much about changes in capabilities that aren't relevant to the organization. For example, if the organization doesn't use a particular flavor of UNIX then metrics regarding new zero-day exploits of that variety are just noise.

As with TEF, intelligence regarding trends in threat capabilities may be operational or strategic, depending on the timeline. In our experience, about the only place to get good leading intelligence regarding changes in threat capability is from commercial threat intelligence providers because they have the resources to do this well (breadth of vantage point and depth of specialization by their staff). This can be expensive though, so you'll want to be sure to evaluate its value against your other opportunities.

From a nonmalicious perspective, sometimes a sudden, large turnover in staff or other events can represent a change in threat capability. For example, as you may remember from the analysis chapter, you can think of every new software release as a threat event (because new releases sometimes result in loss). A significant turnover in development staff could represent a lowered capability, and thus an increased likelihood of losses resulting from faulty software.

Control conditions The first criteria for identifying control KRIs is that only asset-level controls qualify. In other words, variance management and decision management controls will never qualify as KRIs. KPIs yes, but not KRIs. The second rule is that, as we discussed earlier, only those controls applied to particularly important assets should qualify as key. For example, if we've identified a particular set of databases as key, then we'll want to maintain a clear understanding of the resistive, detective, and responsive controls surrounding them.

For the most part, the characteristics we're interested in for these controls are variance frequency, severity, and duration. These metrics help us to understand the level of loss exposure on key assets. There may be some instances however where the intended state of control as defined by policy or standard contributes to an unacceptable level of risk (e.g., an encryption standard that hasn't changed in years and is no longer strong enough to resist common attack methods).

TALKING ABOUT RISK

When we focus on variance, there is an inherent assumption in play that the intended state of these controls (the expectations set through policies and standards) is sufficient to meet the organization's risk needs. For example, if an organization's policies or standards don't set an expectation that logs should collect information to enable event detection, or doesn't require monitoring of the logs, then the problem isn't variance from the organization's formally defined expectations. However, it might represent a variance from executive management's undefined expectations or from an external stakeholder perspective (e.g., regulators). Regardless, when policies and standards are deficient in some manner, that's a decision-management failure, which can be a function of poor visibility, poor risk analytics, poor communication, etc. These decision-making failures can be identified through the root cause analysis process we introduce in the next chapter.

Digging into KPIs

We like to carve KPIs into three categories: visibility, variance management, and decision-making. A good argument can be made that visibility falls into decision-making because it plays a big role in the quality of information decision-makers are operating from. That said, we believe it's an important enough concern to warrant its own KPI category.

Visibility Once an organization has identified its current level of risk landscape visibility, it is extremely important to quickly recognize when key parts of that landscape have changed. This boils down to changes in the things we want to have visibility into (e.g., new network connections, key websites, technologies, etc.) as well as changes in our ability to understand the threat landscape they face and the control conditions surrounding them. For example, CISOs may want a visibility KPI that tells them if important parts of their landscape have changed in some way (e.g., an extension to the network thru an acquisition, new large concentrations of sensitive information, etc.). Another KPI may be one that will let them know if visibility into key parts of the landscape has diminished (e.g., the threat intelligence service provider contract has expired, the DLP product we use to scan systems for sensitive information is on the fritz, or security testing of a key web application has been suspended).

Variance rates As discussed above, as a KRI these metrics fall within the control conditions category because they inform us on the level of risk that exists. As a KPI these metrics inform us about the effectiveness of decision and variance management (expectation setting, communication, support, and motivation). Because these metrics provide such effective optics in both directions—risk and risk management—it is perhaps our favorite metric. It's as close as you will come to the one metric that rules them all.

There will always be some amount of control variance across a set of assets over time. From a KPI perspective, being able to detect when variance increases in frequency, severity, or duration enables us to more rapidly identify and resolve the root causes of variance earlier rather than later, which helps keeps risk management on a more even keel.

Variance causes From an operational perspective, it is crucial that management is aware whenever variance is due to malicious intent or self-interest, regardless of the asset that's involved. Only then can they respond effectively in terms of managing the personnel or organization issues that set the stage for those choices. It also can be important to recognize broken policies, processes, or execution shortcomings that can affect key assets. Other than these, the causes of variance tend to be more a strategic metric.

An example of these metrics from a strategic perspective would include changes in the percentage of variances that are due to a lack of awareness, incorrect prioritization, lack of skills, etc. This information allows the organization to make the necessary systemic adjustments and stay out of groundhog day.

On-time closure rates This metric tends to be more strategic in nature than operational. What it boils down to is that the ability of an organization to consistently meet its commitments in terms of on-time closure of security findings (be they from audits or some other source) can be an important indicator of its overall commitment to risk management. Of course, it can also be an indication that (1) the organization is lousy at estimating how long it will take to remediate a problem (which could be a project management problem), and (2) the organization is lousy at measuring and/or communicating risk. Doing a poor job of measuring and communicating risk often manifests as low levels of commitment by management on remediation efforts. Regardless, if an organization consistently struggles to meet these commitments, some root cause analysis is in order.

High risk acceptances Most organizations will want to keep a very close eye on the rate of high-risk acceptances. This is a lot easier and more pragmatic to accomplish, of course, if the organization is performing good risk analysis (minimizing the signal to noise problem).

Unauthorized risk acceptances This metric can straddle the line between being operational or strategic. From an operational perspective, knowing where within the organization people are making unauthorized risk decisions can be critical if it's occurring around key assets. From a strategic perspective, this indicates that executive management may need to reinforce its position on compliance and risk-taking, or terminate some bad apples. Regardless, keeping tabs on how often personnel are making decisions they aren't authorized to make is pretty important. Also, if people know this is considered a KPI they are likely to be especially careful not to cross the line. To do this effectively does require very clear guidance on who is authorized to approve what.

Analysis quality Metrics regarding the quality of risk analysis are primarily strategic in nature, although they can have operational risk implications when risk decisions are being made regarding key assets. Note that this metric may be one of those that only qualifies as "key" until an organization has become comfortable that it is consistently being done appropriately. For most organizations today, we'd argue that is not the case.

The bottom line for KRIs and KPIs are that they are just the subset of the overall metrics we discussed earlier, focused on those parts of the landscape that we need to pay the closest attention to.

Thresholds

It may come to pass that some KRI or KPI metric has changed sufficiently that we need to do something about it or at least consider doing something about it. The notion of "changed sufficiently" (an alerting threshold, or trigger) is another parameter that has to be established. Most of the KRI/KPI thresholds we encounter are somewhat arbitrarily chosen. By that we mean when we ask people to explain why a certain threshold was chosen, the answers tend to be the equivalent of, "Because it seemed about right." Actually, this is neither surprising nor necessarily bad because at the end of the day these thresholds are mostly about comfort levels—i.e., the point at which stakeholders are worried enough about an issue that they want to be prompted to decision or action. That said, if an organization has set an explicit risk appetite it can more effectively gauge the relevance of changes in KRI's and KPI's and thus calibrate its comfort levels.

DASHBOARDS

You may have noticed that we haven't once uttered the "D" word in this chapter. That isn't because we are "saving the best for last" or because we believe dashboards are inherently bad. No, we've waited until now because dashboards are simply tools for effectively and efficiently communicating the kinds of things we've been discussing throughout this book and especially in this Chapter. In fact, we would argue that you can't effectively leverage dashboards unless you have a firm grasp on what we've covered above. Otherwise, what you can end up with is a bunch of charts and graphs that have limited utility and a low signal to noise ratio. Because there are other good references available on dashboards and data visualization this will be a small section. Besides, we think we've already armed you with much of the information you need to use dashboards well.

Dashboard content

Dashboards should be designed to meet specific information needs of specific audiences. That being the case, your first steps are to identify those audiences and their information needs. Not coincidentally, this aligns well with our discussion regarding KRIs and KPIs. That isn't to say that dashboards should be limited to KRIs and KPIs, but that's where we would start. This especially makes sense if dashboards are supposed to provide fast and simple access to your most important information. So if you know what your KRIs and KPIs are, and what decisions you expect to drive using the dashboard, then knowing what to include in your dashboards is a piece of cake.

TALKING ABOUT RISK

One of the challenges today is that virtually every information security tool seems to come with its own dashboard. As a result, you end up with a bunch of different dashboards, each containing specialized information regarding threat conditions, control conditions, assets, etc. What is missing is the overarching view—the one dashboard to rule them all—that takes all that disparate information and translates it into a single meaningful source of intelligence. Some of the GRC products are trying to play that role, and we're beginning to see movement in this direction with other information security products, but from what we've encountered so far there is a lot of opportunity for improvement in this space.

With regard to a dashboard's look and feel, as we have mentioned above, less is more. By that we mean that a dashboard should be clear and concise and present data in an uncluttered fashion. We are big fans of Dr. Edward Tufte and similar data visualization experts who advocate clean, simple, and intuitive data visualization. 3D charts and lots of busy-ness tend to obscure information rather than make it easier to digest.

Determining whether a metric should be displayed as a bar chart, trend line, spark line, or table should be driven by the nature of the metric and the preferences of the decision-makers who will be using the dashboard. Make no mistake: their preferences matter. Our experience has been that there can be a fair amount of trial and error that takes place before you find the ideal dashboard format for some decision-makers. A helpful shortcut can be to get your hands on dashboards they already use and rely on. Aligning your style to those can streamline the process of acceptance and adoption. Certainly don't assume that they'll accept with open arms any old batch of charts and tables you put in front of them.

TALKING ABOUT RISK

The charts and graphs we generate rarely use multiple colors, and we prefer to reserve red, green, and yellow for those instances where there is a very specific need or purpose. The reason we try to avoid using these colors is because people too easily infer "goodness" or "badness" (or "ho-hum" in the case of yellow) from them. Data should convey meaning on its own. Having said that, if an organization explicitly defines thresholds that delineate levels of concern for a specific metric and want at-a-glance recognition of a particular condition that may need a decision (like in a dashboard), then that is a great time to use these colors.

SUMMARY

We have covered a lot of ground in this chapter and we could have, quite literally, made it a book unto itself (foreshadowing perhaps?). Regardless, even though we haven't gone into great depth on individual metrics or provide as many examples and how-to's as we'd have liked, we hope we have armed you with new insights and clarification regarding information security and risk management metrics. If organizations adopt the GQM framework we've outlined (or some derivative of it) and are thus better able to manage risk more cost-effectively through its metrics, then we'll consider the chapter a success.

There is one last point we would like to make that may seem obvious, but we'll make it anyway. Implementing a metrics program based on what has been described in this chapter might seem overwhelming. That being the case, don't try to eat the elephant all at once. Think about your organization and where it might benefit most, metrics-wise, and start there. Then evolve the program over time as success builds and as you overcome the inevitable hurdles you will encounter. Becoming a metrics-based organization does not happen overnight.

Implementing Risk Management

OVERVIEW

> *"That risk is high risk."*
> **(Lots of people say this.)**

As we said earlier, your organization already does risk management in some fashion, so this chapter is intended to help you identify where your organization operates on a risk management maturity continuum, as well as help you identify opportunities to evolve your organization along that continuum. We attempt to do this in a few ways, by:

- Providing a maturity model for the implicit versus explicit component of risk management. If you're familiar with capability maturity models (CMMs) this will be comfortable territory.
- Introducing you to company X, a hypothetical organization we'll use to illustrate some examples of what it can look like to evolve along the maturity continuum.
- Sharing (at last) our root cause analysis process, which can be very helpful in getting out and staying out of risk management groundhog day.
- Revisiting one of the most important metrics there is and discussing some important considerations that have to be recognized before placing too much faith in the numbers.
- Briefly discussing third-party risk management—one of everybody's favorite topics.
- Discussing growth opportunities we see in many organizations—specifically, regarding the use of governance, risks, and compliance (GRC) products and standards frameworks.
- We have also included a very brief section related to risk measurement ethics.

Of course, not all of the maturity changes require high degrees of explicitness. In some cases, there are clear opportunities to mature while staying primarily implicit in your approach. The bottom line is that every organization will have its own needs when it comes to risk management and we aren't here to dictate the "right" approach for any organization, or any professional for that matter. We're just sharing what we have found to be useful to us in hopes that some of it will be useful to you.

Assuming you've found tidbits of useful information in the earlier chapters, all the concepts, principles, and frameworks in the world would not amount to squat if you don't or won't use them. We want this chapter to make it easier for you to apply what we've covered in the last three chapters to whatever level of maturity fits your needs. As much as possible, we want to provide answers to the question "Where do I start?"

A FAIR-BASED RISK MANAGEMENT MATURITY MODEL

If you're going on a journey, it's a good idea to have a roadmap to help you know where you have been, where you are, where you want to go, and the paths you can take to get there. This chapter is intended to offer an example of the journey from implicit risk management to explicit risk management. This map will take the form of a CMM that models maturity based on the risk management principles described in the previous two chapters. Along the way, we'll also share examples of when performing FAIR risk analyses can make a significant difference in managing risk cost effectively. We'll keep the version of CMM described in this book pretty high-level for two reasons: (1) because to treat this deeply would require many more pages, and (2) it only needs to be a starting point.

The context for the maturity levels in this version of the model is constrained to the probability of decisions within the organization resulting in good risk management. In other words, organizations at lower levels of maturity should have reduced odds of cost-effectively achieving and maintaining the risk appetite of their senior executives. That doesn't mean it can't happen at lower levels of maturity; the odds are just stacked against that happening. Conversely, organizations at higher levels of maturity should have better odds of being cost-effective in their management of risk.

Each maturity level is defined by the condition of the following elements:

*   Terminology
*   Risk concepts
*   Visibility
*   Analysis
*   Decision-maker authority
*   Policies
*   Risk appetite

As with all CMMs, no organization is likely to operate entirely in one level of the model, but instead will have characteristics that span two or more levels. In other words, most organizations will have strengths and weaknesses that are reflected as different levels of maturity in different aspects of the model.

THE LEVELS

Like most CMMs, this one has five levels, with the first level representing the lowest maturity level. With the exception of the first level, the names of these levels will be different from what you might be used to seeing in other CMMs. This was done in order to align with the concept of a continuum related to implicit and explicit risk management. High-level descriptions for each level of the model are described below. Please note that the model shared here is intended to simply illustrate a maturity continuum for risk management decision making. A more complete and refined version will be available on the resources page of the CXOWARE website.

Level 1—chaotic

At this level, decision-making is largely a free-for-all, and based almost solely on intuition and experience. Authority for decision-making is not defined. Decisions themselves are inconsistent and often not aligned with executive leadership needs or expectations. No key risk indicator (KRIs) or key performance indicators (KPIs) have been defined.

Level 2—implicit

Decision-making is primarily guided by rote adherence to policies and standards that may (or may not) roughly align with leadership needs and expectations. Information provided to decision-makers is almost invariably arrived at superficially and very often doesn't stand up to scrutiny. Decision-making roles and responsibilities are unclear and it is common for personnel to make decisions outside of what should be their level of authority. A risk severity scale may have been defined, but the levels of severity are described purely qualitatively. KRIs and KPIs may exist but their relevance from a level of risk perspective is questionable. Foundational risk terminology is used inconsistently. The understanding of risk concepts is superficial or inconsistent.

Level 3—early explicit

Foundational terminology is standardized within the organization and decision-making is supported by information that is more up-to-date and complete. Visibility data is periodically updated. Analyses performed to support decisions are more robust and defensible. Decision-maker authority and accountability are defined but not always strictly adhered to. High-level policy reviews are performed with executive management. A risk severity scale for the organization has been defined that includes quantitative ranges. KRIs and KPIs are defined, and the risk relevance of KRIs is established.

Level 4—mature explicit

Visibility quality is specifically focused on as part of the risk management program. As a result, it is kept up-to-date and the data are actively used in risk analyses. Aggregate views of the organization's risk are developed and risk appetite is set quantitatively against the aggregate view. Risk management policy benefits and burdens are thoroughly reviewed with executive management. Strategic risk management prioritization and solution selection leverages quantitative cost/benefit analyses, KRIs and KPIs are defined, and the risk relevance of both KRIs and KPIs is established.

Level 5—purely explicit

Strategic and operational risk decisions, including policies, prioritization, and solution selection, are evaluated and driven by their effect on the organization's risk posture relative to its risk appetite. KRIs and KPIs are tied to their effect on the organization's position relative to its risk appetite. The level of risk landscape visibility is measured and maintained to support well-informed decision-making.

GAUGING YOUR ORGANIZATION

The questions that follow will provide a way to gauge where your organization stands on this maturity continuum. When none of the choices provide an exact fit for your organization, choose the closest one. If you aren't sure where your organization stands, take your best guess. Nobody is grading this but you.

Terminology

Which of the following describes your organization's use of risk-related terminology?

1. No standard nomenclature has been defined or adopted. If you ask six people in the information security or risk management organization to define foundational terms, you will likely receive different answers.
2. A standard nomenclature has been defined or adopted. If you ask six people in the information security or risk management organization to define foundational terms, you are likely to get reasonably consistent answers.
2. A standard nomenclature has been defined or adopted and personnel are well grounded in its use. If you ask six people in the information security or risk management organization to define foundational terms you will get consistent answers.

Risk concepts

Which of the following describes the level of understanding within your organization on risk-related concepts, like probability versus possibility, accuracy versus precision, and subjectivity versus objectivity?

1. There is an inconsistent level of understanding regarding these concepts among members of the organization. You may get blank stares from some members of the organization if they're asked to explain or apply these concepts.
2. Members of the organization have a clear understanding of these concepts but may be inconsistent in how they apply them.
3. Members of the organization have a clear understanding of these concepts and apply them consistently.

Visibility

Which of the following describe the condition of your organization's risk landscape visibility?

1. The concept of risk landscape visibility is foreign to the organization in any real sense. No active effort is made to maintain data regarding assets, threats, or controls.
2. An asset inventory exists but is not kept up-to-date. The value and/or liability associated with assets are usually not identified. The role of visibility as a key component of risk management is not a distinct element in the risk management program. Threat data may be acquired and used for parts of the landscape (e.g., viruses), but no formal effort is made to define threat data needs for the risk management

program. Control conditions are tested and reported in parts of the organization but no effort is made to develop an overarching view of the control landscape.

3. An asset inventory exists and is relatively up-to-date. The assets representing significant value/liability have been identified. The need to manage visibility as part of the risk management program is recognized. Preliminary visibility estimates have been made and initiatives developed to close gaps to maintain acceptable levels of visibility once they have been achieved. Risk analyses are beginning to leverage the benefits of better data.

4. Risk landscape visibility is an integral part of the risk management program and is considered a strategic KPI. Processes are in place to maintain target levels of visibility. Risk analyses regularly rely on current asset, control, and threat data.

Analysis

Which of the following describes the type of analysis performed on risk issues?

1. No analysis is done. All risk ratings are based solely on a single subject matter expert's estimate. No rationale is documented.

2. Analysis is performed using a defined qualitative method, perhaps using ordinal scales and a rudimentary formula (e.g., threat x vulnerability x impact). Rationale may or may not be provided. Risk ratings may not explicitly have included control conditions, impact, or threat levels.

3. Analysis is based on control conditions, threat levels, and loss magnitude factors, and that supports quantitative measurement and reporting of asset-level risk conditions. Analysis results are expressed in financial terms or in qualitative terms based on a severity scale for the organization. Rationale for analyses is documented.

4. All of the capabilities in the choice above exist in the organization. In addition, an approximate aggregate view of the organization's risk is established. The risk-related effects of variance management conditions are also measured and reported in financial terms (e.g., the loss exposure associated with a systemically broken change management process).

5. In addition to the capabilities described in the third and fourth choices above, the organization is able to quantify the effects of decision-making deficiencies (e.g., the loss exposure associated with poor risk analysis).

Decision authority

Which of the following describes how your organization manages risk decision-making authority?

1. No decision-making roles, responsibilities, or limitations are defined.

2. Unclear or inconsistent definitions exist regarding roles or responsibilities. It is not unusual for personnel to make decisions outside of what should be their authority.

3. Clear definitions exist for risk decision-making roles and responsibilities. It is unusual for personnel to make decisions outside of their authority.

4. Clear definitions exist for risk-taking authority based on levels of risk. These definitions include how much risk may be taken without higher approvals.

Risk appetite definition

Which of the following describes your organization's definition of its risk appetite?

1. Risk appetite has not been defined for the organization.
2. A qualitative risk scale has been defined for the organization and/or an overarching qualitative statement has been made (e.g., "The organization has a moderate-to-low appetite for risk").
3. Quantitative scales for risk severity have been defined for the organization.
4. The organization's aggregate risk appetite has been defined.

Policies

Which of the following describes the level of alignment between your organization's information security policies and executive management?

1. Information security policies were adopted without management involvement or review.
2. Executive management has signed-off on the policies but likely had little or no understanding of how those policies affect the organization's risk.
3. Policies have been reviewed with management who are believed to have a reasonable understanding of why the policies are necessary.
4. Policies were carefully reviewed with management, including a high-level discussion of their risk-related benefits and anticipated burden.
5. Policies are defined to achieve and maintain the organization's risk appetite.

In light of having read this book and answered the questions above, ask yourself if you have a better understanding of how well your organization is managing risk at least from a decision-making perspective. Has this given you ideas for relatively simple changes your organization could make to begin moving up the continuum?

If your organization is immature or inconsistent in foundational risk terminology and concepts, then there's little hope that it can make its way very far up the list. That said, an organization doesn't have to do quantitative analysis in order to gain huge value from good risk landscape visibility. For that matter, just improving the use and understanding of terminology and concepts can bring significant benefit to an organization that otherwise could care less about quantitative analysis. Similarly, tremendous benefits will be realized by organizations that have the opportunity to really sit down with management to review the benefits and burden of information security policies. The point is, you can go a long way without ever touching a program evaluation and review technique (PERT) distribution or Monte Carlo function. That said, as we will see in the following section numbers can make a huge difference.

A RUNNING START

Over the years, we've had the opportunity to consult with a number of organizations as they worked to improve the maturity of their risk management functions. We've been able to support them as they stretch and grow into managing risk in a quantitative fashion and adopting the FAIR frameworks and methods. However, in working with these organizations, we have identified several themes that we felt would be beneficial to the reader as they endeavor to implement FAIR in their own companies. As a result, we've developed the following composite narrative (based on many real-world examples) that will hopefully help you gain an understanding of how an implementation process may unfold in your organization.

Let's imagine that we are the new chief information security officer (CISO) of company X, a reasonably large organization whose leadership believes information security is important but, like most companies, has historically managed risk from checklists and instinct rather than from metrics. In other words, through largely implicit risk management. As a new CISO, we have the opportunity to take stock of what is working and what isn't working, put together a new strategy, and make some changes. Although we've operated in a largely qualitative mode for years, we just read a very cool book on something called FAIR. As the new CISO, we're also expected to make changes so this seems like the ideal time to kick the proverbial quantitative tires. The following is the story of how that transition took place.

Step one—where do we stand?

The book on FAIR had a risk management maturity model in it that seemed to make a certain amount of sense, so the first step we took was to answer the seven questions it posed to see where our organization fell. The results were mixed. We were decent in a couple of things (policies and decision authority), but the organization appeared to be relatively immature overall. Not everyone on the team liked the model though. A couple of people thought it was too strongly biased toward a quantitative view. We discussed it as a team and came to the conclusion that it was indeed biased, but that this should be expected given how it defined risk management. Because we were going to try to become more quantitatively driven as an organization, it made sense to gauge ourselves on a scale of quantitative maturity. We could always choose to stop anywhere along the scale if we found that becoming more quantitative didn't make sense. Besides, some of the improvement opportunities didn't appear to require quantitative analysis. There was no debate, however, that the model and the questions it asked had identified some important opportunities for improvement.

One other thing became clear at this point—not everyone on the team was singing from the same sheet of music, terminology or concept-wise. Just discussing risk and the model became frustrating because nobody else on the team had read the book. We could either tell everyone on the team to read the book (like that would ever happen) or we could bring someone in to train us.

Step two—getting on the same page

We looked into the training options for the team, and there were a few. We could have someone come onsite to train us or have team members take one of the various online training courses. We discovered there was a third option too, and that was to have a FAIR analysis performed by qualified consultants, during which our team would receive a mix of classroom and on-the-job training. We liked this third option because it fit well into some of our other plans. A couple of the team members did buy and read copies of the book (dear reader, you knew we couldn't let that go!), and one of them even opted to take the online training as well because they wanted to get a jumpstart. We found out later that what they really wanted was to become the team's internal subject matter expert on FAIR, which we ultimately indulged. We weren't all on the same page yet, but we had recognized the need and had a plan.

Step three—where do we really stand?

Rather than start with a purely FAIR analysis though, we struck a balance between old school and new school. We brought in an external firm that had solid expertise in information security assessments and they performed a thorough, but traditional, checklist assessment. As expected, their results included a number of "high risk" findings, a lot of "medium risk" findings, and some "low risk" findings. We thanked them very much for their service and sent them on their way.

What they uncovered, of course, were control deficiencies. Everything from an inadequate asset inventory, to inconsistent change control, to users with administrative privileges on their workstations, to unpatched systems, and the list goes on. The risk ratings they assigned to these deficiencies were based on their experience and expertise, but no formal analysis or data were applied.

Our next step was to bring in some qualified FAIR consultants. This is where it got interesting, as follows:

- The first thing they did was provide a half-day workshop on FAIR concepts, terminology, and methods so that we would all be on the same page when speaking with one another. We made sure someone from Internal Audit attended as well because their buy-in would be critical. After the workshop, Internal Audit decided they wanted someone from their group to be closely involved in the analysis both to watch over it (that is their job, after all) and to learn from it. The workshop was eye-opening but not without its challenges. Initially, not everyone in the room was happy with having to learn new ways of thinking about what we do as a profession, and one person in particular was put off by the implication that our previous approaches were deficient in some manner. Several people expressed doubts about being able to find the necessary data to do this kind of analysis. Because I had already stuck my neck out there by kicking this engagement off, we were committed to making a go of it. If it turned out poorly, it was going to fall on me. The team members who had openly expressed doubts were good with that.

- The consultants then helped us scope a set of loss scenarios where the deficiencies identified in the traditional assessment were relevant. With those defined, we did some very quick-and-dirty FAIR analyses to triage which scenarios—and, thus, which deficiencies in our portfolio of findings—were most significant. These analyses simply leveraged the ontology and some critical thinking to identify clear differentiators between higher risk scenarios and lower risk scenarios. This was completed in just a few days. It also served as on-the-job training in FAIR for our team, which we viewed as a bonus. To our surprise, it was relatively quick, painless, and qualitative, which kind of surprised us. It also helped the skeptics get a little more on board with the approach overall. It was hard to argue with the underlying logic of the model.

- Through this exercise we found that several of the "high risk" findings from the traditional assessment did not appear to be high risk. Not even close. We viewed that to be a significant victory from a prioritization perspective. It also made us wonder whether some of the medium findings and maybe even low findings might in fact be "high risk findings" in disguise. To calm nerves, we spent another 2 days scouring the medium and low findings for anything that looked suspicious. The good news? We only found one medium that appeared marginally worthy of being added to the high-risk category.

- From this, we took the most significant scenarios and did in-depth FAIR analyses to quantitatively flesh-out the loss exposure those issues represented. This required more work (three relatively intense weeks, in fact) but we found that the more analyses we did, the faster it went. It helped that a lot of the data we used in the earlier scenarios turned out to be reusable in later scenarios. By this time, most of the team members were becoming comfortable with performing this type of analysis, and were doing them much faster. A couple of the members of the team still struggled with scoping and analysis though. This demonstrated that not everybody acclimates well to this kind of analysis, so we adjusted their roles in order to emphasize their strengths and not try to shoehorn them into doing something that wasn't a good fit.

- This exercise found that the top five scenarios made up just over 85% of the overall total loss exposure. The scenarios that made up the other 15% were still relevant, but, in terms of prioritization, it no longer felt like we were faced with a guessing game.

- In order to evaluate what those analyses realistically represented in terms of aggregate loss exposure, we used a FAIR-based software application to develop joint probability distributions. It also used sensitivity analysis to identify which parts of our risk landscape were most sensitive to change in ways that could hurt or help us, and where higher quality data was most important. This kind of blew our minds because it validated some intuitions we'd had for a long time about things the organization needed to focus on.

- Based on this information, we identified not only which scenarios (and, thus, which deficiencies) were driving the most risk into our landscape, but we also had a first partial (but significant) picture of the aggregate information security risk picture—in financial terms. Another bonus was that we identified things we could do to improve some of the metrics to which the analysis was most sensitive.

- Through the sensitivity analyses and some FAIR-based root cause analyses, we were able to identify what appeared to be our most cost-effective mitigation options. A small number of these were potentially expensive "spot fixes" that required new technology (e.g., logging), while most were more variance and decision-management in nature, including some relatively simple policy and process changes.

- With this in hand, we went to our boss (the chief operating officer) who was cautiously enthused but skeptical. He had known we were planning to do this (and was willing to give the new CISO enough rope to try), but he was still a bit concerned about the credibility of the models and especially the numbers. We explained again the underlying FAIR framework—the model. In his eyes, it didn't hurt that it was also an industry standard and that an industry analyst report on FAIR had been favorable. We also reiterated how we used calibration methods to improve the estimates that went into the model, how we used hard data where we had it, and the fact that the loss estimates came from a combination of incidents the organization had previously experienced, industry data, and the organization's own business subject matter experts (the legal team, marketing and sales, the chief financial officer's office, etc.). Besides, the vice president of Enterprise Risk Management had seen the work in progress and given it a thumbs-up. This calmed his doubts.

So what now? How could we use what had been accomplished from a metrics and analytics perspective?

Given that risk decisions should, in some way, take into account senior executive risk appetite, we had to get their impression of whether the aggregate level of loss exposure resulting from the analysis was acceptable and, if not, how far off it seemed. As it turned out, senior executive reactions were a mixed bag. A couple of them were initially skeptical about how the numbers were arrived at and pushed us hard to defend them. We had anticipated this though, and were prepared. The FAIR consultants sat in the corner of the room to bail us out if need be, but that didn't turn out to be necessary. Other executives accepted the approach at face value. At the end of the conversation though, they all agreed that the process had substantial rigor, in fact, far more rigor than they had ever seen before, and that the level of exposure was unquestionably greater than they wanted it to be, by a fair margin. One of them even commented that for the first time he could wrap his head around the information security problem. This, combined with the cost-benefit analyses we'd done on the various remediation options made for a relatively straight-forward discussion about what our priorities should be, and what resources were going to be required.

Was this approach perfect? Certainly not. Did the aggregate loss exposure results include every possible scenario? No. Was it more effective than the initial third-party risk assessment that would otherwise have driven priorities and funding? That's a rhetorical question.

TALKING ABOUT RISK

There are people in the industry who feel strongly that what we described above is misguided and doomed to failure because it is impossible to:

- Identify all of the vulnerabilities,
- Identify all of the threats,
- Capture all of the losses that might result, or
- Capture all of the mitigation costs.
  They're right about the fact that perfect data is a pipe dream. Our question for them is "How are they making decisions today?" or, put another way, "Compared to what?" Either:
- They have a direct line to some entity who provides them with perfect information (Google is good, but it's not that good), or

- They make their decisions based on the flip of a coin or some other random selection process, or
- Their decisions are based on the same information everybody else operates from.

We suspect it's the third one. But by their logic (i.e., that the absence of perfect data precludes an improved decision) they would be equally happy to put a loaded semi-automatic pistol to their head as they would a revolver with a single bullet in one of the six cylinders. For all they know, the bullet in the semi-automatic could be a dud or its firing mechanism could be broken, either of which would clearly make that gun the better choice for them. But they don't know that, their data is imperfect. Or maybe the next cylinder in the revolver is the one with the bullet and it doesn't matter which gun they choose. Regardless, we'd bet serious money that they'll choose the six-cylinder handgun with an expectation that it represents better odds. In doing so they are measuring the conditions as they know them, imperfectly, and attempting to manage future outcomes (risk management). They aren't predicting anything; they're placing a bet. There's a subtle but critical difference that they seem to miss.

Here is the kicker though, their alternative supposedly avoids the work and messiness of risk management. Yep, just always do exactly what the policy says should be done. This ignores, however, the day-to-day realities in an organization—you have to prioritize. Prioritization involves choice; choice involves one or more comparisons; and every comparison involves measurement. At least on this planet. You can apply some rigor to the process of measurement in an attempt to reduce your uncertainty and, thus, improve the odds of having better outcomes (with no guarantees), you can flip a coin, or you can shoot from the hip. A decision/choice/comparison/measurement will be made regardless.

So the question doesn't boil down to whether or not decisions are made using imperfect data, because one of the few things we can be pretty certain of in life is imperfect data. What it boils down to is how good you are at acquiring data and how well you use the data you have.

So which metrics came into play in the risk assessment effort? Here is a partial list, in no particular order:

- The third-party assessment results (a useful source of data regarding control deficiencies).
- Policy compliance data (from our friendly neighborhood audit colleagues).
- The annual access review process.
- Threat event frequency (TEF) data from both internal logs and a security information and event management (SIEM) service provider.
- System configuration reviews, which provided variance data.
- The asset inventory (even as flawed as it was, it was still useful).
- Vulnerability scan data.
- Anti-virus application data.
- FAIR root cause analysis results.
- Visibility analyses.
- Change control records.
- Incident documentation.
- Industry loss data.
- Data loss prevention tool data.
- A threat intelligence service provider anxious to win our business provided some mobile device security research data at no charge. That gamble is likely to pay off for them, by the way.

Any initial concern of not having enough data to do quantitative analysis was a non-issue by now. There was clearly a lot of room for improvement data-wise, but the results spoke for themselves. In terms of where the organization stood from a maturity perspective, we had moved from an overall rating of "2" to "3." At least as importantly, we had learned a ton and had a different kind of dialogue taking place with management.

Step four—carrying it forward

We had managed an initial pass at establishing risk appetite, refining policy, prioritizing our efforts (for now), and allocating resources. We also had a FAIR tool that took care of a lot of the work in maintaining our risk data. It feels good, but it was only a start. The world does not hold still until next year's risk assessment exercise.

- Within days, one of our KRIs turned red when we received notice that a new zero-day exploit was in the wild. Needless to say, we had to understand as quickly as possible what our exposure was and how aggressively we needed to respond. Reusing some of the metrics from the earlier analyses, we were able to do a rapid FAIR analysis and come to the conclusion that the level of risk, this time, was not substantial enough to put all hands on deck for an emergency patching exercise (which could break some business applications on the desktops, particularly the older desktops). Some changes were made, however, to network logging to provide more rapid detection of the kind of activity this exploit would generate. Of course, management wanted assurance, so we provided a one-page summary of the analysis and steps taken to set their minds at ease.
- Within the next several weeks, our internal audit colleagues completed their review of the organization's financial systems environment as part of the ongoing Sarbanes-Oxley (SOX) compliance effort. Of particular interest to the auditors was segregation of duties, as that had been a problem in the past. It still was. Apparently there were still some developers and system administrators who had access that could allow them to manipulate data used in financial reporting. The good news was that the auditors had been part of the earlier engagement and took a FAIR-based view of the problem. As a result, they worked with us to do a risk analysis on this issue. Part of that analysis included leveraging the logging that had been implemented after the last SOX audit fiasco. This allowed us to demonstrate that illicit activities had not taken place via these privileges (no threat events) and it gave us an opportunity to really think critically about the seriousness of the issue. A root cause analysis regarding why this continued to be a problem identified that there were practical limitations in what access could be excluded from these personnel. As a result, all things considered, the decision was made to make a policy change that recognized these practical business constraints and allow this access.
- Not long after that, one of the projects spun-up from the earlier strategic planning exercise identified a subsidiary organization that had been overlooked in the initial risk assessment. It was also discovered that this subsidiary had unfettered connectivity to the organization's network core. The silver lining was that this whole episode helped us fill gaps in our visibility data, with more gap filling

to be accomplished as network traffic analysis took place, and a risk assessment of the subsidiary took place to see how much additional risk it represented and whether our priorities needed to change. Equally as important, a root cause analysis was performed on this variance to discover how the network connection had eluded us in the first place. The results of this analysis allowed us to improve our processes and metrics for detecting when these kinds of network architecture changes take place.

- A couple of months later, we recognized that we were experiencing a sharp increase in targeted attacks against our primary online transaction Website. Not only that, but the level of sophistication used in the attacks appeared to have increased. A quick review of the most recent vulnerability analysis results for the systems under attack showed that there were some exploitable weaknesses in the web application itself, but that the nature of the attacks appeared to be focused on a different category of vulnerability. This could change at any time, obviously. Because the source of the attacks was not consistent, we couldn't simply block a set of internet provider addresses. Consequently, we worked with the application development management team to accelerate the timeline for remediation. Based on our data and analysis, they made it a top priority. We also adjusted logging and monitoring to identify and immediately alert if the attacks changed in a dangerous direction and added this to our KRIs.

- Soon after the increase in targeted attacks was recognized, we discovered that a set of customer statements had been mailed to the wrong customers because of a malfunctioning piece of equipment. In all, about 1300 customers were affected; not catastrophic, but painful nonetheless. The legal department had to be engaged to help ensure that all of the various state privacy regulations were appropriately accounted for in our response. Customer notifications also had to be sent, credit monitoring offered, and the helpdesk encountered a short period of increased call volume. We also had to inform the regulators and help them become comfortable that we had appropriately identified the cause of the event and minimized the effect on customers.

The way some of this played out may not sound like quantitative analysis and metrics were leveraged significantly or that much differently than you do today. However, let's take a closer look.

Zero day scenario

The fact that we used FAIR to understand how much risk the new zero-day exploit represented is an obvious use of quantitative methods and data. Although the subject matter experts in our organization may have intuitively looked at the situation and come to the same conclusion about the relatively low level of risk it represented, the advantage FAIR presented was the rigor that inherently goes into an analysis (i.e., a lower probability for things to be overlooked and/or biases introduced). Absent this rigor, our experience has been there is a greater likelihood for nervousness to prevail and unnecessary work to be introduced.

SOX scenario

FAIR analysis made a significant difference in how this played out versus the previous time this had been a SOX finding. In the previous instance, we had argued tooth and nail that the exposure was small, but to no avail. It was a SOX control deficiency so it was considered high risk. In this case, we had a rational discussion about the factors, leveraged some data, and made a decision with which everyone was comfortable. Note that if Internal Audit had not been involved in the FAIR project we likely would have had some tough discussions to get through regarding this finding. We might have won the debate based on the strength of our logic—or not. Logic does not always carry the day. This is why it is so helpful to include other stakeholders when implementing FAIR.

Subsidiary scenario

This is an interesting one because it leverages visibility metrics. Specifically, earlier estimates of the organization's visibility into systems, networks, and information had not included the existence of the subsidiary. That said, those earlier estimates had reflected the fact that visibility data regarding the network architecture was sparse and that there could be things like an unidentified subsidiary hiding in the shadows. That's one of the big reasons why a visibility project was spun-up after the initial assessment was done—to discover this sort of skeleton in the closet. This discovery not only provided additional visibility data but also led to root cause analyses that allowed us to improve our processes, which improved future visibility and reduced future variance.

Attack scenario

Having good metrics allowed us to distinguish the increase in attacks, and having metrics regarding normal levels of attack sophistication allowed us to recognize the change in what was being thrown at us. Being able to combine this information with our metrics regarding the deficiencies in the applications meant that we could get management support to take prudent measures without accusations of crying wolf.

Mis-mailing scenario

This one was almost purely about gathering, rather than leveraging, metrics. Loss events, as unfortunate as they may be, are a marvelous and typically poorly leveraged opportunity to better understand what happens when things go wrong. This becomes incredibly valuable as input to future analyses and decisions. By the way, one opportunity we did not mention in the scenario description is the fact that we could track the 1300 affected customers over time to see whether they, as a population, had a higher level of churn than other customers. In fact, if we are incredibly unlucky as an organization, we might at some point have to notify a subset of these customers of a second similar event. If that were to occur, it would be a marvelous opportunity to examine how much less forgiving customers are from multiple events.

Step five—integration

In order to make FAIR an integral part of how our organization manages risk, we had to find ways to bake it into existing processes as well as ways to better leverage existing capabilities within the context of improved risk management. A few things we did were especially important:

- We identified a staff member to be our internal FAIR expert. It isn't that we don't like consultants; we just want someone we can turn to internally for day-to-day issues. We would still leverage external expertise when the need arises.
- We had our internal expert qualified as a FAIR trainer so that we could train newcomers to the team without paying for training.
- We established a peer review process for analyses of particular types and any time an analysis result was over a particular size.
- We established a FAIR-based triage process for audit findings, change management reviews, and project reviews. These triage assessments were quick-and-dirty, but improved our ability to do rapid analysis and not become a boat anchor to the business.
- We trained key stakeholders in making calibrated estimates. This helped people understand where the numbers were coming from and it made getting data from them easier when that need arose. One group in particular that benefited was the project management group.
- We provided short orientation sessions to key executives who might be basing decisions on FAIR analysis results. This helped them understand and become comfortable with the approach and enabled us to better tailor results to their needs and interests.
- We briefed our external auditors and the regulators. The regulators actually liked it right off the bat. The external auditors were more cautious, but after they had a chance to dig into it a bit they gave the thumbs up too.

We hope that these scenarios have helped reinforce the role of metrics and their value. Some of the examples were probably things you already would do and not think of as specifically risk-based or metrics driven, and that is partly our point. As a profession, we are already part way there. We just need to be more explicit and mature about it. You might find it worthwhile at this point to match these metrics against the goal question metric framework we provided earlier to see where each metric fit within the framework. You might also think of other metrics that could have been leveraged in these scenarios based on the framework.

We should also add that not every organization that has attempted to adopt FAIR has been wildly successful with it. In one case we are familiar with, the obstacle was a boss; the CISO thought quantitative results would be well received by executive management only to find that their immediate boss saw the world strictly through an ordinal lens. In another case, there were key stakeholders in the organization that had a strongly different personal view of risk and would not entertain an alternative regardless of how strong the arguments might be. In yet another case, the organization had some strong initial results from its use but its use petered off over time either because of a change in leadership that had their own view of the world or we also suspect there are those who tried to use it and simply decided they preferred the traditional approach. Over the years, we have learned a few things about adoption:

1. Change is not always easy, and adopting FAIR means change. In some cases, it may be better to take a gradual approach to adoption—starting with terminology and concepts, and applying formal analysis sparingly and behind the scenes. In other cases, especially with strong buy-in from a key executive, a running start like what we described above is more effective.
2. It is important to understand the culture of your organization. As much as possible, identify champions and obstacles for adoption. Partner with key stakeholders that will be champions and engage stakeholders that may represent obstacles (who may be peers or even influential people at lower rungs in the organization) in dialogue that finds ways for them to benefit from its use.
3. It can take time for FAIR to become baked into how an organization operates. If there is a change in leadership during this transition period, sometimes the new leader wants to do things their way and not deal with something they aren't familiar with. We get that. Whenever we step into a new leadership role, we prefer to operate with what is familiar to us.
4. People may believe in FAIR and want to use it but they just have not been provided the resources in terms of reference material or software. The Open Group's adoption of FAIR as a standard and the documentation they have developed to support their FAIR professional certification will help with this. Of course this book is intended to solve the problem of reference material definitively.

Even when the quantitative aspects of FAIR have not been successfully applied within organizations, we have consistently heard that the terminology, concepts, and ontology have continued to be helpful. That's at least a step in the right direction.

GOVERNANCE, RISKS, AND COMPLIANCE

These days, no book related to risk management would be complete without discussing GRC. To save some time, we're going to assume that you've had some exposure to GRC so we won't describe it in detail here. Our purpose is to discuss some ways organizations can improve the value they get from a GRC solution. Note that most of these improvements don't require quantitative analysis, although you are almost certain to get more value out of GRC if you go the extra mile.

ONE OUT OF THREE IS NOT GOOD

For years now, we've been hearing about the three promises of GRC solutions:

- That they would help us to more cost-effectively govern our risk landscape,
- Make better-informed risk decisions, and
- Maintain compliance with whatever standards or regulations the organization is subject to.

In this chapter, we'll share five reasons why many organizations are, at best, realizing only one of these objectives (the compliance objective). We'll also share some approaches that can help an organization better realize all three objectives and significantly improve the return on their GRC investments.

GRC SOLUTIONS IN A NUTSHELL

Generally speaking, GRC solutions provide the following features and functions:

- A place to document the "risks" an organization wants to measure and track (often referred to as a "risk register"),
- A place to identify any compliance requirements to which an organization is subjected,
- A place to document audit findings and other reported control deficiencies (sometimes called issues), and a way to associate those deficiencies to the organization's "risks,"
- A place to document and track compliance and remediation activities, as well as the stakeholders associated with those efforts,
- Reporting capabilities for the four bullets above, and
- Workflow capabilities to maximize efficiency in everything listed above.

This doesn't seem like rocket science, so how can we be failing to achieve the three GRC objectives? To understand this, we first need to look a little more closely at each of the objectives so that the problems we describe can be connected to how they affect the value of GRC.

Governance

Ultimately, leadership is expected to cost-effectively govern the organization's risk landscape. Accomplishing this requires setting and communicating expectations, overseeing and facilitating the achievement and maintenance of those expectations, and managing conditions that don't align with their expectations. GRC solutions are supposed to assist with this by providing a way to report where these expectations are and are not being met, within a meaningful business context.

The "R" in GRC

This objective is all about making better-informed risk decisions, which boils down to three things: (1) identifying "risks," (2) effectively rating and prioritizing "risks," and (3) making decisions about how to mitigate "risks" that are significant enough to warrant mitigation. (You'll understand shortly why we've put quotation marks around the word "risks.")

Compliance

Of the three objectives, compliance management is the simplest—at least on the surface. On the surface, compliance is simply a matter of identifying the relevant expectations (e.g., requirements defined by Basel, Payment Card Industry (PCI),

SOX, etc.), documenting and reporting on how the organization is (or is not) complying with those expectations, and tracking and reporting on activities to close any gaps. Most GRC products we've seen seem to do a pretty good job with these functions, which by itself is often of significant value. Chalk one up for the "C" in GRC—maybe. More on this shortly.

OPPORTUNITIES FOR IMPROVEMENT

A "risk" by any other name

Every GRC risk register implementation we've been exposed to is populated, sometimes to a large degree, with "risks" that aren't risks. What do we mean? Let's give you an example. Which of the following would be a legitimate entry in a risk register?

1. Failure to change smoke detector batteries.
2. Smoke detector batteries fail.
3. Building catches fire.

If you chose the last one, congratulations. Why? Well, the last entry is the only one that represents a loss event and, therefore, is the only one you can put a meaningful likelihood and impact estimate to. Unfortunately, much of what we see in GRC risk registers more closely resembles the first two entries—control deficiencies. Don't get us wrong—it is important to document control deficiencies but these should be recorded in a separate part of the GRC product, sometimes referred to as findings or issues (Note: if your GRC solution doesn't provide a way to differentiate between risk entries and control deficiencies, it is broken in a very fundamental way).

The bottom line is that being well informed about risk and making cost-effective risk mitigation decisions (the "R" in GRC), and effectively governing an organization's risk landscape ("G") cannot be achieved if the information those decisions are based on is inaccurate or misleading. For example, we have seen more than one GRC risk register populated with scores of control deficiencies (rather than loss event scenarios)—each with a likelihood and impact rating. When we asked people in the organization how they came up with these ratings, they often shrugged and said those are required fields for risk entries so they entered values that felt right. When we started probing to understand the assumptions and data underlying some of these entries, it became clear very quickly that many of them were nonsense. As a result, much of the risk information being used to inform executive management was fundamentally bad.

The solution to this problem can simply be a matter of reviewing the entries in the organization's GRC risk register and throwing out or refining any entry that does not represent a loss event. This can be challenging in some organizations though, because the notion that control deficiencies are "risks" can be pretty firmly ensconced and difficult to weed out. Once this weeding out is accomplished, what's left is to accurately set likelihood and impact ratings, which we'll discuss below.

TALKING ABOUT RISK

One of our pet peeves is to see the word risk in its plural form—"risks." Keep in mind that, from a FAIR perspective, risk is a derived value, which means a plural form just doesn't make any sense. Risk is a "how much" question and not a "how many" question. If the topic was profit rather than risk, you wouldn't ask "how many profits" nor would you list the profits in a profit register. In a "profit register" you would list the sources of profit, how much profit they are generating, and track the things that increase profit over time. In this way, the register would help you to understand how much profit you have and whether you are hitting your profit objectives. In order to be logically consistent, it should be the same way for risk. The "risks" in a risk register should actually be loss event scenarios, each with a loss exposure value based on likelihood (frequency) and impact. "Findings" within the GRC application would be the conditions within the organization (usually control deficiencies) that are contributing to how much loss exposure exists for each loss event scenario.

We have pretty much given up our naive dream of getting the broader risk management industry to change its ways regarding the use of the term "risks." It seems there is just way too much inertia on the issue. That being the case, all we ask is that if you use the term "risks" you use it as shorthand for "loss event scenarios."

How likely is likely?

If we asked someone to estimate the likelihood that our sun will become a white dwarf star (apparently it lacks the mass to go supernova), by most accounts, the only reasonable answer is "very high" (if not certain). Likewise, if the question is about the likelihood of a malware infection in an organization, the answer would almost have to be "very high" (if not certain) within many organizations because it is almost certain to happen eventually. The operative word being "eventually."

Simply stated, a likelihood estimate by itself is rarely very useful. In order to be useful, it has to be cast within the context of a timeframe (e.g., likelihood this year, in our lifetime, or whatever timeframe is relevant). Unfortunately, many of the likelihood scales we see in GRC implementations don't include a timeframe reference. As a result, there can be a lot of ambiguity and inconsistency in the likelihood values for risk entries, which severely affects the ability to effectively prioritize and report on risk. Without proper prioritization and reporting, effective governance and risk decision-making is a long shot, at best.

This is often the easiest of the problems to fix, as it should simply be a matter of redefining your likelihood scales to include a timeframe reference. Of course, once this has been done all of the entries in the GRC risk register will need to be reviewed to ensure that likelihood estimates are still appropriate.

Likelihood/impact incongruity

So, let's assume that your organization has either fixed or was not subject to the two problems we described above. Before you congratulate yourself too exuberantly you might want to have someone review the likelihood and impact estimates to ensure they are logically aligned with one another. An example might make this clearer.

Let's say that the event in question is personal injury in the workplace. Very often, a risk entry on this topic will have a likelihood estimate of "very high," reflecting the fact that people frequently suffer paper cuts, carpal tunnel, and similar injuries in the workplace. No problem with that. The problem occurs when the impact estimate for a risk entry reflects a worst-case outcome—an event very different from what the likelihood estimate is based on. In this instance, the worst-case outcome for personal injury is "death," which we assume would qualify for a "very high" or "critical" impact rating. Taking this "very high" likelihood rating and "very high" impact rating together, the logical inference is that people are frequently dying in the workplace. If this were true, it would just about have to be the most critical concern in the organization. Odds are though it's not even remotely accurate. The problem is, very often people gravitate toward the most common type of an event for the likelihood/frequency rating, and the worst-case outcome for the impact rating. Almost always, this grossly misrepresents the actual level of risk.

You may not think your organization would make mistakes as obvious as this, but you might be surprised. We see this frequently and it can obviously pose a huge problem in terms of effective prioritization and reporting. Sometimes, we'll see risk professionals "hedge" these situations by overriding a GRC product's programmatically derived risk rating and downgrading something like our example to "medium." Although this may be an improvement in terms of accuracy, the rationale are often not well documented and it shouldn't be necessary if sufficient thought went into the GRC implementation criteria in the first place.

GRC products almost exclusively provide ordinal rating scales for likelihood and impact. If you've gotten this far in the book, you know how severely limiting this is in terms of characterizing risk. It forces you to choose where along the likelihood and impact continuums your rating is going to come from, for example, the maximum or most likely. Whatever you choose, you need to make certain that the likelihood and impact ratings are aligned. For example, if you choose the maximum impact, you need to ensure that the frequency rating matches those maximum impact events.

By choosing just one point along the continuum, you decrease the quality of information about a scenario. Sometimes this doesn't make a material difference, and sometimes it does. Regardless, an organization should make a conscious decision about whether its likelihood and impact estimates are going to reflect worst-case or most-likely outcomes. This need to choose between worst-case or most-likely outcomes reflects a fundamental weakness associated with the simple qualitative scales used in almost all GRC implementations. A simple alternative is to have separate entries and ratings for the most likely scenarios and worst-case scenarios. An even more robust and useful alternative is, of course, to use distributions. Some organizations that have adopted FAIR add fields within their GRC tools for FAIR variables, including the PERT minimum, maximum, and most likely values, as well as a confidence rating. This allows them to import and export values into a spreadsheet or commercial FAIR application to run scenarios and capture results. By the way, at the time this book is being written, one of the major GRC vendors is in the process of licensing FAIR to integrate into their product, and similar conversations are taking place with another vendor.

What does "high" mean?

The fourth GRC challenge has to do with rating scale definitions. It isn't unusual to encounter impact scales where each qualitative rating (high, medium, low, 1, 2, 3, etc.) is described purely in other qualitative terms. For example:

High impact: Any outcome where significant damage occurs to the organization's finances or reputation.

In this example, we defined the qualitative term "high" with the qualitative term "significant." Generally, these kinds of descriptions are very open to interpretation, which results in inconsistent ratings and an inability to reliably prioritize risk.

A better description for high impact might be something like "losses exceeding $10,000,000 (or whatever threshold the business sets) from the effects of reduced market share, increased cost of capital, and/or reduced stock price." Clearly, the specific descriptions will vary based on the size of the organization, its capacity for loss, and management's risk appetite. At the end of the day though, rating scales have to be as meaningful and as descriptive as possible, otherwise input values are more likely to be inconsistent and inaccurate, and decisions are more likely to be misinformed.

Multiplying red times yellow

Last but not least, most people would laugh at the idea of multiplying red times yellow, yet that is exactly equivalent to multiplying 3 times 2 when the numbers are based on an ordinal scale. We don't need to get into the mathematical details of why this is a bad idea, but it is an incredibly common mistake in risk rating systems that often contribute to inaccurate assessments and poorly informed decisions.

TALKING ABOUT RISK

For a great read on the problems associated with doing math on ordinal scales, we suggest you read "*The Failure of Risk Management*" by Douglas Hubbard. In his book, Hubbard describes the reasons why this approach is worse than useless in many instances.

Obviously, the problems we've described above can negatively impact the quality of risk management in an organization. Perhaps not surprisingly, they can also affect compliance because the black-and-white veneer of compliance sits atop an underlying (and sometimes overlooked) need to prioritize compliance gaps and optimize gap mitigation choices. Consequently, if the "R" in an organization's GRC implementation is bad enough, the organization may be checking compliance boxes but it may not be addressing the most important gaps first, or optimizing its gap mitigation choices. When this is the case, an argument can be made that the organization is not fully realizing even the "C" in GRC.

We would also like to point out that the problems we are describing here are to some degree less a function of poorly designed GRC products and more a matter of the inconsistent and sometimes illogical use of nomenclature in our profession combined with organizations simply not giving enough thought to these kinds of risk management considerations. Although it's true that many (if not most) GRC products would benefit from refinements that better facilitate and guide a more mature implementation, their clientele have to set the bar higher before that's likely to happen. It is also crucial to recognize that GRC is a set of processes and not a technology. The technology simply facilitates the processes, and both the processes and technology must support the organization's risk management objectives, or else it's all wasted time, money, and energy.

TAKING GRC TO THE NEXT LEVEL

Organizations that have managed to avoid or fix the problems we've described above will almost undoubtedly be in a better place than most in terms of the value they get from GRC. We believe a thoughtfully designed, implemented, and managed GRC solution can live up to its promises. Achieving this requires that these solutions leverage more evolved methods to provide a much higher level of decision support. Maybe we're biased (of course we are, but that doesn't make us wrong), but GRC would be much more effective if it leveraged the concepts and models we discuss in this book.

RISK FRAMEWORKS

Whether you call them risk assessment frameworks or risk management frameworks, what they purport to do is provide a means for organizations to manage risk better. What we're talking about, of course, are those things we know and love that come from ISO, National Institute of Standards and Technology (NIST), Payment Card Industry (PCI), ISACA, and other such organizations. The International Organization for Standardization (ISO) 27000 series, NIST 800 series, Data Security Standard (DSS), and Control Objectives for Information and Relation Technology (COBIT) standards of the world. To a large degree, these frameworks do provide value in the sense that they provide structure and guidance that help organizations *implicitly* manage risk better. That said, there often are challenges associated with them too, which we'll discuss in this chapter so that you can be aware of and manage their effects. We will also discuss the relationship between FAIR and these frameworks because we often get the question about whether FAIR is intended to replace these frameworks or is complementary to them.

FRAMEWORK CHALLENGES

Before we get into the challenges, we want to reiterate that these frameworks are valuable. In fact, some of them are in many ways quite good. For example, these frameworks tend to be very useful for identifying basic risk management program elements that are missing or deficient. Where these frameworks are less useful are in helping the practitioner determine the significance of deficiencies. It comes back to that explicit thing again. They also tend to have gaps in coverage and very often are not well structured, at least from an efficiency perspective. What this boils down to is there's room for improvement, and that is where FAIR comes in.

A problem with measurement

Most of these frameworks spend very little time on the question of risk measurement. They all say it needs to be done, but, for the most part, they leave it up to the practitioner to figure out how, or they provide very superficial formulas. NIST is the exception to this. The risk analysis method described in NIST's 800-30 document follows a very logical process that should help analysts perform better, more consistent analyses. Clearly, a lot of thought and effort went into its development. That said, there are a few aspects of NIST's method where significant opportunities for improvement exist.

Overall likelihood

The manner in which the NIST method determines overall likelihood of an event results in inaccurate risk ratings in some instances. Specifically, the matrix it uses to combine the likelihood of threat event initiation or occurrence (TEF in FAIR terms) with the likelihood that threat events result in adverse impacts (vulnerability) overlooks a fundamental "law"—the overall likelihood of an adverse outcome cannot exceed the likelihood of the catalyst (threat) event occurring in the first place (see Figure 14.1). To make the point, let's look at an example. Let's say that you are trying to understand the risk associated with some malicious actor running off with sensitive information. You've brought the appropriate subject matter experts together and come up with a likelihood of threat event initiation or occurrence rating of "low." Now the team examines the controls and other factors that would drive the level of likelihood threat events result in adverse impacts and come up with an estimate of "high." Using Table G-5 from the NIST 800-30 standard, you look up the results of combining those two values and arrive at an overall likelihood of "moderate." So what's the problem here? Somehow we started off with a threat event likelihood of "low" but ended up with an overall likelihood of "moderate." How can we have a higher overall likelihood than the likelihood of the threat event itself? Simply stated, logically, we cannot.

Table G-5: Assessment Scale – Overall Likelihood

Likelihood of Threat Event Initiation or Occurrence	Likelihood Threat Events Result in Adverse Impacts				
	Very Low	Low	Moderate	High	Very High
Very High	Low	Moderate	High	Very High	Very High
High	Low	Moderate	Moderate	High	Very High
Moderate	Low	Low	Moderate	Moderate	High
Low	Very Low	Low	Low	Moderate	Moderate
Very Low	Very Low	Very Low	Low	Low	Low

FIGURE 14.1

NIST 800-30's overall likelihood table.

National Institute of Standards and Technology (2012). Guide for conducting risk assessments (NIST Special Publication 800-30 rev 1). Retrieved from http://csrc.nist.gov/publications/nistpubs/800-30-rev1/sp800_30_r1.pdf.

Alternative Table G-5: Assessment Scale - Overall Likelihood

Likelihood of Threat Event Initiation or Occurrence	Likelihood Threat Events Result in Adverse Impacts				
	Very Low	**Low**	**Moderate**	**High**	**Very High**
Very High	Moderate	Moderate	High	Very High	Very High
High	Low	Low	Moderate	High	High
Moderate	Very Low	Very Low	Low	Moderate	Moderate
Low	Very Low	Very Low	Very Low	Low	Low
Very Low	Very Low	Very Low	Very Low	Very Low	Very Low

FIGURE 14.2

Alternate form of NIST 800-30's overall likelihood table.

National Institute of Standards and Technology (2012). Guide for conducting risk assessments (NIST Special Publication 800-30 rev 1). Retrieved from http://csrc.nist.gov/publications/nistpubs/800-30-rev1/sp800_30_r1.pdf.

In order to be accurate, the overall likelihood values in the matrix can never be greater than the likelihood of threat event initiation or occurrence values—even when likelihood threat events result in adverse impacts is high or very high. Given this upper likelihood limit, many of the overall likelihood values need to be adjusted. The table shown in Figure 14.2 provides an example of what an alternative matrix might look like.

Of course, absent a quantitative underpinning, it is ambiguous in both the existing matrix and any alternative matrix as to how much the overall likelihood should drop, as likelihood threat events result in adverse impacts decreases. Still, the fundamental logic seems indisputable regarding the need to limit overall likelihood values based on likelihood of threat event initiation or occurrence values.

Likelihood definitions

The other opportunity for improvement has to do with the definitions within NIST's likelihood of threat event initiation (adversarial) or occurrence (non-adversarial) scales (Tables G-2 and G-3, shown in Figure 14.3).

The descriptions with the likelihood of threat event initiation (adversarial) scale are purely qualitative, using terms like "almost certain," "highly likely," etc. This is no better or worse than most other qualitative likelihood scales. Unfortunately, like many other qualitative likelihood scales, there are at least two concerns:

- No time-scale is given. If something is rated "high" in likelihood, does that mean highly likely this year, this decade, or in our lifetime? Absent a timeframe reference, likelihood is wide open to interpretation and nearly meaningless. As we pointed out earlier, it would be entirely legitimate to state that the likelihood of our sun becoming a white dwarf star is very high—eventually, but (knock on wood) it isn't something we need to worry about in the near future.

Table G-2: Assessment Scale – Likelihood of Threat Event Initiation (Adversarial)

Qualitative Values	Semi-Quantitative Values		Description
Very High	96–100	10	Adversary is almost certain to initiate the threat event.
High	80–95	8	Adversary is highly likely to initiate the threat event.
Moderate	21–79	5	Adversary is somewhat likely to initiate the treat event.
Low	5–20	2	Adversary is unlikely to initiate the threat event.
Very Low	0–4	0	Adversary is highly unlikely to initiate the threat event.

Table G-3: Assessment Scale – Likelihood of Threat Event Occurrence (Non-Adversarial)

Qualitative Values	Semi-Quantitative Values		Description
Very High	96–100	10	Error, accident, or act of nature is almost certain to occur; or occurs more than 100 times a year.
High	80–95	8	Error, accident, or act of nature is highly likely to occur; or occurs between 10–100 times a year.
Moderate	21–79	5	Error, accident, or act of nature is somewhat likely to occur; or occurs between 1–10 times a year.
Low	5–20	2	Error, accident, or act of nature is unlikely to occur; or occurs less than once a year, but more than once every 10 years.
Very Low	0–4	0	Error, accident, or act of nature is highly unlikely to occur; or occurs less than once every 10 years.

FIGURE 14.3

NIST 800-30's threat tables.

National Institute of Standards and Technology (2012). Guide for conducting risk assessments (NIST Special Publication 800-30 rev 1). Retrieved from http://csrc.nist.gov/publications/nistpubs/800-30-rev1/sp800_30_r1.pdf.

- Qualitative likelihood ratings using terms like "almost certain" are inherently upper-bounded at one. In other words, there is no way to easily distinguish between events that are likely to occur once from those that are likely to occur multiple times.

The descriptions within likelihood of threat event occurrence (non-adversarial) appear to have the same time-scale problem noted above but differ in that the descriptions include frequency verbiage such as "more than 100 times per year," "between 10 and 100 times a year," etc. The inclusion of a quantitative frequency range would seem to solve the second problem we noted above regarding being upper-bounded at one event, but introduces (at least) one new problem.

Let's say that we have evaluated two scenarios—one with an adversarial threat community (TCom) and the other with a non-adversarial TCom. Our likelihood rating for the adversarial scenario is "high," meaning that, by definition, the event is highly likely to occur but upper bounded at one. Our likelihood rating for the non-adversarial scenario is "moderate" based on an expectation that the event will occur between 1 and 10 times per year (See Figure 14.4.)

If the impact is the same from either scenario ("high," for example) the resulting risk ratings are backwards in relation to one another. The overall risk rating using

Table I-2: Assessment Scale – Level of Risk (Combination of Likelihood and Impact)

Likelihood (Threat Event Occurs and Results in Adverse Impact)	Level of Impact				
	Very Low	Low	Moderate	High	Very High
Very High	Very Low	Low	Moderate	High	Very High
High	Very Low	Low	Moderate	High	Very High
Moderate	Very Low	Low	Moderate	Moderate	High
Low	Very Low	Low	Low	Low	Moderate
Very Low	Very Low	Very Low	Very Low	Low	Low

Maximum of one event
As many as ten events

FIGURE 14.4

NIST 800-30's level of risk table.

National Institute of Standards and Technology (2012). Guide for conducting risk assessments (NIST Special Publication 800-30 rev 1). Retrieved from http://csrc.nist.gov/publications/nistpubs/800-30-rev1/sp800_30_r1.pdf.

NIST's matrices for the adversarial event will be "high" (based on an apparent maximum of one occurrence) and the non-adversarial risk rating (from as many times as 10 events per year) will be "moderate." Clearly, this isn't logical.

It is important to note that NIST 800-30 is not unique in having these sorts of problems. You don't have to look very far to find other qualitative frameworks that have similar (and sometimes worse) issues. The problem is that these kinds of issues increase the odds of being inaccurate in our measurement of risk and, thus, making poorly informed decisions.

Organizations that use these frameworks are very likely to benefit from using FAIR as the analytic component of the risk assessment process. At the very least, they should carefully examine whatever method they are using and reconcile it against the fundamental principles we've covered in this book to avoid making the kinds of mistakes discussed above.

FRANKEN FRAMEWORKS

Ever heard the phrase "Too many cooks in the kitchen"? When it comes to risk management frameworks the same concept applies, and less than desirable results can materialize in at least a couple of ways.

Terminology

Earlier in the book, we mentioned that inconsistent and imprecise nomenclature was one of the biggest problems our profession faces. That being the case, you would think standards coming out of organizations would help solve the problem. Not so much. Too often, what we see are glossaries in these standards that simply list all of the prevailing definitions for terms like risk, threat, and vulnerability rather than take a stand on a particular definition. We don't know whether they can't agree on a definition, whether they don't want to offend anyone, or whether they just don't recognize that far-flung nomenclature is a real problem in the profession. Regardless, they are perpetuating the problem.

TALKING ABOUT RISK

We should mention that ISACA has tried very hard to normalize the terminology used within its Certified in Risk and Information Systems Control (CRISC) certification, and as a result, it is in much better shape than most. The advantage the CRISC program had is that it was being developed largely from scratch with terminology normalization as a specific objective so this could be dealt with up front. For other well-established certification programs, it is very tough sledding to normalize terminology. If our profession wants to mature though, there has to be that kind of thought leadership commitment from organizations like ISACA, ISO, etc.

We believe that, ultimately, what it will take is for the major industry associations to come together and hash the problem out, once and for all. If that project ever gets off the ground (we are allowed to dream), they will have to exercise real critical thinking in their choice of definitions. By this, we mean that they should *not* get in a room and simply vote on which existing definition is least offensive to the majority. We believe they need to examine the elements of the landscape that need definition and come up with logically consistent definitions. That was our approach in FAIR, and we believe it has served us well. With luck, they would find value in at least some of the existing FAIR definitions. Even if they were inclined to default to FAIR definitions though, we hope they would take the time to examine our definitions critically because there may yet be room for improvement.

Structure and content

It is pretty clear that some of the frameworks were put together by getting a bunch of smart and experienced people in the room who then proceeded to come up with everything they could think of that should be part of an information security program. In some cases, however, it appears there wasn't as much thought put into sifting and organizing the results from an efficiency, coverage, or logic perspective. In addition, in the absence of a model of what risk management is and how it works, the odds are much greater for there to be holes in frameworks.

We know we may be about to step on some important toes again, but let's take a look at the new NIST Cyber Security Framework (CSF) to see examples of some of these challenges. By the way, we are not intentionally picking on NIST through our critiques of 800-30 and the CSF. We could easily have reviewed COBIT, ISO 27000, or PCI-DSS and found some of the same problems and, in some cases, worse problems. NIST's 800-30 and CSF simply were easier to review size-wise within the scope of a chapter like this. Much of what NIST puts out there is very good, and, in fact, there is some good stuff in the CSF but nobody hits a homerun every time they come to bat. In addition, for the record, we provided this feedback to NIST during the CSF review and comment period.

NIST CSF risk focus

The CSF mentions repeatedly that it advocates a risk-focused approach to cyber security management, and it even has some excellent verbiage regarding risk in Section 1.2 of their document. Oddly enough (as far as we can tell), nowhere in the document did it reference NIST's own 800-30 guidance on risk analysis, let alone any other risk analysis resources. As a result, users of the framework appear to have been left to their own devices to figure out how to actually measure the very thing the CSF emphasizes so strongly. As we said above, this is not unique. Many of the frameworks out there speak volumes about being risk-focused but provide very little guidance on risk measurement.

NIST CSF taxonomy

The CSF taxonomy has three levels: functions, categories, and subcategories. There are five functions: identify, protect, detect, respond, and recover, which seem pretty common sense and don't need much explanation (see Figure 14.5).

Within each function there are anywhere from three to six categories defined. For example, within the protect function, the following six categories are defined: access control, awareness and training, data security, information protection processes and procedures, maintenance, and protective technology (Table 14.1).

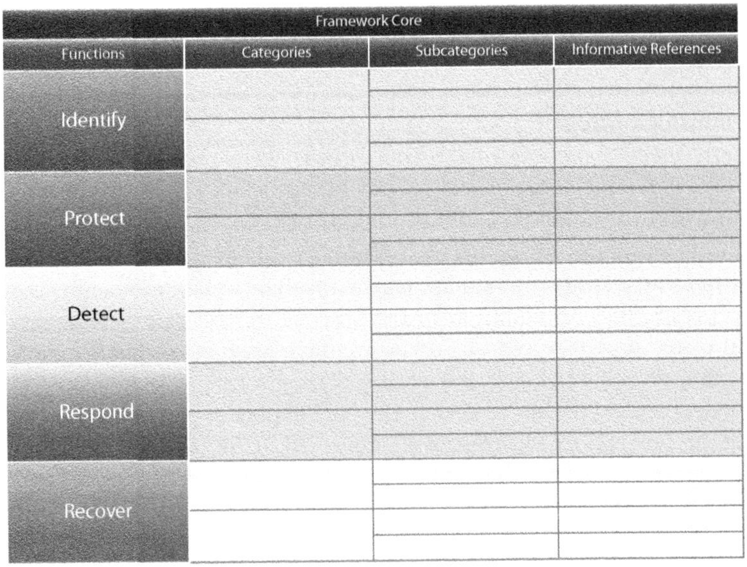

FIGURE 14.5

NIST CSF framework core.

National Institute of Standards and Technology (2014). Framework for improving critical infrastructure cyber-security. Retrieved from http://www.nist.gov/cyberframework/upload/cybersecurity-framework-021214.pdf.

Table 14.1 NIST CSF Protect Subcategories

Protect	Access control
	Awareness and training
	Data security
	Information protection processes and procedures
	Maintenance
	Protective technology

At these two levels of the taxonomy we don't see too much to be concerned about. At the next layer though, the subcategory layer, things begin to get a little problematic.

For the most part, the problems boil down to redundancy. For example, subcategory three under protect/protection technology is "Access to systems and assets is controlled, incorporating the principle of least functionality." Yet subcategory four under protect/access control is "Access permissions are managed, incorporating the principles of least privilege and separation of duties." Although some of the subreferences in each of the subcategories are different, there is significant overlap as well. Some of the other subcategories have similar overlaps.

Another, more subtle dimension of redundancy exists too. For example, the first subcategory under protect/data security is "data-at-rest is protected." This is an objective rather than a control. Many of the other subcategories throughout the taxonomy, such as policy, access control, awareness and training, baseline configurations, etc., are intrinsically intended to help achieve that objective. To have the asset being protected (data-at-rest) defined as a control element that is a peer element to the controls used to protect it is inefficient and doesn't seem logical. In fact, there are a number of these specific "use cases" like data-at-rest, data-in-transit, communications and control networks, etc., all of which are simply parts of the asset landscape where the control-related elements in the CSF taxonomy would apply. We suspect the people putting the framework together simply agreed that these use-cases were of particular importance and needed to be in the framework somehow. Mixing these use-cases with control elements in the taxonomy makes it much more difficult to apply effectively and efficiently. It would be cleaner and more effective if the taxonomy simply contained control elements. A separate asset or use-case taxonomy could be developed that the control taxonomy would be applied to.

This kind of problem related to structural inconsistency and inefficiency is not unique to the CSF, and, as such, it reflects another opportunity for greater maturity and effectiveness in the frameworks our profession uses. Here, again, is where we believe FAIR can be helpful by providing additional clarity and a logical set of principles for building these kinds of frameworks. Of course, another option is to build a framework specifically based on the FAIR ontologies. We are in the process of doing that now, and it will be mapped to the existing major frameworks. So far, what we are finding is that some of the existing frameworks have some gaps. For example, you aren't likely to find references regarding the quality of risk measurement in the existing frameworks, or root cause analysis, yet, as we have discussed, these are very important elements in effective risk management.

TALKING ABOUT RISK

In fairness to NIST, you have to start somewhere. The objective behind CSF is clearly a good one. Given the quality of some of NIST's other materials, we are hopeful that the CSF will evolve significantly over the coming years and overcome at least some of the concerns we described above.

GENERAL STRATEGIES FOR INTEGRATING WITH RISK MANAGEMENT FRAMEWORKS

Although we've spent time here outlining why these frameworks are challenged in their approach to risk, they are not irredeemable. In fact, we would say that most of these frameworks are less methods for risk analysis and more processes for assessing risk (a distinction we have been careful to make throughout this book). In fact, most of the frameworks are either noticeably silent in their discussion of how to compute risk or are capacious in their allowance of any method you prefer. It's for this reason that we often say that FAIR fills a hole in these standards, thus making them inherently compatible.

For example, let's take the overall risk assessment process (Figure 14.6) outlined in the NIST-30 standard we spoke about above. Generally, we agree with the process steps above. Under the first step (among other things), NIST indicates that you should identify the purpose, scope, sources of information, and methodology (we pick FAIR). When conducting the assessment (step two), sources of threats and events are relevant, sure, as too are what they call vulnerabilities (but we know them to really be control deficiencies). Likelihood and impact are important to a FAIR analysis also, even though we know that likelihood is just another word for probability, which is the same as frequency (without a timeline). So we can estimate frequency directly and feel comfortable that we are addressing likelihood as well. The same goes for impact; FAIR just asks you to break down the impact into several categories and assign ranges. Last, the "determine risk" has us coming up with a risk rating. Interestingly, in another part of the document (a section entitled 2.3.2 Assessment Approaches), it indicates that:

> *"Risk, and its contributing factors, can be assessed in a variety of ways, including quantitatively, qualitatively, or semi-quantitatively."*

It then proceeds to call out some pros and cons of each approach. As a result, it is clear that this framework is compatible with quantitative methods like FAIR, as it indicates any approach may be used, so long as it fits with the organization's preference. Further, the process steps above call out that at a certain point, someone has got to choose a risk ranking. They give examples using a basic qualitative probability impact graph, however, the standard does not expressly prohibit other methods.

Our brief treatment here ignores some of the finer points of implementation obviously. There are things that will need to be worked out regarding terminology,

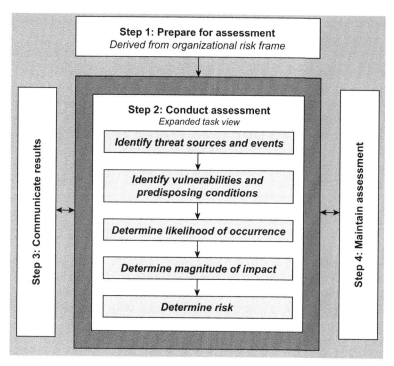

FIGURE 14.6

NIST 800-30's overall process.

National Institute of Standards and Technology (2012). Guide for conducting risk assessments (NIST Special Publication 800-30 rev 1). Retrieved from http://csrc.nist.gov/publications/nistpubs/800-30-rev1/sp800_30_r1.pdf.

nuance, and flavor of one particular standard over another. However, our point here was to call out some of the high-level approaches that make FAIR compatible as an engine for risk analysis within most frameworks. Last, if you are interested in a more complete treatment of integrating FAIR with a popular risk assessment framework, then we recommend reading The Open Group's publication C103: *FAIR—ISO/IEC 27005 Cookbook*. It is a very complete guide for integrating FAIR within the ISO 27000-series guidelines for risk assessments. We will tell you the secret of how the authors did this: the ISO 27005 standard defines the process for risk assessments, but allows you to pick your own tool for computing risk. How about that?

ROOT CAUSE ANALYSIS

Your wait is over. We've been alluding to this throughout the last three chapters so it's about time we fulfill our promise. If there is any question in your mind about the purpose for root cause analysis (RCA) it boils down to limiting the number of times throughout the year that you have to utter the phrase "Dude. Again? Really?" What we sometimes refer to as the DAR problem. Said another way, this is about reducing variance by attacking the causes of variance.

In our experience, one of the most frustrating aspects of being an information security professional is facing the same "mistakes" made repeatedly by personnel. Whether it's failure to install a security patch on a system, writing vulnerable web applications, clicking on obviously questionable e-mail links, sending unencrypted sensitive information over e-mail, leaving a laptop openly on the backseat of your car, or any number of similar snafus, it is these kinds of things that create most of the unintended loss exposure in an organization.

Most of the time organizations play whack-a-mole on these issues rather than spend the time to understand and resolve the root causes. Even when organizations do try to fix the source of the problem, very often they only address a proximate cause. For example, perhaps the issue is that an organization repeatedly fails to keep systems at current patch levels. Well, clearly, this means the system administrators aren't making this a priority, so let's reprimand them. Or maybe we recognize that they are working as hard as they possibly can but still can't keep up with all of the "critical" and "high risk" vulnerabilities. Therefore, instead of reprimanding them, we extend the timeframes they are expected to patch within. Whew. That's much better. With a timeframe of 90 days instead of 30, they are finding it easier to patch all of the critical and high-risk issues on time. They're still not keeping up, but they are closer. Of course, the organization just tripled the windows of exposure on these systems, probably without serious consideration of the risk implications. It just swapped poisons.

THE RCA PROCESS

The RCA process will be presented as a set of flowcharts. An infographic version entitled "Cage the Beast" (meaning the groundhog) is available as a download from the CXOWARE Website (www.cxoware.com/resources). It's more entertaining than a flowchart but does not fit as well within the pages of a book.

In its simplest application, you use the RCA process to determine and resolve the root cause of a single issue—perhaps a single instance of a system not being up-to-date on patches. The greater power in RCA though, comes from applying it to a portfolio of "unintended conditions." What typically happens when you apply this to a set of issues is that you discover one or two prevailing and systemic problems in how your organization manages risk that are driving most of the variance—and, thus, most of the risk—into the organization. By attacking those root causes, you can have a profound effect on the organization's risk profile.

As you can see from the first part of the flowchart (Figure 14.7), the process begins by categorizing the nature of the problem as expectation related, awareness related, capability related, or choice.

Expectation

We've covered expectation setting earlier in the book, and how it is often not very well done in various respects. Whether it is obscure, hard to find, or hard to read

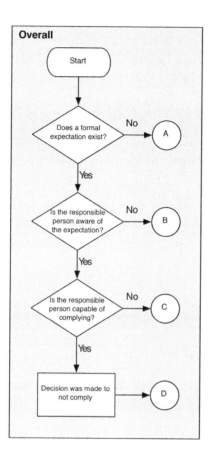

FIGURE 14.7

RCA process flow.

policies and standards, or the complete absence of documented expectations, it is remarkable how often something so basic contributes to variance. When expectations have been decently defined, it boils down to poor awareness, communication, or risk analysis (see Figure 14.8).

Awareness

Sometimes it feels like you can't go a week without reading or hearing someone say that inadequate user awareness training is a critical problem within their organization. It may be, but we don't see very many organizations attack the problem realistically or effectively, and it doesn't typically boil down to insufficient resources. What we see most of the time are awareness efforts that focus on some basic issues for the general user audience. You know, choosing good passwords, not leaving your laptop unattended in an airport, and not clicking on sketchy e-mail attachments.

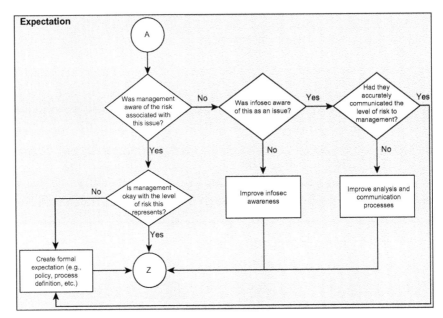

FIGURE 14.8

RCA expectation process flow.

More and more these days, organizations have implemented web-based training on these topics that all employees must go through every year. In some cases, they have to check a box in the web application attesting that "yes" they will not do stupid stuff. In other cases, they have to take a quiz on the material. Regardless, this approach can be effective on the topics it includes. The problem is that many of the DAR events we encounter are related to decisions that aren't covered within the usual material. For example, deploying systems without being configured in accordance with organizational policy or standards, implementing new network connections without engaging information security, or letting executive administrative assistants use their executive's e-mail accounts. The point is, much of the necessary awareness (and subsequent accountability) is a matter of communicating specific expectations to specific audiences (see Figure 14.9).

TALKING ABOUT RISK

As a CISO, I (Jack Jones) always made certain my awareness program identified specific key audiences (e.g., network administrators and engineers, system administrators, developers, administrative assistants, helpdesk, etc.) and the specific information they needed to know in order to avoid DAR. We then considered and used the communication media likely to be most effective for each audience (e.g., e-mail, web-based, classroom, etc.). In some cases, we were even able to make completion of the material a requirement within the first week for new employees. Besides improving their awareness of the expectations, this focused attention also makes the awareness process more efficient (e.g., executive administrators do not have to read about server patching requirements) and it helps to enforce the notion that the organization considers this to be an important subject.

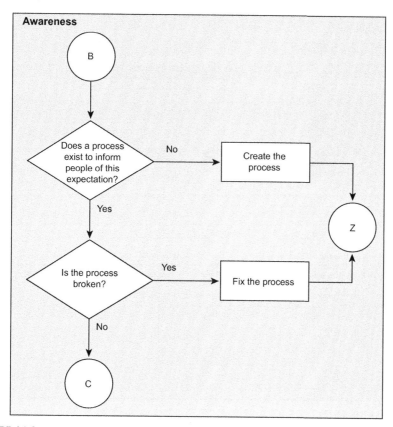

FIGURE 14.9

RCA awareness process flow.

Capability

Skills and resources—that is what capability is all about (see Figure 14.10). That said, even though this is part of the root cause analysis structure, we rarely find capability deficiencies to be a significant DAR problem. Oh, you might get people saying they just didn't have the time to do whatever it was they were supposed to do, but that is virtually always a matter of prioritization (choice) rather than a lack of capability. To qualify as a lack of capability, it has to be a matter of insufficient skill or some form of technical/operational incapacity. For example, we did encounter one company that had a root cause that fell into this category. There was a well-communicated and well-known policy that required the use of encryption when sending sensitive e-mails. However, they had failed to deploy any software that would allow for secure e-mails to be sent. Effectively, although everyone knew they should be encrypting sensitive e-mails, there was no capability with which to accomplish the task. This is a great example of why this aspect of the root cause framework needs to be considered. Having said that, we doubt you will find this to ever be a heavy contributor to your DAR challenges.

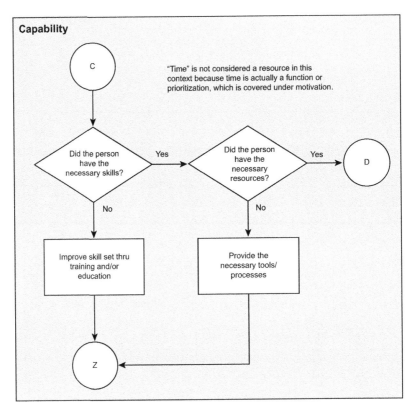

FIGURE 14.10

RCA capability process flow.

Choice

Call this choice or motivation, it all boils down to someone making a decision to not comply with the established expectation. As you will see in Figure 14.11, these decisions will be driven by malicious intent (rarely, in our experience), the individual's self-interest, or other business imperatives. You'll notice that human error is accounted for in this part of the RCA process, essentially as the last possible cause for variance. We put it here because, in our experience, human error is otherwise too quickly fallen back on as the cause. We would submit too, that human error occurs most commonly on things people don't view as a priority. In fact, in an earlier version of the RCA we didn't even include error as an option, reflecting this stricter view of human error as a function of low prioritization.

Documentation and metrics

Of course, after you've determined the root cause of a variant condition, you need to document what you found as well as what you did, or plan to do, to resolve it.

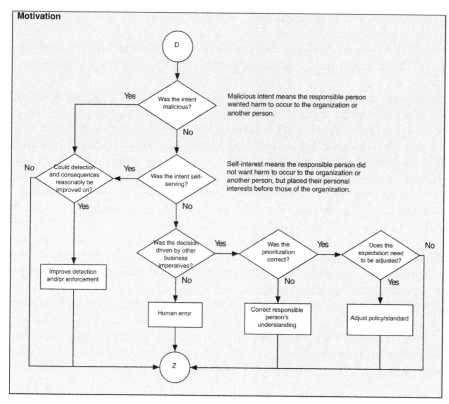

FIGURE 14.11

RCA motivation process flow.

Doing this across a portfolio of variances is when you begin to generate metrics that inform you of systemic sources of risk within the organization. If you are looking for a particularly meaningful metric, you will be hard pressed to find one better than this. Over time, you'll also be able to evaluate the efficacy of your remediation efforts. In some cases, this may stimulate additional root cause analyses for ancillary causes.

A most useful metric—maybe

Out of all of the metrics we've discussed, we believe variance metrics on asset level controls are (or at least can be) the most informative. In other words, if we only had the resources to focus on one metric category, we would focus on asset level control variance metrics (e.g., the percentage of systems that are compliant with configuration standards, etc.). Why? It's because these metrics provide clues into both the level of loss exposure, as well as the efficacy of variance management and decision-making controls. Therefore, if we're seeing significant variance in asset level controls, it may be reasonable to infer that we have higher levels of risk without necessarily having to directly measure risk in every case. In addition, significant levels of asset level control variance also suggest that variance management and perhaps decision-making aren't working well. Be forewarned though, that there is a key assumption being made here: inferring that variances are relevant from a risk, execution, and decision-making perspective presumes that the baselines the variances are measured against are appropriate. Let's look at an example.

One of the most common information security metrics is the percentage of system and application patches applied within policy-defined timeframes. Typically, these timeframes are broken out by severity (e.g., "critical" patches must be applied within seven days [or whatever timeframe the organization has set], "high" severity patches within 30 days, etc.). If we looked at patching metrics in many organizations, we would likely see that a lot of patches aren't being applied within their defined timeframes (i.e., the frequency of variance against this policy is high), such as "In the last reporting period on average only 2 out of 10 patches were applied within the required timeframe." Not only that, but it's not unusual to find that some patches are applied well beyond their defined timeframe. For example "On average, patches that are applied late are applied 75 days after the defined timeframe," which tells us the degree of variance in a second dimension. On the surface, metrics like this suggest that the organization likely has an unacceptable level of risk. We also might assume that the organization's system administrators need a kick in the pants to get patching done on time. Unfortunately, these inferences regarding risk and execution would be incorrect in many organizations, for at least a couple of reasons:

- As we noted earlier, today's vulnerability scanners tend to use models that inflate (sometimes grossly inflate) the amount of risk associated with vulnerabilities. As a result, assumptions regarding the loss exposure associated with patching variance are often incorrect.
- Patching timeframe requirements are often not aligned with operational reality. Too often, the information security organization defines patching timelines without working closely enough with the people who have to do the patching, or with the business stakeholders who depend on the systems and applications. Consequently, assumptions may be wrong regarding the ability to achieve the timeframes, or that the timeframes are even appropriate from a business perspective given the potential for aggressive patching to make systems and applications unstable. This would be an example of broken decision-making (i.e., information security should not be setting those timeframes), not at least without better information regarding what is realistic and acceptable from a business perspective.

In order for us to confidently and accurately interpret the relevance of variance in a metric, we first have to do our homework. We have to ensure that measurements are reasonably accurate and that defined expectations accurately represent stakeholder needs. Unfortunately, too many of the risk metrics we see organizations using suffer from both poor accuracy and/or misalignment with stakeholder desires.

All of this is to say that, although variance metrics can be marvelously useful and can provide solid optics into risk, variance management, and decision-making, those optics are only useful if the underlying expectations are appropriate and the measurements are accurate.

THIRD-PARTY RISK

One of the most challenging and important aspects of information security today is managing third-party risk. Whether it's your business partners, onsite vendors, offsite vendors, or some form of "the cloud," organizations have come to realize that there can be significant risk associated with these relationships. When organizations have hundreds or even thousands of these third-party relationships, it becomes an incredible burden to manage the associated risk. It's no "party" for the third parties either because they often have many customers or business partners, all of whom come to the table with their own custom information security requirements and checklists. With this process representing such a huge burden on both sides of the table, you have to ask the question: "Is it working?" Are the processes and checklists commonly being used effective at managing third-party risk, or is it just a bunch of very expensive hand waving and due diligence box checking? From our experience, it depends.

Some of the checklists we've encountered are reasonably good. They are relatively concise and seem to focus on risk management practices rather than things like obscure server configuration settings or encryption key lengths. Others, however, are nothing short of ridiculous—many hundreds and sometimes thousands of questions that get way down into minutia. The objective, apparently, is to leave no stone unturned. But the information value (i.e., your reduction in uncertainty) regarding the level of risk a third party represents begins to fall way off after the first couple of dozen questions (if they are the right questions). In fact, it could be argued that long checklists actually impede risk management because the resources applied (on both sides of the table) to deal with those next-to-useless questions are resources that cannot be applied to do far more important things.

We've seen efforts to establish broadly accepted standard checklists. This is a marvelous idea except for the fact that most of what we've seen proposed as a standard falls into the minutia-focused category. Although this might reduce the current schizophrenic nature of every checklist being unique, it wouldn't be much of an improvement in understanding third-party risk. Too much noise, not enough signal.

Based on the material covered in this book, we believe there are, for most organizations, just a handful of concerns that should be focused on when gauging the information security risk associated with a third party:

- The value/liability of the information (your information) they have access to.
- The connectivity their networks and systems have to yours.
- The third-party's decision management practices (especially visibility and prioritization).
- The third-party's ability to manage variance.

If an organization can gauge those elements effectively, then we believe it has what it needs in order to know how much to worry about a third party from an information security perspective. The value of everything beyond this in a checklist should be considered carefully to make sure it is providing sufficient value, information-wise, for the level of effort involved.

Although full treatment of third-party risk management is better left to a book dedicated to explicit risk management practices, we suggest you consider leveraging the questions we asked earlier in this chapter. Consider how much you could learn about a third party from those. Also, we suggest you reference the chapter on KPIs in the chapter on metrics. That should provide a good starting point for what matters because whether you are dealing with your own organization's risk management or another's, the most important risk management performance elements are going to be the same or very similar.

ETHICS

Risk measurement is all about informing decisions, but this means it can be incredibly powerful in influencing decisions as well. It is for that reason the question of ethics must be covered, even if only briefly. Frankly, it does not require a lot of verbiage to reinforce that our job is simply to help our stakeholders make well-informed decisions. *It is not to influence them to make the decision we think we would make if we were in their shoes.* FAIR, like any other analytic method, can be gamed and leveraged to drive a personal agenda. The good news is it is a dangerous game to play and can turn on a perpetrator in an instant if someone starts probing into the rationale behind the numbers. At best, they come off looking foolish or incompetent. At worst, they are exposed as dishonest.

There is another angle regarding ethics that may be less obvious. When we perform risk analyses, the analytic perspective is almost invariably from the organization's perspective (i.e., the loss exposure *the organization* has from whatever scenarios are being considered). Sometimes, however, these scenarios also represent significant loss exposure potential for persons or entities outside the organization— the community at large. When these external stakeholders are in a position to react negatively in a way that hurts the organization (e.g., lawsuits, spending their money elsewhere, etc.), the secondary loss exposure component of an analysis will capture this. As a result, decision-makers will at least be aware of the effect on those external stakeholders and can factor that into their decision based on altruistic or selfish principles. In other cases, affected stakeholders may not be in a position to hurt the organization, either because of legal constraints or due to a lack of political or market influence. When this is the case, an analysis would not inherently capture the scenario's effects on those stakeholders. As ethical professionals, if we encounter a scenario like this, we have a duty to ensure that the decision-makers are aware of those broader damages that, although not material to the organization's bottom line, are still important.

Last, it is important to disclose any aspects of the analysis with which you have an inherent stake or bias. For example, if analyzing a risk scenario that would potentially place your assets at greater risk (even if as a subcomponent of a superset of assets), it is important to declare that and make sure that you describe how you have accounted for this bias in your analysis. For example, many employees will be customers of the organizations for whom they work; they partake in the banking, insurance, or other products and services offered by their employer. Although the relationship may be trivial from an overall perspective, just like investment advisors, a risk analyst should disclose their holdings (so to speak) before claiming their opinion is unvarnished truth.

IN CLOSING

We've covered a lot of ground in this book and tried to strike the right balance between concept and application on the topics we believe are most critical. We've also tried to make the material as easy to read and absorb as possible. Regardless, we suspect you invested significant time in getting this far (unless, of course, you've just skipped ahead to this point or skimmed). If you did read all the way through – thank you, sincerely. We hope that means you found the material interesting and useful.

If you choose to apply some, most, or all of the principles and methods we've shared, we hope you experience the same success and value that we've had. That said, we also predict (did we just use the word, "predict"?) that there will be instances where you will struggle. That's to be expected when applying an approach that may be new to you. The good news is that if your experience with it is similar to ours, the struggling part passes relatively quickly and you find yourself answering questions you couldn't before. Not only that, but your level of confidence in how you approach your work may be stronger than ever.

We also anticipate that you'll have questions we haven't answered here. Or you may have ideas for improvements or ways of applying the material that we haven't covered or perhaps even thought of. Regardless, whether it's to ask questions or share ideas, please don't hesitate to reach out to us. FAIR is constantly evolving, or at least we intend for it to, and a good part of that evolution will come from questions and feedback.

Best regards,
Jack & Jack

Index

Printed and bound by CPI Group (UK) Ltd, Croydon, CR0 4YY

08/06/2025

01896868-0011